LET JUSTICE ROLL

Biblical Devotions on Conscience and Justice

LET JUSTICE ROLL

AN IMPRINT OF *MESSAGE*, 2021

Carmela Monk Crawford, *Editor Message*

Edward Woods, III, *Chair, The Conscience & Justice Council*

Patrice Thomas Conwell, *Proofing Specialist*

■■

Cover and Book Design by Howard Bullard Graphic Design

Printed in the United States of America

DEDICATION

The Conscience & Justice Council dedicates this book to anyone interested in knowing the biblical foundations for conscience and justice. We pray that this morning devotion stirs the Holy Spirit within you to strengthen you and make a difference within your family and community for liberty of conscience & justice for all. ■■

ACKNOWLEDGEMENTS

The Conscience & Justice Council offers its heartfelt praise and gratitude to the Lord, the Author and Finisher of our faith. We believe that our ministry models Christ's method of evangelism, strengthens communities around local churches, respects humanity, and prioritizes our relationship with Christ Jesus.

In an era of pandemics, Covid-19, systemic racism and police brutality, and economic uncertainty, God continues to show up and show out. Our volunteer authors poured their hearts into this project as they challenged us to reflect Christ in the conscience and justice ministry. We know that God wants to equally save the victims of injustice and their perpetrators as well. Please reach out to the authors and let them know how they blessed your soul.

We extend our appreciation and applause to Adventist HealthCare, *Liberty* Magazine, *Message* Magazine, North American Division Ministerial Department, North American Division Public Affairs and Religious Liberty Department, North American Religious Liberty Association, and the Office of Regional Conference Ministry for their continual support. Special shout out to Carmela Monk Crawford, *Message* Magazine editor, for collaborating with the Conscience & Justice Council on this project. Because of you, we can authentically share the unadulterated gospel of Jesus Christ and give the trumpet a certain sound.

Finally, we would like to thank you for making an investment and buying this devotional book. Knowing sanctification is the process of a lifetime, we pray that this devotional book empowers you to see Christ in ways you have never seen Him before.

In Christ's peace and love,

Edward Woods III, Chairperson
PARL Director, Lake Region

Cryston Josiah, Vice Chairperson
PARL Director, Central States

Lawrence Brown
PARL Director, Northeastern

Elton DeMoraes
Vice President, Southwestern Union

Moses Edwards, Jr.
PARL Director, South Atlantic

*Kerwin Jones
PARL Director, Southwest Region

Martin Lister
PARL Rep. At-Large

Kingsley Palmer
Regional PARL Rep, Pacific Union

Melissa Reid, Executive Director
North American Religious Liberty Association

Jerome Hurst, Vice Chairperson
PARL Director, Allegheny West

Amerih Al-Haddad
PARL Director, Southern Union

Mark Brown
PARL Director, Southeastern

Jackson Doggette, Jr.
PARL Director, Allegheny East

Paul Goodridge
PARL Director, South Central

Derek Lane
Regional PARL Rep., North Pacific Union

Nicholas Miller, Professor of Church History
Seventh-day Adventist Theological Seminary

Zdravko Plantak, Professor of Religion
Loma Linda University

*Stephen Brooks
PARL Director, Southwest Region

*During this project, Elders Stephen Brooks and Kerwin Jones held the Public Affairs and Religious Liberty Director (PARL) positions for Southwest Region.

TABLE OF CONTENTS

FOREWARD

Heightened partisan banter among people of faith created this opportune moment. Knowing our identity in Christ supersedes partisan persuasion, we knew it was time to let the Bible speak for itself as it relates to matters of conscience and justice.

What does the Bible say about oppression, exploitation, and discrimination? What does the Bible say about protests and advocacy? Are there biblical characters who speak to conscience and justice? How did Jesus deal with conscience and justice? Why would it not be okay to say "Black Lives Matter, Too"?

In the Seventh-day Adventist Church, public affairs and religious liberty represents the work of conscience and justice. As found in the Gospels, we embrace Christ's method of relationship-building: be present with the people and seek to meet their needs, first, before other invitations or appeals. We believe relationships matter, whether people join the church or not.

Thus, we implement seven aspects of Public Affairs and Religious Liberty wrapped in prayer. The seven aspects include:

- conscience
- discipleship
- engagement
- fellowship
- Holy Spirit
- love, and
- prophecy.

Throughout this morning devotion, you will see each of these themes covered in a month. In addition, we'll address the biblical characters for conscience, the biblical characters for justice, thanksgiving, and the Gospel of Jesus Christ.

Through prayer and guidance of the Holy Spirit, we believe the biblical foundation for conscience and justice will be made clear, respecting all people made in the image and likeness of Christ.

Knowing that everyone counts, and everyone matters to Christ, we pray that this morning devotional inspires you to ensure that everyone counts and everyone matters to you and within your sphere of influence. ▮▮

The Conscience & Justice Council
Message Magazine

JANUARY

PRAYERS OF JUSTICE

The administrators of the Seventh-day Adventists, pastors, and members of the North Pacific Union Conference territory in the Pacific Northwest of the U.S. are grateful to share devotional thoughts centering around the theme of social justice and religious freedom, with an emphasis on prayer.

Often prayers are intercessory and offered on behalf of the poor, the widow, the orphan, or the stranger, or what one writer called, "the quartet of the vulnerable." Some are corporate prayers and offered on behalf of God's people; some for the nation and national leaders.

We are grateful to the North American Division, Public Affairs and Religious Liberty, the Conscience and Justice Council, and *Message* Magazine, for the opportunity to share how prayer has affected our journey. We pray for that day when justice, indeed, will roll down like water, and righteousness like a mighty stream. In the meantime, stay encouraged, watchful, and faithful.

These daily readings are shared with the hope that we will live meaningful, spirit-led lives as we navigate the unseen struggle and tension between what is and what is yet to be. We look forward to that day when, as the prophetic writer John penned and George Frideric Handel set to music, the "kingdoms of this world are become the kingdoms of our Lord, and of His Christ; and He shall reign for ever and ever." ■

— DEREK LANE
Regional Representative,
North Pacific Union Conference of
Seventh-day Adventists

JANUARY 1

WHERE ARE YOU?

"Then the Lord God called to Adam and said to him, 'Where are you?'" (Genesis 3:9 NKJV).

The first conversation between God and man following sin was initiated by God. Prayer took the form of a conversation, but this one was different. Instead of responding to His voice, they hid themselves "from the presence of the Lord God" (Genesis 3:8).

Did God know where Adam was? Of course He did; God is all-knowing. We cannot hide from Him. God did not ask the question because He needed the information. He wanted Adam to understand the consequences of his actions and where disobedience leads. Straying from His will leads us to the loss of relationship with God. It leads us to guilt and shame.

While it was over 40 years ago, I remember it like it was yesterday. It was during the time of the infamous Atlanta child abductions. It was a typical bright, sunny day in upstate New York and my mother called out looking for my sister but could not find her. She asked the entire family to help search for her, but could not find her. With each passing minute we heard the growing angst, fear, and desperation in our mother's voice. Our sister was lost and could not be found! We expanded our search to outside and began combing the neighborhood while my mother contacted the local authorities. By this time, our initial, casual response had grown to a fevered pitch of desperation, and we solicited the help of our neighbors and friends.

Finally, my brother and I came back home without success. My sister was only 11 years old, where could she have gone? Nearly three hours had passed and still no sign of her. The side door entrance to our home opened into the dining room. We had a breakfast nook built into the wall, and when the door was opened it actually concealed a portion of the u-shaped seating area. As we were standing in the dining room trying to figure out what to do next, we heard someone stirring behind the door. It was her! She had been lying on the wrap-around seating the whole time, fast asleep! She never knew we had been looking for her.

Adam heard God's voice but chose not to respond. My sister didn't hear our voices and couldn't respond. But God calls out to each of us today. Can we hear His voice? Praise God my sister was found!

May we exert our energies and efforts to find our brothers and sisters today. ∎

— DEREK LANE

JANUARY 2

ABRAHAM'S PRAYER FOR SODOM TO BE SPARED

"Then he said, 'Let not the Lord be angry, and I will speak but once more: Suppose ten should be found there?' And He said, 'I will not destroy it for the sake of ten'" (Genesis 18:32 NKJV).

Abraham had separated from his nephew, Lot, because of the size of their respective flocks and herds. Lot had chosen the incredibly beautiful fertile valley that was home to the two cities of Sodom and Gomorrah. Initially he pitched his tent outside of the city, but as time went on the convenience and excitement of the city enticed him to move there.

The Lord had heard of the wickedness of the city and now had come down Himself to investigate the matter to see what should be done. On His way to Sodom, He stops by Abraham's home to visit and bring him up to speed of His and the two angels' mission.

When Abraham hears what the plans are, he immediately begins a prayer that quickly becomes a negotiation to plead with the Lord for the sparing of the cities.

"Lord what if fifty righteous are found there?" Abraham asks.

"I will spare the city on account of fifty," Jesus answers.

"What if only 45? How about 40? Would you destroy on account of 30, 20, or 10? "

"No, I will not destroy the city even if only 10 are found to be righteous there" (Genesis 18:23-32).

The Scripture shares an account with us of how depraved the cities had become in their lawlessness and lack of human compassion. Sadly, not even 10 righteous could be found to believe the angels and leave the city with Lot and his family. Abraham could now see that his Lord had done all He could to try to save Sodom and Gomorrah.

There are a few important points we can learn from this story:

1. We should always be willing to intercede for others and not stop praying for them.

2. We, just like Abraham, now can see the mercy of the Lord in destroying sin and those clinging tightly to it. Otherwise it will only continue to spread.

3. Even though the cities were destroyed, the Lord—in His mercy—was able and is able to save His people from the coming destruction.

Please Lord Jesus, come soon. Please spare our cities where only a handful of Your faithful servants can be found. We trust You to be just and merciful, and to save all who want to be saved. By the power of Your Holy Spirit please keep Your people faithful to You. Amen. ▮▮

— KEVIN SCOTT

JANUARY 3

A PRAYER OF SELF-ADVOCACY

"I am not able to bear all these people alone, because the burden is too heavy for me" (Numbers 11:14 NKJV).

Moses was tired. He had left his quiet life to advocate for an enslaved group of people; fighting for their freedom and taking a leadership role that pushed against the boundaries of his comfort zone. His reward? A camp full of disgruntled, griping, and nit-picking people.

The noble fight for justice is not as glorious and victorious as many of us hope for. Instead, it can be tedious and tiresome. Our best efforts are unappreciated and even openly despised, as those we work for slip back into the familiar habits and decisions of the "good old days." This is where we find Moses in Numbers 11, and his response is anger and discouragement—a familiar place for many justice workers.

Our proximity to pain and suffering can leave us crushed under the weight of need and frustration. If left to fester, feelings of being overwhelmed can turn into anger and cynicism, like Moses'. Guilt, fear, avoidance, or physical breakdown are also common symptoms.

Exhausted, Moses accepts the people's blame, taking responsibility to produce results that he is both unable to provide and are not his responsibility. Consequently, Moses goes on the offensive with God. He accuses God of punishing him and asking too much of him. He states he would rather God kill him than to be publicly humiliated by failure.

While Moses' reaction is a bit dramatic, it is also familiar. Have you been there too? Have you felt that your calling to justice ministry was a curse, rather than a blessing? Have you felt you were on the brink of failure with everybody waiting to condemn you? Facing high expectations with low resources?

However belligerent it was, God welcomes Moses' prayer. God is never afraid of our honesty and, significantly, this time Moses is advocating for himself. His efforts to alleviate others' needs blinded him to his own personal vulnerability. As a leader, do not forget to champion your own cause. Have compassion on yourself and stretch your hand out to God in the same spirit of advocacy that you offer others.

As always, God responds with compassion to Moses' cries for help and bridges the gap between his perceptions and God's reality. God points out the 70 other faithful and capable leaders who stood ready to share the weight of the work.

The weight of the world is not for you to bear. You are no better, no stronger, no wiser than those you serve. Do not forget to approach God on your own behalf, and His compassion and mercy will be poured out on you. ▮▮

— COLETTE NEWER

JANUARY 4

THE CALL OF ABRAHAM

"Now the Lord had said to Abram: 'Get out of your country, from your family and from your father's house, to a land that I will show you'" (Genesis 12:1 NKJV).

Many Bible scholars associate this text with the initiation of the Abrahamic covenant. It is spoken of in theological terms and discussed in the context of God's covenant relationship with His people. Yet there is a personal, human side of this story that we sometimes overlook.

The Lord spoke to Abram and asked him to take his family and move from his childhood home to a land he had never seen before. It must have been a stressful and challenging time for him and his family. Modern research has shown that six out of 10 people cite moving as the most stressful of life events.

At 10 years of age I remember moving from England to my father's country in Trinidad. It was exciting and frightening all at the same time! I remember having to adapt to a new country, a new climate, a new school, and new friends. And while it was a major transition in my life, I realize now that God was simply preparing me for my life's journey.

God had plans for Abram, who would later become Abraham and the patriarch of three world religions—Judaism, Christianity, and Islam. I am sure it was not an easy journey for him. He was not shown the dangers, trials, and challenges ahead.

Likewise, God has not unveiled the scroll for us to see our future. Yet He challenges us to take the journey and trust Him along the way. And because God knows His creation's needs, He gave Abram some additional words to encourage him along the way. God promised to honor his name and bless him. He promised to protect him and make his name great (Genesis 12:2-3).

God will not leave us alone. As we journey through this experience called life, whether it is across the seas or through the years, we have the promise of His presence. Although we may not have a clear destination in mind, we can trust God through it all.

Looking back now, I see my early transition as preparation for another one. After finishing high school, I had the privilege to take another journey from my island home to the United States. And God has been with me along the way and has honored His word. And He will be with you.

My prayer for you today is that you will trust Him when you cannot trace Him. Entrust your life and your future to Him. And like the promise He made to Abraham, He will bless you in ways you cannot imagine. ■■

— TONI B.

JANUARY 5

THE PRAYER OF MOSES AND SONG OF DAVID

"So it was, whenever the ark set out, that Moses said: 'Rise up, O Lord! Let Your enemies be scattered, and let those who hate You flee before You.' And when it rested, he said: 'Return O Lord, to the many thousands of Israel'" (Numbers 10:35-36 NKJV)

The children of Israel were on their journey through the wilderness and heading towards the Promised Land. A journey that typically takes less than two weeks ended up taking 40 years and pitching camp 42 times along the way. Although they encountered both internal challenges and external threats, God's will was to guide them into the promised land of Canaan. Like Israel of old, God desires to grant us His presence as we traverse this wilderness called life, toward our heavenly Canaan home.

As Israel journeyed with the ark of God, Moses took the time to thank God at each stop along the way. Today's text was the prayer Moses prayed whenever they pitched or broke camp. Moses took the time to acknowledge God's providential leading and protection.

Eighteen years ago, I left New York City and my job of 14 years to travel with my family to the Pacific Northwest. It did not take 40 years to get to my final destination, but like the children of Israel, there have been challenges along the way. And even now, in my new assignment and territory, I continue to seek God's guidance and protection for our family. I follow the lesson and example of Moses and thank God at each transition along the way.

Years later the psalmist David, perhaps inspired by the prayer of Moses, set to composition the prayer of Moses, and sang, "...Let God arise, let His enemies be scattered: let them also that hate Him flee before Him" (Psalm 68:1 NKJV).

As we make this journey toward our promised land, injustice and challenges will confront us along the way. As we navigate crises great or small, may our prayer continue to be, "Let God arise, let His enemies be scattered..."

As God has kept and preserved me and my family, may He protect you and yours. May we sense His presence and guiding hand as we navigate these tumultuous times in which we live. And may those that rise up against you be scattered. ■

— KEN BUCKNOR

GOD OF THE IMPOSSIBLE

"These are the ones who were numbered of the children of Israel by their fathers' houses. All who were numbered according to their armies of the forces were six hundred and three thousand five hundred and fifty" (Numbers 2:32 NKJV).

Six hundred thousand males were numbered for military service out of 2 to 3 million people—the suggested number of Israelites. Imagine trying to lead a newly formed nomadic nation through a barren, hostile wilderness for 38 years. Logistics is the fine art of getting food in every mouth, sandals on every foot, water in every leather-skin canteen, and every head pointed in the right direction. To survive in this wilderness, one would also need UV protection during the day and warmth for desert nights.

If you were standing on Sinai looking out upon the tents of Israel, you might think to yourself, "Wow. That is a lot of people." However, if you were standing on Sinai looking out upon the tents of Israel, and you were responsible for them, you would probably think to yourself, "Wow. This is a logistical nightmare."

There are many well-crafted arguments aimed at debunking the historicity of the Bible. Among these is the simple observation that maintaining this number of people in the desert for four days, much less 40 years, is as impossible as parting the Red Sea.

This was, I believe, precisely God's point. It is impossible. Yes, of course; completely impossible, without Him. When God calls people, He frequently calls them beyond their capacity so that they have no recourse but to put their faith in Him. God taught Israel how to access the "impossible" through prayer.

Was Moses, in looking down upon all of these people, feeling overwhelmed and inadequate? How do you even pray for these people? Two times in Scripture God taught people how to address Deity in prayer. (*See Numbers 6:24-26 and Matthew 6:9-13.*)

God instructed Moses to teach Aaron and his sons this prayer:

"'Yahweh bless you, and keep you; Yahweh make His face shine on you, and be gracious to you; Yahweh lift up His face on you, and give you peace.' So they shall place My name on the sons of Israel, and I will bless them" (Numbers 6:24-27, translation and emphasis added).

Millions of people, innumerable problems, a vast barren wilderness, an overwhelmed and inadequate mind that might expect more complexity, but there it is. We can face the impossible when we are looking upon God's face and calling out in God-given prayer. Salvation in all its phases is solely the work of God.

"There is salvation in no one else! God has given no other name under heaven by which we must be saved" (Acts 4:12 NLT). "They will see His face, and His name will be on their foreheads" (Revelation 22:4 NASB). ▮▮

— JOHN KURLINSKI

MOSES FOR A NEW LEADER OF ISRAEL

"Then Moses spoke to the Lord, saying: 'Let the Lord, the God of the spirits of all flesh, set a man over the congregation, who may go out before them and go in before them, who may lead them out and bring them in, that the congregation of the Lord may not be like sheep which have no shepherd'" (Numbers 27:15-17 NKJV).

In 2011 it was obvious that Apple, Inc. was facing a transition as its co-founder, Steve Jobs, was resigning from his post during his final stages of pancreatic cancer. For the previous seven years, Tim Cook was in second chair, serving as chief operating officer. With his extensive experience, Cook appeared the most likely choice to succeed Jobs. This decision was presented to, and ratified by, Apple's board of directors in August 2011. Only two months later, at the age of 56, Jobs died on October 5.

Succession of leadership for Apple and for Israel seemed quite obvious. There was a "right hand man" who had been observing closely all that the primary leader had been doing for quite some time. Both Moses and Steve Jobs were reaching the end of their leadership season and looking to hand off the football to their trusty counterpart. And yet, in the Biblical case and in modern times, it was imperative to keep the mission front-and-center when it came time for musical chairs.

Planning for the future in leadership is difficult even when things appear constant. The year 2020 was one of change, uncertainty, and adaptation in which most leaders were driven to the point of having to admit, "I don't know what to do next." This is why it is so crucial to keep focused on mission, redefining and constantly improving our focus on our priorities and identities.

In earthly terms, Joshua had been serving for almost 40 years as Senior Vice President of Military Operations and Chairman of Promised Land Procurement. He represented the most likely candidate in line for the role of CEO to follow Moses. And yet, even as qualified as he was, it was the Lord's mission that needed to remain in clear focus. No single person—even a shepherd of sheep—is the sum total of God's will and purpose. Each of us must choose to wisely use the freedoms we have in a responsible manner that honors God.

May God direct your leadership decisions, today, that keep mission in clear focus as leaders come and go; for each of us is to serve faithfully for a season. ▮▮

— CRAIG CARR

MOSES ASKS TO GO INTO CANAAN

"I pray, let me cross over and see the good land beyond the Jordan, those pleasant mountains, and Lebanon" (Deuteronomy 3:25 NKJV)

Moses, from the time he was a young man, had felt the calling to help deliver God's people from Egypt. Now at 120 years old he had played a huge part in doing just that. He had witnessed the mighty miracles God had performed over the course of 40 years in delivering, sustaining, and protecting His people as they journeyed to the Promised Land.

Now, very close to the borders of Canaan, Moses, instead of speaking to the Rock as he had been instructed, struck the Rock twice in anger and made the claim that he was the one bringing water from that Rock. Because of this sin of presumption, because he had misrepresented the Lord to His people, Moses is told that he will not enter the Promised Land.

This is news that Moses finds very hard to accept. He begs God to let him pass over the Jordan into Canaan, but the Lord, angry now at Moses, tells him to stop speaking about the matter and go to the top of Pisgah. There, God shows Moses the Promised Land before he dies. It is a very spectacular view. Moses could see all the way to the Mediterranean Sea, all of the West Bank to the north, and all of the Dead Sea and desert areas of Southern Israel.

Moses died and Jesus buried him on Mount Nebo, but Moses' work was not over. Just as Moses needed the Lord every step of the way while leading His people, Jesus, at a point in His ministry, needed encouragement from Moses.

It had been 1,500 years since Moses had died on top of that mountain. Now, he was with Jesus again at the summit of another Mount, this time joined by another great prophet of old, Elijah. There they both encouraged Jesus to continue on and complete His earthly mission. Elijah spoke on behalf of all those believers who will be alive when Jesus returns, and Moses spoke on behalf of all the believers who have fallen asleep since the beginning of time. Both spoke for all believers who would not have a hope of everlasting life if Jesus did not finish the mission He started.

Moses had thought the punishment of not being able to enter Canaan was too harsh. The Lord knew that the immense blessing He had in mind for Moses would literally drown any perception of harshness.

So it is in each one of our situations. None of us knows the extent of what Jesus has planned for us. We may look at our own lives and believe that we are being treated unfairly, but just as it was in Moses' case, so it is in our own. Jesus has wonderful, glorious, magnificent plans for each one of us. We may have to trust Him, even through death, before we see the implementation of those plans.

Here is the good news—Jesus' plans for us are far better then what any of us can imagine. Pray not for our situations to change, but that Jesus' plan will be fulfilled in all of our lives. ■

— KEVIN SCOTT

JANUARY 9

JOSHUA'S PRAYER FOR THE SUN AND MOON TO STAND STILL

"Then Joshua spoke to the Lord in the day when the Lord delivered up the Amorites before the children of Israel, and he said in the sight of Israel: ' Sun, stand still over Gibeon; and Moon, in the Valley of Aijalon'" (Joshua 10:12 NKJV).

God had fulfilled His promise in giving the land of Canaan to His people. Now, Joshua and the Israelites were faced with a formidable coalition of five Canaanite kings who wanted to remain in the land and destroy God's people. God had kept His word that day in fighting for His people by sending great hailstones down on their enemies. More died from the hail than from the sword of Joshua's army. In spite of the additional help, Joshua saw that the day was about to end allowing many of the enemies to escape in the darkness. Joshua knew that for God's will to be fulfilled on that day, something miraculous had to happen.

"Sun, stand still over Gideon, and moon, over the valley of Aijalon" (Joshua 10:12 HCSB).

I was preaching a series of evangelism meetings in South Haven, Michigan. It was Sabbath evening and the topic for that session was, "What Happens When You Die." A fairly severe thunderstorm had rolled through off of Lake Michigan that afternoon. Cindy and I thought little of it as our area had not been affected. But as we were driving to the church, we noticed the area around the church was very dark.

When we arrived we discovered that the power was off at the church. Some members were encouraging us to cancel the meeting, but I was sensing otherwise. Immediately we gathered in a room and prayed a prayer.

"Lord these are Your meetings, not ours. These are Your people that are coming out, not ours. You must provide the power for our equipment for us to continue."

Several members were in the construction industry and had lighting and extension cords. Another had a generator. All the cords were laid out, all the lights were plugged in. Sydney, who owned the generator, spoke up.

"Pastor I used my generator all day yesterday and I know how long a tankful lasts. There is no fuel in that generator."

"It's too late to get gas now," I responded. "We must start the meeting, so fire up the generator."

The generator started and continued to run for 1 1/2 hours until the end of the sermon and the people were being dismissed. At that moment, the generator stopped and the electricity came back on.

When we know God's will, we can feel confident in His ability to solve any challenges we may face—even if it's causing the sun to stand still or a generator to run on fumes.

Lord, please increase our faith. ■

— KEVIN SCOTT

ONE LAST VICTORY

"He called out to the Lord: 'Lord God, please remember me. Strengthen me, God, just once more. With one act of vengeance, let me pay back the Philistines for my two eyes'" (Judges 16:28 HCSB).

Woody was the best friend of an elderly man my parents took in when my grandmother told us about her neighbor's medical condition. When we got to the home where Woody lived with other elderly people, it was saddening. The place was dark, chilly and, while clean, had only basic amenities for them.

We listened to Woody's story and situation. He received minimal care; dinner was a piece of cake and a cup of coffee; breakfast and lunch were not much better. The tenants were treated as a nuisance rather than with compassion and dignity. They were verbally abused when they physically could not follow orders, and were forcibly pushed or pulled into positions that the caretaker wanted.

My father spoke to the caretaker to express his displeasure. In response, we were told that we could never come back. We contacted Elderly Protective Services, and later found out that they found nothing wrong with the home and we still could not return. Woody died a year later.

How terrible when one's actions for justice do not get realized, or when a voice is raised and there's still silence, or, in turn, it becomes worse for others. After victories over the Philistines, Samson the judge— who could conquer any enemy—fell because he could not conquer his inner "me." Betrayed, he finds himself helpless in captivity, blinded, and put into forced labor. He finally is brought forth for public ridicule (Judges 16:21-25).

Samson prays, "Lord GOD, please remember me. Strengthen me, God, just once more. With one act of vengeance, let me pay back the Philistines for my two eyes" (Judges 16:28 HCSB). This prayer seems to indicate that he had turned fully to God. The mention in Judges 16:22 of his hair growing back demonstrates that Samson was fulfilling his Nazarite vow.

Yet raw humanity is still there. The second part of his prayer calls for God to act based on personal vengeance, not for God's glorification. It can be comforting to know that in our pain and frustration about what we see happening or what has happened to us, even though there may be elements that are not fully given 100 percent to God, God still sees us by our calling (Hebrews 12:32).

When our actions of justice seem to weaken us, let us not grow weary in doing good (2 Thessalonians 2:13), for God will not sit on the sidelines. As with Samson, when God's faulty servants are being humiliated, God takes it personally and will act, even when our intentions are selfish. He is faithful to do justice. ■

— DAVID SALAZAR

OPEN HIS EYES

"And Elisha prayed, 'Open his eyes, Lord, so that he may see.' Then the Lord opened the servant's eyes, and he looked and saw the hills full of horses and chariots of fire all around Elisha" (2 Kings 6:17 NIV).

God had to pry Elisha's servant's eyes open! There is a tension that immediately arises from the text because Elisha is praying for something that should be obvious. The servant is questioning, or doubts the ability of God to deliver and protect in this situation.

Can we really blame him?

After all they are unskilled, unprepared, and surrounded by their enemies. They are in a hopeless situation where relief seems impossible.

Can't you identify with this servant? How many times have we been in situations where we are stuck and cannot see a possibility of deliverance?

I boarded a packed bus and headed to school. Like most riders, I squeezed into a little spot to avoid a man who stood coughing and sneezing next to me.

I later got a seat close to the window at the back of the bus and close to the engine. However, I realized that the seat was a little warm. I began to sweat and I felt something was wrong, but I adjusted my body and remained calm. As the trip continued, the seat became unbearably hot and I could smell burning fabric. I shot out of my seat in a panic and screamed out.

"Driver, stop the bus!"

Immediately the driver swerved to the roadside and looked back. My seat was smoking and sparking. I thought I was going to die. All the passengers rushed and pushed to the exit. It was a challenge to get out. The seat burst into flames and fire started to engulf the bus. I could not see a way to escape and thought this would be the end!

Suddenly, the driver grabbed the extinguisher to put out the fire, but to no avail. Flames poured out of the seat and into the bus like hot lava from an erupting volcano. We finally hopped off the bus and onto the roadside.

All passengers stood away from the vehicle to view the aftermath. The bus became a ball of black melted metal and charred debris, within minutes.

That experience is a reminder to me that God cares and protects. God sometimes chooses moments where we are stuck in potentially deadly situations, to reveal His power and ability to deliver. Difficult moments make it hard to see clearly. However, may our eyes be opened to see that those who protect and provide for us outnumber our enemies. ∎

— GARTH DOTTIN

JANUARY 12

THE PRAYER OF JABEZ

"Jabez was more honorable than his brothers. His mother had named him Jabez, saying, 'I gave birth to him in pain.' Jabez cried out to the God of Israel, 'Oh, that you would bless me and enlarge my territory! Let your hand be with me, and keep me from harm so that I will be free from pain.' And God granted his request" (1 Chronicles 4:9-10 NIV).

The prayer of Jabez is one of the shortest, yet most effective prayers in Scripture. It is also perhaps one of the prayers most misunderstood. Upon first glance, it looks like a selfish prayer. It looks like a prayer for self-aggrandizement. It is one thing to express gratefulness for God's blessing. It seems appropriate to offer thanks for the material blessings of life. But it just seems antithetical to the call for humility and resistance of pride to actually pray for blessings and more territory!

We can better discern the true import of Jabez's words upon closer examination. The penitent is only mentioned in one chapter of the Bible. We are introduced to Jabez as a man more honorable than his brothers. His name is associated with the birth pangs his mother experienced. In Hebrew, his name literally means, "he causes pain." In Jewish culture, a name is often associated with one's birth, character, or destiny.

With this backdrop in mind, Jabez and his prayer seem more clearly defined. His request to be blessed is not strange. There are many prayers and requests in Scripture asking for a blessing. One only has to think of Esau and Jacob as examples of others who specifically requested to be blessed.

But Jabez also requested an "enlarged territory." Territory does not have to be associated solely with physical territory. Jabez is concerned with enlarging the influence and impact he could exert for the kingdom and glory of God.

He also requested for the "hand" of God to "be with me." The hand is often associated with one's livelihood or work. Jabez's request is an acknowledgement of his own limitations to fulfill his true purpose on his own, and his inability to save himself by the works of his own hands.

Finally, Jabez asked to be kept from harm, "so that I will be free from pain." Remember, his very name means, "he causes pain." So, what is Jabez really asking God? Is it possible that he is requesting to be emptied of self, emptied of Jabez? The word "pain" in Verse 10 is the Hebrew term for "evil."

In the Lord's model prayer in the New Testament there is also a request for blessings—the blessings of "daily bread," as well as a request to be "delivered from evil."

May God grant us, like Jabez, the boldness to make our requests known to Him and the humility to be delivered from ourselves and our carnal nature as we seek justice. ▮▮

— DEREK LANE

WALK HUMBLY WITH GOD

"If my people who are called by My name will humble themselves, and pray and seek My face, and turn from their wicked ways, then I will hear from heaven, and will forgive their sin and heal their land"
(2 Chronicles 7:14 NKJV)

•

Humility seems to be in short supply among leaders today. Arrogance and an attitude of superiority seem to characterize the demeanor of a majority of leaders. Words that fit with humility include modest, meek, and without pride. Today, humility is seen as weakness. Therefore, God's appeal to us in Micah 6:8 and the text for today, seems as counter cultural as salmon swimming upstream.

2 Chronicles gives us a cluster of actions and attributes that seem to go well with, and may help define, the kind of humility needed by God's people:

• **PRAY:** You cannot truly pray without faith and trust in God. Hebrews 11:6 says, "He who comes to God must believe that He is, and that He is a rewarder of those who diligently seek Him" (NJKV). Proud and haughty people do not pray, except in dire circumstances, because they do not believe they need to. They feel they can do just fine using their own wisdom and ingenuity.

• **SEEK MY FACE:** As sinful human beings, knowledge of sin should humble us and motivate us to seek the grace of God. However, even Adam and Eve—who had an intimate relationship with God before their sin— after their sin, hid from God rather than coming to Him. Fear and shame stood in the way. God had to seek them out.

• **TURN FROM THEIR WICKED WAYS:** The tendency of many Christians, and especially Christian leaders, is to justify their actions and double down on their unwise and unholy actions. Turning from wickedness presupposes an attitude of humility and a recognition that God is the only one who is all wise and all powerful, not us. Pride and arrogance keep people from turning toward God.

When we learn to pray, learn to seek God's face, and learn to turn from our wicked ways, we will begin to develop the kind of humility needed to walk, like Enoch, with our God. ■■

— BYRON DULAN

JANUARY 14

THE PRAYER OF THE DISTRESSED

"We do not know what to do, but our eyes are upon you" (2 Chronicles 20:12 NKJV).

Two years ago, when the ball dropped in Times Square announcing the arrival of the new decade, a fresh wave of hope and optimism swept over our nation. The year 2020 was going to be a year of new vision and new opportunities.

Then suddenly, an invisible invader—a "novel" Corona virus—landed on our shores and attacked with a merciless vengeance. Our distress at the advance of the devastating pestilence was not unlike that of King Jehoshaphat's at the advance of the vast and "novel" allied armies of Moab.

Jehoshaphat and the armies of Judah would surely be overrun, just like the virus overwhelmed many of our cities, maxing out our hospitals, and striking hardest at our communities of color. In great distress, Jehoshaphat proclaimed a fast and sought the Lord in corporate, urgent prayer.

Jehoshaphat's prayer is a model for any people, group or nation in distress. First, He focused on the person of God (2 Chronicles 20:6). When you are in distress, remember that *nothing is too hard for God.* Trust Him for the future, based on His trustworthiness in the past.

"We have no power to face this vast army that is attacking us," Jehoshaphat prayed. "We do not know what to do, but our eyes are upon you" (Verse 12). To know the strength of God's resources, we must admit the weaknesses of our own. The simplest cry, "Lord, save me," is all that is necessary to move the arm of God in swift deliverance. (See Matthew 14:30-31.)

Through the prophet the Lord responded, "Do not be afraid or discouraged . . . . for the battle is not yours, but God's" (Verse 15). What made it God's? It was His people, His promises, His Name, and His power under attack. And when we call on Him, He defends it all, including us. (See Psalm 50:15.) When in distress, *realize the battle is the Lord's.*

Because the battle was the Lord's, He made this promise: "You will not have to fight this battle. Take up your positions; stand firm and see the deliverance the Lord will give you" (Verse 17). In response to the praises of the people that were prompted by their trust in His promises (Verse 21), God defeated their enemies. Prayers of distress became praises of deliverance.

We, too, will overcome the enemies of injustice and pestilence the same way Jehoshaphat overcame Moab—by the blood of the Lamb and by the word of our testimony. And our testimony is, "His love endures forever." ■

— RANDY MAXWELL

JANUARY 15

JOB PLEADS FOR A FAIR HEARING

"Oh that I knew where I might find Him, that I might come to His seat? I would present my case before Him, and fill my mouth with arguments. I would know the words which He would answer me, and understand what He would say to me" (Job 23:3-5 NKJV).

Have you ever been falsely accused? Have you ever looked to your friends for support and they only made things worse?

How many have sought vindication for false accusations and were met only with condemnation and judgment? I have been there, and reading the story of Job left me with a special kinship to someone who shared similar circumstances.

Instead of encouraging Job or giving him the benefit of the doubt, Job's friends became, not his witnesses or unbiased sounding boards, but his jury and judge. They did not have evidence of his guilt, but assumed he must have done something wrong because the scale and intensity of the calamities he experienced were often seen as a judgement from God. His friends challenged him to come clean and confess whatever it was that he had done wrong. And when his friends could not see or understand the spiritual drama behind the scenes as Job maintained his innocence, they assumed he was hiding something.

Like Job, I have longed for vindication; to have my case tried before an unbiased, neutral jury of my peers. And when I could find no comfort, solace, or listening ear, I had no other choice but to turn to an All-knowing, Righteous Judge, and lay my burdens on Him in prayer. He knows our innermost secrets. He knows the travails of our souls. He knows what it is like to be misunderstood as He, too, experienced false charges from the 'accuser of the brethren." What a sweet relief to be in the audience chamber of the Most High and know that He, indeed, is "touched with the feelings of our infirmities."

So the next time you experience trials or trauma you don't understand, the next time you seek comfort from the arm of flesh, remember the prayer of Job. Know that it is okay to voice your frustrations and burdens to God. It is wonderful to know that we can take them to the Lord in prayer. We can lay out our case before Him; we can share the burdens of our hearts.

Do you have a troubled heart? Is it burdened by the weight of misunderstanding and false accusation? Like Job, take it to God in prayer. He will hear your cry and the travail of your soul. The promise of Isaiah 59:1 still rings true! "Behold, the Lord's hand is not shortened, that it cannot save; nor His ear heavy, that it cannot hear." ■■

— JOYCE MATTHEWS

JEREMIAH PRAYS FOR THE OPPRESSED PEOPLE OF JUDAH

"Turn us back to You, O Lord, and we will be restored; renew our days as of old" (Lamentations 5:21 NKJV).

One Sunday, while churches were still restricted from gathering during COVID-19, I visited an Ethiopian Christian church that gathered in Othello Park in Seattle, Washington where I live. Having recently moved there, one of the things I appreciate about the area is its rich diversity. Seattle is home to one of the nation's largest East African communities. According to recent census data, an estimated 25,000 East Africans live in King County, Washington (the county which encompasses Seattle). It consists of mostly recent immigrants and refugees from countries like Ethiopia, Somalia, and Eritrea.

We lease space in our church on Sundays to an Ethiopian group. Many of the believers in the park that day were from that group. I asked them about what brought them together. Beyond their religious connection, the majority of them were refugees seeking to escape ethnic tensions and violence in their homeland. It was powerful to hear their stories of sacrifice to find peace and respite in a new land.

Judah also represented an oppressed people and Jeremiah describes their grief following the fall of Jerusalem and subsequent Babylonian captivity. The whole book of Lamentations is a beautiful, poetic tribute to the full range of the human experience of pain, loss, and the hope of redemption through the mercies of God.

Judah had strayed from God's will and the prophetic message of Jeremiah warned of God's coming judgement. While he was denounced and persecuted for his message of calamity and call to repentance, he maintained fidelity and love for his people and their land.

The first four chapters of Lamentations follow an acrostic style that corresponds to each of the twenty-two letters of the Hebrew alphabet. Chapter 3 has 66 verses. Every three verses pay homage to each letter of the Hebrew alphabet. There is no such acknowledgement in Chapter 5. The last chapter is a prayer. It is a cry for mercy under the agonizing weight of sin. It is a prayer of intercession and forgiveness. One writer suggested that any technical literary expression would be inadequate to express the depths of their despair.

Jeremiah, often called the weeping prophet, models for us what it means to share "the truth in love." While he was called to proclaim a message of coming judgement, he remained committed to their ultimate transformation and redemption.

In our call to proclaim an end-time gospel message, we too can remain hopeful in the justice of a sovereign God who desires our good and extends mercy to all who come to Him by faith. ■

— DEREK LANE

JANUARY 17

DANIEL PRAYS A CORPORATE PRAYER FOR FORGIVENESS

"O Lord, hear! O Lord, forgive! O Lord, listen and act! Do not delay for Your own sake, my God, for Your city and Your people are called by Your name" (Daniel 9:19 NKJV).

It had been 66 years since the Jewish exile to Babylon. The Babylonian empire had fallen to the Medes and Persians. Daniel was aware of the prophecies of Jeremiah 25:11, and he knew the time to return to Jerusalem was near. He was also well-aware of the reasons God allowed them to be led away in the first place. Israel had fallen away from God. During their 500-year reign, they had killed His prophets, caused injustices, and profaned his Holy Temple with the erection of foreign gods.

While Daniel shared no part in the infraction of his people, he took responsibility. That is what makes his prayer in Daniel 9:1-19 so special! Daniel intercedes for Judea. He understands that before any rebuilding takes place, God's people must repent. Daniel pleads, "O Lord... we have sinned and committed iniquity, we have done wickedly and rebelled, even by departing from Your precepts and Your judgments...we have sinned, we have done wickedly!" (Verses 4a, 5, 15b).

In the year 2020 we saw some terrible events. It is palpable that this nation is still healing from its dark history. As a nation, we cannot turn a blind eye to the atrocities of the past nor present. The church must take the prayerful stance of Daniel by standing in the gap. We should be willing to intercede for forgiveness, even if we were not directly responsible, and take a stand to make a difference. Before any action can occur, we must pray for healing and redemption.

As a church, we must seek opportunities to minister to others' needs—even for those who are non-Christians. The best place to begin is in prayer. There is no better prayer than intercessory prayer. With our current context in mind, we can pray the same prayer as Daniel, substituting our nation in place of Jerusalem.

"O God, hear the prayer of Your [church], and their supplications, and for the Lord's sake cause Your face to shine on [this nation] which is [divided]. O my God, incline Your ear and hear; open Your eyes and see our [division], and this [nation that was founded] by Your name; for we do not present our supplications before You because of our righteous deeds, but because of Your great mercies. O Lord, hear! O Lord, forgive! O Lord, listen and act! Do not delay for Your own sake, my God, for Your [nation] and Your people. Amen" (Daniel 9:17-19 NKJV). ▮▮

— ROME ULIA

JANUARY 18

A PRAYER FOR GOD TO ACT

"O Lord, how long shall I cry, and You will not hear? Even cry out to You, 'violence!' and You will not save" (Habakkuk 1:2 NKJV).

Very little is known about Habakkuk except his name, which means either "the embracer" or "the wrestler." Habakkuk was the embodiment of his namesake. He was one who wrestled with the injustices of his day, as we do today.

The burden he carried has been one Black people have carried for centuries. "O Lord, how long shall I cry, and though wilt not hear, even cry out unto thee of violence and though wilt not save." (Habakkuk 1:2 KJV).

My grandparents and generation after generation prayed that prayer, and I am still praying it today! What will it take to stop the brutality and violence? When will the final steps be taken that lead us out of the dark and dismal dreggiest of racism and injustice into a present reality where race is not a factor in our institutional and societal practices?

Yes, indeed I pray for God to act, and to act soon! Systemic racism must be challenged and addressed. Policies and procedures that perpetuate racial discrimination must be crucified and laid to rest.

I continue to pray and inquire as Habakkuk did. His inquiries were deeply rooted in hope and trust as he waited in anticipation for God's reply (Habakkuk 2:1). God did not answer right away, but He did assure him that he would understand things better by and by.

As I pray—as we all pray—for God's intervention, like Habakkuk we must not forget to offer up prayers that express faith and trust in God.

"But the just shall live by his faith" (Habakkuk 2:4 KJV).

"Although the fig tree shall not blossom, neither shall fruit be in the vines; the labour of the olive shall fail, and the fields shall yield no meat; the flock shall be cut off from the fold, and there shall be no herd in the stalls: Yet I will rejoice in the Lord, I will joy in the God of my salvation. The Lord God is my strength, and he will make my feet like hinds' feet, and he will make me to walk upon mine high places" (Habakkuk 3:17-19 KJV).

While we may not always understand God's ways, we must trust that God is completely wise and sovereign in all His dealings. Hence, we pray that God will not only act, but that He will act through us as we faithfully wrestle with the enemy to carry out His will for a fair and just society. ▮▮

— EUGENE LEWIS

JANUARY 19

A PRAYER OF REJOICING

"Though the fig tree may not blossom, nor fruit be on the vines; Though the labor of the olive may fail, and the fields yield no food; Though the flock may be cut off from the fold, and there be no herd in the stalls—Yet I will rejoice in the Lord, I will joy in the God of my salvation"
(Habakkuk 3:17-18 NKJV).

In life there are times when it is kind of easy to trust in God's goodness and to praise Him because He has been good to us. Yet there are other times when things are falling apart. These are times when sorrow fills our hearts and we wonder if God really cares about us. In such times, can we still trust in God's love? How can we be joyful in pain, COVID-19, rejection, or distress? Is it possible to rejoice when we are going through tough times?

Today's Bible text is an account of the prophet Habakkuk who got to a point in his life (and the children of Israel as well) when things were bad. They were in difficult and depressing times. But rather than murmur or worry, Habakkuk chose to rejoice in the Lord God. Even with things falling apart, he chose to rejoice. The future looked bleak, but his heart bloomed with joy. Difficulties could not dictate his joy.

The word "still" in this context means regardless of what is going on, I will rejoice in the Lord. It also means however and regardless of the situation and circumstance, I will be glad in the Lord. Other meanings for "still" in this context are, notwithstanding, in-spite-of, despite, yet, but, though, although, and until now.

The word "rejoice" means to delight, glory, exult, joy, triumph, gladden, delight, be glad, cheer and enliven. The Bible commands us to rejoice always for the joy of the Lord is our strength. No storm should keep us downcast.

May God continue to revive us with His promises. ■

— RICHARD KURTZ

FINDING FREEDOM IN OUR TRUE IDENTITY

"In this manner, therefore, pray: Our Father in heaven, Hallowed be Your name" (Matthew 6:9 NKJV).

Often called, "The Model Prayer," it is one that many the world over can repeat from memory, conjuring up memories of family or corporate worship. But why not make "The Lord's Prayer" personal, as if it only applies to me and "My Father in heaven"? Let's take that liberty, perhaps just this once, and find new blessings in this iconic prayer.

When the disciples appealed to Jesus saying, "Lord, teach us to pray," He answered them, "In this manner, therefore, pray: Our Father in heaven, Hallowed be Your name" (Matthew 6:9 NKJV). It has always struck me that Jesus, our Elder Brother, is sharing His holy, heavenly Father with me, inviting me to claim Him as mine. My father. This intimate relationship is the context of this prayer and life itself, and our identity as sons and daughters of our heavenly Father.

"Your kingdom come. Your will be done. On earth as it is in heaven" (Matthew 6:10 NKJV). Not only is He our Father in heaven, let Him be in charge. His kingdom, His will, in what we see and know around us (on earth), as well as in the unseen claimed by faith (in heaven). This humbly reminds us of God's sovereignty and engagement in our lives.

From the high and lofty big picture, we turn to our day-to-day living. "Give us this day our daily bread. And forgive us our debts, as we forgive our debtors. And do not lead us into temptation but deliver us from the evil one" (Matthew 6:11-13a NKJV).

It is easy to think that we earn a wage to buy our food and thus provide for our own needs. But our daily bread comes from our heavenly Father in physical, spiritual and emotional sustenance. We depend on God for every breath we take. And with regard to forgiveness and temptations, we are reminded that God's love and grace offer us a new identity in Him. We are no longer slaves to the evil one. The Lord is our Master, our Sustainer, our Advocate, our Deliverer, in Whom we can place our very souls as our Keeper.

The grand finale, when sung to the traditional music written by Albert Hay Malotte in 1935, builds up to a melodic highpoint: "For Yours is the kingdom and the power and the glory forever. Amen" (Matthew 6:13b NKJV). The prayer ends just as it began, with the recognition of God as the One Who is in charge of all things; His kingdom, His power, His glory forever to be enjoyed by all of His children today and forever.

He is calling us home. ▮▮

— CRAIG CARR

CENTURION PRAYS FOR HEALING OF HIS SERVANT

"The centurion answered and said, 'Lord, I am not worthy that You should come under my roof. But only speak a word, and my servant will be healed'" (Matthew 8:8 NKJV).

Philanthropy is a challenging but rewarding field. Whether one is soliciting assistance for projects or causes or deciding which ones to support, it can be a rewarding experience for both the recipient and the donor. Most of my career I have had the wonderful privilege to help organizations fulfil their mission.

One such organization was a Christian community development ministry in Mendenhall, Mississippi. We hosted groups of volunteers who were interested in serving the needs of those less fortunate. They would travel from around the country to engage in short-term mission trips to repair homes, work on the farm, or visit residents to pray, offer hope, and provide emergency assistance or support where needed.

We were extremely grateful to the many individuals and groups from throughout the U.S. who took the time to sacrifice their own creature comforts to provide relief and hope to a small, rural impoverished community. And the response we received from everyone who visited was the same. They would leave saying, "We have received so much more than any material or financial help we have provided."

Indeed, it is more blessed to give than to receive. In fact, studies show how charitable giving, volunteering, and assisting others can have residual and measurable benefits for the health of those who serve. Altruistic behavior releases endorphins—chemicals that are naturally produced in our bodies that help relieve pain, reduce stress, and provide an overall sense of well-being.

One of the blessings of serving in that small rural town was the pleasant surprise of knowing that there are generous, kind-hearted people, blessed with material and financial means, who count it a joy and privilege to serve others less fortunate.

This reminds me of the centurion ruler. He was in a position of authority and influence. I am sure the loss of one servant would not have affected his bottom line. But he was relationally connected and interested in the health and well-being of his servant. His appeal to Christ was an intercessory prayer on behalf of someone he cared for. He expended time and energy to find help for one of his servants. He exhibited a spirit of humility and did not expect or demand favors based upon privilege, or use it as an excuse from serving the least of these.

May God grant us such a spirit. And may this ruler's example appeal to all who have been blessed with a measure of health and means. Lord, grant us such a selfless spirit of service. Amen. ■

— DEREK LANE

A WOMAN PRAYS FOR HEALING OF HER DAUGHTER

"Then she came and worshiped Him, saying, 'Lord, help me!'" (Matthew 15:25 NKJV).

Children are a blessing from God. They are entrusted to parents/guardians to protect and take care of them. We are their advocates. The mother in today's text is doing exactly that; she is advocating for her daughter. Have you ever been in a predicament as a parent when you felt as if you were going to lose your child? I have, and in a very poignant way I can identify with the woman in the Scripture lesson.

My daughter was diagnosed with Discoid Lupus while attending college to become a nurse. She had to withdraw from the nursing program and postpone her education.

As the disease progressed and began to take a toll on her health, I went into "protection mode." I wanted my daughter to live a fulfilling life and receive the best care possible. The disease changed her life in so many ways. We celebrated many holidays with her in hospital rooms. She was in and out of remission. At one point she was taking nearly 40 pills of prescription medication per day, and required out-patient procedures for pain management.

One particular day I will never forget. I asked to have a conference with her primary care physician. I wanted us to explore ways to reduce her medication regimen, as they seemed to keep her in a lethargic state. At some point during the conversation he broke the news and said, "Your daughter only has about three years, give or take, to live. Why not make her time here on earth comfortable? Let her remain on the current medication regimen that I now have her on."

I literally could not speak, but summoned the energy to cry out, "Jesus give me strength!"

How does it feel to have your plea dismissed, ignored, or countered with more bad news? I can relate to the mother in our text. What do you do?

We can take a lesson from the mother's response. In spite of her treatment and Jesus' seeming lack of compassion, the text says, "she came and worshiped Him."

Maybe your situation does not result in the answer you expected. Perhaps your intercession on behalf of loved ones does not yield the results you desire. But you can still worship and leave the results with God. It has been 13 years and my daughter's condition is in remission. She is living a happy, fulfilled life today.

When life seems unfair, when people seem aloof to the struggle of others, we can always worship. We can continue to trust and leave the results with God. ■

— MAE ALDRIDGE-LANE

JANUARY 23

A PRAYER FROM THE CROSS

"And about the ninth hour Jesus cried with a loud voice, saying, ' Eli, Eli, lama sabachthani?' that is to say, 'My God, my God, why hast thou forsaken me?'" (Matthew 27:46 KJV).

One cannot help but think—black people in particular—that like Jesus, we often feel that God has forsaken us. Consider how long we have suffered at the hands of slavery and Jim Crow, and how long we have been handcuffed physically and economically in ways unimaginable.

And what about the religious bigotry and betrayal we have felt from white evangelical theocrats and black theological impotent and greedy power-hungry preachers who have equally sold the black community out to the money changers of our day? It would be hard not to believe if one did not feel forsaken at one time or another.

However, for as much as the cross was meant to be an "emblem of suffering and shame," we look to the cross for relief. For Jesus' prayer is not without hope. Outside of love, hope may be the greatest gift to humankind. It gave our ancestors the will to live, and it did the same for Jesus as He was dying on the cross.

Remember, Jesus was a victim of brutality and injustice. On the surface, His prayer would appear to be without hope; "Father why has thou forsaken me?" But it wasn't! It was pregnant with possibilities.

Hope may not be spoken, but it was demonstrated by the way Jesus died. He died for all people who are on the slippery slope of sin, prejudice, brutality, and injustice. He addressed the perpetual pandemic of racism, brutality, and injustice. When Jesus gave up His life in exchange for ours, He showed us a better way through love, hope, and a prayer of forgiveness.

Jesus' prayer, if not rightly understood, by all appearances could be misleading. God did not forget Jesus, nor has He forgotten us. When we read further in the closing verses of Matthew 27, after Jesus died, hope sprang to life. The graves in and around Jerusalem gave up the righteous dead to life and life eternal. Jesus followed three days later.

The cross has always been central to our faith and prayer life. As we continue to fight racism and injustice wherever it may be found, I pray—we pray—"Father into thy hands we commit our spirit." ▮▮

— EUGENE LEWIS

JANUARY 24

UNSEEN BLESSINGS

"Then, looking up to heaven, He sighed, and said to him, 'Ephphatha,' that is, 'Be opened'" (Mark 7:34 NKJV).

God wants to surprise us. He delights in pouring out blessings for His children.

When our children were young, we had a family tradition on New Year's Day. We reviewed God's blessing from the previous year and shared what we anticipated in the year ahead.

One year had been particularly difficult for us. We prayed for God to open windows and work things out on our behalf. That was a year we will never forget. He went beyond our wildest imaginations and poured out unseen blessings on our behalf!

God did the same thing in the story of the healing of the man who could not hear or speak. His friends brought him to Jesus in hopes that Jesus would extend compassion and pronounce upon him a blessing, or simply share an expression of encouragement. They did not expect Jesus to heal him, as evidenced by their response.

Before the healing took place, the Bible says He "took him aside from the multitude." Often God does His work for us, and in us, away from the crowd. Sometimes our most intimate spiritual seasons are experienced when we are away from human interaction.

The narrative then describes the healing process. Jesus "put his fingers in his ears" and "spat and touched his tongue" (Mark 7:33 NKJV). Jesus touched the man in the areas that needed healing. When God steps in and begins to heal the broken places in our lives, it is more than an intellectual experience; it is also an experience we can feel.

Finally, in Verse 37 the Scriptures tell us that when Jesus "looked up to heaven, He sighed." It is only one of a few prayers in Scripture where a prayer was uttered without words. The sigh was an inward groan and a compassionate response to the pain and sorrow sin has brought into this world. It was also a prayer to the Father for healing. Romans 8:28 also describes how the Holy Spirit intercedes on our behalf with groanings "which cannot be uttered."

Isn't it wonderful to know that God sighs over us? He pities our condition, and desires that we experience life, and life more abundantly. Often He moves in our lives in ways that allow us to experience blessings we didn't ask for, favors we didn't anticipate, and a touch we didn't expect.

May our relationships with God grow as we seek to know Him more, and as He continues to open the windows of heaven! ▮▮

— DEREK LANE

JANUARY 25

WHERE ARE THE NINE?

"And they lifted up their voices and said, 'Jesus, Master, have mercy on us!' So when He saw them, He said to them, 'Go, show yourselves to the priests.' And so it was that as they went, they were cleansed. And one of them, when he saw that he was healed, returned, and with a loud voice glorified God, and fell down on his face at His feet, giving Him thanks. And he was a Samaritan. So Jesus answered and said, 'Were there not ten cleansed? But where are the nine?" (Luke 17:13-17 NKJV).

Expressing gratitude is a choice. It is also a voluntary, selfless act of appreciation. Research has shown that the most grateful people tend to live happier, longer, and more fulfilling lives.

In the Bible story above, Jesus heals 10 lepers. What is interesting is that they do not experience healing until they act on His word. The story says, "as they went, they were cleansed." How often have we prayed to God to move in our lives but have not acted on His Word?

The Bible also makes a point to identify the nationality of one of the recipients of healing. The Bible says he was a Samaritan. The Samaritans and Jewish people did not get along. They resented one another and tended to disassociate from each other.

The Samaritans were originally strangers who amalgamated with the Jews during their Babylonian captivity. When the Jews were allowed to return to their homeland, they refused to allow the Samaritans to worship with them at the temple. So the Samaritans erected a rival temple on Mount Gerizim, which was subsequently destroyed. The enmity between the Jews and Samaritans continued during the time of Christ. John 4:9 says the Jews had "no dealings with the Samaritans."

Do we have racial and ethnic tensions like that today? Do we treat or disassociate ourselves from people based upon their traits, customs, or beliefs? This story also highlights an irony of sorts. Although a Samaritan was among those healed, Jesus commanded all to show themselves to the Jewish priest; but only the Samaritan returned to show thanks.

God's church is comprised of people from every "race, kindred, tongue, and people." What if we could model a spirit of kinship and fellowship that reached across ethnic, racial, and cultural divides? When only the Samaritan returned to show thanks Jesus asked, "Where are the nine?" That's a good question. Why didn't the others return to show thanks? The Bible does not tell us.

Likewise, where are those today who are willing to reach across superficial divides and celebrate the goodness and mercy of God? Where are those willing to cultivate an attitude of gratitude, and rejoice in the mercies of God for His healing and manifold blessings in our lives?

My prayer today is that we would take a moment to celebrate the diversity of creation and the mercies of God. Our prayer should be that we allow His Spirit to help us see one another as children of our heavenly Father.

Where are the nine? ■

— DEREK LANE

JANUARY 26

I WANT MY HAM

"Now there was a widow in that city; and she came to him, saying, 'Get justice for me from my adversary'" (Luke 18:3 NKJV).

In March of 2018, I played the character, "Hambone" in August Wilson's play, Two Trains Running. Wilson wrote several Pulitzer Prize-winning plays and is perhaps best known for ten of them, often referred to as his "century cycle." Each of these ten plays is about a different decade of Black life in the 20th century. One of my goals, as an actor, is to perform in all ten of Wilson's century cycle plays. So far I've performed in three of them. Seven more to go!

Two Trains Running is Wilson's 1960's installment of the century cycle. The play is set in 1969 in a diner in Pittsburgh, Pennsylvania. The owner of the diner is the play's protagonist, Memphis Lee. The diner is set to be condemned and Memphis refuses to be short-changed for the price that the city is offering him for his property. He wants fair value and he won't settle for less. The story is told through the daily activities of the diner; activities which unfold in the Black lives of those who frequent the diner as its faithful patrons.

Hambone is one of those patrons. He is promised a ham if he paints a fence for a white butcher whose shop is across the street from the diner. Hambone paints the fence, but upon completion the white butcher offers him a chicken instead. Hambone tells the white butcher, "I want my ham."

Hambone wants his ham so badly that every day for nearly ten years he meets the butcher outside of his shop when he comes to open it and says, "I want my ham." Hambone dies before he gets his ham; But he dies trying.

Hambone represents the entirety of the 400-year African-American political experience; he abides on the receiving end of a broken promise. Hambone doesn't want a handout. Hambone wants what was promised him, and he's determined to get it.

Similarly, whether it is the lofty rhetoric of America's founding documents or the broken promises of "forty acres and a mule" during reconstruction, time and again African-Americans have been promised the ham of justice, only to be offered the chicken of broken promises.

As you meditate on social justice today, consider Hambone and the parable of the widow and the unjust judge found in Luke 18:1-8. The spirit of importunity embodied in both Hambone and the widow helped them relentlessly pursue justice. Pray today that God blesses you with a fervent spirit of importunity on behalf of others that you may do likewise.

I want my ham. How about you? ∎

— TIMOTHY GOLDEN

JANUARY 27

IF THESE HOLD THEIR PEACE

"But He answered and said to them, 'I tell you that if these should keep silent, the stones would immediately cry out'" (Luke 19:40 NKJV).

It was late in the afternoon on a Friday. A "good lady" was just picking up a couple of items at the grocery store before the sun went down. The lines were long and she was five people back from the cash register. Checking out in front of her was an old woman and an old man.

The "good lady" didn't really pay any attention at first, but it soon became obvious that something was wrong. The old woman was going through her purse and pulled out some cash. The "good lady" could not hear the words, but it seemed as if the old woman did not have enough cash. She was going through all of the pockets in her purse. She turned to the old man and asked if he had any money. He must have said "no" because she said something like, "You never have any money with you."

Bits of conversation went back and forth. The "good lady" could only hear snippets, as she was several places back in the line. In the "good lady's" mind she was thinking, "I wish I were closer so I could help." What an audacious thought. The "good lady" was only five people away.

She watched the scene in front of her eyes. Without hearing the words, she knew what was going on, but she stood motionless. If it had been a movie, the audience would have been chanting in their heads, "help her."

The "good lady" wanted to help, but she stood there and watched, as if detached from the story. The people behind her were getting upset because the line wasn't moving. The "good lady" wanted to turn and say to them, "The old woman doesn't have enough money." Instead, she stood there thinking, "I wish I was closer so I could help."

That Friday afternoon she left the store, ashamed and without feeling the joy from the blessing of service. When we fail, when we operate in the mode of business as normal, God's plan can still prevail. The old woman's needs were met. The cashier, against company policy, gave of her own money to help the old woman. God had his will accomplished.

"Good" people, with no malcontent in their mind at all, can easily fail to be the hands of Jesus in this world. Esther was told that if she held her peace, that respite and deliverance would arise from another place (Esther 4:14). Jesus says, "If these should hold their peace, the stones would immediately cry out" (Luke 19:40 NKJV). ■■

— PAM SCOTT

JANUARY 28

THE CHURCH'S RESPONSIBILITY TO THE POOR

"Then Peter said, 'Silver and gold I do not have, but what I do have I give you: In the name of Jesus Christ of Nazareth, rise up and walk'" (Acts 3:6 NKJV).

In Acts, Chapter 3, we encounter the story of Peter and John as they were making their way to the temple to pray. We know the story well.

A certain man, lame from birth, was carried by his friends to the temple gates to beg of the crowd. As Peter and John approached the gate, they were impressed to engage this lame man who lived in poverty. Peter called his attention saying, "Look at us." The man looked up and locked eyes with the disciples. Then Peter said those immortal words in today's text: "Silver and gold I do not have, but what I do have I give to you. In the name of Jesus Christ of Nazareth, walk" (Acts 3:6). The disciples then took him by the hand, helped him to his feet, and the man began to walk.

In his book, The Book of Acts, F.F. Bruce recounted a legendary tale of an interaction taking place over 1,000 years after the story of the lame man at the gate. The medieval theologian and philosopher, Thomas Aquinas, was called on by Pope Innocent II (around 1135 A.D.). By this time, the Roman Catholic Church had established a monolithic presence in Europe as both the religious and political authority.

As Aquinas approached the Pope, he found Innocent II counting a large sum of money. Looking up, the pope said, "You see, Thomas, the church can no longer say, 'Silver and gold have I none.'" Thomas Aquinas's reply was immediate; "True, holy father, but neither can she now say, 'Rise and walk'" (Bruce, 1988).

Without a doubt, the healing of the lame man and the power of the resurrected Jesus Christ is the central theme of Acts, Chapter 3. However, as a subtext of that chapter, Peter and John encounter the misguided scorn of the religious authority who don't see their act as service, but as a threat. Similarly, Bruce sheds light on the dangers of a religion driven by greed rather than service. In both stories, the church seems to marginalize the marginalized.

The early church was blind to the clear miracles that were happening in their midst, just as the medieval church was blinded to the true ministry and mission of Jesus. Both saw the plight of the poor as a social problem removed from the duties of high church office.

When we look at our world today, what blind spots do you see that represent opportunities for ministry? Are there individuals or groups in our world today that are calling for help? What is the reaction to their call by the church, by society, and by you? ▮▮

— CRAIG MATTSON

JANUARY 29

A MESSAGE OF COURAGE AND PRAYER OF COMPASSION

"While they were stoning him, Stephen prayed, 'Lord Jesus, receive my spirit.' Then he fell on his knees and cried out, 'Lord, do not hold this sin against them.' When he had said this, he fell asleep" (Acts 7:59-60 NIV).

For marginalized communities and persons of color it is almost inevitable. Inescapable. Eventually, there will come a time when those of us who identify with these groups will be confronted with the ugly stain often associated with the suffix, "-ism." Racism. Sexism. Classism. It happens when we are mistreated for traits, characteristics, or circumstances that we have little or nothing to do with.

Stephen, as one of the first deacons of the early Christian church, was associated with, what could best be described at the time, a religious minority of the Jewish sect.

Christianity was in its embryonic stages and often misunderstood by the community at large. What made this all too familiar, yet a painful beginning in the history of the church, is that Stephen was being stoned by religious people. He was being persecuted by believers with whom he had once enjoyed fellowship. Experiencing mistreatment is hurtful enough; but when it is initiated or perpetrated by religious people, it can be extremely harmful and contradictory to the gospel mission and witness.

I experienced this 16 years ago in the aftermath of Hurricane Katrina that ravaged the gulf coast of the U.S. My church at the time, along with other area churches, was composed predominantly of people of color. As part of assisting with the long-term disaster recovery efforts, we managed a donations warehouse and coordinated volunteer activities with fellow white believers in the Southern region.

Tensions arose when our white counterparts assumed administrative and leadership roles, while area members—who happened to be persons of color—were assigned labor-intensive tasks and responsibilities. Differences also ensued over the appropriation and distribution of donated items.

Eventually the conflict was resolved, but it highlights the fact that the church is not immune from experiencing issues of fairness and justice. It also underscores the need for the church to acknowledge and confront challenges whenever and wherever they exist, and create an atmosphere where healing and reconciliation can take place.

We all are called to be "ministers of reconciliation." With his dying breath, Stephen was able to rise above the bitterness and animosity that is often associated with incidences of unfairness and injustice.

May we have the courage to acknowledge, confront, and excise any actions, behavior, or attitudes that cheapen or treat others with less dignity than they deserve as children of God. And may the Lord grant us the courage of Stephen to confront, speak truth to power, and advocate for the work of justice; and the compassion to forgive and resist the temptation to harbor bitterness and animosity. ■

— DEREK LANE

JANUARY 30

A PRAYER OF RESURRECTION

"But Peter put them all out, and knelt down and prayed; and turning to the body he said, 'Tabitha, arise.' And she opened her eyes, and when she saw Peter she sat up" (Acts 9:40 NKJV).

I believe we shortchange Tabitha (Dorcas) by reducing her to a simple do-gooder and missing the strength of her leadership and advocacy for the vulnerable. However, the distress felt by those she left behind tells a different story.

When Peter arrives after her death, the widows rush at him with the physical evidence of Tabitha's influence. The clothing they show him represents more than her kindness; it represents economic assets, physical well-being, and hope. The widows' distress demonstrates that losing Tabitha goes beyond heartache. They have lost an advocate who brought stability and comfort to their lives.

In a beautiful web of support, the widows advocate for the one who had once advocated for them. They come to Peter crying out for help. Peter responds by advocating for Tabitha's restoration.

Often we, as ministry leaders, prefer to see ourselves as the helper, rather than the one who needs help. We fail to see ourselves as being as frail as those we serve. But we all need to lean on others to bring fresh perspective, renewed vigor, and new life to our work and humanity. Who is in your web of support, bringing advocacy to you and whom you advocate for?

After clearing the room, Peter prays. The text does not give the full script of the prayer. In fact, it might be easy to skip over the prayer except that the command Peter gives next is a part of that prayer; a prayer for restoration and wholeness.

"Tabitha, get up!"

These words are a prayer for God's mercy and healing. Tabitha's eyes open. She sees Peter and sits up, renewed in body and soul to continue her life of service. To separate Peter's prayer from his command for Tabitha to get up would be a mistake. It is only in prayer that we can speak words of wholeness and change.

Too often we leave God in our "prayer closet" as we go out to do the work that needs to happen in our churches and communities. But your work is itself a prayer. That prayer is fulfilled as God brings life to our work.

Whether you are marching in the street, sewing clothes, distributing food, or visiting prisoners, do your work and speak your words as a prayer. Speak your desires, and behind the words pray that the God of the universe will bring your service to life. Pray that Jesus, Himself, will breathe transformation and wholeness into the work you do and that life will flourish from them. ▮

— COLETTE NEWER

JANUARY 31

THE PRAYER OF THE MARTYRS

"And they cried with a loud voice, saying, 'How long, O Lord, holy and true, until You judge and avenge our blood on those who dwell on the earth?'" (Revelation 6:10 NKJV).

The theme given for this devotional's text was made into the title but given the punctuation of a question. Do martyrs really want vengeance? Is this the longing expressed in their tears and their subsequent spilled blood? An examination of the passage in its setting and in the context of Scripture may suggest something else.

Martyrs were killed with violence for sharing good news, "the word of God and the testimony [of Jesus] which they possessed" (Revelation 6:9). They cried out "as loud as they could" (phōnē megalē), questioning the policy of permission. They don't doubt God's character, but they do question His methods. It seems so unjust. It feels like God is indifferent to their plight. He is sitting on His hands while they are taking it on the chin. Their "prayer" is better described as a scream.

"When will You act?"

Are they screaming to God to punish their enemies? Does the blood of Abel cry out to God to "let Cain have it?" Would punitive action make it all better? Does Job cry out to God to slaughter the Sabeans and Chaldeans? Does King David celebrate at the death of Saul? Does Stephen long for the stone-throwing mob to be slaughtered? Is this what Jesus prayed while hanging on the cross? How far and how long are the words, "Father forgive!," applicable?

If the loud crying of gospel-living, gospel-proclaiming victims falls in line with the prayer of the One called, "the Faithful Martyr" (Revelation 1:5), then perhaps what is in mind is the outcome. What we are hoping for is an earth made new where righteousness dwells. No more trafficking of children, forced labor, unjust wages, or abuses based on gender or race. The issue is one of time, and it seems so long.

Will evil, experienced in deception and violence, ever end? God's thoughts and methods are counter-intuitive to human solutions.

Vindication will come but in God's' time. Patience in waiting for the justice of God is one of the hallmarks of the faithful. (See Revelation 14:12.)

Revelation reveals that while we are hurting and hollering, God is sealing. And perhaps the most evocative picture of ultimate justice is found in the phrase, "and God [the Father, the One who sits on the throne] will wipe away every tear from their eyes" (Revelation 7:17). This is ultimate justice writ large. This is what the martyrs are praying for. ■

— JOHN KURLINSKI

FEBRUARY

SOCIAL JUSTICE

This month I prayerfully enter into sharing devotions around a subject that incites both anxiety and fervid sentiment in our current social climate. This topic is social justice, and I must admit that in facing the influence of a myriad of positions, it is usually easiest to succumb to feelings of reluctance and to avoid the conversation altogether. However, one cannot share the gospel without addressing the inherent dignity of each and every human being.

Throughout this month, it is my prayer that as you read the daily devotional thoughts you will be informed, challenged and inspired. God calls us to be His hands and feet here on earth; so, in us exploring our feelings for others we are in turn exploring the heart God has for His people. This isn't a new concept. God's people have been caring for those less fortunate for thousands of years.

Amos, the prophet who wrote the Old Testament book, was a big advocate for social justice. He spoke up about the harsh treatment those in power had over those less fortunate. God calls us from the same heart today. He still desires to see all people treated equally and He still calls us to be His hands and feet to do it. There is a group of people God has put on your heart. What can you do to stand up for them today?

As you read may you reflect on the words Dr. Martin Luther King, Jr.: "We refuse to believe that the bank of justice is bankrupt. We refuse to believe that there are insufficient funds in the great vaults of opportunity of this nation. We have come to remind America of the fierce urgency of now! Now is the time to rise from the dark and desolate valley of segregation to the sunlit path of racial justice. Now is the time to open the doors of opportunity to all of God's children. Now is the time to lift our nation from the quick sands of racial injustice to the solid rock of brotherhood." ▮▮

— JEROME HURST
Director of Public Affairs and Religious Liberty,
Allegheny West Conference of Seventh-day Adventists

FEBRUARY 1

YES, GOD DOES CARE ABOUT SOCIAL JUSTICE

"The people of the land have used oppressions, committed robbery, and mistreated the poor and needy; and they wrongfully oppress the stranger" (Ezekiel 22:29 NKJV).

According to today's Scripture, in various translations, "those who are looked upon as important people of the land have practiced extortion and have committed robbery. They have oppressed the poor and mistreated the immigrant. They have also oppressed and denied equal justice among the people."

In the Bible there are several passages of Scripture that remind us of this type of behavior. Ezekiel 22:29 is just one example. This particular verse appears in a chapter where God specifically alludes to the fact of how the people have sinned. Throughout much of the chapter, God focuses on Israel's leaders, which include those in authority. It appears the problem is their disregard for God's commandments, not only through their worship, but also how they treat others with oppressive tactics—specifically those who are immigrants—while also denying the rights of orphans and widows.

Once again, in Verse 29, the writer says, "the important people of the land have practiced extortion and have committed robbery. They have oppressed the poor and mistreated the immigrant. They've oppressed and denied justice." Actually, in the Hebrew this means "important people of the land" which actually refers to ordinary people.

Continuing the same practice of their leaders, they had taken advantage of the feeble and deprived each other. They practiced discrimination in order to benefit themselves and had neglected to look after, or do the right thing by others. Therefore, just like their leaders, the people stood under God's reasoning.

This verse clearly depicts the desire of God to ensure that all are treated equitably. Yes, He does care about social justice in society, and He judges those who fail to put it into practice. It appears that those who are scripturally minded have a sincere desire to follow God's lead to treat everyone as God commanded us in the Ten Commandments. Yet, when we are devoted to a particular subject—and in this case social justice—we are not required to politically take sides. When you analyze the difference, the way we develop a passion for justice in the political sphere will vary, depending upon our varied views that have nothing to do with Scripture.

I often say that Jesus was a social justice preacher. Why? Because He decided to remain in the presence of those who were considered the least, the left out, and the lost. ■■

— JIMMY GATES

FEBRUARY 2

BORN TO BE FREE

"For I consider that the sufferings of this present time are not worthy to be compared with the glory that is to be revealed to us" (Romans 8:18 NASB).

As we celebrate Black History Month, the apostle Paul directs our attention to a passage of Scripture that gives us a sobering wakeup call: We are all in bondage.

Now I know it doesn't look that way, at least not in the way we typically think of bondage, and sometimes it doesn't feel that way, but God's creation is in bondage. Paul, in Romans 8:18, identifies it as "present sufferings." He is not speaking of a difficult period in history, but rather the entire present age. The whole history of creation, since man's disobedience, is marked by suffering.

Global warming, natural disaster, food shortages, violence inflicted on the innocent, etc. All these present issues are the result of man's fall into sin. And now, Paul describes all creation as "groaning" as a woman in labor pains, wanting to be free from this burden. But just like a woman who gives birth, the end result always outweighs the pains that precede it. Paul wants to remind us; there is always another side to our pain.

From suffering comes glory; from labor pains there is birth; from the present there is eternity; from adoption there is kinship; and from bondage there is freedom. This is the hope that should anchor us as we live on this side of eternity—understanding that nothing we are going through lasts forever. Our present struggle, our bondage to this decaying body, will all be ended when creation is restored, and there will not be any violence or death.

Maybe you, today, have found yourself in a place of pain and suffering. A loved one has died, a job offer fell through, or perhaps you just find yourself saddened as you listen to all the reports of devastation and destruction happening on a daily basis. You may find yourself trapped in a sick body that doesn't want to cooperate, leaving you sidelined. Or possibly your dreams and aspirations haven't come to fruition and you feel like you've missed your opportunity.

In these moments the temptation is to feel trapped and hopeless, thinking that the way things are is how they always will be. But Paul reminds us that we were "born to be free" despite our current circumstances, and what we see is a better day is coming.

We are to live with this hope, knowing that the present sufferings of today cannot compare with the glory that God will reveal/birth in us! ■■

— BRYANT SMITH

FEBRUARY 3

JUSTICE FOR RIGHTEOUSNESS SAKE

"But let justice run down like water, and righteousness like a mighty stream" (Amos 5:24 NKJV).

During the time of Amos, the Northern Kingdom of Israel had allowed their religious practices to become disconnected from real life. Though this disconnection existed, they still carried out their ritualistic rites of religious routine.

After this "performance" was over, they treated each other without regard for what God wanted in their relationships. This lack of justice and righteousness, especially in relation to the poor and needy, angered God. He sent Amos to warn the Israelites of the impending judgement that was to come upon them.

God gave Amos a message for the people. Amos 5:21 says, "I hate all your show and pretense—the hypocrisy of your religious festivals and solemn assemblies" (Version). God says, I'm not impressed with all your dressing up, praise teams, and preaching. He says what impresses/interests him is, "a mighty flood of justice, an endless river of righteous living" (Amos 5:24).

God says, I am more interested in justice. From today's text, there seems to be a connection between justice and righteousness. In the Bible God makes it quite clear that He is deeply concerned about justice and fairness in the way society should be organized. Proverbs 29:7 says, "The righteous care about justice for the poor, but the wicked have no such concerns" (Version).

The kingdom of God is a kingdom of justice, but it's people must do more than be religious. They (we) must be the hands and feet of Jesus to the poor, outcast, oppressed, hungry, needy, sick, and even to people that are difficult to deal with. Without this component we will fall short of what it means to be God's people and dwell in a kingdom of God's justice. ∎

— JEROME HURST

FEBRUARY 4

THE WILDERNESSES WE KNOW NOTHING ABOUT

"Behold, I will do a new thing, now it shall spring forth; Shall you not know it? I will even make a road in the wilderness and rivers in the desert" (Isaiah 43:19 NKJV).

Although we talk about the wildernesses we have been in and through, and give God praise for having gotten us through, the fact is that we really do not know the number of wildernesses we have actually been in. James Weldon Johnson wrote, "We have been over a way that with tears has been watered..." but we do not know how often that "way" has been constructed just for us to help us to wither and fall under the weight of white supremacist oppression.

Isaiah, Chapter 43, is one of the most beautiful in the Hebrew Scriptures. From the beginning of the chapter, the words speak to us about the presence of God, saving us, lifting us, and protecting us.

But years ago, after the successful uprising in Haiti led by Toussaint L'Ouverture against the French, Christian missionaries in England grew worried. They did not want enslaved Africans to believe they had the right to rebel against their condition. They needed them to believe that God had created them to be enslaved.

And so they decided to do all they could to prevent enslaved Africans from seeking freedom. Among the things they did was create a Bible just for "Negroes," which they called, "The Slave Bible." Nearly 90 percent of the Hebrew Scriptures, and 50 percent of the New Testament, was deleted. In the Protestant, King James Version (KJV) of the Bible, there 1,189 chapters; but in the Slave Bible there are only 232. None of the psalms were included. The Book of Exodus excludes the story of the exodus; in fact, in the Slave Bible only Chapters 19 and 20 are included in the Book of Exodus, as opposed to the 40 in the KJV. The Gospel of Mark was excluded, as was the entire book of Revelation and all of the Minor Prophets

Thus, African Americans were fed a manipulated Bible, constructed to keep them in their place. Anything that suggested that God wanted all people to be free was taken out. The 43rd Chapter of Isaiah was not included, which means that the words about newness springing forth and about God making a way in the wilderness were not in the Bible the enslaved were taught from.

People of African descent were thrust into a wilderness within the wilderness of a racist country, a way 'that with tears has been watered," but they persisted and hung on. Regardless of what the oppressors tried to do, they could not take the will and the word of God out of the hearts of the Africans. They knew a God of love and of liberation and freedom. Not even the wilderness of white supremacy, fed by a people who were so intent on controlling them that they thought nothing of altering a sacred text, could keep them—our ancestors—from moving forward.

Regardless of the obstacles we face because of a world that hates us, we have God, God who has never left us nor forsaken us. And we always will. Amen and amen. ▮▮

— DR. SUSAN SMITH

WHAT DO YOU SEE?

"When it was evening, His disciples came to Him, saying, 'This is a deserted place, and the hour is already late. Send the multitudes away that they may go into the villages and buy themselves food.' But Jesus said to them, 'They do not need to go away. You give them something to eat'" (Matthew 14:15-16 NKJV).

Deitrich Bonhoeffer, Desmond Tutu, Nelson Mandela, Susan B. Anthony, Malcolm X, and Martin Luther King, Jr. are some of the greatest social justice activists & warriors this world has ever known. Yet the greatest one of them all is often times not even considered a social justice activist and warrior at all, and that is Jesus Christ of Nazareth.

Jesus understood that there is no gospel outside of social justice. Whether or not you consider it the same or as something different, at its very core the gospel and social justice focus on the same thing— compassion for people. This is why Jesus declared that, "He has anointed Me to preach the gospel to the poor; He has sent Me to heal the brokenhearted, to proclaim liberty to the captives and recovery of sight to the blind, to set at liberty those who are oppressed" (Luke 4:18 NKJV).

In the book *Wishful Thinking*, author Fredrick Buechner describes compassion as, "The fatal capacity for feeling what it is like to live inside somebody else's skin. It is the knowledge that there can never really be any peace and joy for me until there is peace and joy finally for you too."

Speaking of compassion, I'm reminded of the passage of Scripture in Matthew 14 where Jesus is with His disciples and He sees a crowd. And because He sees them the Scriptures say that He was moved with compassion for them and He healed their sick. It's the story of the feeding of the 5,000.

Yet there was almost no miracle that day. The disciples wanted to send the people away hungry and tired even though they had followed Jesus all day. Even though they had witnessed and performed ministry that day, they never really saw the people. They didn't feel their hunger; they didn't feel their pain. That's why they were so willing to send them away hungry because they never saw them, and as a result, they had no compassion.

We're not much different today than the disciples. Many of us are doing ministry, but we're not seeing people. But not Jesus, He saw people. He saw them that day and He told His disciples don't send them away; we'll feed them. Jesus took what was available—two fish and five loaves of bread—and blessed it, and brake it, and— you know the rest of the story.

But it all started because Jesus saw people, and had compassion for them. The question is what do you see? ▮▮

— JASON RIDLEY

FEBRUARY 6

COLORISM

"Then Miriam and Aaron spoke against Moses because of the Ethiopian woman whom he had married" (Numbers 12:1 NKJV).

Colorism, or having biases against people that are a darker hue or lighter hue than you, is real. In slavery, some were separated by their color; the lighter or whiter you were, the better job you got on the plantation. The darker you were, the harder job you got on the plantation.

This is the beginning set up for classism amongst blacks in America. E. Franklin Frazier wrote a book in 1955 titled, The Black Bourgeoisie, which does a great job outlining aspects of colorism. But this form of prejudice is found in the Bible, too.

Moses takes a wife—and we are unsure if this wife is Zipporah, the daughter of Jethro, or if he takes another wife—but Numbers 12 states that Miriam, his sister and Aaron, his brother, had an issue with the woman "because she was an Cushite" (Numbers 12:1). Remember, Cush means Ethiopia. The woman was darker in color than they were. Aaron and Miriam could probably pass the brown paper bag test; Moses' wife probably couldn't.

Moses' own siblings began to plot against him because of the color of his wife. They murmured and complained, and said, "God does not only speak to Moses, he speaks to us too!" (Numbers 12:2 paraphrased). And Moses, being meek, sits there and says nothing (Numbers 12:3).

But God sees this and God calls both Miriam and Aaron out on it, and rebukes them and reminds them, "whom I call, don't you question!" After that encounter, God made Miriam a leper, white as snow (Numbers 12:10). It is Moses, the husband of the wife she talked about, who had to intercede on her behalf. Moses pleaded to God to heal her, but God didn't want to hear it. He said, "if her father spit in her face would she not be locked out for seven days? Put her out the camp for seven days and she shall be returned to herself! (Numbers 12:12-14).

That is what colorism and racism do to us as children of God. It makes us sick, as it did Miriam. It makes us focus on the wrong things about people, forgetting that they, too, were created by God. The very thing Miriam thought she was, lighter, became the curse that she had!

Colorism is real. Be mindful how you treat those of darker colors or different cultures. God loves them too! Remember God is love. ■

— VINCENT E. STOKES

FEBRUARY 7

GOD'S HANDS

"Humble yourselves, therefore, under the mighty hand of God so that at the proper time He may exalt you" (1 Peter 5:6 ESV).

"God of our weary years"

Lord, touch me! Touch me with Thy healing hands, loving hands, caring hands, keeping hands, providing hands, praying hands, stirring hands, prosperity hands, delivering hands, reaching hands, victorious hands, participating hands, selfless hands, comforting hands, encouraging hands, helping hands, hosting hands, mighty hands, creating hands, teaching hands, timeless hands, protecting hands, withered hands, massaging hands, blessing hands, blessed hands, fighting hands, redeeming hands, knowing hands, working hands, forgiving hands, covering hands.

"God of our silent tears"

Today, touch me Father with Thy freeing hands, connected hands, connecting hands, restoring hands, still hands, strengthening hands, compassionate hands, bronze hands, cotton-picking hands, old and tired hands, equipping hands, believing hands, courageous hands, Holy hands, naming hands, great hands, stretched hands, pierced hands, bloody hands, factory-stained hands, resting hands, resurrected hands, living hands, anointed hands, praising hands, righteous hands, raised hands, saving hands, arthritic hands, shielding hands, feeling hands, advocating hands, justice hands, powerful hands, trusting hands, calloused-with-good-news hands, hands like my hands.

"God of our silent tears"

Lord, touch me with Thy victorious right hand, hands that made all things, keeping hands, hands of You who "has done great things." Thank You for Your empowering, delivering, discipline hands in whom I have chosen to "entrust my life."

God "who has bought us thus far on the way," whose image I am made in, walk with me, talk to me, touch me, Lord, so that I might "lift (my) voice and sing ... to march on till (in Your name) "victory is won." Amen. ▮▮

— LESLIE WATSON WILSON

FEBRUARY 8

GOD'S FAVOR FOR ALL

"'The Spirit of the Lord is upon Me, because He has anointed Me to preach the gospel to the poor; He has sent Me to heal the brokenhearted, to proclaim liberty to the captives and recovery of sight to the blind, to set at liberty those who are oppressed; to proclaim the acceptable year of the Lord'" (Luke 4:18-19 NKJV).

From the very beginning of Jesus' ministry, He very clearly enunciated his agenda. No one was left in doubt as to the main thrust of his portfolio, except of course for the Pharisees! It was always God's plan to restore and free humanity from the shackles of sin.

Consequently, everywhere Jesus ministered there was always a vast crowd of sick, indigent, poor, homeless, crippled, blind, and demonic individuals, adulterers, prostitutes, and others that followed Him. Why was this?

Jesus made it abundantly clear that He was an advocate for the disenfranchised. He boldly declared that He was "anointed" by the Holy Spirit to bring restoration, freedom, and healing to all who were victimized and held captive by any circumstance in life. In fact, His calling was to pronounce "favor" on all and to break down walls that divide and separate.

We live in an age where injustice, unfairness and unkindness have assumed a new normal. We have become so desensitized to various types of inhumane acts hurled at each other that we no longer flinch. If we do feel any outrage, its life span is equivalent to the time it takes for the muscles of the eyebrow to be raised and then to resume their normal posture. A chaplain in Kansas USA, at the opening of the Senate sessions, declared in his speech that as a people, "we have lost spiritual equilibrium and have reversed our values." What an indictment!

In her book, *A Call to Stand Apart*, Ellen G. White assures us that this problem can be corrected when we put into practice the notion that "Good deeds are the fruit that Christ requires us to bear: kind words, deeds of benevolence, of tender regard for the poor, the needy, the afflicted....When the naked are clothed, the stranger made welcome to a seat in your parlor and a place in your heart....an answering strain is responded to in heaven. Every act of justice, mercy and benevolence makes melody in heaven" (White, 2011, p. 60).

The Father sent His Son, Jesus, to proclaim healing for all, to bring the good news of salvation to the poor in spirit, a category which describes each of us. This message of deliverance is particularly captivating to those who are shunned by society because of ethnicity, poverty, or physical inabilities. There is absolutely no room in God's thinking for discrimination.

So in the words of Jesus, let us rise up and "proclaim the year of the Lord's favor" to everyone we meet. ▮

— V. O. COX

FEBRUARY 9

PROSPER AND GOOD HEALTH

"Beloved, I wish above all things that thou mayest prosper and be in health, even as thy soul prospereth" (3 John 1:2 KJV).

One of the popular healing sayings in the African-American religious tradition is, "by the stripes of Jesus, thou art healed," from the text in Isaiah 53. In many ways, it is used to declare the healing power (and desire) of God through His Son, Jesus Christ. The healing comes through a heavenly engagement and an earthly engagement. It occurs through the miraculous touch of Jehovah-Rophe, the Healer. It comes about through the intentional and permissive will of God. This is the heavenly engagement.

The earthly engagement of healing comes through the intentions and actions of humankind; through our wise, effective and productive actions. Here, the healing comes about through our healthy eating, active living, and also through quality health care. The Johannite text tells us that God wishes us to prosper and be in good health, but a large part of this healing engagement is in our hands and based upon our actions. We take intentional steps to eat better and take care of our bodies through Godly wisdom and even obedience, to protect our physical temples.

But there is more. It also involves the will and intentions of the government and people of power. It is fair and people-centered public policy and action. Thus, this form of earthly engagement involves quality health care and health coverage for all. Yes, quality, affordable and accessible health coverage for all, supported by all who hold public office and positions of power and influence. But there must be the will and the desire of government and people of power and influence to care for all and serve all. They must take intentional action.

Dr. Martin Luther King Jr. famously stated that, "of all the forms of inequality, the injustice in health coverage is the most shocking and inhumane." While that was over 50 years ago, his words ring loudly today. Our question as a "people of faith," is simply what steps are we going to take to turn it around?

May we, as followers of Christ, remember His words, "inasmuch as you have done it unto the least of these, you have done it unto me" (Matthew 25:40 KJV). Let us take steps to organize, advocate, and even agitate to ensure that God's desire for us to "prosper and be in good health" comes about.

May we join Christ and pick up our cross and follow Him by "tearing down the structures and systems" that hinder prosperity and good health. ■■

— TONY MINOR

FEBRUARY 10

SPEAK UP

"'The Spirit of the Lord is on Me, because he has anointed Me to proclaim good news to the poor. He has sent Me to proclaim freedom for the prisoners and recovery of sight for the blind, to set the oppressed free, to proclaim the year of the Lord's favor'" (Luke 4:18 NIV).

On June 17, 2015, Dylann Roof opened fire in the Emanuel African Methodist Episcopal Church in Charleston, South Carolina. The shooting resulted in the death of nine African Americans. Members of that church had gathered that Wednesday evening, as they did every week, for Bible study. A visitor walked inside, sat through the entire service, only to open fire near the end. When asked what the reason was behind his actions, reports indicated his response was that he was there "to shoot black people."

Our country has been marred by oppression and discrimination against people of color. In the face of that reality, the question must still be asked, "What responsibility do believers play in all of this?"

I would suggest that in matters of social justice, God's people should have a strong voice, if for no other reason than the fact that Jesus Himself was on the front lines of social justice issues. There is no way to separate social justice and the gospel, because the essence of the gospel is to set free individuals who have been held captive and enslaved by sin. Everything we see in the world around us that is evil is nothing more than a symptom of the overall problem, which is sin. Unfortunately, racism and oppression will not be done away with until sin is done away with.

In the meantime, believers are not expected to sit silently. We have a responsibility. Jesus' entire ministry was spent speaking up for, and helping, the poor, oppressed, and disenfranchised. There are many characteristics we could use to describe Jesus, but passive is not one of them. Jesus was actively involved in the liberation of all people. He had no issue calling out anyone who tried to use religiosity as a way of escaping their moral and spiritual responsibility. We should not have to wait for oppression to knock our door down before we sense our need to quench it.

Whether that means protesting, petitioning or voting, we have the responsibility of being present in matters of injustice and inequality—regardless of who it affects. In the words of Mamie Till, "Two months ago I had a nice apartment in Chicago. I had a good job, I had a son. When something happened to the Negroes in the South I said, 'That's their business, not mine.' Now I know how wrong I was. The murder of my son has shown me that what happens to any of us, anywhere in the world, had better be the business of us all." ▮▮

— NATHANIEL DREW

FEBRUARY 11

WHO'S YOUR NEIGHBOR?

"But he, wanting to justify himself, said to Jesus, 'And who is my neighbor?'" (Luke 10:28 NKJV).

Social justice and social issues affect all, no matter the culture, skin color, nationality or ethnicity. We are all connected in one form or another. Being a part of God's creation simply puts us in the same gene pool with one set of parents, Adam and Eve. God's plan of salvation included cohabitating in an environment where we all depend on Him and help one another.

The parable of the Good Samaritan is riddled with the trappings of racial divide, economic disparity, and a confluence of immigration assumptions. Moreover—most won't admit it—there is a natural disdain for those who are different; especially for those who are poor, frail, indigent, and down on their preverbal fate.

The Gospel of Luke exposes the essence of racial inconsistency. The question is, "Who is my brother and what part do I play in this thing called life?" The traveler who is stripped of clothing, beaten and left for dead alongside the road was in the wrong place at the wrong time. First a priest and then a Levite come by, but both avoided the human being in anguish. Finally, someone who was neither Republican or Democrat, and possibly not even Independent, happens by and tends to the wounded traveler.

The moral of the Good Samaritan is that everyone, even those normally considered an enemy, is your neighbor. It doesn't matter if you are Jew or Samaritan, White or Black, the haves or the have nots, we are all neighbors—brothers and sisters—and we have a responsibility to each other.

The parable offers a vision of life rather than death. It evokes 2 Chronicles 28, which recounts how the prophet Obed convinced the Samaritans to aid their Judean captives. It insists that enemies can prove to be neighbors, that compassion has no boundaries, and that judging people on the basis of their religion or ethnicity will leave us dying in a ditch.

There is an old joke that goes something like this: Why did the chicken cross the road? It was not to get to the other side. It was because he was chicken (afraid)! The reason why most individuals don't like to deal with social justice issues is because they're afraid. Getting involved means they must sacrifice something. Most are territorial, selfish, and basically live in their own world.

The Bible says in Luke 6:27 NLT, "But to you who are willing to listen, I say, love your enemies! Do good to those who hate you." ▮▮

— GLEN ALLEN

FEBRUARY 12

JESUS' MISSION STATEMENT

"'The Spirit of the Lord is on me, because he has anointed me to proclaim good news to the poor. He has sent me to proclaim freedom for the prisoners and recovery of sight for the blind, to set the oppressed free, to proclaim the year of the Lord's favor'" (Luke 4:18-19 NIV).

It was the Sabbath day, and the Bible declares that Jesus was in the synagogue as His custom was. Not only was Jesus in the synagogue, we are also told that Jesus participated in the service. Jesus takes the scroll and stands up and announces that, "The Spirit of the Lord is on me, because," Jesus continued, the old words flowing from His mouth, ringing with new meaning, "he has anointed me to proclaim good news to the poor. He has sent me to proclaim freedom for the prisoners and recovery of sight for the blind, to set the oppressed free, to proclaim the year of the Lord's favor" (Luke 4:18-19 NIV).

He completes the reading. "Today, this scripture is fulfilled in your hearing" (Luke 4:21 NIV). This occasion marks the beginning of Jesus' earthly ministry. What this text does is state the mission statement of Jesus. Jesus declares, here is why I am here. This is My Mission. Now we read this Scripture from Luke 4, however Jesus is quoting from Isaiah 61:1-2. Those who heard Him that day were well aware of Isaiah's prophecy.

They understood that these words referred to the Messiah and to the year of Jubilee. The Jews had a custom, ordained by God, that not only would every seventh day of the week be the Sabbath, a day of rest, but that every seventh year would also be a Sabbath, when the land would not be farmed, and so on... After every seventh Sabbath year (that is, every 50th year), there would be, what was called, the "year of Jubilee." In that year, all slaves would be set free, and all men whose poverty had forced them to sell their lands would receive them back again. Those who had lost family members into slavery or imprisonment would be reunited with their loved ones. You can see why it was called "The Jubilee!"

Jesus' mission statement makes one thing abundantly clear; people are His priority. And Jesus expects His agenda to be our agenda. We can measure how well we are fulfilling the agenda by how lives are being changed. Are we busy preaching the good news, proclaiming freedom, bringing healing, releasing prisoners, and compassionately meeting people's needs? That is the Spirit of Christ!

Let me ask you, what is the agenda for your life? What are you doing that will last forever? What is God calling you to do? What are you waiting for? ■■

— JEROME HURST

JESUS AND ECONOMIC JUSTICE

"Defend the poor and fatherless; do justice to the afflicted and needy. Deliver the poor and needy; free them from the hand of the wicked" (Psalm 82:3-4 NKJV).

The alleviation of poverty should be a significant part of a Spirit-led, social justice agenda. Throughout His ministry, Jesus was greatly concerned about economic justice. However, some Christian communities preach so much about the blood and death of Jesus that they neglect the justice principles Jesus taught during His life.

While looking at economic equality in today's America, we can be saddened by how minorities are treated; from gun violence to police brutality, to not being able to reach the American homeowner's dream. Minorities face predatory lending to predatory utilities. The recent legal issues with cable companies and their practice of charging minorities for the same service that others receive at a lower cost truly expresses, "we have not inherited the land."

Economic injustice involves the state's failure to provide individuals with the basic necessities of life, such as access to adequate food and housing, and its maintenance of huge wealth discrepancies. In the most extreme cases of maldistribution, some individuals suffer from poverty while the elite of that society live in relative luxury. Such injustice can stem from unfair hiring procedures, lack of available jobs and education, and insufficient health care. All of these conditions may lead individuals to believe that they have not received a "fair share" of the benefits and resources available in that society.

As the Psalmist declares, God is concerned about the justice for the lowly, the destitute, the orphan and the poor. Although many of our politicians may not be concerned about the poor, including the working poor, they stand at the center of God's heart. Knowing this to be true, the Psalmist implores God to rescue all who are caught in the grip of the wicked. That is, those who use and oppress the poor for their own benefit.

Jesus blessed the poor and cursed the conditions that made people poor. At its core, economic injustice is an assault upon the dignity of God. In the name of Jesus and through the power of the Holy Spirit, Christians should have a holy urgency to alleviate, if not eradicate, poverty. We can do more than run revivals, put on prayer breakfasts and sponsor fashion shows. Hopeless, homeless, hungry people need us to enmesh, or "enflesh" our faith.

According to James 2, Christians should "flesh out" a social justice agenda by fighting poverty. He says, "What good is it, my brothers and sisters, if you say you have faith but do not have works? Can faith save you? If a brother or sister is naked and lacks daily food, and one of you says to them, 'Go in peace; keep warm and eat your fill,' and yet you do not supply their bodily needs, what is the good of that? So faith by itself, if it has no works, is dead" (James 2:14-16).

— ANDREW MOBLEY

FEBRUARY 14

JESUS AND HEALTH CARE

"Jesus went through all the towns and villages, teaching in their synagogues, proclaiming the good news of the kingdom and healing every disease and sickness" (Matthew 9:35 NIV).

The year 2020 was like no other year that I have experienced in my lifetime. We have lived through a world pandemic that has completely changed the way we go about everyday life. The most tragic fact of 2020 is that over 250,000 individuals lost their lives as a result of COVID-19. This pandemic placed a spotlight on the inequalities of health care to the Black and Brown communities. According to the statistics, Black, Indigenous and Latino Americans all had a COVID-19 death rate of triple or more than White Americans.

Amidst the pandemic, and people dying daily, there are those in government who've been trying to do away with the Affordable Care Act that provides health insurance to over 23 million people. And yet, there are so many who are still uninsured. In America, the richest nation in the world, thousands die every year because they are underinsured or uninsured. And thousands more, many with health insurance, face bankruptcy because they are broken by health care costs that insurance would not cover.

It seems so obvious to me that health care reform is a moral imperative. Jesus was in the forefront of health care reform. The kind of health care Jesus provided, and commanded His followers to provide, put no limits on what sicknesses it covered or whom it covered. It was health care for whomsoever.

Notice these Scriptures:

• And large crowds came to Him, bringing with them those who were lame, crippled, blind, mute, and many others, and they laid them down at His feet; and He healed them (Matthew 15:30).

• And He healed many who were ill with various diseases… (Mark 1:34).

Jesus was going through all the cities and villages, teaching in their synagogues and proclaiming the gospel of the kingdom, and healing every kind of disease and every kind of sickness (Matthew 9:35).

It is clear that Jesus was in the business of health care. The issue of providing health care to those who do not have access to such care, because of the exorbitant costs, is not a political or economic issue. It is a moral issue that calls us to re-envision how we see life and human dignity. The test of faithfulness to Jesus is always in how we treat the vulnerable of society.

Proverbs 29:7 says, "The righteous care about justice for the poor, but the wicked have no such concern" (NIV). ▮▮

— JEROME HURST

FEBRUARY 15

DREAM BIG!

"And Joseph dreamed a dream, and he told his brethren: and they hated him yet the more" (Genesis 37:5 KJV).

Dr. King had a dream that one day black and white people would come together, and though racism still exists, his dream came to pass. Today, we have black and white students in the same class; we have black and white couples getting married and having children; black and white players on the same sports teams; black and white children playing on the playgrounds; black and white children holding hands and praying together in Vacation Bible School and Pathfinders.

Just in case we may have forgotten his words, Dr. King said, "I have a dream that one day little black boys and girls will be holding hands with little white boys and girls." Today, we see that his dream came to fruition.

Just like Dr. King, the book of Genesis tells about a little boy named Joseph, who also had a dream. His dream came in twos. His first dream was expressed in Genesis 37:7.

Joseph told the dream to his brothers, who hated him for it. He said, "For, behold, we were binding sheaves in the field, and, lo, my sheaf arose, and also stood upright; and, behold, your sheaves stood round about, and made obeisance to my sheaf" (KJV).

Joseph's brothers hated him, and sold him to foreigners who took him to a strange land where he was a slave. Joseph ended up thrown into prison for not sleeping with his master's wife. However, Joseph never gave up his faith in God, and God was with him in his oppression.

Joseph's brothers did end up bowing before him years later, when they found out that he was the ruler in Egypt who supplied their food in a time of famine. Joseph's dream came true—not about his brothers serving him—but about uniting and restoring his family in a time of famine.

God looked through the peephole of time and made sure that this dream grew in Joseph's mind so that we can glean from it today.

We are living in a world among those who oppress us. Are you feeling oppressed by things of this life? Remember, God is with you every step of the way. Joseph's dream united his family in their toughest time. Dr. King's dream united us during the civil rights movement. But God will unite us all in heaven.

Today, if you are going through rough times, remember God is with you and that it won't last forever. Remember that both Joseph and Dr. King went through rough times as well, but their dreams were realized.

Whatever you are going through, dream big! Keep the faith! Stay faithful! Don't give up! And God will make sure your dreams come to fruition as well. ▮▮

— PAUL LAWRENCE

FEBRUARY 16

THE STRENGTH OF NIMROD

"Cush begot Nimrod; he began to be a mighty one on the earth" (Genesis 10:8 NKJV).

Black folks are a people who have strength. Today I want to talk about Noah's great grandson, Nimrod!

Nimrod was the son of Cush, who was the brother of Canaan, who was the son of Ham, who was the son of Noah. Ham is believed to be the father of blackness in the world, after the great deluge. His sons were Egypt, Put, and Canaan.

Is it strange that strong, long-lasting African regions were birthed from Ham? I think not; God ordained it to be such. Cush's name is synonymous with, "Aethiopia," which literally means, "land of the black!" When you look at the map of Africa and how it was broken up at the Berlin council in 1886, Dutch South Africa, Belgian Congo, American Liberia, French Guinea, German Kenya—every country in Africa was colonized—except Ethiopia!

Of course they tried, but the strength of Nimrod was in those people! Nimrod, according to Scripture, was the first on Earth to be a mighty man! (Genesis 10:8). Nimrod used his strength for God, and in generations gone by his strength was still there, and is still there! Being the son of one whose name means black, Nimrod brings to blackness a badge of pride and a badge of honor, to be a man of might before God.

And don't you know God has still blessed the black man and woman with that might? The Greeks went to Africa, stole what Imhotep did in math and put "Pythagorus Therum" on it, and called it Hellinistic. Iron was first mined in Africa. They still can't figure out how the pyramids were built by Africans. Our presence is so great they even want to take Egypt out of Africa because of our greatness!

All of that came from Noah's grandson, Cush, and his great grandson, Nimrod! You are of greatness, and don't you forget that! ▮▮

— VINCENT E. STOKES, II

FEBRUARY 17

NEW DAY RESOLUTION

"Through the Lord's mercies we are not consumed, because His compassions fail not. They are new every morning; Great is Your faithfulness" (Lamentations 3:22-23 NKJV).

How many of you made New Year's resolutions? How many of you have already lost sight of your goal? I will confess—I am guilty.

There was a time when I enjoyed running and became rather fascinated with its meaningful life lessons and spiritual applications.

My first race was running 5 miles in the winter of Cleveland, Ohio. Over 5,000 people participated with smiling faces, high hopes and positive affirmations. Prior to beginning, I received a text from my trainer saying, "stay the course, go your own pace, and I'll see you at the finish line."

Each mile marker was a victory and finishing was my most pressing goal. As I began mile 4, my legs began to feel heavy and my toes were freezing from my snow soaked socks! The large crowd was gone and the handful in my reach were tired and cold, all focused on our own journeys towards the finish line. I was too far into the race to go back, but not close enough to see the end. I was stuck in the middle of the road and exhausted!

How can God's people stay focused when we're stuck in the middle of this Christian race and exhausted? Hebrews, Chapters 11 and 12 remind us:

1. The race is achievable and others have succeeded. Paul literally gives us a list of a "great cloud of witnesses" that have been in our shoes of frustration, uncertainty and exhaustion. We are not alone and we are in good company!

2. We must persevere. Don't give up. The only thing quitting guarantees is that we'll never reach our goal.

3. Focus on Jesus! "Therefore, since we are surrounded by such a great cloud of witnesses, let us throw off everything that hinders and the sin that so easily entangles. And let us run with perseverance the race marked out for us, fixing our eyes on Jesus, the pioneer and perfecter of faith" (Hebrews 12:1-2a NIV).

Don't get discouraged by looking at the "big picture." Focus on the task before you, guided by the One who loves you. Today's text in the ESV says, "The steadfast love of the LORD never ceases; his mercies never come to an end; they are new every morning; great is your faithfulness."

No need to burden yourself with overzealous yearly commitments. Model after Christ and let your resolution of obedience to His will be made new every single day. ■

— CHARDE' HOLLINS

FEBRUARY 18

WON'T HE DO IT

"Forget the former things; do not dwell on the past. See, I am doing a new thing! Now it springs up; do you not perceive it? I am making a way in the wilderness and streams in the wasteland" (Isaiah 43:18-19 NIV).

Our nation is desperate for healing and the church cannot be silent. Currently there is much conversation on race relations. While some progress has been made, we still have a long way to go. As Christians, it is important that as we have these conversations we keep in mind that: 1) God has never made a person He doesn't love; 2) Race was God's idea; 3) Racial reconciliation is at the heart of the gospel; and 4) How you and I treat other people matters deeply to God.

Notice 2 Chronicles 19:7: Be careful what you do, for there is no injustice with the LORD our God, or partiality (paraphrased). "Partiality" is an old English word for racism and prejudice; "racism" means treating one group of people better than another group.

Proverbs 22:2 (NIV) reminds us that, "rich and poor have this in common, The LORD is the maker of them all." Might I add, the white and the black, the Jew and the Gentile, the educated and the uneducated—we all have this in common—the Lord is the maker of us all. Not only is He our Maker, but we each are made in His image.

Now it is sad, but true that in 2021 there is still injustice against Black Americans, and other minority groups. As followers of Jesus Christ, we cannot be silent. We must be on the front lines in this quest for equality. We must have the hard conversations.

All Christians must hold out the hope of Christ as our banner for justice. We must continue to believe that our best days are ahead. We must greet every day expecting God to bless us.

We must continue to believe in the dream of Dr. Martin Luther King Jr. that, "one day on the red hills of Georgia, the sons of former slaves and the sons of former slave owners will be able to sit down together at the table of brotherhood."

Hold on to the promise of Isaiah 43:18: "Remember ye not the former things, neither consider the things of old. Behold, I will do a new thing" (KJV).

Despite what it looks like we must have faith that God is going to do a "new thing!" When there seems to be no way, the Lord will create a way. When there seems to be no present hope, the Lord will give us hope.

As the preachers say, "Won't He do it!" ■

— JEROME HURST

FEBRUARY 19

BLACK AND BEAUTIFUL

"I am dark, but lovely, O daughters of Jerusalem, Like the tents of Kedar, Like the curtains of Solomon" (Song of Solomon 1:5).

In our text today, we find the wife of Solomon making a bold statement that she is black and beautiful like the tents of Kedar. She not only tells us that she is black, but she also tells us how black she is.

Kedar is the name of a North Arabian Bedouin tribe who were in the habit of making tents out of goat's hair. The particular goats that were indigenous to that region were extremely black. So, she is telling us that she is not just sun tanned, but she is black—extremely black.

While in that region there were individuals whose color were deep black and others were dark brown, Solomon's bride describes her husband as being ruddy in complexion. As a matter of fact, Solomon's father, David, is also described as being ruddy in complexion (1 Samuel 16:12; 17:42), meaning reddish-brown.

There is no doubt that the Bible states that David is ruddy and handsome, and Solomon's bride is black and beautiful; so we must concur that there is nothing wrong with being Black.

However, in society black is mostly associated with negativity. Here are a few examples:

- When Hollywood actors or performers are shunned or ostracized for taking a controversial stand, they are said to be "blacklisted."
- When children grow up to become bitter disappointments to their families, they are called the "black sheep."
- The political candidate who is expected to lose an election is often referred to as the "dark horse."
- On Monday, October 19, 1987, when the stock market took a nose dive causing a lot of people to lose a lot of money, it became known as "Black Monday."
- An acceptable and forgiving lie is called a "white lie," but the worst lie anyone can tell is a "black lie."
- If you go to the bakery and ask for an Angle's Food Cake, the baker will give you a white cake; if you ask for a Devil's Food Cake, the baker will give you a "black cake."

We must not allow society to convince us that we are some obstinate group, or out of step with everyone else because of our skin color. We are not left in the dark as to who we are and to whom we belong. We, as black people, should not allow anyone to convince us that we are nobodies and that we must look like others to be accepted or to be viewed as good looking. We do not need to act like others to fit in; but we must be true to God and our responsibility to serve Him in spite of the hardships and persecution we endure.

Jesus endured persecution for all of us so that we would not allow our history to dictate our destiny. A time will come when all of God's children will be in one place, on one accord, without color barriers and no more distinctions. We—the people of God—will stand on the sea of glass with harps, praising God and singing the song of Moses. ▮▮

— JACK MCCRARY

FEBRUARY 20

WHY ON EARTH ARE YOU HERE?

"You are worthy, our Lord and God, to receive glory and honor and power, for you created all things, and it is for your pleasure that they exist and were created" (Revelation 4:11).

Do you know why you were created? According to the text, you exist for God's pleasure. What exactly does that mean? The word pleasure is defined as "a feeling of happy satisfaction and enjoyment" (Source). That means, dear friend, that you exist for the express purpose of bringing God joy.

Now, ask yourself, "What does God enjoy? What makes Him happy?" Who better to answer that question than God? He said, "And now, Israel, what does the Lord your God ask of you but to fear the Lord your God, to walk in obedience to him, to love him, to serve the Lord your God with all your heart and with all your soul" (Deuteronomy10:12 NIV).

Pleasing God relates directly to our pursuit of holiness. When we say no to sin and yes to righteousness, we bring our Heavenly Father pleasure. God is not apathetic to our obedience; He has committed His own joy to it.

When sin sings its siren song, we'll hear another voice saying to us, "Well done; enter into the joy of your Master" (Matthew 25:21 ESV). That thought should inspire the motivation we need to pursue holiness. Knowing that our obedience has the ability to bring happiness to the God of the galaxies is incredible motivation. And knowing that our disobedience can bring God grief and sorrow keeps us from treating sin lightly.

Every decision that you make, every choice that you have in front of you to pursue sin or to pursue righteousness, is a chance to bring happiness to God himself. We need the static element of union to keep us from doubting. We need the dynamic aspect of communion to keep us pursuing. Both are for our joy. Let's make it our pleasure to please Him. ▮▮

— CAROLYN HENRY-HURST

FEBRUARY 21

YOUNG GIFTED AND BLACK WOMAN

"I commend to you our sister Phoebe, a deacon of the church at Cenchreae, so that you may welcome her in the Lord as is fitting for the saints, and help her in whatever she may require from you, for she has been a benefactor of many and of myself as well" (Romans 16:1-2).

Phoebe only appears in this periscope of Scripture. From these two verses we know that Paul instructs the church to be hospitable to her because she has been a helper to many, including the apostle himself. Paul's commendation of Phoebe makes it clear to us that the work and worth of the women of God in the ministry is invaluable.

It is for this reason that as Black women, we must seek God to understand what it means to serve. There are so many untapped gifts that we possess that can be useful for doing the work. It may feel uncomfortable for you because for almost an entire year, the church has not been on the inside of four walls. However, Phoebe did not have a formal position in the church, yet her work was meaningful and commendable.

As Black women, we have always carried our churches in ways that cannot be quantified. Our gifts, money, talents and time have also been the backbone of the movement for the liberation of our people. For example, when it comes to voting, black women are the most represented population of voters. In all of that, God is calling us to more because there is still yet work to do.

What is the meaningful and commendable work that God is calling you to do in light of this Black History Month? What would it look like for you to bring awareness to an issue for which you are passionate? Perhaps, God is calling you to the work of mentoring a young person as they finish the virtual school year strong. Could God be giving you a new vision to bring change to your locale?

Let this encouragement ignite your fire: Go forward young, gifted, and black woman; and serve! ▮▮

— SHEENA MARIE CAMERON

FEBRUARY 22

A BLACK MAMA

"So the woman conceived and bore a son. And when she saw that he was a beautiful child, she hid him three months. But when she could no longer hide him, she took an ark of bulrushes for him, daubed it with asphalt and pitch, put the child in it, and laid it in the reeds by the river's bank...Then Pharaoh's daughter said to her, 'Take this child away and nurse him for me, and I will give you our wages.' So the woman took the child and nursed him" (Exodus 2:2-3 & 9 NKJV).

A black mama will do all she has to do to protect her black child. In Exodus 2 we meet Jochebed, the wife of Amram, and the mother of Moses. The government put a bounty on the heads of all boy children, but Jochebed broke the law and hid her baby for three months.

When she finally could not hide him any longer, she made Moses a bassinet and had his sister send him down the Nile River to float away to his watery grave. But while the bassinet was floating it got caught in the high reeds of the Nile River and the baby began to cry. Pharaoh's daughter saw the child and had compassion, and the sister of the child asked her, "Then his sister said to Pharaoh's daughter, "Shall I go and call a nurse for you from the Hebrew women, that she may nurse the child for you?" (Exodus 2:7 NKJV).

Pharaoh's daughter ends up paying Jochebed, Moses real mother, to do what she would've done for free anyhow. A black mama knows how to protect her children, but she knows how to prosper her family as well. Jochebed made a living off of the oppression of the Egyptians.

You have to wake up early in the morning to get over on a black mama! Praise God for our mothers, our grandmothers, the sisters who mother us, and the aunts who provide for us! Praise God for your mother and your children's mother, and any woman who has mothered you! ■■

— VINCENT E. STOKES, II

MARCH ON UNTIL YOUR WALLS COME DOWN!

"By faith the walls of Jericho fell, after the army had marched around them for seven days" (Hebrews 11:30 NIV).

As the children of Israel journeyed closer to the land of Canaan, they encountered an obstacle—the walls of Jericho. Joshua, who became Israel's leader after the death of Moses, received the promise from God that He had already delivered Jericho into their hands. (See Joshua. 6:2.) Knowing that God is faithful to His word, Joshua trusted God, and he and the people were submissive to God's promises even when it looked impossible. (See Joshua. 6:3-10.)

Despite the massive walls of Jericho, the Israelites marched around the walls once a day for seven days. The promised miracle did not happened on day one or on day five. But on the seventh day, on the seventh trip around the city, the horns start to blow and at the appointed time the people shouted, and in one miraculous moment "the walls came a tumblin' down."

Joshua and the people had crazy faith with legs. I have discovered that people who have crazy faith simply live by faith; living by faith means acting on belief. I truly believe that exercising this type of faith allows one to experience more of God's amazing miracles, bringing every wall in life down, in God's time. When we walk in obedience to God, He always shows Himself mighty to save.

Throughout history, God has torn down many walls for His people. Over 100 years ago, like Joshua and his brave army, our African-American ancestors marched on (and shouted) until the walls of slavery were abolished and the slave ships stop sailing.

They marched on until the walls of segregation were annihilated. They marched on until black men and black women were treated equally in the eyes of the law and were given an opportunity to vote.

They marched on until our beautiful black boys and girls were allowed to sit and study at the same school and in the same classroom with their white counterparts. They marched on until blacks were able to enter the front doors of any restaurant and drink from the same water fountains that Caucasians drank from.

They marched on until blacks were allowed to sit anywhere on the bus without having to get up and move to the back of the bus in order for a Caucasian person to have the front seat. They marched on until blacks were elected to serve as CEOs, professors, lawyers, judges, and even the president of the United States of America.

Yes, life was hard for our ancestors, yet they did not give up. Rather, they pursued after righteousness; they strove for success and excellence; and because they did, the Lord performed wonders in their lives. And if God did it for them, surely, He can do it for you. ■

— CLAVAL HUNTER

FEBRUARY 24

THE LAND ON LAYAWAY

"Let not your heart be troubled; you believe in God, believe also in Me" (John 14:1 NKJV).

After the Civil War in 1865, Army General William Sherman met with 20 black Baptist and Methodist ministers to chart the best course for the newly freed men. Led by Rev. Garrison Frazier, himself a former slave who purchased freedom for himself and his wife with $1,000 in silver and gold, the ministers suggested adding "a mule" to General Sherman's Special Order No. 15, which granted 400,000 acres of land for exclusive settlement and governance for and by blacks.

Rev. Frazier was quoted as saying, "The way we can best take care of ourselves is to have land and till it by our own labor...and we can soon maintain ourselves and have something to spare. We want to be placed on land until we are able to buy it and make it our own."

President Lincoln approved the order. But his successor, Andrew Johnson—a southern sympathizer—reneged on it, seized the lands and returned them to the families of the former slave owners, thus handicapping the cornerstone of the Reconstruction land ownership.

In Genesis 12, God calls Abram and tells him to leave his native land for a land promised. The Lord established a covenant with him by promising three elements: blessing, seed (nation), and lands. For God, the cornerstone of the covenant is the land promised. Without land, the covenant is useless. So when God promised Abram the land, and as he sojourned through it, he knew by faith that it would be his. While the writer of Hebrews tells us that Abraham died not having obtained the promise, he looked for a city whose builder and maker was God.

Like the former slaves in the 19th century South, we too were once in bondage. Our freedom has been purchased with the blood of Jesus Christ. Not only has our freedom been purchased, but the Lord Himself has said, "In My Father's house are many dwelling places... I go to prepare a place for you..." (John 14:1 NASB).

In the covenant Christ has made with His believers, land is a cornerstone element. John the Revealer saw a new heaven and a new earth, and he saw where God moved His dwelling place to earth to be with humanity. (See Revelation 21:1-4.) We can rejoice because our land is on layaway, promised and purchased by the blood, and no prejudicial power can reverse that special order. ▮

— SAM JEUDEN

FEBRUARY 25

HELP US

"During the night Paul had a vision of a man of Macedonia standing and begging him, 'Come over to Macedonia and help us'" (Acts 16:9).

In our Scripture we find the citizens of Macedonia calling out for help. They had done all that they could do. They needed more than just prayer. They cried out, "Please come over to Macedonia and help us."

Not much has changed. As I walk through our communities I hear the call, "Help Us." Why do they cry out? They cry out because many are unemployed, uninsured, receiving subpar education, and impacted by high crime rates. Yes, while many of us celebrate the accomplishments of the past, the question is how will you respond to the cries of those less fortunate?

Notice what the text says about how Paul responded. "After Paul had seen the vision, we got ready at once to leave for Macedonia" (Acts 16:10, NIV).

We, like Paul, must be obedient without hesitation to the cry of help from a lost and dying nation. "We must quickly carry out the tasks assigned us by the one who sent us. The night is coming, and then no one can work" (John 9:4, NLT). Martin Luther King, Jr once preached that, "We are now faced with the fact, my friends, that tomorrow is today" ("Beyond Vietnam: A Time to Break Silence").

Our Scripture does not permit us to sit still, to wait for God to call to us a second time. Today is the day; this is the hour, the minute when we say yes to God's call to us to live as His disciples. God has called all of us to go to Macedonia. God has called us to hear the cries of those crying out, "help us!"

We cannot allow those who are crying out, "help us," to wallow in the valley of despair. Our brothers and sisters wait eagerly for our response. And while God is faithful to answer these cries that touch His heart, the question is will we be obedient to the cries, "Help us?" ▮▮

— JEROME HURST

FEBRUARY 26

GO WITH GOD

"So He said, 'I will certainly be with you. And this shall be a sign to you that I have sent you: When you have brought the people out of Egypt, you shall serve God on this mountain" (Exodus 3:12 NKJV).

As we evaluate all that needs to be done to make our lives better, to make our families better, to make our churches better, to make our communities better, to make the world better, it can become overwhelming. We hear the voice of God calling us to do something. We want to say yes. Yet we feel like we are so inadequate for the task. And because we want to be obedient to voice of God, we say, "Yes Lord, I will go." Even while the words, "Here I am," are coming out of our mouths, we feel self-doubt and uncertainty well up inside.

That's how Moses felt when he heard God call him to go and liberate the Israelites from Egypt. Look how Moses replies to God in Exodus 3:11 (NKJV): "But Moses said to God, "Who am I that I should go to Pharaoh, and that I should bring the children of Israel out of Egypt?"

Here we see Moses doubting his abilities. I would like to suggest that is a good thing when faced with the task of liberating people from the things that bind them. That will push us back on God. Our self-doubt will teach us to depend on what God has given us, and not to jump out there and be false heroes.

There are a lot that people need to be liberated from; poverty, addictive behaviors, and emotional oppression. But most of all they need to be set free from the burden of sin. The fact is, God is calling us to be available to go and set the captives free. And I've discovered that it is OK to have a little healthy self-doubt, and like Moses, ask, "Who am I that I should ... bring my people out?"

When you do, you will find the same answer that Moses found: that God will be with you. God will prepare you. God will show you the way. God will fight it with you. God answers Moses in Verse 12, "And God said, "I will be with you."

And I declare just like God was with Moses, He will be with you. The difference is the presence of God, and with His presence comes His power. It is not your ability, your knowledge, your talent, or the size of your gift or the beauty of your gift that matters. All that matters is, God with you. When God is with you, that's enough! Amen. ■

— JEROME HURST

FEBRUARY 27

MY DEOXYRIBONUCLEIC ACID

"Then the word of the Lord came to me, saying: 'Before I formed you in the womb I knew you; Before you were born I sanctified you; I ordained you a prophet to the nations'" (Jeremiah 1:4-5 NKJV).

Throughout this month, the black culture is challenged to intentionally reflect on our heritage and the sacrifices of our ancestors; their highs and the lows, their trials and the triumphs. We are called to remember the strength, wisdom, and royalty inside our DNA.

In 2017, musical artist, Kendrick Lamar, released a song entitled "Inside My DNA." After hearing a young person casually reciting the lyrics to himself, I took an interest and searched online for the song. These were the first words I saw:

I got loyalty, got royalty inside my DNA
Cocaine quarter piece, got war and peace inside my DNA
I got power, poison, pain and joy inside my DNA
I got hustle though, ambition, flow, inside my DNA

I read the lyrics in full, and after reading I began to think about how the artist was actually saying something of meaning. Away from the head-nodding beat and a few choice words, there was a real message that resonated with me and made me stop to think; what is inside my DNA?

Our DNA is similar to a blueprint, and each aspect of the design significantly matters. In today's text, God lets us know that He took His time in creating each one of us, making sure that everything we needed was already included in our blueprint.

Even through our struggles and disappointments, we must remember what's in our DNA: Moses, who led thousands and parted the Red Sea; David, who defeated a giant with a small stone and a slingshot; Samson, who slayed hundreds with his bare hands; and Jesus, who conquered death and holds the keys to all of heaven and hell!

Beloved, regardless of any difficult situations, mistakes or burdens carried, we must always remember that there is greatness in our DNA. You have favor, power, strength, and unimaginable greatness in your bloodline.

I got worrisome, abandonment inside my DNA
I got bitterness and hopelessness inside my DNA
But God put the Holy Spirit up inside my DNA
He's the King of kings and Lord of lords of my DNA
He's Jehovah Jireh, my provider of my DNA
I got purpose, peace and happiness inside my DNA
I got Jesus' Blood, from up above, inside my DNA
Got God's loyalty, His royalty, God is my DNA! ■

— CHARDE' HOLLINS

NO ROOM

"And she brought forth her firstborn Son, and wrapped Him in swaddling cloths, and laid Him in a manger, because there was no room for them in the inn" (Luke 2:7 NKJV).

Can you believe it? Jesus, the Savior of the world, is being born and no one had room for Him? Read today's text again: "And she brought forth her firstborn son, and wrapped him in swaddling cloths, and laid him in a manger; because there was no room for them in the inn."

Is it sad that no one offered to give this pregnant lady their room, or make room for her at least, seeing the condition she was in? Jesus, the owner of everything, and yet treated as if He owned nothing. He comes from heaven to earth and He discovers a "No Vacancy" sign in one of His own motels.

But then, things haven't really changed much have they? How many in society are told there's no room for them:

- Because they had no health insurance;
- Because they became pregnant out of wedlock;
- Because they were homeless; or
- Because they were an illegal immigrant?

And can you believe that:

- Even after the story has been told millions of times in a million ways;
- Even though Christ's miracles have been well documented and recorded;
- Even though the life, death, and resurrection of Christ has been preached for more than 2,000 years;
- Even though the mysterious works of Christ have been experienced by believers for centuries; and
- Even though many have been healed, delivered, saved, and blessed by Jesus; remarkably, Christ still struggles to find room in many people's lives?

The question we each must answer is have you made room for Jesus in your life? And if you do not have room for Jesus, then what is filling that space? Is that space filled with anger, pride, envy, jealousy, lust, bitterness, resentment, insecurity, greed, doubt, selfishness, prejudice, hatred, sorrow, bad memories, fear, hunger, unforgiveness, loneliness or darkness? Jesus says, If you make room for me, I can be whatever you need me to be.

As we end this month I appeal to you to make room for Jesus. If you want a meaningful life, you ought to make room for Jesus Christ. When you make room for Jesus, you will have peace. When you make room for Jesus, you will have joy. When you make room for Jesus, you will have everlasting love. When you make room for Jesus, you will have mercy. When you make room for Jesus, you will have victory. ▮▮

—JEROME HURST

MARCH

HEALTHY FELLOWSHIP

When God made humanity, we were made to be social beings. Though we were created to have dominion and interaction with all of creation, God ordained us to have fellowship with Him and each other. Such a relational connection shows fellowship on a vertical as well as a horizontal plain.

The vertical plane is humanity's connection with God. The horizontal plane, is humanity's relationship one to another. Looking at this configuration one can see the sign of the cross. However, I must hasten to point out that the sign of the cross must first have a vertical structure before being able to sustain a horizontal one. In order for humanity to have a strong and meaningful connection with each other, there must be a good relationship with God.

Healthy fellowship is what our heavenly Father exemplified as He visited Adam and Eve in the Garden of Eden on a daily basis. Healthy fellowship strengthens the relationships that we have with each other. Each relationship is prone to weakening if we allow the enemy, called sin, to come in and erode it. Therefore, we should be forever mindful of the ill effects that sin has on our relationships. We should always strive to cultivate positive acts of kindness as we fellowship with each other in our various relationships.

This month we will look at some healthy and unhealthy forms of acts and fellowship, in the context of our relationship with God and with each other. As we do, bear in mind that we are all brothers and sisters because we are from one set of parents, Adam and Eve, with God as our Creator. So how we act or interact with each other is always under the umbrella of social justice or social injustice. ■

— MARK A. BROWN, PH.D.
Southeastern Conference of Seventh-day Adventists

MARCH 1

A PRAYER AND THIRTY-FIVE DOLLARS

"The steadfast love of the Lord never ceases; his mercies never come to an end; they are new every morning; great is your faithfulness" (Lamentations 3:22-23 ESV).

My husband and I decided very early in our marriage that we were going to be totally committed to our two sons receiving a Seventh-day Adventist Christian education. Armed with that commitment, we knew we had to trust God to supply all of our needs.

God has always been faithful to us, but somehow we seemed to forget that when difficult times rolled around. As a stay-at-home mom and fulltime student with two children in elementary school, each day seemed like a financial challenge.

This day in particular, my faith was tested to its limit. With my husband being the sole provider, stuck in a job without any upward mobility or any future salary increase, this was not the first time I was traveling down this path. But that day in question, the path seemed impassable.

The refrigerator contained just a few items that would not last more than a day. The pantry was also bare, and we were about 10 days away from my husband's next paycheck.

That day, while the boys were at school and my husband was at work, I decided to have a faith talk with God. After agonizing with Him, I was prompted to start dusting the furniture. As I dusted the nightstand, I was urged to remove the lamp and the doily in order to do a thorough cleaning. As I lifted the doily, I was pleasantly surprised to find neatly folded bills in the sum of $35.00. It was enough to sustain our family until my husband's next paycheck. All I could do was cry to God with joy, while wondering how it got there.

That day in the store it seemed like the money multiplied like the widow of Zarepthath's meal and oil. "For thus saith the Lord God of Israel, the barrel of meal shall not waste, neither shall the cruse of oil fail, until the day that the Lord sendeth rain upon the earth" (1 Kings 17:14 KJV).

I remembered how earlier that morning I had agonized with God about providing for us and now I realized, again, He was faithful to us.

That was over 25 years ago. However, there have been many instances since then where I have experienced God's faithfulness over and over again. I've never doubted God's provision, and I will always remember that He remains faithful to me. God promises to do the same for you. Just trust Him. ▮▮

— BARBARA DAVIS

MARCH 2

BE STILL

"The Lord will fight for you; you need only to be still" (Exodus 14:14 NIV).

When Moses was leading the children of Israel out of Egypt, there is that well know impasse when they reach the Red Sea. Pharaoh and his army are fast approaching behind them and the mighty Red Sea is right in front. Many argue that they should have given up; they are anxious and feeling desperate and alone.

Life has a way of causing us, as Christians, to feel scared, desperate and alone. There are many days, many months, sometimes even years when we do not see a way out of our problems. There's no light at the end of the tunnel; times when we see only darkness, in front and behind us.

However, listen to what the great leader Moses says to his now troubled and panicked people: "Do not be afraid. Stand firm and you will see the deliverance the Lord will bring you today. The Egyptians you see today you will never see again. The Lord will fight for you; you need only to be still" (Exodus 14:13-14 NIV). Moses is full of faith when it should be so easy to be afraid. He is mirroring what we read in Psalm 46:10, "Be still and know that I am God."

The idea of being still leaves room for God to do something bigger than we are. It gives us time to ponder, to listen and to wait. Being still means that we know that God is with us, leading us, and we have yielded to His direction for our lives.

The deeper meaning to being still is that we will have to trust God. The people of Israel were going to have to trust that God would part the waters of the Red Sea. Remember, the command to keep moving was given before the waters separated. They had to believe that the walls of water would not tumble down on them. It wasn't doing "nothing"; it was walking by faith, not by sight.

If we are moving in the direction of God, if we are following His plans for our lives, if we are being obedient, we don't have to fear the outcome. We don't have to worry about the provision of God for our journey. We don't have to wonder if God will do as God said He will do. He has our back! He has the ultimate triumph. We can rest in Him. We can be still—one simple action that holds so much silent, purposeful meaning. ■

— SANDRA GORDON

MARCH 3

PRAYER IN ANY LANGUAGE

"As she kept on praying to the Lord, Eli observed her mouth. Hannah was praying in her heart, and her lips were moving but her voice was not heard. Eli thought she was drunk" (1 Samuel 1:12-13 NIV).

Often in my alone time with God I have stopped, awestruck, reflecting on the fact that while I was calling on my Father, there were billions of other believers also calling on Him. What is my awe of it? That He hears my tiny cry above all the other voices. He does not confuse my call with another. He knows me, He knows you, and He answers with no mistakes.

Do you pray aloud? Do you whisper? On the other hand, do your lips just move as Hannah's did that morning? While Eli was confused and rebuked Hannah because he thought she was acting in drunkenness, God heard her every unspoken word and blessed her. Isaiah 65:42 says, "And it shall come to pass, that before they call, I will answer; and while they are yet speaking, I will hear" (KJV). God immediately started the process to answer Hannah's prayer because her request pleased Him.

A few years later, as Hannah presented the answer to her prayer— Samuel—to God and to Eli, the old priest could not contain himself. "He worshipped the Lord there" (1 Samuel 1:28 KJV).

Our Father deserves worship. He wants to build an unshakeable relationship with every one of His creatures. He hears when we call, and He hears when all we can do is groan. When the words just cannot be uttered, He hears our heart's cry.

Written by The Carters and sung by The Louvin Brothers, the story in the song, The Drunkard's Plea, reminds us that God hears sincere pleas, even the drunkard's:

I walked one day by an old country church, I saw a drunkard stagger and lurch,
And as he reached his mother's grave, I saw the drunkard kneel and pray.
"Lord have mercy on me," was the kneeling drunkard's plea
And as he knelt there on the ground I know that God from heaven looked down.
"Bring my darling boy home to me," Was his mother's dying plea,
And as he staggered through the gate, at last he was one day too late.
Three years have passed since she went away, her son is sleeping beside her today,
I know that in heaven his mother he'll see, for God has heard that drunkard's plea.

Today, like with Hannah and the drunkard, He will hear your plea, spoken or unspoken. He will answer. Remember, God has time in His hand, you do not. He is waiting, watching, and longing to hear from you. Give Him a call; do not delay. ■

— OWEDA DAVIS

MARCH 4

FACE TO FACE WITH GOD

"Now when Joshua was near Jericho, he looked up and saw a man standing in front of him with a drawn sword in his hand. Joshua went up to him and asked, 'Are you for us or for our enemies?' 'Neither,' he replied, 'but as commander of the army of the Lord I have now come.' Then Joshua fell facedown to the ground in reverence, and asked him, 'What message does my Lord have for his servant?'" (Joshua 5:13-14 NIV).

Joshua is the son of Nun, grandson of Elishama, chief of the tribe of Ephraim. From a young age, Joshua was the servant of Moses. God chose Moses to lead Israel out of Egypt, and gave him the tablets of the law and the ordinances governing Jewish worship.

Joshua was a man of great faith, of firm and courageous character. With Caleb, he gave a favorable report on Canaan based on what he had seen as a spy. Faced with opposition from the ten other spies, Joshua said that with the help of God the Israelites would be able to conquer the country.

We find the first mention of Joshua in Exodus 17:8-16, during the battle against the Amalekites. He was undoubtedly a good soldier. He was given the responsibility of leading the fight while Moses interceded for them with God on the top of the mountain. Thanks to the intercession of Moses, Joshua won the victory over the Amalekites. Joshua is an outstanding example for us today.

In the same way, the Lord supports us in the battles that we are waging on this earth against Satan and against the flesh. " Yet in all these things we are more than conquerors through Him who loved us" (Romans 8:37 NKJV).

By his preparation and experience, Joshua was a man with exceptional natural qualities. Still, his highest quality was being a man who was clothed with the Holy Spirit.

After crossing the Jordan, in the plain of Jericho, Joshua gathered the people to give them a new strategy to invade Jericho. While he was near Jericho, a warrior appeared to him. Joshua had come face to face with God.

This meeting was a special union because God could have sent an angel, but He chose to deliver this message Himself. In so doing, Joshua is reassured that God would be with him, just as He was with his predecessor and mentor, Moses.

The meeting called for reverence: "Then the Commander of the Lord's army said to Joshua, "Take your sandal off your foot, for the place where you stand is holy." And Joshua did so" (Joshua 5:15, NKJV). To contemplate the victory of God in our lives this year, we must remove our shoes that symbolize the sins that surround us.

This was a special message because it was reassuring. The experience gave Joshua the courage he needed to lead the people where God wanted them. Just like Joshua, the messages we get from God's Word today are specific, relevant, and should be obeyed if we are to obtain the victory. ▮▮

— NICHOLAS LEWIS

MARCH 5

PERSEVERANCE

"And let us not be weary in well doing: for in due season we shall reap, if we faint not" (Galatians 6:9 KJV).

Genesis 26:18-22 tells the story of Isaac re-digging the wells that his father Abraham had made. The first well he called Esek, for the herdsmen of Gerar contended with him that the water belonged to them. Isaac then dug another well and called it Sitnah, and again, there was contention as with the first. He then moved and dug a third well and called it Rehoboth, and for this one there was no striving. Isaac said, "For now the Lord has made room for us, and we shall be fruitful in the land" (Verse 22).

God will sometimes use our enemies to move us from a place of our own choosing to a place of His choosing. He will move us from a place of self-reliance to a place of God-dependent living.

Isaac then went up to Beersheba and the Lord appeared to him that same night and said to him, "I am the God of Abraham thy father: fear not, for I am with thee, and will bless thee and multiply thy seed for my servant Abraham's sake" (Genesis 26:24 KJV).

God's timely appearance to Isaac was no accident. God wanted to commune with Isaac, but the turmoil in Isaac's life robbed him of the blessed communion with God. Isaac had to transition from places of conflict to a place of quiet rest. There he heard the voice of God. There he was assured of God's abiding presence—"I am with thee..." He came to know that in God's presence there are blessings— "...and will bless thee..." and that his boundaries would increase— "...and multiply thy seed."

Too often we lose out on our blessings because of our stubbornness. Isaac could have dug in his heels, and then decided not to re-dig any other wells because he was entitled to the existing ones. However, through the spirit of peace, he decided to move further afield, and there he was a recipient of God's richest blessings.

When Isaac was at rest, when he was still, God spoke to him. The heart hears nothing during its moment of crying. In the stillness, in quiet contemplation and in earnest listening, we too can and will hear the voice of God. God will then reveal Himself to us and satisfy our deepest need. If only we would learn to be still, we would come to know the power of God's presence. Psalm 46:10a says, "Be still, and know that I am God" (KJV). ■

— RAYMANO GRANT

MARCH 6

THE MOMENT OF GRACE

"When Jesus had lifted up himself, and saw none but the woman, he said unto her, 'Woman, where art those thine accusers? Hath no man condemned thee?'" (John 8:10 KJV).

Have you ever been in the wrong place at the wrong time? I would say that was an understatement for the woman in John 8 who had obviously violated the law by her sinful act of adultery. But what's interesting, even outrageous, is that although she was caught in the very act, she is the one subjected to sexual exploitation by the scribes and Pharisees.

She alone suffered the humiliation and social injustice of being dragged before the people early in the morning and being placed within their midst to ensure everyone got a glimpse of her. No doubt, she was probably sparsely clothed since she was taken in the act of her indiscretion. What's worse is that the people didn't even care about her. She was simply used as a pawn for a broader, more devious plan to trap Jesus, which had nothing to do with her.

How much of our world is like that today? Undoubtedly, the world and the church are full of people who make mistakes, but somehow there seems to always be individuals who feel it is their duty to magnify the "sins" of others. The idea that this type of hypocrisy and injustice still happens today is utterly abhorrent. Rather than man attempting to dispense his version of condemnation, there must be more grace and mercy extended; the kind that Jesus gave to this poor woman. Jesus reminds us that we are not "all that" ourselves.

We have all fallen short of the glory of God; we just don't have our sins on display for the world to see. The accusers who put so much effort into shaming this woman did not realize their sinful deeds would be exposed as well. Despite their intent to harm her, one by one they disappeared due to their own sins, leaving no one to condemn her. By the sweet words of Jesus, the moment of grace had finally come for this woman as He said to her, "neither do I condemn thee. Go, and sin no more" (John 8:11 KJV).

Have you ever been in the right place at the right time? It's when you have an opportunity to offer grace and mercy to another human being, rather than judgment and condemnation. This, after all, is how the world will know we are Christians—by our love for others; the love that rests within the heart of everyone who claims to be a follower of Christ. ▮▮

— MITHRA WILLIAMS

THE VERTICAL AND THE HORIZONTAL RELATIONSHIPS

"That which we have seen and heard we declare to you, that you also may have fellowship with us; and truly our fellowship is with the Father and with His Son Jesus Christ" (1 John 1:3 NKJV).

We serve a God who is the God of fellowship and relationship. This fellowship and relationship must be translated in our worship. Slavery and bondage did not stop our forefathers from worshipping. The church is not short on what to preach, how to preach, or whom to preach. However, the church comes up very short in its ability to translate the preached word into the lived word.

There must be a living connection between the pulpit and the pew. The people may not say it, but they can certainly see it, feel it, and experience when there is a spiritual and social disconnect between the preacher and the people.

There are only two types of relationships; the vertical relationship between man and God and the horizontal relationship between man and his fellowmen. A sermon that is lived is always more effective than a sermon that is preached. Christianity is about modeling the life of Christ and the life of Christ is about fellowship and relationship. People can be abused from the pulpit by pastors who have lost connection with the Power Source. They can be taken for granted, and experience social and religious injustice even in church.

If we lose sight of the basic need for fellowship and relationship, we are simply playing church and will be numbered among those who will hear from the Savior's lips, "depart from me I never knew you" (Matthew 7:21-23). Life is all about relationships. An individual's relationship with God must be translated into the relationship he has with his fellowmen. God did not ordain the hermit life.

You cannot live your Christian life in recluse because, whether in bondage or freedom, you must "let your light so shine before men that they may see your good works and glorify your Father in heaven (Matthew 5:16). It calls for Christ-like humility, the kind that is rarely seen today.

Ellen White states it clearly: "If we would humble ourselves before God, and be kind and courteous and tenderhearted and pitiful, there would be one hundred conversions to the truth where now there is only one," (*Welfare Ministry*, p. 86). Let us translate this into our worship; and since God has willed it, we can achieve it by cooperating with the Holy Spirit.

So let us make this year the year to embrace a paradigm shift in fellowship and relationships. By this, I mean we must find more creative and innovative ways to have fellowship with each other and so enrich our relationship with God. ▮▮

— DOLPHY CROSS

MARCH 8

COVENANT KEEPERS

"Then Jonathan and David made a covenant, because he loved him as his own soul" (1 Samuel 18.3).

A covenant, according to the *Webster's Dictionary*, is a solemn and a binding agreement.

Covenant keepers are hard to find in today's society. We live in a disposable culture which says, "If it is broken, let's throw it out and get another one." This ideology has seeped into our relationships with humanity. With the advancement of technology, we have the ability to friend and un-friend a person with just a key stroke. Our world is sinful, fickle and unstable.

Thanks to Facebook and other social media platforms, some claim to have thousands of friends. However, the majority of them are not true friends, and would be unable to help if you were in need. The Bible states, "A friend loveth at all times, and a brother is born for adversity" (Proverbs 17:17).

As Christians, we sometimes forget that One God created us all and we are related to each other; therefore, we should be a covenant-keeping people.

This covenant that Jonathan and David made between each other was that of a friendship for life. It was a bond that no family's disapproval, circumstances of distance, time or death could change. For even after Jonathan's death, when David became king, he took care of Jonathan's son (Mephibosheth) as his own.

Prince Jonathan, the son of King Saul, did not have to befriend David. He could have had, humanly speaking, good reasons not to like him. David was younger, and showed up at the battlefield one day and showed out. Not dressed in battle armor, he defeated Goliath, the enemy of Israel. This victory catapulted David to instant fame.

Although Jonathan was next in line to be king from a linage standpoint, he recognized some attributes in young David that he was willing to acknowledge and help David achieve. Jonathan did not envy or hate David because God had anointed David to be the next king of Israel. Unlike King Saul who was envious and jealous of David, Jonathan was a protector and preserver of David's life, especially in light of his father's intent to kill David. Because of Jonathan's covenant with David, his posterity was blessed.

We should all take note that we all are our "brother's keeper." Thus, as Christians, let us stop spreading envy, hate and jealousy. Let us all be covenant keepers to protect and preserve the lives of all for whom Christ died and rose to save. ■

— MARK A. BROWN

MARCH 9

DEPLETED AND DELETED! BUT GOD!

"But he said to me, 'My grace is sufficient for you, for my power is made perfect in weakness'" (2 Corinthians 12:9a NIV).

I was so wrapped up in maintaining my image, I was missing the point. I remember thinking how God wanted me to serve Him with my whole heart and not with relational holes in my spirit. Moreover, just as He did for Abraham when He dispatched him to unknown parts, God was preparing specific instructions for me. But would my heart be submissive?

Too often have I seen believers whose hearts are fatigued from toting the weight of toxic relationships on their shoulders. There is no joy in their journey. There is no peace in their hearts. Their smiles are contrived and their testimonies are stunted. Their sweetness has been turned into sourness. They forget that toxicity is of the enemy and there is no redeeming value in enabling it.

This is familiar territory for me since I, too, was now walking away from a toxic relationship after years of secret pain. Though many looking on would never understand the toxic aspects of my day-to-day life, I knew I was backed into a proverbial corner. I had to choose between missing eternal life and losing a relationship in which I had invested so much.

This was my journey of faith in which my devotion to God would be severely tested. There I was, on the brink of a new sunrise, wondering what Abraham's fate would have been had he stuck his finger in the eyes of God and ignored instructions to leave everything behind and embark on a mysterious journey. He could have made all the excuses in the world; I am 75 years old, my family lives here, this is the only place I have ever known, You haven't given me a destination, and the list goes on.

I left, though the road ahead was strewn with spikes! There was never a single moment when God was not reminding me of His precious promise, "My grace is sufficient for you, for my power is made perfect in weakness." My response? "Therefore I will boast all the more gladly about my weaknesses, so that Christ's power may rest on me" (2 Corinthians 12:9 NIV).

Dear Father, as we seek to manage our human relationships, may we depend completely on Your guidance; for with You as our Guide we can never stray from Your designated path. Amen! ▮▮

— DOREEN PRISCILLA BROWN

MARCH 10

CHAMPIONS FOR JUSTICE

"He will bring justice to the poor of the people; He will save the children of the needy, and will break in pieces the oppressor" (Psalm 72:4 NKJV).

This Psalm entitled, "A Psalm for Solomon," is King David's prayer as he reflects on his life and reign. The decision regarding his successor has been made and this Psalm is his prayer for his son, Solomon, the new king of Israel.

David covers all the bases; the blessing of God, peace and prosperity, increase in territory, submission of his enemies, respect and homage from the kings of other nations. These are typical requests to God from a king for himself, and certainly for his progeny. But David wants his son to be a good king. His request therefore, has another component; one in which a despotic tyrant or self-indulgent potentate would have no interest.

David prays that his son would, "bring justice to the poor of the people" and "save the children of the needy." David prays that Solomon would hear the cause of those who have no representation, no voice, no vote, and little hope. Evidence of its importance to David is seen in its repetition in Psalm 72:12-14. "For he will deliver the needy who cry out, the afflicted who have no one to help. He will take pity on the weak and the needy and save the needy from death. He will rescue them from oppression and violence, for precious is their blood in his sight" (NIV).

The word translated, "justice" from the Hebrew, has multiple meanings and applications; one of them is to vindicate. To vindicate is to justify, support, and defend. David wants his son to "save the children of the poor." The word "save" suggests deliverance, liberation, victory in battle. David is asking God to make his son a crusader for justice. This is not a passive approach to the cause of the poor and the needy. This is the language of warfare, made even more vivid by what David expects Solomon to do to the oppressor of the poor; break them in pieces.

Jesus declared himself the friend of the poor and oppressed when He proclaimed His mission statement, "The Spirit of the Lord is upon me, because he hath anointed me to preach the gospel to the poor; he hath sent me to heal the brokenhearted, to preach deliverance to the captives, and recovering of sight to the blind, to set at liberty them that are bruised" (Luke 4:18 KJV).

As Jesus' followers, it is our responsibility to fight for justice for the poor and needy of the people. ▮▮

— NICOLA STODDART

ENCOURAGING ONE ANOTHER

"Therefore, encourage and comfort one another and build up one another, just as you are doing" (1 Thessalonians 5:11 AMP).

"You need to be aware of what others are doing, applaud their efforts, acknowledge their successes, and encourage them in their pursuits. When we all help one another, everybody wins." — Jim Stovall

We live in a self-serving, self-centered, and self-obsessed modern day rush-rush society filled with negativity and constant tearing down of others. If we really want to make a difference, we need to focus on building others up.

Are you a taker or a giver? A consumer or a builder? Too many believers choose a church based on what they get out of it. While it is important that we be fed and encouraged as a part of a local body, there should be more to it than that.

Are other believers stronger and more secure in their faith because of us? Are we making a positive difference in the lives of others? This charge to encourage and build up is not given just to pastors and teachers; it is given to all believers.

Encourage one another and be a builder. Let us not be satisfied with being just consumers. Invest in the lives of your fellow believers. After all, the health of the church is dependent on the working of each member.

As we aim to build each other up in Christ, let us be wise in our speech; be encouraging; be quick to forgive; be understanding; avoid gossip; share knowledge; stay humble; stay positive; esteem others higher; and above all else, love others according to 1 Corinthians 13:4-8a, 13:

"Love is patient, love is kind. It does not envy, it does not boast, it is not proud. It is not rude, it is not self-seeking, it is not easily angered, it keeps no record of wrongs. Love does not delight in evil but rejoices with the truth. It always protects, always trusts, always hopes, always perseveres. Love never fails ... And now these three remain faith, hope and love. But the greatest of these is love" (NIV).

Let us go one step further, by envisioning whom and how we can build one another up, encourage, and inspire change in the church and each other. Then work on making these changes a reality.

Today, let us make a promise that we will continue to encourage and build each other up. Only then will we see growth and advancements in our spiritual and personal relationships to our fellow believers. ■

— SANDRA GORDON

MARCH 12

BURGER KING ACQUAINTANCE

"Therefore, all things whatsoever ye would that men should do to you, do ye even so to them: for this is the law and the prophets" (Matthew 7:12 KJV).

I remember visiting California and walking down Hollywood Boulevard. I was amazed at the sights, but more so I saw individuals from all walks of life; the rich, the poor, the kempt and the unkempt. Not knowing the needs and hearts of the people I saw, I tried not to be judgmental.

It was a long day and being famished I went to Burger King to eat. I was standing in line trying to place an order. I kept noticing a well- dressed man pacing back and forth. I kept watching because he seemed out of place in a Burger King.

After I placed my order and sat down to eat, I noticed he had finally made his way to the counter. He was attempting to get some water, but he was being ignored. My mind was racing. Was he hungry, did he not have money for food? No one seemed to notice or care.

God was, indeed, tugging on my heartstrings. I got up from my seat and approached this well-dressed man at the counter where he stood. I asked if I could assist him in any way. It was at that point that I realized he had no money for food, and I placed an order for him. He thanked me kindly. God had given me the opportunity to bless someone who was in need.

When he received his food he sat at a table by himself, and again I thought he didn't belong there. I wondered how someone so well-dressed lacked the ability to feed himself. But again, I reminded myself not to judge, as I did not know his circumstances and it was not Godly.

After eating I left the restaurant and went on walking down Hollywood Boulevard. To my surprise, my Burger King acquaintance approached me on the street and thanked me once more for providing his meal. It made me realize that even the relationship we have with acquaintances reflects who we truly are, and it goes a very long way.

The Scriptures remind me of the love of God and His love for us. We should have the spirit of God, of love, and kindness each day. We should seek opportunities to touch the lives of others going through greater sorrows and distress than we are. We should purpose in our hearts to treat others as we would have them treat us. ■

— SHEREE N. BROWN

MARCH 13

HEROES

"When Reuben heard this, he tried to rescue him from their hands. 'Let's not take his life,' he said. 'Don't shed any blood. Throw him into this cistern here in the wilderness, but don't lay a hand on him.' Reuben said this to rescue him from them and take him back to his father" (Gen 37:21-22 NIV).

True heroism is remarkably sober, very undramatic. It is not the urge to surpass all others at whatever cost, but the urge to serve others, at whatever cost. — Arthur Ashe

In the story of Joseph's rise to power, we find an interesting episode which highlights an unassuming antihero, Reuben. Of the 12 sons of Jacob, Reuben is the oldest. By default, he should be his father's apprentice, his brothers' leader, his sisters' protector, and a morally authoritative voice. Sadly, when the most pivotal moment arrives, he is unable to fulfill his assignment.

Several of Joseph's brothers have agreed to lay hands against him. They are considering a plot to kill him and dispose of his remains. Reuben succeeds in stalling the plan by diverting them to throw him into a cistern. His plan was to return to the cistern and retrieve Joseph, and return him home. As the story goes, the brothers have already sold Joseph to Midianite merchants by the time Reuben returns to sneak him out.

Joseph was in need of a hero. Daily, duty calls someone to action. God answers prayers through people—ordinary people. We call them heroes.

Here are three lessons that I draw from Joseph's story:

1. Heroes act! To be a hero you have to learn to be a deviant, because you're always going against the conformity of the group.

2. Heroes are leaders. Reuben abdicated his authority as a leader and forfeited his claim to the birthright. (See 1 Chronicles 5:1-2.) As a result, he no longer had the moral authority that the other brothers would follow.

3. Heroes are selfless. When the moment arrives, heroes are willing to pay the sacrifice, accept potential loss, and face challenges, regardless of the loss.

God's will prevails in spite of Reuben's failure. God uses the vengeful hearts of the brothers to deliver Joseph into the hands of the Midianite merchants who will help Joseph fulfill his destiny.

Ultimately, God is the Hero. He acts through us all. He came in the person of Jesus the Christ. Jesus was not hesitant to act in saving humanity. Jesus was a leader whose character was above reproach. Jesus was so committed to the rescue mission for the world, that no sacrifice could separate [them] from the love of God.

You are the hero that the world is waiting for. You are called to be His hands and His feet. ■

— PIERRE FRANÇOIS

DIVINE IRONY

"But Ruth replied, 'Don't urge me to leave you or turn back from you. Where you go I will go and where you stay I will stay. Your people will be my people and your God my God'" (Ruth 1:16 NIV).

Can you recall a time in your life when you would do anything for that one person that you love? Here is a story that portrays love and devotion.

Ruth was a native of Moab, descendants of Lot and his first daughter. Moab was a country that hated the living God, instead, worshipping Chemosh, the god protector of their nation. History shows that the Moabites were always in conflict with Israel. Saul fought against the Moabites; and David sought asylum in Moab, then later fought against them and forced them to pay heavy taxes. The irony is that a Moabite woman was David's great-grandmother.

Ruth and her mother-in-law, Naomi, moved back to Naomi's hometown where everyone believed in the true God. In our modern culture, mothers-in-law and daughters-in-law seek autonomy from each other. However, these two widows—who had lost the love of their lives—decided to start life anew together.

Ruth kept her promise that Naomi's people would be her people and Naomi's God, her God. Ruth even wanted to be buried with Naomi's people when she died. Ruth had no way of knowing that her way of blessing Naomi would eventually become a blessing in her own life. Ruth fell in love and married an Israelite who taught her and, I am sure, showed her by example, the Living God.

Divine irony also comes into play through Naomi and her husband and sons fleeing their country to greener pastures, only to meet with tragedy. Naomi lost both of her sons and her husband. This tragedy left Naomi feeling bitter. However, God stilled loved her. She gained a daughter-in-law who was able to go to the fields and glean for her, as she was too old to provide for herself. Ruth was a handworker and caught the eyes of Boaz who, ironically, was Naomi's cousin. Ruth discovered, firsthand, the generous, loving and loyal nature of God when she married Boaz, and then had a son. Through this lineage, Jesus was born.

Luke 6:38 says, "Give, and it will be given to you. A good measure, pressed down, shaken together and running over, will be poured into your lap. For with the measure you use, it will be measured to you" (NIV).

Thank God for giving us the ability to form deep and lasting relationships, and for keeping His promise to us. Remember that no matter what the situation is, we need to trust and believe that God is working everything out for us. He will do His part. We need to do ours. ■

— SANDRA BROWN

MARCH 15

HOW DO YOU HAVE FELLOWSHIP?

"For I have not spoken of myself; but the Father which sent me, he gave me a commandment, what I should say, and what I should speak. And I know that his commandment is life everlasting: whatsoever I speak therefore, even as the Father said unto me, so I speak" (John 12:49-50 KJV).

The Bible is replete with information on how to have fellowship with God and others. The concept of fellowship is so pervasive and necessary that the subject can be found in every verse, chapter, and book of the Bible.

After God created Adam and Adam failed, the last Adam—Jesus (1 Corinthians 15:45)—was sent to show us how to fellowship with God and each other. This was a practice that He demonstrated daily, as seen in our Scripture for today. Your fellowship with the Lord must be just as steadfast so that you are always carrying out His will, and that must not be by praying, only.

The greatest explicit instruction on fellowship is found in Acts 2:37-47. I found 30 ingredients necessary for fellowship. They are not in any specific order, and it would be a good exercise for you to try to find all 30, and possibly, more. Understand that you don't need all 30 ingredients for fellowship to take place. The fact that the ingredients for good fellowship are found all over the Bible testifies about its importance, and the simplicity of fellowship.

Here is a summary of the ingredients found in Acts 2: Your heart must be pricked; that is, convicted, and should ask, "Lord, what shall I do to be saved?" You do what Peter says in his response: repent and be baptized in the name of the Father, Son and Spirit; then, your sins will be forgiven and you will receive the Holy Spirit. Why? Because God called you and you responded. Then you testify and exhort others, and they will be baptized. You then make the Word of God your own, and desire to fellowship with those God brings into your life.

You will be able to perform signs and wonders, and those who don't know the Lord will experience fear, that is, reverence or awe; and you, with the help of the Holy Spirit, will lead them to Jesus. Then you will have all things in common with them. You will only say what the Spirit tells you, in order to help others who are in need. You should notice, also, that prayer comes way down on the list.

Fellowship is fluid and does not take on a set pattern. If you want to lead people to Jesus daily, and your church wants to baptize daily, this concept of fellowship must be understood, taught, and practiced. ▮▮

— KENNEDY VANTERPOOL

MARCH 16

IT'S YOUR TIME!

"For if you remain silent at this time, relief and deliverance for the Jews will arise from another place, but you and your father's family will perish. And who knows but that you have come to your royal position for such a time as this?" (Esther 4:14 NIV).

We live in a world where it seems that so many are just trying to find their way, trying to fit in, and trying to establish themselves in society. We can easily recognize this by one's style of dress, the color of their hair, or even the language they use to express themselves.

For some, identity is disguised based on political culture, biases, racial tones, and social pressures. Many people today are confused, perplexed, and depressed; some contemplating what the world would be like if they were no longer in it. Unfortunately, for those who fall into this category, they are searching in all the wrong places and, perhaps, for the wrong reasons.

God has purpose and fulfilment on His mind for each person He has created. One's gift to the world is as unique as a snowflake or fingerprint, and every voice must be heard. It is just that the world has distorted the truth, and people search for earthly recognition and acceptance rather than the approval of God. Once we recognize who we are in Christ and that we are royalty, we are in a position for Him to use us for something magnificent, if we let Him.

Esther, this beautiful queen—a Jew in truth—probably felt her own measure of unworthiness, which undoubtedly contributed to her reluctance in going before the king. As difficult as it must have been for her to take a stand, Esther stood at a great precipice. The words of her cousin Mordecai rang loudly in her ears: "who knows that you have come to your royal position for such a time as this?"

Once those penetrating words reached Esther's heart, she realized that the truth could not only make her free but it could save an entire nation! No longer would she have to hide who she was; no longer would she have to maintain a persona. What powerful lessons of courage and strength we glean from the story of Esther.

Have you ever considered the fact that, just maybe, God got it right when He created you? In addition to doing so, He is preparing you—yes, you—for something great. It is your time!

Rather than succumb to feelings of fear and doubt, or listening to society's ever-changing views on identity, find your true purpose and identity in Christ. His truth will make you free! ■■

— MITHRA WILLIAMS

MARCH 17

LEAVING A LEGACY

"Fear not, for I am with you; Be not dismayed, for I am your God. I will strengthen you. Yes, I will help you. I will uphold you with My righteous right hand" (Isaiah 41:10 NKJV).

The promise of being a constant companion to His followers is a comforting promise God gave to all His people. As Jesus was about to depart from this earth, He reassured His disciples that He would send them the Holy Spirit to be a Comforter to, allowing His legacy to live on. Likewise, we should all endeavor to leave a positive legacy.

Losing someone you love makes you think about your own life. It may prompt you to ask yourself, how are you going to live your life from this moment on? We contemplate the choices they made and the opportunities they gave up so we could have a better life than they experienced. We want to make sure that our loved one's life was worth the sacrifices they made for us during their lifetime.

The legacy my mother left, when she passed recently, was a living example of a faithful wife, loving mother, trustworthy sister, and friend. Her greatest legacy was her faith and trust in God. She walked by faith, not by sight. Faith was the title deed to what she was hoping and looking for. Faith allowed her to interact with and share God's love with others. Faith led her in solitude with God. She was like the woman who reached out in faith and touched the hem of Jesus' garment, knowing she would be healed by that simple, yet courageous act.

How would our lives change if we received the diagnosis of a terminal illness? Yet, we do have a diagnosis from King Jesus. Paul says, in Romans 6:23, "For the wages of sin is death, but the gift of God is eternal life in Christ Jesus our Lord" (NKJV). We just don't know if we have three weeks or three years left. Either way, how will we use the short time we have left?

Losing someone you love is not the end; it should the beginning of a closer relationship with God. It is high time for us to take inventory of the life we now live, and the legacy that we will leave for those left behind.

What kind of legacy are we leaving for our children and those around us? We need to focus our lives on leaving a positive impact on those we interact with daily; our families, neighbors, friends, those we work with, and even those we are not aware of as they pass through our lives sporadically. ▮▮

— KEITHA HATCHER

KNOWLEDGE AND RELIGIOUS FREEDOM

"To the Jews who had believed him, Jesus said, 'If you hold to my teaching, you are really my disciples. Then you will know the truth, and the truth will set you free'" (John 8:31-32 NIV).

Religious freedom is intrinsic in the consciousness of the human being and awakens with the knowledge of the truth. The full truth is Jesus Christ. Jesus could rightly tell His audience of Jews that they needed the knowledge of the truth to be free from impure thoughts; to be free from pernicious traditions or sinful impulses that ruled their actions, and did not allow them to understand and accept the contrasting beauty of His message.

In the same way, we need the knowledge of the truth; to drink from the inexhaustible source of knowledge that emanates from Jesus' words and His outpouring of love. That knowledge can only be acquired when we intentionally seek a constant and intimate relationship with Him.

Through the study of the Bible and the observation of nature, we contemplate Jesus and His love for humanity. His companionship becomes necessary to the point of our not being able to live without Him. Living the life of Jesus means living in the peaceful, natural, and inevitable joy of freedom.

I remember in my home country of Cuba that a number of us, as Christian students, were forced to endure acts of persecution for professing our Christianity. Most of us, at the time, were between the ages of five and six. We endured acts of public repudiation. Our teachers even paraded us in front of our other schoolmates, and made fun of our Christian beliefs and fun of our God. They tried desperately to weaken and ruin our faith. But their actions only served to strengthen us in our beliefs. The knowledge of Jesus Christ set us free, and in our choice to follow Him, we found the reason to live with hope.

The study and understanding of the life and work of Jesus Christ helps us to be good and educated Christians. Being good makes us happy, understanding that, like Jesus, we find happiness when we make others happy. Being educated makes us free because by accepting and meditating on the message of Jesus, we realize that there is forgiveness and redemption for each person. Those who acknowledge their mistakes and decide to repent from their sins can live in freedom.

Through a thorough study of God's word, we come to a serving knowledge of the real meaning of freedom. Because true freedom can only be obtained as we surrender our lives to the will and ways of Almighty God. ■■

— JUAN GONZALEZ

MARCH 19

LOVE AND FORGIVENESS WILL COVER A MULTITUDE OF SIN

"Finally, brothers, whatever is true, whatever is honorable, whatever is just, whatever is pure, whatever is lovely, whatever is commendable, if there is any excellence, if there is anything worthy of praise, think about these things" (Philippians 4:8 ESV).

A pastor, several years ago, was pastoring a very difficult congregation in a small community. This congregation was known to be challenging for its pastors (dating back many years). During his ministry, this pastor encountered issues among the leaders of his congregation that not only bordered on the question of a lack of integrity, but also issues that were, indeed, a display of the same. This was very heartbreaking for the pastor who had never encountered anything like it, before entering this pastorate.

Some of the things that happened in that congregation—like direct attacks on the pastor himself—brought him to tears. Other things that happened caused him to think seriously about asking the conference leaders to transfer him to another assignment.

However, as he evaluated the history of his congregation and his experience at the time, he understood how a leader—and a Christian in general (without the gift of love and forgiveness)—could develop resentment for the people he served.

Despite the lies that were told, the undermining that took place, the personal attacks, and other un-Christ like actions of a strong contingent in his church, the pastor stayed true to himself and his integrity. He continued to pastor his members without resentment, without hatred, and without retaliation against anyone.

Despite what your relationships might be, or in spite of how others may be persuaded to treat you, never let go of your hold on God. Never allow other people's actions and conduct to make you into something you were not intended to be.

When you are oppressed and abused by the people in your life, follow the advice of Paul and think good thoughts about them, and pray for them. Follow the advice of Jesus who tells us, "You have heard that it was said, 'You shall love your neighbor and hate your enemy.' But I say to you, love your enemies, bless those who curse you, do good to those who hate you, and pray for those who spitefully use you and persecute you, that you may be sons of your Father in heaven" (Matthew 5:43-45 NIV).

When it was time for the pastor to leave that pastorate, one of the members who had caused him significant pain, confessed, "Pastor despite all that I have done to you, you have never treated me any differently."

Love and forgiveness, if given a chance, will cover a multitude of sin. ■

— JIM DAVIS

MARCH 20

MOTIVATING JOY

"...let us run with endurance the race that is set before us, looking unto Jesus, the author and finisher of our faith, who for the joy that was set before Him endured the cross, despising the shame..." (Hebrews 12:1b–2a NKJV).

The sprinter crossing the finish line in first place. The actor receiving the Golden Globe. The scientist receiving the Nobel Prize. The musician receiving the Grammy. The CEO presenting the new product on the world stage. These iconic individuals are often what the media promotes as the epitome of success. But behind the glitz and the glamor are the years of hard work, sacrifice and preparation.

The athlete couldn't cross the finish line in first place without years of training. The actor, but for a few exceptions, couldn't walk that red carpet without first enduring failed auditions and years of struggle. The scientist could not celebrate the joy of the prize without first persisting through many failed experiments. The musician would first perform in small, no-name venues before ever lifting the gilded gramophone. The CEO could only present the amazing new product after many iterations of not so amazing prototypes.

What was the drive that helped them endure failure and hardship, and sometimes ridicule? They had a vision of a future that was worth enduring the pain of the present.

One of my favorite movies is Shawshank Redemption. It is the story of an innocent man wrongly imprisoned who, after years of having his appeals rejected, focuses on gaining freedom through other means— escape. While enduring the everyday hardships of prison violence, mistreatment at the hands of the guards, and abuse by the warden, he patiently tunnels through the walls, discarding the evidence in the prison yard one pocketful at a time.

On the day of his escape, he successfully navigates his way through the large sewer pipes and crawls to freedom through, "five-hundred yards of human excrement, smelling foulness I can't even imagine...500 yards... that's the length of five football fields..." His desire for freedom is so strong that it propels him through any inconvenience or hardship to get to it.

The model of endurance for Christian believers is Jesus, "who for the joy" of seeing His followers saved, endured the excruciating and humiliating execution of death by crucifixion. The cross has become a metaphor for hardship, and the Apostle Paul challenges us to take up our cross, face our hardships, and endure through them. In order to endure, you must have a hope, a joy that is set before you.

What is the goal to which you are striving? What are your joys that make fulfilling those goals worthwhile? You must identify them, because when you do, you'll be unstoppable. ▮▮

— MARK STODDART

MARCH 21

MOVING FORWARD TOGETHER IN THE WAY

"And it came to pass, when Pharaoh had let the people go, that God led them not through the way of the land of the Philistines, although that was near; for God said, Lest peradventure the people repent when they see war, and they return to Egypt: But God led the people about, through the way of the wilderness of the Red sea: and the children of Israel went up harnessed out of the land of Egypt" (Exodus 13:17-18. KJV).

There is always strength in togetherness. Togetherness helps to preserve values and enhances growth. It is hard for the enemy of our souls to defeat us when we work in tandem and move together.

God liberated the Israelites out of an oppressed environment and purposed that He did not want them to change their minds and return. God foresaw that through challenges and difficulties, the freed Israelites would be afraid and scared of Pharaoh and his army, and would one day choose to return rather than to fulfill the promise made to their forefathers. (See Exodus 14:10-13.)

We must never forget that our God cannot lie, so we can trust Him to keep His promise to us. The children of God will never perish because they find themselves in a cul-de-sac. Our God will always provide a way of escape out of any temptation or situation. (See 1 Corinthians 10:13.)

Today, although times have changed, the situations that confront God's people remain the same. The requirements to go to heaven remain the same: strict obedience and live, or disobey and die; love your enemies and do good to them that hate you; render to Caesar the things that are Caesar's and unto God the things that are God's; take care of the poor and needy among us; and happy are they that do His commandments that they may have right to the tree of life and may enter in through the gates into the city.

Fairness and impartiality are Christian principles that form the foundation of social justice. Social justice is against human rights abuse. The Egyptian bondage and slavery of the Israelites may have been in the past, but today we are still seeing its debilitating effects being played out in our culture and other cultures around the world.

An example is the African American who was thrown out of a Double Tree Hotel in Oregon in 2019, which was a breach of social justice. The incident was a form of racial profiling and resulted in an unnecessary lawsuit. There were so many ways in which that incident could have been handled differently. "There is neither Jew nor Greek, there is neither slave nor free, there is neither male nor female, for you are all one in Christ Jesus" (Galatians 3:28 NKJV).

Let us, as God's people, strive to put into practice the things of God we know in theories. Let us strive to treat those around us, especially within the household of faith, as brothers and sisters. ■■

— DOLPHY CROSS

MARCH 22

RELATIONSHIP AND TRUST

"Put not your trust in princes, nor in the son of man, in whom there is no help" (Psalm 146:3 KJV).

For those looking on, my life appeared perfect. I was adored and praised for my beauty. Yet I lived in fear of being punished by an abusive husband if someone so much as complimented or admired me. My home became a prison. Only my close friends knew what I had to endure. I lived a life of servitude for years. The truth was I lived through a brutal existence, and was the object of anger and inhumane treatments. My lifestyle was one of pretense and silent suffering.

The turning point came when my brother found me crying one day on the steps of my mother's house. He put his arms around me and assured me that I was better than being treated this way. Being a Christian, his comforting arm reminded me of what God would do for His children. I found comfort in knowing that God was not a sleeping giant.

As the Bible says, I knew I had to "trust in the Lord with all thine heart; and lean not unto thine own understanding. In all thy ways acknowledge him, and he shall direct thy paths" (Proverbs 3:5-6 KJV).

The word "trust" is mentioned 134 times in the Old Testament and 13 times in the New Testament. Obviously, being mentioned these many times in the Bible, the word must be of great importance and a vital ingredient for our relationships with humanity and with God.

Trust can be defined as the ability to hold one's self accountable. However, to be able to do this one needs to know who they are and the magnitude of their limitations. When trust is expressed, it is often the outgrowth of being truthful. All thriving and healthy relationships have these elements. Truthfulness is vital to any healthy relationship, as well as properly established boundaries. These boundaries must respect personal space and individuality. We were created to be involved with each other and with God.

There are so many other stories like mine about social injustice levied on others. So many are living and suffering in silence; many not knowing we have a God in whom we can trust in times of great peril. I thank God today for my mental support and guidance through those troubled years. Looking back on those days when I was so depressed because of my choices, today I can truly say, without a doubt, that I am a woman, naked and not ashamed.

To have a successful relationship, there must be trust and respect. ■■

— JULIA ROBINSON

PLEAD MY CAUSE, OH GOD

"Plead my cause, O Lord, with them that strive with me: fight against them that fight against me" (Psalm 35:1 KJV).

Psalm 35 is one of the imprecatory psalms. It is David's cry of distress when men, who were formerly his friends and who now returned his love with intense hate, were persecuting him.

We were never promised a smooth path or an easy road. Life will not always be glamorous and full of glitter. There will be points in our lives when trials will come our way. They will come unexpectedly and without warning. Those whom we strive with and for will rise up against us and plan our demise. From the moment we were born, the devil started to plan and scheme. Obstacles are constantly placed in our paths.

My story is similar to David's; one of gross injustice against me in the workplace. Several years ago, I felt God calling me into church ministry. I left the corporate world, knowing I would be earning significantly less. However, being called into God's service, I worked diligently and tirelessly in my job; at times going above and beyond the call of duty. Not for monetary compensation or human accolades, but because I felt I was doing the will of God.

Those for whom I rooted, cheered on, and championed tried to block my professional development. Several times, I was uprooted from my comfort zone; sometimes because of job realignment, other times because of personal relationships with other coworkers, but never because I was performing unsatisfactorily.

The spirit of retaliation rose up within me. I wanted to lash out with the same intensity of fury that was levied against me. However, I knew that was not what God wanted me to do. He has always promised to take care of all my needs, and I promised God I would give it my all to make it work.

I have proven God to be faithful in all aspects of my life. In this instance, it has been no different. My mindset was that when God gives you something, no man can ever take it away. So I decided to sit patiently and wait on God's deliverance, and for fairness to prevail.

We do not serve a God who ever slumbers or sleeps, so I know that in all things He will be victorious. For those who strive with me, I look forward to our day of celebration. In addition, for those who fight against me, I pray that God will extend mercy and grace. ▮▮

— TONI-ANN CARR

MARCH 24

WHAT ARE YOU SEARCHING FOR IN LIFE?

"But if we walk in the light, as he is in the light, we have fellowship one with another, and the blood of Jesus Christ his Son cleanseth us from all sin" (1 John 1:7 KJV).

You were made in God's image and likeness; thus, you will need, want, and desire the same things He does. Remember the Kingdom principle God established in Genesis 1:11-12, 21, 24-25: kind can only produce kind; therefore, whoever God is, and whatever He likes, wants, or desires, so you are and do.

Yes, sin has marred the image of God in you; however, deep down within you remains the desire to be like God. It is just like your children who are made in your image and likeness (Genesis 5:1-3); they normally end up doing the same things you have done, even though they may not have seen you do them. That is what I believed happened in the case of Abraham and his son Isaac. They both, at one point, lied that their wives were their sister. (See Genesis 20 & 26.)

Not knowing what your wants, needs, and desires are, you are not sure what you are searching for and, therefore, you will not be able to find them. Furthermore, you will be looking in the wrong places.

Do you know that one of the main reasons you got married or want to get married, why you have children, why you hang out with friends or party, and go to church—whether you are aware of it or not—is for fellowship? God created you to have fellowship, and He wants you to have fellowship with Him and others.

We already established that we are interrelated and interconnected, because we all came out of God. If, through His Spirit, you can understand that, imagine how much we would love the Lord and one another. Fellowship would intensify our love.

Without fellowship, you would literally go crazy and eventually die. You are always craving it. If you experience fellowship in a way that is positive and wonderful, it's great. If, however, you cannot experience genuine fellowship, you will settle for the negative, such as joining a gang or being incarcerated, because you cannot live without fellowship. It is in your DNA.

God designed you for fellowship. That is why solitary confinement is so effective for the prison system, but detrimental to the individual. Numerous studies have documented the effects of solitary confinement on prisoners. For example, some develop Special Housing Unit Syndrome (SHU), which also includes post-traumatic stress disorder (PTSD). We dislike being alone, because we were not designed to be that way.

Therefore, seek after fellowship with God and each other. ■

— KENNEDY VANTERPOOL

MARCH 25

WHAT'S IN YOUR HAND? SHARE IT!

"And if anyone gives even a cup of cold water to one of these little ones who is my disciple, truly I tell you, that person will certainly not lose their reward" (Matthew 10:42 NIV).

"One sprinkle of kindness could color the world golden." — Doreen Brown.

When a single mother got word that her run-down home had been selected for a major renovation, she broke down in tears. She and her 16-year old autistic son found themselves on the receiving end of an unselfish church and its caring pastor.

The Extreme Home Repair program is an outreach ministry of the Church in the Valley Seventh-day Adventist Church in Langley, British Columbia, Canada. The details of the project were ingeniously kept secret from the needy mother. Imagine how that one act of kindness would forever change the lives of an entire community long after a large school bus, which had purposely shielded the house from view, was moved.

The stakes could hardly be higher for God's people at a time when socio-economic conditions require those in the family of God to become protectors of each other. Moreover, isn't that what Christ demands of us? "My command is this: Love each other as I have loved you" (John 15:12 NIV). Therefore, we love because love is of God and God is love. We "give back" because we have received so much from our Heavenly Father.

In *Thoughts From the Mount of Blessing,* author Ellen G. White says, "We are to give in sincerity, not to make a show of our good deeds, but from pity and love to the suffering ones. Sincerity of purpose, real kindness of heart, is the motive that Heaven values" (White, 1896).

Selflessness and having a heart for God go hand-in-hand. Even as we reflect on Christ, who is a friend of the needy, we pay tribute to our Statue of Liberty (Lady Liberty) and Emma Lazarus' much-recited poem engraved on Lady Liberty's plaque:

"Give me your tired, your poor, your huddled masses yearning to breathe free, the wretched refuse of your teeming shore. Send these, the homeless, tempest-tossed to me; I lift my lamp beside the golden door!"

If this appeal seems to be a call for genuine brotherhood and sisterhood, it is! 1 Corinthians 2:9 states, "But as it is written, eye hath not seen, nor ear heard, neither have entered into the heart of man, the things which God hath prepared for them that love him" (KJV). Therefore, may God help us to model what it means to be each other's protector.

Lord, prepare me to be a vessel useful in Your vineyard to bless even the least among us. Amen! ▮▮

— DOREEN PRISCILLA BROWN

MARCH 26

WHAT IS THE BIBLE ABOUT?

"The earth is the Lord's, and the fulness thereof; the world, and they that dwell therein" (Psalm 24:1 KJV).

Understanding what the Bible is about has revolutionized my life. At first, I thought that it was about developing relationships with God and my fellowmen. Then one day, while I was engaged in a discussion with my buddy, God revealed His truth to me.

My friend told me that my concept of the Bible's overall objective was wrong! He said that the Bible is not about relationship, but fellowship! The moment he said that, the Spirit revealed to me that my friend was correct. Still, I prayed and asked for clarification in understanding this concept.

As I began studying the Bible on this subject, here is what the Lord revealed to me: Adam came out of God, Eve out of Adam, and every human being came out of God through Adam and Eve. Therefore, we all are related one to another, and thus, have a relationship with God and each other.

Furthermore, since God created all, everything in God's Kingdom is interconnected and interrelated with everything else. So, a relationship already exists among God and all mankind, and each other. However, because of the separation caused by sin, we must accept Jesus Christ as our personal Lord and Savior to restore the original spiritual relationship. Interestingly, even this restoration is accomplished through fellowship!

Here is something else I discovered: relationships cannot die. There is nothing that can destroy them. Death or divorce cannot change the marriage relationship. Consider this text: "And David dwelt with Achish at Gath, he and his men, every man with his household, even David with his two wives, Ahinoam the Jezreelitess, and Abigail the Carmelitess, Nabal's wife" (1 Samuel 37:3 KJV).

Abigail's husband, Nabal, had been dead since 1 Samuel 25:37, yet the Bible refers to her as "Nabal's wife." This is repeated in 1 Samuel 30:5, 2 Samuel 2:2 and 3:3. That is one of the reasons for the use of the terms "ex-husbands" and "ex-wives," because one cannot change a relationship once it is formed. Although my father died in June 2015, he is still my father.

We do have some control over, and can change our fellowship. Hence, what God wants us to do is to learn to develop intimate fellowship with Him and each other. He does not leave us in the dark as to how this can be accomplished. The Word of God—His manual on how to live—is pregnant with the 'how to' of fellowship with the Lord and our fellowmen. ▮▮

— KENNEDY VANTERPOOL

MARCH 27

YOU WERE CALLED FOR FELLOWSHIP

"God is faithful, by whom ye were called unto the fellowship of his Son Jesus Christ our Lord" (1 Corinthians 1:9 KJV).

One of the reasons God called you is to have fellowship with His Son, Jesus Christ. In other words, the Apostle Paul is saying that one of the main purposes for which God created you, and for Him sending His Son Jesus, is for Jesus to have fellowship with you.

What is fellowship? It is spending time with others in communion, interaction, communication, socialization, intimacy, and much, much more. It is how you relate daily with others to enhance your relationships. Fellowship determines the type of relationships you have. It qualifies our relationships. Fellowship is what you can change and have control over. On the other hand, relationship is something that, once established, nothing can change.

Why are you called to fellowship? It is a potent principle that God created, and is a natural part of our lives. It is like listening, which is one of the most powerful forces in the entire universe. Human beings may engage in fellowship with one another or with God. Let me show you an example of how powerful fellowship with each other can be.

Here is what God said of the antediluvian people: "And the Lord said, Behold, the people is one, and they have all one language; and this they begin to do: and now nothing will be restrained from them, which they have imagined to do" (Genesis 11:6 KJV).

The people were about to build the Tower of Babel to reach the height of the clouds, and they could have. Why? Because of their fellowship with each other. They knew their gifts, purposes, roles, and responsibilities, and stuck to them. They did not attempt to do what they were not gifted to do. Hence, fellowship is most effective when you know who you are and what you are capable of doing. The antediluvian people understood this, and if God had not come down and confounded the language, nothing would have hindered them from accomplishing their objective.

Businesses, governments, schools, gangs, and communities who operate on the concept of fellowship are, and will be, successful. When you begin to understand this concept of fellowship, and use it to bring honor and glory to God and to advance His Kingdom, you will, with the help of the Holy Spirit, destroy strongholds, break yokes, begin to experience a freedom like you have never done before, and live abundantly. You will then fellowship with the people that God brings in your life and they, too, will begin to experience the fantastic fellowship you are enjoying. ■

— KENNEDY VANTERPOOL

MARCH 28

WITH WHOM DO YOU NEED TO FELLOWSHIP?

"That which we have seen and heard declare we unto you, that ye also may have fellowship with us: and truly our fellowship is with the Father, and with his Son Jesus Christ" (1 John 1:3 KJV).

The Apostle John declares that our fellowship begins with one another, and he is right. Before birth, fellowship occurs between the mother and the child. Studies have shown that the environment in the womb affects the child. After birth, this fellowship continues with the family.

However, John realized that because we are born in sin and shaped in iniquity, our fellowship could have selfish purposes. This would not accomplish God's purpose for fellowship. Thus, John declared that truly our fellowship is with the Father and the Son.

Why do we need to first fellowship with the Godhead before we can experience effective and meaningful fellowship with each other? Because there can be no true fellowship without the One who initiated relationships, that are qualified by fellowship. The Lord will help you to have, and enjoy, fellowship with Him and your fellowmen.

Human fellowships are not enough or complete until you have fellowship with the Father and the Son. Can you comprehend that? No world leader would consider us of any significance for them to interact with; yet, the King of kings wants to have fellowship with us! This characteristic is not strange or foreign to Him. This is what God does. He used to come down daily to have fellowship with His children in the Garden of Eden (Genesis 3:8).

The Father and the Son want to fellowship with you and me so badly that Jesus was sent to live here on earth among us. One reason was to show us who our Father is and to restore the original fellowship. That is why when Philip asked Jesus to show him the Father, He said, "he that hath seen me hath seen the Father" (John 14:9 KJV). God has always manifested Himself to His children.

You will notice that another characteristic of the Godhead is that when Jesus came to earth, He spoke about His Father and the Spirit. The Scriptures make it clear that we need to fellowship, not only with God the Father and God the Son, but with yet another member of the Godhead: "If there be therefore any consolation in Christ, if any comfort of love, if any fellowship of the Spirit, if any bowels and mercies" (Philippians 2:1 KJV). It is the Holy Spirit who will lead you to the right people with whom you need to develop loving fellowships. ▮▮

— KENNEDY VANTERPOOL

MARCH 29

THE NEVER-CHANGING GOD

"For I am the Lord, I change not; therefore, ye sons of Jacob are not consumed. Even from the days of your fathers, ye are gone away from mine ordinances, and have not kept them. Return unto me, and I will return unto you, saith the Lord of hosts. But ye said, wherein shall we return?" (Malachi 3:6-7 KJV).

People are changing all over the world. Even governments have broken their promises and trust has become a relic of a bygone era. As people change, the world changes also. It is not the world that changes people. It is people who change the world. However, we serve a never- changing God whom we can trust to be constant.

Therefore, we must be careful and intentional as we present the gospel to a people who are in constant change mode. Prayerful planning and care must be taken to ensure that we are not adulterating the gospel to suit the whim and fancy of an increasingly fickle society. God's people should not be afraid of criticisms, therefore the gospel must not be compromised to please the populace.

In the last days, the Scriptures tell us that men and women will have itching ears for their own gospel. 2 Timothy 4:3-4 says, "For the time will come when they will not endure sound doctrine; but after their own lusts shall they heap to themselves teachers, having itching ears; And they will turn away their ears from the truth and shall be turned unto fables" (KJV).

Itching ears is a figure of speech that refers to the earthly and mundane desires of people who go to church. They will only want to hear that which enhances and goes along with their present ways of life. These churchgoers will ultimately reject sound doctrine and anyone who calls sin by its right name. Speaking the unadulterated truth will eventually open the doors for religious persecution and social injustice.

We are a people of light, therefore there is always a way to present the truth to be heard. There was a time when progressive people who made things happen were considered people who "think out of the box." Today, however, the term "thinking outside of the box" is actually outdated. Progressive people are now considered "contrarian thinkers." If everybody is doing it, maybe it is time to do something different and be bold about it.

Jesus and the apostles used this "out of the box" thinking method. "And they continued steadfastly in the apostles' doctrine and fellowship, and in breaking of bread, and in prayer...so continuing daily with one accord in the temple, and breaking bread from house to house" (Acts 2:42, 46a).

God's message did not change, so we should not change. Times may change and we may be forced to change the method, but not the message. ■

— DOLPHY CROSS

MARCH 30

RIGHT RELATIONSHIP, RIGHT FELLOWSHIP

"And Michal Saul's daughter loved David: and they told Saul, and the thing pleased him" (1 Samuel 18:20 KJV).

One of the most used words in the English language, and yet an abused word, is the word "love." Today's verse gives, in 15 words, the concept of genuine love, and at the same time, vengeful hatred couched in the chasm of acceptance.

This verse has the appearance of genuine love mutually shared by all the parties involved, but not so. We should seek to know, by the power of God, the motives of those who claim to accept us in their family.

David won the love and affection of King Saul's daughter, Michal, and with pure motives she wished him to be her husband. When King Saul realized that his daughter had genuine feelings for David, he decided to fulfill a promise he'd made to anyone who was brave enough to defeat the champion of the Philistines. Any such brave warrior would get his daughter's hand in marriage.

Heartfelt love would mutually grow from this union. How ironic that genuine love flowed from Saul's son (Jonathan) and daughter towards David. They both wanted to align themselves with one who carried around so much divine favor, because they could see the favor of God upon him. Yet their father (Saul) tried everything to destroy David.

Why would a father want to kill a husband who is the joy and pleasure of his daughter? Why would a father want to make his daughter a widow, knowing full well that she loved and adored her husband? David was a man who respected her father and was the best friend of her brother. Why would a king make a fugitive of the most beloved man in the community? One who rid them of their nemesis; one who, through his victory over the enemy, brought back joy and singing to the community? To get away from Saul, David had to fain madness so that he could find refuge in the enemy's camp.

David ran from King Saul to spare his life. He ran because even though the king was out of God's favor, he was still God's anointed. David was not afraid of King Saul; he ran because he wanted to spare the king's life.

Being in a right relationship with God is far better than any place or position that one can have or hold. Being in a right relationship, and fellowship, with one who has the favor of God evident in their life, is better than the company of the elites who have no connection with the Almighty God. ■

— MARK A. BROWN

THE GOSPEL EXPOSES RELATIONSHIPS

"For I am not ashamed of the gospel, because it is the power of God that brings salvation to everyone who believes: first to the Jew, then to the Gentile" (Romans 1:16 NIV).

Through our relationship with others, we expose the potency of the gospel in our lives. Jesus declares that our love for one another provides the true test of discipleship. Relationships continue to play a pivotal role on this Christian journey for believers and non-believers alike.

Comparing the Civil Rights Movement with Black Lives Matter Too, we hear the same concerns about white churches standing on the sidelines spewing sentimental and compassionate rhetoric, labeling social issues as having nothing to do with the gospel while giving eye-opening explanations that allow systemic racism to continue.

Consequently, nearly 60 years later the same excuses are still offered today, even though Dr, King appears more revered now, in death, than he was in life.

In Dr. Martin Luther King, Jr.'s Letter from a Birmingham Jail, he lamented, "In the midst of blatant injustices inflicted upon the Negro, I have watched white churchmen stand on the sideline and mouth pious irrelevancies and sanctimonious trivialities. In the midst of a mighty struggle to rid our nation of racial and economic injustice, I have heard many ministers say: 'Those are social issues, with which the gospel has no real concern.' And I have watched many churches commit themselves to a completely other worldly religion which makes a strange, un-Biblical distinction between body and soul, between the sacred and the secular."

The Civil Rights Movement utilized television to showcase disparity. Black Lives Matter Too maximized social media to broadcast the disparity. *Business Insider* produced 26 charts to illustrate how racism is still a problem in America. The charts include disparities relating to employment, income, education, access to capital and healthcare, police shootings, and the criminal justice system.

In order to address systemic racism, we need Christians—Blacks and Whites—working together to exemplify the gospel. During the Civil War, we had the Abolitionists. During the start of Civil Rights Movement through the Montgomery Bus Boycott, we had Pastor Robert Gaetz. We know the winning formula calls for whites and blacks to not be ashamed of the gospel. In the Adventist church, we need this now more than ever to ensure the message that Black Lives Matter too.

We compromise and secularize the gospel in pushing the status quo, remaining silent, and prioritizing our self-interests. The world and our kids see the hypocrisy, and view us as being ashamed of the gospel. Instead of us changing the gospel, let's empower the gospel to change us. Consequently, we restore the potency of the gospel through our relationships with one another as brothers and sisters in Christ. ▮▮

— EDWARD WOODS, III

APRIL

LOVE

In dying for our sins, Jesus continues to represent the greatest love story on earth. We call this good news, the gospel.

In the Christian community, you can listen to the gospel being proclaimed weekly on either a Saturday or Sunday. Through responding to the love of Jesus, it transforms us to love one another as Jesus loves us.

As you explore the love of Jesus this month, we hope you take an introspective look at your life and can testify how you experience the love of Jesus. We hope that you will share the love of Jesus. Through sanctification, we pray that you become the love of Jesus.

We celebrate love by studying the love of Jesus. We celebrate love by our compassion for one another. We celebrate love through seeking forgiveness. Through our trials and triumphs, we celebrate love by praising Jesus. ▮▮

APRIL 1

TRUSTING THE WORD

"And when Jesus was entered into Capernaum, there came unto him a centurion beseeching him, and saying, 'Lord, my servant lieth at home sick of the palsy, grievously tormented.' And Jesus saith unto him, 'I will come and heal him'. The centurion answered and said, 'Lord, I am not worthy that thou shouldest come under my roof: but speak the word only, and my servant shall be healed'" (Matthew 8:5-8 KJV).

God's Word is powerful! There is no substitute for the word of God. I don't need to ask God to come down on a cloud and rain down bolts of lightning. I don't need to ask God to part the Red Sea. I just need to rely on the Word of God. Just speak the word! My sickness will be healed. My family will be mended. My needs will be met.

Just speak the word, Lord.

"The Lord is my Shepherd I shall not want," (Psalm 23:1).

"My God will supply all of your needs according to His riches in glory," (Philippians 4:19).

"God is our refuge and strength, a very present help in trouble," (Psalm 46:1).

Just speak the word, Lord!

"[A]ll things work together for good . . ." (Romans 8:28a).

I am more than a conqueror, (Romans 8:37).

I can do all things through Christ who strengthens me, (Philippians 4:13).

Just speak the word, Lord!

Trust in the Lord with all thine heart and lean not unto thine own understanding. In all thy ways acknowledge Him and He shall direct thy path," (Proverbs 3:5, 6).

"For the word of God is quick, and powerful, and sharper than any twoedged sword, piercing even to the dividing asunder of soul and spirit, and of the joints and marrow, and is a discerner of the thoughts and intents of the heart," (Hebrews 4:12).

The Word of God is the only offensive weapon that you have in your armor. Use it. Pick up His Word. Study His Word. Follow His Word. Rest in His Word. Trust in His Word. ▮▮

— MARTIN LISTER

APRIL 2

WHAT'S THE WORD?

"In the beginning was the Word, and the Word was with God, and the Word was God" (John 1:1 KJV).

"What's the Word?" Anyone who has spent any considerable amount of time with me has heard me open a conversation with this question. I like this question. In my mind it is an opportunity to enter into a discussion on what is most important to you at any given point in time. I must have asked this question well over a thousand times in my life and I always enjoy hearing the varied responses to this open-ended question.

One of my favorite responses to this question was by a poetic friend of mine while I was in college. Whenever I asked, "What's the word?" he would cleverly respond, "Love's the word, now spread the word."

I really liked his answer. It was creative, profound, and if applied would make a tremendous impact in our lives. If we are to thrive and survive in this cursed world, we have got to learn how to love.

Jackie DeShannon had it right, "What the world needs now is love, sweet love. It's the only thing that there's just too little of." But do we know what it means to love? There are so many definitions of love and if we are to find peace and joy, we must actuate love in its truest form.

So upon reflection, as wonderful as my friend's answer was to my oft asked question, it still falls short of the answer hinted in today's verse. Jesus is the word. And not only did He teach love, He is the source of love. If we are to understand love, we must learn of the Word and He will show us what it means to love.

Today's text says it best; "In the beginning was the Word, and the Word was with God, and the Word was God." Jesus is a powerful Word. Philippians 2:10-11says that it is at the name of Jesus every knee shall bow and every tongue confess that He is Lord. There's something about the name Jesus, it is the sweetest name I know. Jesus is the Word.

Now, spread the word! ■■

— MARTIN LISTER

APRIL 3

CAN I BE LIKE YOU?

"Be ye therefore followers of God, as dear children; And walk in love, as Christ also hath loved us, and hath given himself for us an offering and a sacrifice to God for a sweetsmelling savour" (Ephesians 5:1-2 KJV).

The word "rabbi" means respected teacher, when roughly translated to English, but it is a rich, Hebrew concept that means much more. One of the defining aspects of a rabbi was that he had disciples who followed him. Often, from a western standpoint we tend to equate "disciple" as being a "student," and the "rabbi" as "teacher." However, this falls short of the cultural richness of this relationship. A student wants to know what the teacher knows. A disciple wants to be what the rabbi is. This cannot be overemphasized!

In order to fully appreciate the role of the rabbi in Jewish culture and spiritual formation, consider the educational system that was in place for young Jews at the time of Christ in order to teach their children about Torah. Between the ages 4-12, young Jewish boys participated in Bet Sefer, memorizing the books of Torah. After Bet Sefer, most children would go to work in their family trade.

However, the most talented boys continued their Torah studies. This level of education, called the Bet Midrash included memorization of the prophets and writings, along with the interpretation and application of Torah.

After completing bet midrash, the student would approach a rabbi in an attempt to further his study. He would do this by approaching the rabbi and asking him, "Can I be like you?"

Can I be like you? This is the probative question that every disciple must consider in his or her journey of discipleship. What does it mean to look like Jesus, to walk like Jesus and to talk like Jesus? And the question of greatest import, as it relates to each of our own spiritual journeys is, do I look like Jesus? It is my prayer that during this month, you will discover a clear picture of who our Rabbi is and what it means to be like Him. ▮▮

— MARTIN LISTER

APRIL 4

JUST ORDINARY PEOPLE

"And Jesus, walking by the sea of Galilee, saw two brethren, Simon called Peter, and Andrew his brother, casting a net into the sea: for they were fishers. And he saith unto them, 'Follow me, and I will make you fishers of men.' And they straightway left their nets, and followed him" (Matthew 4:18-20 KJV).

Isn't it great to know that God uses ordinary people? Yesterday, we learned that Jews had an educational system with three stages; Bet Sefer, Bet Midrash and formal discipleship from a rabbi. What is interesting to me is that after Bet Sefer, if it was clear that a young Jewish lad was not cut out to be a teacher of the law, they would be encouraged to take up the family trade.

Young boys would take up carpentry, business, farming, tent-making, fishing, and a host of other respectable professions. There was no shame in it. But it is also true that within this society, there was a certain amount of respect that was given to those who progressed in their training of Torah.

Now consider the story from today's text. One day, early in Christ's formal ministry, but after it is clear that He was a spiritual leader in Judea, Jesus was walking by the Sea of Galilee and He saw two brothers who were fishers. He invited them to "Come follow me."

This is significant for two reasons. First, they were fishermen. Jesus invited two brothers who had gone back to their family trade to come and follow Him. With a bit of deductive reasoning, we can determine that at an early age they weren't cut out to be teachers of the law. They were not cut out for discipleship. But Christ saw something in them.

Second, He invites them to come follow Him. Normally, potential disciples would seek out a rabbi for their training. It was a great honor to learn from a master of the Torah, akin to going to the Ivey League schools of today. Indeed, Christ was approached throughout His ministry by others who wanted to sit under His tutelage. Consider for example the rich young ruler. But in the instance of these two brothers, Christ saw something in them and invited them to "Come follow me."

Obviously, this is an invitation at which these two brothers jumped. What an honor! They left their nets, their jobs, and their homes because what they were getting was so much more than what they were leaving behind.

And the same is true for us. Softly and tenderly, Jesus calls for us "ordinary people" to come follow Him. May we be willing to leave everything behind to follow the Master Teacher. ▮▮

— MARTIN LISTER

APRIL 5

JESUS' AUTHORITY

"And they were astonished at his doctrine: for he taught them as one that had authority, and not as the scribes" (Mark 1:22 KJV).

From the Biblical record, we have note of seven different groups or types of people who refer to Jesus as "rabbi" or "teacher:" His disciples (Mark 9:5); Pharisees (John 3:1-2); John the Baptist's disciples (John 1:35-38); common people (Mark10:51, John 6:24-25); Torah teachers (Matthew 8:19); Herodians (Luke 3:12); and Sadducees (Matthew 22:23-32). Additionally, Christ refers to himself by this title (John 13:12-14, Luke 22:10-11).

Our text for today lets us know that the religious leaders of Christ's time were astonished at His doctrine, for He taught them as one that had authority, and not as the scribes. So what is a scribe? A scribe is someone who had an understanding of Torah; however, they were not able to interpret Torah. You might find them debating Scripture, parroting other people's thoughts, but they had no following. They had no disciples, they had no authority.

Authority meant that the rabbi had disciples and was able to interpret Torah. Jesus had authority. People would come from across town to listen to Christ teach. They would come by the thousands and would sit for hours listening to Him teach from Scripture. He had a word that people wanted and needed to hear, and ministered in a way that commanded the respect of a nation.

People wanted to be around Him. They wanted to hear His words, follow Him to seashore, touch the hem of His garment, climb up in a tree to see Him, and break open ceilings in order to get close to Him. His enemies argued against Him in order to understand His reasoning. They were threatened by Him and plotted to kill Him. Christ had authority!

Christ is the most consequential figure in human history. Time is divided by His life. Volumes of books have been written about Him. Billions of people profess Him as their Lord and Master. Christ has authority.

The question that I wonder then is, does Christ have authority in your life? Do you follow Him? Do you study His teachings? Do you long to be around Him? Will you climb up a tree or tear open a roof to see Him? My fear is that most people that profess Him as Lord and Master do not fully know what it means to be a disciple.

I pray you will continue in your journey to study His life and character, so that you may be more like Him. ▮▮

— MARTIN LISTER

APRIL 6

JESUS' YOKE

"Come unto me, all ye that labour and are heavy laden, and I will give you rest. Take my yoke upon you, and learn of me; for I am meek and lowly in heart: and ye shall find rest unto your souls. For my yoke is easy, and my burden is light" (Matthew 11:28-30 KJV).

Every rabbi had a yoke. A yoke was their method of interpreting Scripture, in which they would order the commandments from greatest to least.

In Judiasm, there are 613 commands given by God in the Torah. As a result of the variety of real life, there were often times where one or more of these commands might come into apparent conflict with other commands

For instance, what if an animal fell into a pit on the Sabbath (which was required to be kept holy)? Getting it out would require work (violating Sabbath), but to leave it in the pit would be cruel (in violation of the commands against cruelty to animals). In such cases, which was the greater (heavier) command and which was the lesser (lighter) command?

The yoke of a rabbi would help his disciples determine how to interpret Torah correctly, so as to best hear and obey God in everyday situations where one commandment might conflict with another. According to Matthew 11, Jesus' yoke was easy and its burden was light.

The simplest way of learning the heart of a rabbi's yoke was to ask the rabbi, "What is the greatest commandment?"

In Mark 12:28-33, one of the teachers of religious law was standing there listening to the debate. He realized that Jesus had answered well, so he asked, "'Of all the commandments, which is the most important?' Jesus replied, "'The most important commandment is this: 'Listen, O Israel! The Lord our God is the one and only Lord. And you must love the Lord your God with all your heart, all your soul, all your mind, and all your strength.' The second is equally important: 'Love your neighbor as yourself.' No other commandment is greater than these'" (NLT).

Jesus' yoke can be characterized by one simple word, love! Love for God and love for our fellow man. Indeed, every other commandment must be filtered through this core principle. And this is more radical than you could ever imagine. Do you know what it means to love? Is love the dominant principle that dictates how you relate to others and to God? ■■

— MARTIN LISTER

APRIL 7

SHEMA

"Hear, O Israel: The Lord our God is one Lord"
(Deuteronomy 6:4 KJV).

"Shema" is a Hebrew word that simply means "listen," and is the first word in this powerful mantra of Jewish life and culture. This is perhaps the greatest call phrase for the people set apart to the God of Abraham, Isaac and Jacob. Here, Jews were commanded by God to reflect on the Shema when they lie down and when they rise up. Every morning and every evening they would recite this mantra and declare that the God of Israel is the One and only Lord.

When you analyze this powerful mantra in its entirety, you will find that God makes several demands of His followers. Consider the following examples:

Shema demands your children. "And these words, which I command thee this day, shall be in thine heart: And thou shalt teach them diligently unto thy children, and shalt talk of them when thou sittest in thine house, and when thou walkest by the way, and when thou liest down, and when thou risest up" (Deuteronomy 6:7 KJV). Shema demands that we raise our children in and around the concept of Shema.

Shema demands exclusive worship. Do you remember when Jesus was tempted in the wilderness and the devil offered the world in exchange for Christ's worship? Well, Christ quoted from the Shema in order to withstand the attack of the enemy. Jesus answered and said unto him, "Get thee behind me, Satan: for it is written, Thou shalt worship the Lord thy God, and him only shalt thou serve" (Luke 4:8 KJV). (See also Deuteronomy 6:13.) The Shema demands exclusive worship. No other gods besides Me.

But what is Shema? What are we called to listen to? Shema is the love that God demands from His followers. The Bible says, "Love the Lord your God with all your heart and with all your soul and with all your strength" (Deuteronomy 6:5 KJV).

God demands that we love Him. Isn't that radical? In fact, all of the law and the prophets are built on this command to love God. Do we love God with all of our Heart, soul and strength? ▮▮

— MARTIN LISTER

APRIL 8

THE SILVER RULE

"Thou shalt not kill. Thou shalt not commit adultery. Thou shalt not steal. Thou shalt not bear false witness against thy neighbor" (Exodus 20:13-16 KJV).

Throughout history, the "Silver Rule" has dominated ethical practice. The Silver Rule simply states, "One should not treat others in ways that one would not like to be treated." This maxim is similar in meaning to the Hippocratic Oath. Hippocrates wrote, in his Epidemics, Bk. I, Sect. XI. "make a habit of two things—to help, or at least to do no harm."

The Code of Ur-Nammu (Originating from Mesopotamia circa 2100-2050 BC) is the oldest known law code surviving today (300 years older than Hammurabi's Code). The preamble sets forth that the basis for which this law was established by Ur-Nammu is in accordance with his principles of equity and truth. This code was written on tablets of stone which contains laws that discouraged murder, robbery, kidnapping, rape, adultery, assault, perjury, conversion, and negligence.

You are familiar with another code written on tables of stone, popularly characterized as the Ten Commandments, or the Decalogue (circa 1450 B.C.). This code also contains several laws related to social practice, which begin with the phrase, "Thou shalt not."

The essence of the Silver Rule can be summed up by the words of the legal philosopher, Zachariah Cafee, Jr. Writing on the subject of liberty, he states, "Your right to swing your arms ends just where the other man's nose begins."

The Silver Rule mandates that we should not harm one another. It is a terrible thing, indeed, to prey on others, to take advantage of others, to kill, steal, or hurt others. Beneath those acts of transgression is a fundamental lack of respect for others. To betray the Silver Rule is to suggest that my needs and my desires are above yours. And in order to secure my prosperous end, I have the right to trample upon you.

This is Satanic. This is wickedness in its purest form because it speaks to the sin of pride and arrogance. I wonder how many people struggle with this basic rule of humanity. Human trafficking, racism, economic inequality, are all symptoms of the fact that this basic moral principle is cherished in our society. How many struggle to not take advantage of others or look down upon other. Decency cries out, we must respect one another.

Where is your humanity? ▮▮

— MARTIN LISTER

THE GOLDEN RULE

"Realizing how much the man understood, Jesus said to him, 'You are not far from the Kingdom of God.' And after that, no one dared to ask him any more questions" (Mark 12:34, NLT).

The Golden Rule states, "One should treat others as one would like others to treat oneself." The first time we find the Golden Rule codified in civic law is in ancient Jewish culture (circa 1450 BC) in a well-known verse, "You shall not take vengeance or bear a grudge against your kinsfolk. Love your neighbor as yourself: I am the LORD" (Leviticus 19:18, NLT).

To give an example of what it means to love this way, consider these: When you harvest the crops of your land, do not harvest the grain along the edges of your fields, and do not pick up what the harvesters drop. It is the same with your grape crop—do not strip every last bunch of grapes from the vines, and do not pick up the grapes that fall to the ground. Leave them for the poor and the foreigners living among you. I am the Lord your God (Leviticus 19:9-10.)

Do not take advantage of foreigners who live among you in your land. Treat them like native-born Israelites, and love them as you love yourself. Remember that you were once foreigners living in the land of Egypt. I am the Lord your God (Leviticus 19:33-34).

The difference between the Silver Rule and the Golden Rule is subtle, but significant. The Silver Rule states that we should not hurt others. The Golden Rule requires us to be kind to others.

In Mark 12, we find Christ talking to a lawyer who asks Him which is the greatest commandment. Christ answers, "The most important commandment is this: 'Listen, O Israel! The Lord our God is the one and only Lord. And you must love the Lord your God with all your heart, all your soul, all your mind, and all your strength.' The second is equally important: 'Love your neighbor as yourself.' No other commandment is greater than these" (Mark 12:29-30, NLT).

So here is where it gets interesting. The teacher of religious law replied, "Well said, Teacher. You have spoken the truth by saying that there is only one God and no other. And I know it is important to love Him with all my heart and all my understanding and all my strength, and to love my neighbor as myself. This is more important than to offer all of the burnt offerings and sacrifices required in the law" (Mark 12:32-33, NLT).

Realizing how much the man understood, Jesus said to him, "'You are not far from the Kingdom of God.' And after that, no one dared to ask him any more questions" (Mark 12:34).

In this passage, Christ seems to suggest that even keeping the Golden Rule is not enough. It gets us close to the Kingdom of God, but it does not get us in the Kingdom of God. If we are to be like the Rabbi, we need a deeper understanding of love so that we may live according to the Kingdom of God. ▮▮

— MARTIN LISTER

APRIL 10

THE PLATINUM RULE

"A new commandment I give unto you, That ye love one another; as I have loved you, that ye also love one another. By this shall all men know that ye are my disciples, if ye have love one to another" (John 13:34-35 KJV).

So here is where the rubber meets the road. In John 13 we find the story of the Last Supper. Christ washes his disciples' feet and declares that Judas is going to betray him. Judas leaves the room and Christ, the rabbi, drops this deep teaching.

He says, "Now I am giving you a new commandment." What Christ is about to teach is completely new to philosophical, ethical and moral thought. Jesus says that His disciples are to, "Love each other. Just as I have loved you, you should love each other. Your love for one another will prove to the world that you are my disciples."

This is beyond radical, for at least two reasons. First, Jesus is adding to the 613 commands that the Jews are familiar with and have identified as the rules that govern human morality. He is giving a new commandment. Let that sink in. Jesus essentially states, I not only have authority to interpret the law; I have the authority to add to the moral law. This is huge!

Christ here indicates that I AM not only the Supreme Court, I AM the House of Representatives, I AM the Senate, I AM the Mayor, I AM the Governor, I AM the President, I AM prophet, I AM priest, and I AM king. I AM. And similar to God handing down the Ten Commandments to Moses on Sinai, Christ is handing down a new commandment for his disciples to keep. That's a big deal!

The second reason why this is a big deal is found in the substance of the command. Here, Christ redefines what it means to love. This definition determines whether we are or are not representing Him well as His disciples. Jesus states that His disciples should love others the same way He loves us. This standard is higher than the Silver Rule. It exceeds the Golden Rule. Jesus says we must love the same way He loves. What an audacious concept!

Now, we have an objective standard of what our love must look like if we are to be disciples of Jesus, the Rabbi, the greatest Teacher our world has ever known. We must learn of Him. We must look like Him. We must be like Him. And He not only taught love; He is love! ■■

— MARTIN LISTER

APRIL 11

CHRIST'S LOVE

"But God demonstrates His own love toward us, in that while we were still sinners, Christ died for us" (Romans 5:8 NKJV).

I can imagine you are asking, "What does it look like to love like Christ?" Well, there are many passages to choose from to illustrate the love of Christ. Most of us have memorized John 3:16 which reads, "For God so loved the world that he gave his only begotten Son that whosoever believeth in him should not perish but have everlasting life" (KJV). What a beautiful passage that shows God's love for us.

Another one of my favorite texts that show the magnitude of God's love is our key text today, which specifically shows what Christ's love looks like. It says that God demonstrates His own love toward us, in that while we were yet sinners, Christ died for us. Just analyze this text closely and you will find exactly what Jesus' love is like.

Christ's love is unhuman. Read the text, again. It begins with these words, "But God." If we are to love like Christ we have to realize that it is a God thing. It is not a human thing. We are simply unable to have Godly love in our own power. We are too selfish, too proud, and too arrogant to be able to love the way that Christ loves. It is a God thing.

Christ's love is unconditional. The text continues by saying, "while we were yet sinners." Did you know that Christ loves us in the midst of our sin? He does not wait until we are righteous or converted. He loves us just as we are, warts and all.

Christ's love is unlimited. Keep reading the text. Christ died. Christ gave up everything to demonstrate His love. He left heaven. He took on humanity. And He died the worst kind of death imaginable in order to show His love for humanity. There is no greater love!

Christ's love is under authority. Notice how Christ dies in order to show God's love. In other words, Christ sacrificed His life because the Father gave the instruction for Him to do so. Philippians puts it this way: Christ was obedient even to the point of death.

I am a member of the United States military, and something that is drilled into us at an early point in our development is the importance of following the orders of a commanding officer. Christ demonstrates His love through obedience. His love is not based on emotion; it is not even based on reason. Christ's love is based on principle. The Father told Him to die and so He sacrificed His life. Christ abides in the Father, who shows Him love, and Christ is compelled to love as a response of obedience. Christ's love is under authority.

In the same way, if we are called to be Christ's disciples, our love must be unhuman, unconditional, unlimited, and under authority. May we study at the feet of Jesus. May we abide in the vine of Jesus so that we may understand very clearly what it means to demonstrate His magnificent love. ■

— MARTIN LISTER

APRIL 12

JESUS OUR ATTORNEY

"And I will pray the Father, and he shall give you another Comforter, that he may abide with you for ever" (John 14:16 KJV).

The Greek word for comforter is "parakletos," which is really a compound word with two parts. "Para" means "alongside," and "kletos" means "to call." Altogether, a comforter is someone who is called alongside. Parakletos actually has legal implications, as it can also be interpreted as an advocate, or a counselor. This is why when we read John 14:16, depending on which version you use, Christ says, I will send you another comforter, advocate, or helper.

One of the favorite professions, perhaps the favorite profession that people enjoy making fun of, is lawyers. There are a million lawyer jokes. For instance: What's the difference between a good lawyer and a bad lawyer? A bad lawyer might let a case drag on for several years. A good lawyer knows how to make it last even longer.

Or how about this one: A man went to a lawyer and asked what his fee was. "One hundred and fifty dollars for three questions," answered the lawyer. "Isn't that a little steep?" asked the man. "Yes," said the lawyer. "Now, what's your third question?"

Just one more: How many lawyer jokes are there, anyway? Only three. The rest are true stories.

All jokes aside, have you ever wondered why people will spend, $200, $300, $400 and even $500 an hour to have an attorney? Everyone talks bad about attorneys, until they need one. Not only is an attorney a master of the law, an attorney is an advocate that comes to your side in your time of greatest need. Attorneys stand up for you when the world seems to be against you and things are at their worst. The attorney looks to see things from your perspective. Attorneys fight for you and make a way of escape when you thought there was no way of escape. When you look at it closely, it's no wonder why people will pay big bucks for an attorney.

That's what Jesus, our parakletos, does when we cry out to Him! Jesus comes to our side. He sees things from our perspective. He fights on our behalf. And He makes a way of escape when we thought there was no way of escape. And here is the kicker—Jesus doesn't charge us. It pays to serve Jesus!

The old hymn says, "What a friend we have in Jesus, all our sins and griefs to bear, what a privilege to carry, everything to God in prayer." Jesus is the best friend we could ever have. He sees us. He cares for us. He loves us.

Shouldn't we find comfort in having a friend like Jesus? He is happy to walk alongside us, but first, we must call out to Him. Why not call on Him today? ▮▮

— MARTIN LISTER

APRIL 13

THE BODY OF CHRIST

"Now ye are the body of Christ, and members in particular" (1 Corinthians 12:27).

The Bible presents several metaphors of the Church. 1 Peter 2 describes the church as a temple with living stones. Ephesians 5 likens the church to Christ's bride. But the word picture that perhaps most are familiar with is the metaphor identifying the church as the body of Christ. In Christ's body we find several parts which must be understood.

The mind of the body is Christ. The mind tells the body what to do. Several Scriptures demonstrate the headship of Christ in the body. For instance, Ephesians says, "And hath put all things under his feet, and gave him to be the head over all things to the church, Which is his body, the fulness of him that filleth all in all" (Ephesians 1:22-23 KJV). Colossians says, "And he is the head of the body, the church: who is the beginning, the firstborn from the dead; that in all things he might have the preeminence" (Colossians 1:18 KJV). Christ is the head of the church and, as such, has authority in the body of Christ.

The members of the body are us—the members. The members' jobs are to submit to the authority of Christ as the head. I love the story in Genesis when Abraham brought his son to be sacrificed. Just in the nick of time, God sent an angel to stop Abraham: "And Abraham lifted up his eyes, and looked, and behold behind him a ram caught in a thicket by his horns: and Abraham went and took the ram, and offered him up for a burnt offering in the stead of his son" (Genesis 22:13 KJV).

I know it's simple, but I want you to note that the body of the ram was unable to leave the head. As much as it may have wanted to escape, it was caught by the head. The body went where the head went. It was attached to the head. In the same way, the members of the body must remain attached to the head, which is Christ.

The motive of the body is unity. We all work together for a common goal. We all need each other, whether we are the hands, feet, eyes, ears, or mouths. We must be motivated to work together for the edification of the body.

The message of the body is love. God calls us to love. It is love that flows from the mind of Christ to the members of Christ to the world. Notice that right after we learn of the body of Christ in 1 Corinthians 12, we find the greatest gift of love in 1 Corinthians 13. Love is the message that the mind shares with the body, to share with the world.

But we need one more thing. We need a medium that connects the mind of Christ to the body of members motivated by unity in order to share a message of love. That medium is the Holy Spirit. The Holy Spirit is the nervous system, that is, the chief controlling and coordinating system of the body. It controls and regulates all voluntary and involuntary activities of the body. It is the Holy Spirit that connects us and gives us power to share the message of love with the world. ▮▮

— MARTIN LISTER

THE FOURTH GROUP

"And one of the malefactors which were hanged railed on him, saying, 'If thou be Christ, save thyself and us.' But the other answering rebuked him, saying, 'Dost not thou fear God, seeing thou art in the same condemnation? And we indeed justly; for we receive the due reward of our deeds: but this man hath done nothing amiss.' And he said unto Jesus, 'Lord, remember me when thou comest into thy kingdom.' And Jesus said unto him, 'Verily I say unto thee, Today shalt thou be with me in paradise'" (Luke 23:39-46 KJV).

When I consider the cross of Christ, I find that with all of the people who witnessed the crucifixion of Christ, they can be consolidated into one of four groups.

The first group is the group that started with Jesus and ended up against Him (e.g. the multitude at the triumphal entry of Jesus, and Pilate). In terms of numbers, this group was the second largest group and represents the fallen angels led by Lucifer, now Satan, the arch enemy of our souls.

The second group is the group that started with Jesus and ended up with Him (e.g. Mary the mother of Jesus, John the beloved, and the women at cross). In terms of numbers, this group was the second smallest group and represents the good angels, like Gabriel who is identified in Luke as an angel that stands in the presence of God. (See Luke 1:19.)

The third group is the group that started against Jesus and ended up against Jesus (e.g. mob, priests, rulers, scribes, Roman Soldiers, wicked thief on cross). In terms of numbers, this group was the largest group and represents sinful humanity who will die in their sins.

The fourth group is the group that started out against Jesus and ended up with Him (e.g. thief on cross). In terms of numbers, this group was the smallest group and represents saved humanity.

Consider this quote from the timeless book, *Desire of Ages*: "For long hours of agony, reviling and mockery have fallen upon the ears of Jesus. As He hangs upon the cross, there floats up to Him still the sound of jeers and curses. How grateful then to the Saviour was the utterance of faith and love from the dying thief! While the leading Jews deny Him, and even the disciples doubt His divinity, the poor thief, upon the brink of eternity, calls Jesus Lord. Many were ready to call Him Lord when He wrought miracles, and after He had risen from the grave; but none acknowledged Him as He hung dying upon the cross save the penitent thief who was saved at the eleventh hour" (White, 1940, p. 750).

Aren't you glad that Christ waited long enough on that old rugged cross to hear this penitent thief declare his faith in the Savior? His story reminds us all of the amazing love of Christ, who loves us so much as to wait as long as possible to save a wretched sinner like me. We all should be so wise as to be a part of this elite group. ■

— MARTIN LISTER

APRIL 15

NO MORE SECRETS

"Whoever conceals their sins does not prosper, but the one who confesses and renounces them finds mercy. Blessed is the one who always trembles before God, but whoever hardens their heart falls into trouble" (Proverbs 28:13-14 NIV).

What are you hiding from Jesus? What is that one thing or habit that is hard to give up? Perhaps you don't want to let it go, even though you know Christ doesn't approve.

Imagine your life like rooms in a house. When you allow a guest over, you only allow them in one room, maybe the bathroom if you cleaned it. As you get to learn the guest better, you allow them in the living and dining rooms, maybe let them fix their own plate in the kitchen.

After a while, you offer them your extra house slippers and allow them to get comfortable. You take them to the garage to see the riding mower, the tools, or the project car. Or maybe you sit and knit a hat or sweater with them over a cup of coffee or tea. Eventually, you allow them more and more access to your home as you become more relaxed. How about the master bedroom? Not a chance, right! What about your computer or its history?

What is the room (area) of your life that you don't want Christ to touch and change? We've sung, "Lord, I love you more than anything," but do you love Jesus more than your secret sin? Which one sits on the throne of your heart?

We need to practice self-examination. Self-examination is required before we participate in Holy Communion (1 Corinthians 11:28), so we can have pure hearts and clean consciences before partaking of His body, and His blood; knowing that we're forgiven and are Holy as He is. After all, He already knows our thoughts from afar (Psalm 139:2), so we're not informing God. Rather we're acknowledging that what we did was wrong, and our need to turn away from that sin. With His help we will resist the evil one so he will—not may—flee (James 4:7).

There's no need to be ashamed, for "If we confess ours sins, He is faithful and just to forgive us our sins, and to cleanse us from all unrighteousness" (1 John 1:9 KJV). I'm not asking that you confess your sins to any person, but unto the One who already knows and is ready to forgive you: Jesus Christ.

If you have a confidant or accountability partner that you can trust to keep your business, then feel free to obey James 5:16 which says, "Therefore confess your sins to each other and pray for each other so that you may be healed. The prayer of a righteous person is powerful and effective" (NIV).

Finally, have the courage to take the necessary steps to "pluck out" (Mark 9:47) whatever tempts or causes you to sin. If that means moving residences, do so. If that means deleting contacts from your cell phone or social media, delete them. If that means cutting out friends who don't want you to live a righteous life in Jesus Christ, tell them about Jesus. If they don't accept Christ, then let them go! At least you told them about Jesus; you've done your part. What good would it be to "gain the whole world, and lose your soul" (Mark 8:36, KJV). ■

— WILLIAM MALLORY

APRIL 16

IT WAS GOOD

"And the earth was without form, and void; and darkness was upon the face of the deep. And the Spirit of God moved upon the face of the waters" (Genesis 1:2 KJV).

I once read a meme that said, "Smooth roads don't make exceptional drivers! Smooth seas don't make exceptional sailors! Clear skies don't make exceptional pilots! A problem free life won't make a strong & exceptional person! Be strong enough to accept the chaos of life. Don't ask life, 'Why me?' Instead say, 'Try me.'"

Sometimes life is chaotic. One of the things that I remind myself of as I go through difficult moments in life is this simple fact: growth often occurs in the valleys of life. Reminding myself of this fact doesn't change the fact that life is difficult right now, but it helps me value the difficult days a bit more. Life gets hard sometimes—really hard. Storms come and seem to put everything in disarray. But whenever the storm clouds come, I determine in my heart to say, all things will work out for my good.

Today, one could easily characterize the state of the world as being in a state of chaos; it would be difficult to find an argument that would suggest otherwise. In Genesis 1:2, we see the only appearance of the Hebrew expression, "toho vavohu," meaning "without form and void"; the word translation in English being "Chaos." We can find hope in the part that says, "And the Spirit of God was hovering over the face of the waters" (NKJV). Amid earthly chaos, Scripture assures us that our God, our Father, is always near, hovering.

Furthermore, the believer can find beauty in that God spoke peace into chaos, resulting in a heavenly declaration; "it was good" (NKJV). God will soon bring this season to an end through the manifestation of His work, during the chaos of our lives too, as He declares "It was good."

Father God, there is none like you. Help us, your people, to see the manifestation of your heavenly work in the midst of life's chaos. Every trial you have chosen for us, we shall count it all joy! We rejoice in knowing that all things work together for good to them, who love you and are called according to your purpose. This too shall pass, and we shall declare, "It Was Good." Amen. ■

— TONY BROWN

APRIL 17

PUT YOUR JESUS FACE ON

"My Father is glorified and honored by this, when you bear much fruit, and prove yourselves to be My [true] disciples" (John 15:8 AMP).

Recently I asked my youth Sabbath School class what it meant to live like Jesus. It came as a complete surprise when one of the students responded with the blunt remark, "Christian adults are just fake."

My first thought was to dismiss the comment as the student's attempt to be controversial. But the comment stuck with me. I couldn't shake the feeling that maybe that's how other people see us, too. Is this the example we reflect to others? Are we living as Jesus-like as possible, or do we just profess to live like Him, and then act like everybody else?

To really live like Jesus is a full-time thing. If we put on our Jesus face to attend church, and then quickly take it off for the rest of the week, we aren't fulfilling His mandate—the one where He told us to glorify and honor God by being His true disciples. Sure, we're going to fail. There're going to be days and times when we are far away from what He wants for us. But that's when we accept grace and try again. We need to have Jesus in us when we're happy and when we're sad; in our thinking and planning; in absolutely everything.

When we do this, when we have that love of Jesus in everything, that is when people around us will see that we are His disciples. Only then will we come to "a full understanding and expression of the love of God and the patient endurance that comes from Christ" (2 Thessalonians 3:5 NLT). When we carry the love of Jesus around with us at all times, we'll want to live better, pray harder, love deeper and profess to anyone who will listen the truth about the amazing God we serve.

We owe it to the generations that will follow us to set the example, to keep the standard raised high. We owe it to ourselves to dig deeper, to aim for a tighter hold on the Lord and His word than ever before. And we owe it to Jesus, the original love-giver, to share that love with everyone around us.

So today, I challenge you to take up the love of Jesus and put your Jesus face on. With Him, victory is assured. ▮▮

— JACKIE GONZALEZ-FEEZER

APRIL 18

FREE TO CHOOSE AND FREE TO LOVE

"For God so loved the world that He gave His only begotten Son, that whoever believes in Him should not perish but have everlasting life" (John 3:16).

"Cease your Anabaptist heresy and do not baptize adults anymore!" said the jailer as he hurled Balthasar into one of the dirty jail cells in the city of Zürich. The year was 1525, and the city of Zurich had been divided in a nearly three-year struggle over the question of adult baptism. The city had just recently overthrown the city's Catholic establishment and embraced Protestantism with its teaching on the centrality of the Bible.

Despite this, the citizens of Zürich in the early 1520s still held on to the Catholic practice of infant baptism. Providentially, a group of believers emerged who, through their diligent study, recognized and began preaching the teaching of adult baptism. Their critics labeled them "Anabaptists," meaning "re-baptizers," since they believed that they were baptizing "again" those who had received baptism as infants.

Sadly, the same Protestants who desired toleration from their Catholic oppressors were not as willing to embrace the message of adult baptism or to grant this group of believers the freedom to baptize their faithful. Consequently, the Anabaptists faced persecution from none other than Huldrich Zwingli, leader of the Reformation in Zürich and one of the heads of city council. Balthasar Hubmaier was one of their leaders and was imprisoned for his belief in adult baptism.

After being tortured under a rack and imprisoned under subpar sanitary conditions, Hubmaier penned the following words, "I may err, I am a human being—but a heretic I cannot be—for I constantly ask instruction in the Word of God."

The sufferings of Hubmaier and the thousands of other Anabaptists who died as a result of religious bigotry and persecution were not in vain. Through them many have inherited the truths of adult baptism and separation of church and state. The Anabaptist commitment to civil disobedience would inspire Martin Luther King Jr. in the struggle against racial segregation and in favor of civil rights for all. Most importantly, the testimony of Anabaptists, like Balthasar Hubmaier, reminds us that faith can only exist where there is love, and love can only exist where there is freedom. ▮▮

— GUILHERME BRASIL DE SOUZA

APRIL 19

RECOVERING FREEDOM

"The Lord builds up Jerusalem; he gathers the outcasts of Israel. He heals the brokenhearted and binds up their wounds" (Psalm 147:2-3 ESV).

Freedom to choose. Is there any more basic right that we value and protect? Yet, no matter where in this world you go, there are multitudes of people who have lost this freedom. Yes, even in the "land of the free." And they don't even realize it.

To understand this shocking reality, we must consider the cognitive process involved in how we make decisions. Our brains were created to absorb information from our senses in order to experience joy and pleasure. The limbic system, where these are processed into memories and emotions, involves several regions of the brain that communicate through chemical signals, passing the data from one area to the next. The prefrontal cortex finally compiles the information and decisions are made, determining whether or not the experience was good and how to respond.

But for some people, these areas of the brain have undergone severe changes that remove their ability to understand situations clearly and to make positive choices. Addiction to a substance such as drugs, and tobacco, or behavior such as gambling, lying, sex, shopping, and eating, have direct effects on these regions of the brain. The changes worsen over time and cause an unrelenting dependence on the addictive substance or behavior. The result is that sound decisions regarding life and beliefs are more difficult to process. Ultimately, according to the American Society of Addictions Medicine, addictions lead to specific biological, psychological, social and spiritual problems (www.asam.org).

The recovery process, however, restores the abilities of the brain. It can be rewired and revitalized over time. The book, *Mind, Character, and Personality, Vol. 1* makes this hopeful statement: "The love which Christ diffuses through the whole being is a vitalizing power. Every vital part—the brain, the heart, the nerves—it touches with healing. By it the highest energies of the being are aroused to activity. It frees the soul from the guilt and sorrow, the anxiety and care, that crush the life-forces. With it come serenity and composure. It implants in the soul, joy that nothing earthly can destroy—joy in the Holy Spirit—health-giving, life-giving joy"(Ellen G. White, p.115).

Support from peers, family, and professionals are key to complete recovery from addictions. Unrelenting love from others, especially those who themselves have experienced the transforming power of God, is a necessary agent of change. It is in our power to help bring freedom back to those who have lost it. And it is our calling. ■■

— ANGELINE B. DAVID

APRIL 20

GOD IS LOVE

"Can a mother forget the baby at her breast and have no compassion on the child she has borne? Though she may forget, I will not forget you!" (Isaiah 49:15 NIV).

It has been said that three-year-olds fit the profile of a psychopath. They act irrationally, lack empathy for others, and have no remorse for their actions. As a parent of a young child, I laughed when I heard this. But, as with all humor, it is funny because there is a kernel of truth within. I was simultaneously amused and scared for this child I was raising. Then I came across a story that gave me a lot of comfort.

James Fallon, a neuroscientist from the University of California, Irvine School of Medicine, used brain imaging to find anatomical patterns in the brain that correlated with psychopathic tendencies in the real world. In a serendipitous series of events Fallon found that his own brain fit the profile for patterns that correlated with psychopathic behavior. He tells his story in his book, *The Psychopath Inside.*

At first, he thought his "hypothesis was wrong and that these brain areas are not reflective of psychopathy or murderous behavior." But after further testing showed Fallon also had genetic markers that pointed in this direction, he came to view that he is, what scientists call, a pro-social psychopath.

Fallon reflected on why he did not turn out to be a serial killer, rapist, or go down some other scary path. "I was loved, and that protected me," he says. Partly as a result of a series of miscarriages that preceded his birth, he believes the exceptional amount of love he was given directed the paths of his life.

What an incredible illustration of the power of love. In 1 John 4:16 we read that God is love. God's love is true, unconditional love. Nothing can separate us from God's love. Romans 8:38-39 tells us, "For I am persuaded, that neither death, nor life, nor angels, nor principalities, nor powers, nor things present, nor things to come, nor height, nor depth, nor any other creature, shall be able to separate us from the love of God, which is in Christ Jesus our Lord" (KJV).

As much as I love my child and find comfort in the fact that my love can protect my child from future ills, God loves my child more. How humbling it is to think that God loves my child more than I do. How incredible to think that God loves me that much too. God loves you in the same way. ▮▮

— KATE WOLFER

SIT AT THE TABLE

"Contribute to the needs of the saints, practice hospitality. Live in harmony with one another. If possible, so far as it depends upon you, live peaceably with all" (Selected from Romans 12:9-21 RSV).

The second decade of my life brought important transitions. At age 11, I was baptized and began the journey of being a disciple-maker for the Kingdom. At age 17, I headed to Andrews University for my first year of college. It was there that my desire to "live for Jesus today" took root, and I discovered the promises of Romans 12:9-21. As I said "yes" to Jesus every day, I knew He would help me live out the values of His kingdom and in that life I would find my greatest joy and help through difficult times.

One of the phrases that has stayed with me through the decades is, "practice hospitality." When we feed others, we meet a basic necessity of life. It sets the table for the other things God wants to accomplish through us and among us. By sharing a meal we have the opportunity to listen, tell stories, experience new seasonings, come to a richer understanding of one another, and become friends.

In my sixth decade, I attended some committee meetings where the group was politely but keenly divided. One particular day was very difficult for me. I cried silently with frustration, anger, and helplessness as I listened to several presentations of those with a different view than mine.

After choosing my "comfort foods" in the supper buffet line, I approached the closest table. It had one empty chair. Glancing around the table, I saw only the faces of my "adversaries." I wanted to move on, but I chose to sit. It is likely my presence changed the nature of the conversation, but more importantly, the new conversation changed my nature. The organizers of the meeting had wisely "set the table" for hospitality—a place where we would listen to each other, tell stories, experience the different seasonings we each brought to the table, and become friends (again).

As those who seek to live for Jesus each day, let us think about our tables—who will sit at my table today? What new tables do I need to explore? Through the act of biblical hospitality let us set the table for God to build His kingdom through and among us every day, through all the decades of our lives. ■

— ESTHER F. RAMHARACKSINGH KNOTT

APRIL 22

CARING ENOUGH TO TELL THE TRUTH

"Faithful are the wounds of a friend; but the kisses of an enemy are deceitful" (Proverbs 27:6 KJV).

Grandpa was my hero. I've never seen anyone reflect God's unconditional love so consistently. I had the honor of being with my Grandpa the last week of his life. He had difficulty breathing, so he couldn't talk much. But shortly before he died he said something I'll never forget. He looked at me lovingly and whispered, "You are an encourager."

Grandpa's comment meant the world to me. I've always wanted to live up to the title he gave me. It's a beautiful gift to be able to encourage others with our words and actions. Encouragement relieves suffering. Jesus was an encourager, and I want to be one too.

Jesus was also a truth-teller. He wasn't afraid to tell the truth even when it cost Him. When Jesus saw people hurting themselves or others, He lovingly spoke up. Throughout Scripture, God also sent the truth-telling prophets to give messages that were desperately needed, but often difficult to share.

Most of us feel comfortable encouraging and affirming people. It's much more difficult to talk directly to someone about how their decisions are destructive or their habits are causing pain. But sometimes this is exactly what Jesus calls us to do.

Speaking of the importance of truth telling, the ancient King Solomon wrote, "Faithful are the wounds of a friend; but the kisses of an enemy are deceitful" (Proverbs 27:6 KJV).

Sometimes we're called to speak the truth in big ways: denouncing injustice, standing up for the oppressed, or defending the teachings of Jesus when they are under attack. But truth-telling is a muscle that grows over time. If we practice telling the truth in small ways, we'll be more prepared to stand for what's right when it's most difficult.

What might everyday truth-telling look like?

- Sharing with a friend that her habit of gossiping has hurt you or others.
- Speaking up for a coworker who is being mistreated.
- Telling a parent that you've noticed their child has an unmet need.
- Supporting biblical principles, even if you're misunderstood or labeled.

May God empower us to "speak the truth in love," in ways that bring justice and healing to the people around us. ▮▮

— ELISE HARBOLDT

APRIL 23

DON'T JUDGE ME

"Judge not, that you be not judged" (Matthew 7:1 NKJV).

Developing an appreciation for religious pluralism and a recognition of it as a means to effectively co-exist is becoming more and more important in today's diverse society. Religious pluralism is not the dismissal of one's tenets of faith, but rather an ability to accept others without apprehension.

Part of my responsibility as a chaplain in the United States Navy Chaplain Corps is to conduct worship services of various Protestant faiths. This opportunity allows me to minster in a diverse environment without respect of persons or religions, and without judgment. These times provide me with opportunities to serve a variety of faith groups with unconditional acceptance.

Religious pluralism has a long history that reaches from antiquity to contemporary trends in post-modernity. One of the earliest examples of religious pluralism is documented in the "Cyrus Cylinder," which describes how Cyrus, a Persian king, promised freedom of religion and worship for the diverse religious groups of people living in the Persian Empire. Cyrus was an outstanding advocate of religious pluralism, and is referred to as "God's anointed" (Isaiah 45:1).

The Founding Fathers of America believed in religious pluralism, and many migrated to America's shores in search of religious tolerance. Religious pluralism is protected by the First Amendment of the United States Constitution, which states, "Congress shall make no law respecting an establishment of religion or prohibiting the free exercise thereof..." Religious liberty, as it is defined, guarantees that multiple religions can worship peacefully.

One of the most powerful ways of demonstrating the love of God is ministering to others without regard to their religious beliefs. Both the Bible and more modern history offer examples of people who understood and respected religious pluralism. Take, for example, the apostle Paul, David Livingstone and Mother Teresa. They exemplified Christian love in diverse religious settings unconditionally and without judgment. Of course, Jesus Christ is the best example of One who not only ministered to all people, but gave Himself as a sacrifice of unconditional love for all.

We are called upon to do the same as we share His love with a world that is in great peril. ■

— WASHINGTON JOHNSON, II

APRIL 24

BETTER THAN BUBBLES

"Your love for one another will prove to the world that you are my disciples" (John 13:35 NLT).

Sometimes I like to share stories of life-before-the-smart-phone with my Gen-Z friend. She can't believe that one of the highlights of my college life was blowing bubbles—sitting outside the Student Center on Friday afternoons with friends. Technology has its wonders, but nothing like good conversation, bubbles, and avoiding homework and room cleaning.

Perhaps some of the greatest displays of God's grace in our lives are these moments of wonder. The incredible artwork of a sunset over an expansive tropical ocean or majestic mountain peaks. The silence of snow. The surprise of spring. A grandparent's stories, or an older sister's lullabies. Watching someone's life transform for the better.

Wonder is never far away, but I think it comes closer when we make space for it in our lives—especially when we make space for others. Sometimes I attend a local gathering of women mostly from Ahmadiyya Muslim, Jewish, Church of Jesus Christ of Latter-day Saints, and mainline Christian backgrounds. Over time, I've gotten to know some of the women, and even though I'm probably the only Seventh-day Adventist in the room, I never feel alone. And I experience plenty of wonder.

As I hug my Muslim friends, I find wonder realizing that strangers are becoming friends. When I listen to personal stories from different faith backgrounds, finding something in each I can relate to, I find wonder. Realizing that every woman in that room is a beloved daughter of God, and feeling His movement of love in my heart for them, I find wonder.

As I leave these gatherings, refreshed and strengthened in my own faith, I remember Jesus' words to His disciples; that the world will know who He really is because of our love for one another. "One another" begins with our families, friends, and faith communities. But love does not stop there. It is always seeking to open the circle to others. It does not hide from those who are different—it embraces, it welcomes, it smiles, it risks being misunderstood and misunderstanding.

Basically, love just shows up—like Jesus did. When we're running on that kind of love, there is so much wonder waiting for us—even better than smart phones or blowing bubbles. ▮▮

— ANDREA KEELE

APRIL 25

WHEN OUR MESSAGE IS NOT WELCOME

"Be happy with those who are happy, and weep with those who weep. Live in harmony with each other. Don't be too proud to enjoy the company of ordinary people. And don't think you know it all! Never pay back evil with more evil. Do things in such a way that everyone can see you are honorable. Do all that you can to live in peace with everyone" (Romans 12:15-18 NLT).

As efforts to censor Christian viewpoints online and in the public space intensify, we may be tempted to respond in a way that doesn't represent the character of Christ. However, Jesus calls us to be a practical witness, one that puts Him on display in all aspects of our lives, and that is not so easily censored.

Jesus sought first to fulfill people's needs; He then invited them to follow. We can use our digital and social influence to gain insights and focus on meeting the mental, physical, and spiritual needs of those around us. Once relationships and trust are built, we can invite them to "taste and see that the Lord is good" (Psalm 34:8, NIV). The gospel of action can further our ministry of hope and wholeness, even when words of truth are silenced.

Practically, this means when someone online expresses sadness, anxiety about a life challenge, or excitement about a happy event, empathize with them. Engage with their post and/or send a personal message to let them know you're with them along the way, that you're there if they need help. Be consistent in building relationships with others who may have very different beliefs. Once they know how much you care, they are more likely to come and reason with you over truth.

People share a surprising amount of information online. It's up to us to act upon that knowledge. Modern technology gives us the opportunity to reach into gated communities and closed-off hearts, allowing us to build bridges on common ground. Every post represents a real-life person, their experiences, and their needs. What prayers can we answer by simply paying attention?

We can change hearts and minds by living out Jesus both online and offline. When our voices are silenced, know that the Holy Spirit is still at work. In faith, step out and share God's love without reservation. Trust God to perform the miracle. ▮▮

— JAMIE DOMM

APRIL 26

ADDRESSING SECURITY NEEDS

"You will keep in perfect peace all who trust in you, all whose thoughts are fixed on you!" (Isaiah 26:3 NLT).

While talking to a friend about the topic of dating, I was unexpectedly asked if I had any insecurities. My immediate response was a firm, "No!" but the question challenged me to examine all other aspects of my life—work, finances, ambitions, and friendships. The question lingered in my mind, leading me to dig into what it actually means to be "insecure." In a nutshell, insecurity is a manifestation of uncertainty. A more literal meaning is to perceive a lack of security.

One of the most famed psychologists from the early 20th century, Abraham Maslow, developed a theory that broke down the hierarchy of needs for every human being. The theory is illustrated by a five-tier pyramid that leads to what Maslow thought to be every human's ultimate goal—self-actualization. The foundation of the pyramid is made up of basic or physiological needs such as food, water, shelter, and air. However, right above basic needs is "safety needs" which go beyond physical safety. Maslow believed safety needs also include financial, social, vocational, and psychological or emotional security needs. With that in mind, it would be dishonest to say I have not struggled with thoughts of insecurity. It's easy to get consumed with worries in areas of life that seem to be out of my control. This is especially true when life's stressors, such as debt, shaky relationships, tragedies, and illnesses, seem to be more constant than transient. This would naturally prompt us to question our security. Further, it would be easy to have our thoughts shift to hopelessness in the face of insecurities.

Thankfully, God's love compels Him to protect us not only from external struggles, but internal griefs. His love is unfailing and perfect. 1 John 4:18 says, "perfect love expels all fear" (NLT).

The peace you will feel when you give your insecurities to God is beautifully outlined in Proverbs 3:24-26: "Your mind will be clear, free from fear; when you lie down to rest, you will be refreshed by sweet sleep. Stay calm; there is no need to be afraid of a sudden disaster or to worry when calamity strikes the wicked, for the Eternal is always there to protect you. He will safeguard your each and every step" (VOICE).

When overcome with insecurities, we need to remember to bring our awareness to the One who loves us so much that He looks out for all of our security needs. He guarantees this is one area of life we never need to be insecure about.

God "will keep in perfect peace all who trust in [Him], all whose thoughts are fixed on [Him]!" (Isaiah 26:3 NLT). ■■

— MYLON MEDLEY

APRIL 27

LOVE FERVENTLY

"Seeing ye have purified your souls in obeying the truth through the Spirit unto unfeigned love of the brethren, see that ye love one another with a pure heart fervently" (1 Peter 1:22 KJV).

As it relates to our daily interactions with others in a general sense, Paul wrote "If it be possible, as much as lieth in you, live peaceably with all men" (Romans 12:18 KJV). I would surmise that the majority of those who don't even consider themselves Christians abide by this standard. Living in a peaceful community and having great neighbors would be acceptable to almost anyone.

But as it relates to "the brethren," our fellow brothers and sisters in Christ, Peter does not give any wiggle room regarding our emotional commitment toward those who are members of the family of God. He unapologetically wrote to those who have been purified by the Spirit to "see that you love one another with a pure heart fervently" (1 Peter 1:22 KJV).

Peter did not qualify the word "brethren" with any of the following modifiers—kind, respectful, forgiving or cheerful. He doesn't suggest that the "brethren" have any qualification to receive this intense emotional outpouring except their relationship to us in Jesus Christ. Is such a biblical revelation even worth considering? Does it make sense to not only put this counsel on the back of the stove, but take it off of the stove completely? Or was he considering the new commandment Jesus uttered, "As I have loved you, that you also love one another" (John 13:34 NKJV)?

Would anyone suggest that the love of Jesus for us was effete or lacking in anyway? Does not the cross of our Lord and Savior make it clear that He gave His all for us? But to love in such a manner is inconceivable from a natural point of view. Therefore, in the following verse Peter wrote, "Being born again, not of corruptible seed, but of incorruptible, by the word of God, which liveth and abideth for ever" (1 Peter 1:23 KJV). The seed of our first birth brings forth "bitter envying and strife . . . is earthly, sensual, devilish" (James 3:14-15 KJV).

In contrasting human love and divine love, Ellen White wrote, "Love is a heavenly attribute. The natural heart cannot originate it. This heavenly plant only flourishes where Christ reigns supreme. Where love exists, there is power and truth in the life. Love does good and nothing but good. Those who have love bear fruit unto holiness, and in the end everlasting life" (*The Youth's Instructor*, January 13, 1898). ▮▮

— DAVID A. LONG

APRIL 28

KNOWING HIS RESURRECTION POWER

"That I may know Him and the power of His resurrection" (Philippians 3:10 NKJV).

Jesus was crucified on Friday, the sixth day. He rested in the grave on the seventh day Sabbath. And early Sunday morning, the first day of the week, He came forth from the tomb a conqueror over death.

Roman guards stationed at His sealed tomb were helpless to stop Jesus from resurrecting.

Evil angels did all they could to keep Jesus locked down, but they too were powerless to prevent His resurrection. Jesus said in John 10:18, No one takes it from Me, but I lay it down of Myself. I have power to lay it down, and I have power to take it again. This command I have received from My Father" (NKJV).

God desires all of us to experience His resurrection power in our daily lives. That's why the Holy Spirit inspired Paul to write about it repeatedly:

• Philippians 3:10: "that I may know Him and the power of His resurrection" (NKJV).

• Ephesians 1:19-20: "that ye may know the exceeding greatness of His power to us-ward who believe, according to the working of his mighty power, which he wrought in Christ, when he raised him from the dead..." (KJV).

• Ephesians 2:4-6 "But God, who is rich in mercy, ...even when we were dead in sins, hath quickened us together with Christ, (by grace ye are saved;) And hath raised us up together, and made us sit together in heavenly places in Christ Jesus" (KJV).

Grace is more than unmerited favor. The favor is that God has continually made available to us His Resurrection Power, through His Spirit.

Through God's Resurrection Power, those dead in sin can be resurrected to newness of life.

Through God's Resurrection Power, dead relationships can be resurrected to newness of life.

Through God's Resurrection Power, physical health can be resurrected to newness of life.

Through God's Resurrection Power, dead careers can be resurrected to newness of life.

Through God's Resurrection Power, dead financial conditions can be resurrected to newness of life.

Claim God's resurrection power for your life today.

Lord, thank You for raising me up with Christ, and making me sit together with Him in the heavenly realms, in Christ Jesus, so that in the coming ages You may show forth the indescribable riches of Your grace expressed in Your kindness towards us in Christ Jesus. In Jesus' name, Amen. ▮▮

— WILLIAM S. SMITH

APRIL 29

CHILDISH LOVE

"When I was a child, I spake as a child, I understood as a child, I thought as a child: but when I became a man, I put away childish things" (1 Corinthians 13:11 KJV).

As a child in elementary school, I was certain that Mrs. Maggie James did not love any of her students. She wasn't abusive in her language, she did not give that many "spankings," although she was not opposed to doing so and did so from time to time. But the reason I was sure she didn't love us as students was because of her unwillingness to allow us to get away with mediocre or less than acceptable homework assignments.

During that time, I was sure that I would never have a different point of view regarding her teaching methods or her strict adherence to excellence. In my mind, it was overbearing, completely unnecessary and devoid of love. But after I left her fifth and sixth grade class and entered the seventh grade, I was more advanced than I realized because she refused to give me "love" as I understood it in my limited thinking. This brings to mind the words of Paul, "When I was a child, I spake as a child, I understood as a child, I thought as a child, but when I became a man I put away childish things" (1 Corinthians 13:11 KJV).

Sometime ago my wife and I were looking to buy a home. We came across a home that we really liked and we were excited about the location. It wasn't that far from our employment, and even more importantly, the price was in our range. We were convinced that was the house God had for us. But it didn't work out.

At the time I was sure God failed us. I couldn't find a reason in my mind why He let that slip through our fingers and get past His eyes that never sleep or slumber. Even though my wife accepted God's leading, I was very disappointed and shared my frustrations with the Holy One of Israel.

Sometime later we found the home that God had chosen for us. It was over 25 miles away from what, I thought, was the perfect location. He placed us in an area that was convenient for many of the activities in our life that were important to us. The "perfect house" would have been a nightmare. What I thought wasn't "love" because of my limited thinking, truly was love. ▮▮

— DAVID A. LONG

APRIL 30

THE SACRIFICE OF THE VINE

"My command is this: Love each other as I have loved you. Greater love has no one than this: to lay down one's life for one's friends" (John 15:12-13 NIV).

Jesus has some very repetitive themes going on during His last few hours before His trial and crucifixion. Along with giving His disciples hope and courage and speaking so much about God the Father, Jesus continues to speak about the nature of love.

Christ had prepared Himself to be the sacrificial lamb, but He was also preparing His disciples to understand that as well. He knew it was the plan that He would lay down His life to redeem us all.

As the fingers of COVID-19 reached around the globe, gripping the world in the first pandemic of this millennium, pet stores and pet adoption agencies soon ran out of dogs for people to adopt. Waiting lines of pre-approved applicants starting filling up. As several of my own siblings acquired puppies into their homes, the wonder and joy of puppy days began filling our family social media threads.

From the first minute of holding the puppies, to that weird but sweet minute when a mostly fully-grown puppy still wants to be held like a baby, these new family pets exhibit that type of love that God has for us and that we should have for Him—agape love. It's that unconditional love that requires nothing and exists from the very beginning. Just like puppy love.

In those final hours leading to His crucifixion, Christ wanted us to understand just how important it is to love. Our humble, meek and mild Savior gave a command in the upper room. He commanded that we love like He loves. Greater agape love has no one than this; that he lay down his life for his friend.

As we celebrate a risen Savior this weekend, as we give thanks that His sacrifice for us was accepted by God, let us remember to also celebrate love and to share our love (and the love of God) with those who come into our sphere of influence.

Dearest Jesus: Thank you for your unbounded love to us and your sacrifice on our behalf. No one loves us better than You. May we each lead a life worthy of both Your love and sacrifice. We rejoice as we serve a risen Savior. Amen. ■

— AMIREH AL-HADDAD

THE HOLY SPIRIT

The theme for the month of May is the Holy Spirit. This third person of the Godhead has a tremendous impact on the life of a Christian. Without the Holy Spirit, we would not be cognizant of our true condition or be convicted that we need to be converted. The Holy Spirit not only points the way to God, but gives us the desire, courage, and ability to turn to God.

Throughout this month, we will look at several aspects of the Holy Spirit. We will begin with examining the person and presence of the Holy Spirit. We will then discover how the Holy Spirit uses whomever He wills to accomplish His purposes. We will next explore the work of the Holy Spirit in our lives. We will see how the Holy Spirit seeks to save us, sanctify us, grow us, and speak to us. Following that, we will spend some time looking at what it means to follow the Holy Spirit as He leads us. Then we will marvel at the power of the Holy Spirit and His desire to share that power with us. Finally, we will look at the peace that comes from trusting in the Holy Spirit.

As you reflect on each day's devotional, you will read expositions and experiences of people from all walks of life: pastors, students, teachers, and ordinary men and women. You will discover that what they all have in common is an encounter with, and appreciation for, the Holy Spirit. ■■

— PAUL GOODRIDGE

MAY 1

AN EVER-PRESENT PRESENCE

"And I will pray the Father, and He shall give you another Comforter that He may abide with you forever; even the Spirit of truth whom the world cannot receive because it seeth Him not neither knoweth Him: but ye know Him; for He dwelleth with you, and shall be in you" (John 14:16-17 KJV).

The Holy Spirit has been present since the creation of the world. Genesis 1:2 states, "the Spirit of God moved upon the face of the waters" (KJV). Not only has He been present from creation, but He has also been active from creation. He is unseen, like the wind (John 3:9), but His mighty power can be felt.

He is also termed, the Holy Ghost, as referred to in Luke 1:35 as the source of the Virgin Mary's conception (KJV); as a dove at Jesus' baptism (Luke 3:22 KJV); and as a rushing mighty wind at Pentecost (Acts 2:2-4 KJV). He also inspired the prophets to write and proclaim God's words.

When Jesus was about to offer His life for the salvation of the world, He told His disciples He would go to prepare mansions for them and then return to take them and others who loved Him to be with Him. In His absence, He would send the Holy Spirit, or the Comforter, who would lead them into all truth and would bring back to their remembrance things He had told them.

The Comforter, or Holy Spirit, is the third person of the Godhead. This ever-present presence is a person who can be grieved, but not seen. Paul warned, "and grieve not the Holy Spirit of God whereby ye are sealed unto the day of redemption" (Ephesians 4:30 KJV). We can grieve the Spirit by refusing to listen to His promptings, and failing to read or listen to God's words.

M.M. Wells, the song writer, penned these words: "Holy Spirit, faithful guide, ever near the Christian side. Gently lead us by the hand, pilgrims in a desert land."

As end-time Christians, our deepest need today is to pray for an infilling of the Holy Spirit so that our lives will reflect the life of Jesus. And like the disciples at Pentecost, we will proclaim the everlasting gospel wherever we go. Then the work will be finished, and the Savior will return to take His faithful children home with Him.

It is now time for full surrender, because tomorrow is not promised to us. Let us, like the Apostles, pray for this power in our lives that will enable us to live for Christ and to be ready for His soon return. ■

— BERYL C. MARTIN

MAY 2

PREPARING FOR THE OUTPOURING OF THE HOLY SPIRIT

"Be patient, therefore, brothers, until the coming of the Lord. See how the farmer waits for the precious fruit of the earth, being patient about it, until it receives the early and the late rains. You also, be patient. Establish your hearts, for the coming of the Lord is at hand" (James 5:7-8 ESV).

The outpouring of the Holy Spirit is one of the most important subjects in the Bible, but it is also one that is not well understood. Not only are we living in the last days, but we are also living in the dispensation of the Holy Spirit, and He has a special work to do to prepare us for Christ's second coming.

As we study the work of the Holy Spirit, we see that there are three aspects of His work: the initial gift (Acts 2:38), the early rain (Acts 1:8), and the latter rain (Joel 2:23). The initial gift of the Holy Spirit is received with repentance and baptism. The early rain was received by the early Christians at Pentecost. The latter rain will be received after the passing of the National Sunday law.

The early reign cultivates the spiritual soil and helps us to get rid of all known sin in our lives. However, though we have been in the time of the latter rain since 1888, most of us are still struggling with the work of the early rain. Therefore, we are not ready to receive the letter rain.

The latter rain is the power of the final loud cry. It will give power to the loud voices of the three angels' message found in Revelation 14:6-12. The final loud cry is the announcement that Babylon has fallen (Revelation 14:8; 18:1-4). Babylon falls completely when the National Sunday Law is enacted. Thus, the latter rain follows the passing of the National Sunday Law.

With this in mind, there are seven conditions for receiving the latter rain: (1) We must be a victorious people; (2) we must be an enlightened people; (3) we must be a loving people; (4) we must be a praying people; (5) we must be a working people; (6) we must be a temperate people; and (7) we must be a Sabbath-keeping people.

This should be our daily focus. As we go through each day, let us pray for God's help in preparing for our Savior's soon return and the outpouring of the Holy Spirit. ▮▮

— GABE H. TAYLOR, JR.

MAY 3

THE POWER OF PRAYER

"If ye then, being evil, know how to give good gifts unto your children: how much more shall your heavenly Father give the Holy Spirit to them that ask him?" (Luke 11:13 KJV).

The greatest need a Christian has is the indwelling of the Holy Spirit. Through the Holy Spirit, sins are confessed, lives are changed, and power is given to do great things for God. However, God has never—and will never—forced Himself on those who do not ask Him to come into their lives. Therefore, it is critical that we not just hope for the Spirit's presence, but that we daily pray for it.

More often than not, we reduce prayer to some rhythmic habit we've inscribed into our daily comings and goings, a routine conversation we have with ourselves. As such, we are missing out on communicating with the Love of our lives, and He with us.

Consider two passages in scripture: Daniel 10 and 2 Chronicles 7:14. Daniel 10 tells us about the young Hebrew prophet, Daniel, who is in 'mourning' for three weeks, searching for wisdom and understanding in regard to the visions which he had received. For 21 days Daniel's heart was fixed on this, and when the angel arrives, he tells him, "from the first day that you set your heart to understand, and to humble yourself before God, your words were heard; and I have come because of your words" (Daniel 10:12 NKJV).

Later in the text we learn that it took 21 days because there was, quite literally, a cosmic conflict which held the angel up. But note, because of Daniel's words the angel came. This reminds us of one crucial thing: our prayers precipitate action in heaven (with the very important caveat that we humble ourselves).

2 Chronicles 7:14 similarly shows this exact idea of God responding to our prayers. However, in this case God expresses a longing to bless His people; and according to Romans (4-8), we are His people through the saving work of Christ. God is literally just waiting for us to humble ourselves and pray so that He can pour out His Presence. Before the day of Pentecost, the disciples found themselves deep in prayer for 10 days. In Testimonies to Ministers and Gospel Workers, author Ellen White tells us that for 10 days the disciples prayed (White, 1962, p.170), and added to this was Christ's intercessory work. This unlocked the outpouring of The Holy Spirit.

As we pray for the presence and power of the Holy Spirit, trust that our prayers are not just heard, but consequential. ▮▮

— JOHANS ROMERO

MAY 4

THE UNEXPLAINABLE WORKING OF THE HOLY SPIRIT

"When they saw the courage of Peter and John and realized that they were unschooled, ordinary men, they were astonished and they took note that these men had been with Jesus" (Acts 4:13 NIV).

Jesus called commoners to be His helpers, the bearer of the words of truth that He so often preached to the people that came to listen to Him. These helpers were unschooled, as the leaders of the Jews expected them to be. They had no special calling, no special office; they were just called "common men." Today, we would call them idiots. What the Jews failed to acknowledge, or is unexplainable, is that the Holy Spirit brings change to individuals who seem of little worth in human estimation. God had to remind Samuel that, "The Lord looks not on his countenance ... but on the heart" (1 Samuel 16:7-8 KJV).

Two young Galilean fishermen stood before the same formidable tribunal which, a few weeks before, had condemned their Master. They might well have quailed. Evidently, "Annas, the high priest, and Caiaphas, and John, and Alexander, and as many as were of the kindred of the high priest" (Acts 4:6) KJV, were very much astonished that their united wisdom and dignity did not produce a greater impression on these two contumacious prisoners. They were "unlearned," knowing nothing about rabbinical wisdom. They were "ignorant," or, as the word ought rather to be rendered, "idiots." They had no kind of official dignity. And yet there they stood, perfectly unembarrassed and at their ease, and said what they wanted to say— all of it, right out.

So, as great astonishment crept over the dignified ecclesiastics who were sitting in judgment upon them, they remembered what, of course, they knew before, only it had not struck them so forcibly as now in explaining the Apostles' demeanor. They had been with Jesus. So they said to themselves, "Ah, that explains it all! There is the root of it. The company that they have kept accounts for their unembarrassed boldness."

Can you or I explain the working of the Holy Spirit? The results we see around us are all evident: ignorant men bring people to Christ. Illiterate individuals who cannot read their ABC run evangelistic crusades and people come to know Jesus. Praise the Lord for the unexplainable working of the Holy Spirit. We will understand this in the kingdom, and we will have all eternity to discover how this transformation works.

By God's grace, let us get there. ■

— EVETHE CARGILL

MAY 5

THE UNSEEN POWER OF THE SPIRIT

"Do you not know? Have you not heard? The Lord is the everlasting God, the Creator of the ends of the earth. He gives strength to the weary and increases the power of the weak" (Isaiah 40:28-29 NIV).

In the United States, Cinco de Mayo has become associated with the celebration of Mexican American culture. However, the origin of the commemoration of the date goes back to May 5, 1862 when under the leadership of General Ignacio Zaragoza, the much smaller Mexican army defeated the much larger French Empire at the Battle of Puebla. This miraculous feat of the smaller defeating the bigger, or the weaker defeating the stronger, is a theme that has been celebrated throughout history.

Even Hollywood has cashed in on the notion of the "underdog" with movies such as Rocky, Remember the Titans, The Karate Kid, Invincible, Hoosiers, Rudy, Sea Biscuit, the Mighty Ducks, Miracle on Ice, and Erin Brockovich. We also see this theme throughout the Bible, namely in such stories as Joshua vs. Jericho (Joshua 6), Gideon's 300 vs. the Midianites (Judges 7), Samson vs. the Philistines (Judges 16:23-31), and David vs. Goliath (1 Samuel 17), just to name a few.

However, the reality is that in many of these miraculous victories, the miraculous actually happened. The Spirit of the Lord took over and collapsed the walls of Jericho. The Holy Spirit caused the Midianites to turn on each other and kill themselves. The Spirit of the Lord fell on Samson and gave him the strength to collapse the building in which the Philistines were celebrating. The Holy Spirit fell on David and guided his stone to kill Goliath.

It's easy to think that our strength, abilities, cunning, education, or expertise accomplishes the impossible, incredible, or unbelievable. But behind the scenes, God—through the Holy Spirit—works in mysterious ways to perform supernatural acts.

Unlike many of us who would be quick to accept praise and recognition for our accomplishments, the Holy Spirit does not look for these when He works on our behalf. Instead, He concurs with Jesus who said that our works should lead others to glorify God (Matthew 5:16).

The next time we are tempted to think that we aced the test, overcame obstacles, or defeated giants in our lives, we would do well to remember that there is an unseen power, the Holy Spirit, moving, working, guiding, directing, and acting behind the scenes on our behalf, performing miracles. ■

— PAUL GOODRIDGE

MAY 6

AN UNLIKELY SOURCE

"The wind blows wherever it pleases. You hear its sound, but you cannot tell where it comes from or where it is going. So it is with everyone born of the Spirit" (John 3:8 NIV).

Here I was, at the beginning of another semester with only £500 (British pounds sterling = $630 U.S. dollars) to my name to go back to Oakwood University to continue my studies in Theology. I wondered how God was going to get me through this time. Bear in mind, I was an international student, so I didn't qualify for financial aid, scholarships, or student loans like American nationals. My concerned parents were telling me that maybe I should consider cheaper options like staying off campus. But, I was adamant that I would get into school and get back into my room, though I secretly didn't know how.

The two Sabbaths before returning to Oakwood, I was scheduled to preach at two different churches. The first Sabbath I was invited by a lady to be the guest speaker. I preached a sermon on faith, and while preaching, I noticed a particular lady in the congregation. After I finished preaching, the lady who invited me told the congregation that she felt impressed to take up an offering to help me get back into school. After the service, while shaking hands, the lady I had noticed in the congregation came to me and asked me how much I needed for school.

I had no idea what was about to happen nor why she was asking. Considering I had three semesters to go before graduation, I told her I needed about £35,000 ($45,000). She said, "OK," and just walked away. She came back about two minutes later and timidly asked if £10,000 ($12,000) would help. I was in a state of shock because that amount would enable me to get back into school and into my room for the next semester.

I was even more shocked when the lady explained that the Spirit told her give me the money. She continued that while she was not rich, nor did she have the expendable finances to give to anybody, she sensed the calling of God was on my life. What was even more incredible was that this woman was not a Christian, or a believer. This was her first time in a church, let alone an Adventist church, since she was a young lady.

More than a year later, as graduation approaches, I am still amazed at how the Holy Spirit will use anybody as He wills, even unlikely sources, to do His will. ■

— JESSE SAMUEL

MAY 7

GOD MOVES IN MYSTERIOUS WAYS

"For he will order his angels to protect you wherever you go" (Psalm 91:11 NLT).

Growing up as a young girl in Barbados, I used to hear my mom repeat these words, "God moves in mysterious ways His wonders to perform." At the time, it held no significance.

Fast forward to some years ago, when my three daughters and I were driving to Atlanta where we would spend the night and fly the next day to Barbados to visit my family. Two hours into our four-hour trip, my car began to slow down then came to an abrupt halt. Immediately I prayed that God would help us. Having limited knowledge about cars, I turned on the hazard lights, stopped and lifted the hood. I stood outside the car, flagging down passing vehicles, but no one stopped. My heart was beating fast, and I became concerned because it was getting dark.

Our plan was to leave our home in Huntsville, Alabama early that afternoon, but we left a few hours later than expected. Now, here we were stuck on the highway. Without thinking it through, I told the girls to stay in the car while I walked to the nearest exit to find help. It didn't occur to me that my decision was extremely risky. I instructed them not to open the door for anyone. One of my girls decided to come with me. As we ran on the highway, I continued to pray and flag down vehicles; however, they just zoomed by.

But God is so merciful and gracious! Looking ahead, we saw that a truck had stopped. From the lights of passing vehicles reflecting on it, I saw a man with white wooly hair exit the truck and start walking toward us. As we got closer, he called out.

"Woman, are you crazy? Don't you know it isn't safe to walk on the highway in the night?"

I explained what happened, and he said that he would help us. He drove us back to our car. Another truck was parked behind it. The two drivers discussed the situation and decided that the second driver would help us. I thanked the driver who'd taken us back to my car, and he departed. The truck driver took us to the nearest telephone booth to call my husband and a wrecker.

When we arrived at the auto repair center, the owner said that he was planning to leave early, but for some unknown reason he was still at work. Only the Holy Spirit could have orchestrated something like that. The truck driver stayed with us until our car was fixed. We arrived very late in Atlanta, but we were safe.

God certainly moves in mysterious ways, His miracles to perform! ■

— SHIRLEY C. IHEANACHO

MAY 8

THE POWER OF A PRAYING MOTHER

"In her deep anguish Hannah prayed to the Lord, weeping bitterly. Hannah was praying in her heart, and her lips were moving but her voice was not heard. Eli thought she was drunk.... 'Do not take your servant for a wicked woman; I have been praying here out of my great anguish and grief.' Eli answered, 'Go in peace, and may the God of Israel grant you what you have asked of him'" (1 Samuel 1:10, 13, 16-17 NIV).

Often times, because we read the Bible and see men as priests or taking the spiritual lead, we assume that only the men can or should lead out in family worship. However, in my family I first saw God and the characteristics of God through my mother.

Growing up, my dad worked a job that caused him to be overseas often. This forced my mother to take on many more roles than, perhaps, she would have liked. This included leading out in worship as the spiritual leader of the home. I remember her calling my brothers and me for worship, even when we didn't want to come, and calling us to pray, even when we didn't see the need. I can recall hearing my mother praying diligently for us, even when we weren't praying for ourselves.

My mother is English by nationality but Caribbean by heritage. Often times when one would speak to her, she would respond with Scripture. Unbeknownst to my mom, many times the Holy Spirit would speak to me through her, to give me exactly what I needed at that particular time in life.

I remember one specific time, when I was probably at my lowest spiritual state. I was preaching on my college campus almost every week, but I felt far from God. My mother "happened" to call me one day and started to share her testimony of how God had recently blessed her.

She then "randomly" started sharing words of encouragement. She reminded me that God is big enough to handle our mistakes and redeem us so that not only do we think we may be wanted by Him, but that we are actually wanted and loved by God. Only the Holy Spirit knew what I needed to hear at that exact moment, and He used my mother to speak to me.

On this Mother's Day, let us take the time to reflect on our mothers or mother figures, whom the Holy Spirit has used to speak to us or pray for us when we could not, or would not, pray for ourselves. ▮▮

— JESSE SAMUEL

MAY 9

THE HOLY SPIRIT IS NO RESPECTER OF PERSONS

"And he saith unto them,'Follow me, and I will make you fishers of men.' And they straightway left their nets, and followed him" (Matthew 4:19-20 KJV).

Jesus made a simple call to two sets of brothers (James and John, Peter and Andrew) to follow Him, and they did not hesitate to leave all and follow Him. There must have been a dynamic or charismatic presence to this simple carpenter, who probably was a stranger to the brothers, to have caused them to leave their families, to give up job security, to abandon their assets, and to follow Him. When the call was issued, Jesus did not have some earthly business or workshop in which to employ these men. Yet, they perceived that He had a higher, or spiritual mission, that they should follow.

This perception did not come through the power of their natural deduction or intellectual expertise, because these men were uneducated. They were fishermen, who understood and used the language of the street. Instead, their perception came through the influence of the Holy Spirit on the lives of these unconverted men. This is made even clearer when Jesus asked these same men who they thought He was. Peter exclaimed that he thought Jesus was the Son of God. Jesus then exclaimed that, "flesh and blood has not revealed this" to him, but His Father in Heaven (Matthew 16:17 NKJV).

This interaction lets us know that the Holy Spirit is available to all of us, despite our station in life. He is no respecter of persons. No matter who we are, He has the power to sharpen our intellect, to enhance our perception, to clean up our thoughts, and to direct and guide us on the path to righteousness.

Today, Jesus offers to us the same call He extended to the disciples, "Follow Me." And this call has similar objectives and extended promises. He will make us fishers of men and will also give us "rest" (Matthew 11:28-29). Unlike the call to the disciples to follow this itinerant preacher without a home or a track record, we have evidence of the power and capacity of this Christ to fulfill His promises to save us from eternal loss.

Jesus is waiting for you to accept His call and to let the Holy Spirit have His way in perfecting your life. Won't you let Him into your life today? ▮▮

— STAFFORD W. CARGILL

MAY 10

TREASONOUS TESTIMONY

"No wonder our hearts have melted in fear! No one has the courage to fight after hearing such things. For the Lord your God is the supreme God of the heavens above and the earth below" (Joshua 2:11 NLT).

Most military leaders would probably not have used her as a strategic asset. Her reputation was not one of fidelity. Given the kind of people she associated with, she would require frequent background checks. As the story unfolds, Rahab, the harlot, could probably be tried and convicted of treason, for she colluded with the enemy.

Yet the testimony of Rahab is one of the most powerful in the Bible. Joshua, head of military operations, sent two men to spy out Jericho. As they crossed the Jordan River and moved closer, they did not sneak in unnoticed. The sentinels on duty saw them and went to report the matter to the king. When they returned, the spies were gone. The Jericho intelligence agents questioned Rahab, since it looked like they came in her direction. She admitted to having seen them, but said they went in another direction.

The truth was that they were hidden in her apartment. Once the men were gone, Rahab—who appears to have been waiting on this opportunity—began to testify.

"I know your God has given you this land," she says. "He has been with you since you left Egypt. We heard how you crossed the Red Sea on dry land. You serve a mighty God. When you come to conquer Jericho, please spare my family" (Joshua 2:8-12 paraphrased).

If one were to parallel Rahab's lifestyle practices with her testimony about the power of God to lead in the affairs of men, the two are incongruous. But it appears Rahab was aware of the God who is in the life transformation business. She wanted to break out of her immoral matrix. This was her opportunity.

When Rahab's name appears in the lineage of Jesus (Matthew 1:5) and in the Faith Hall of Fame (Hebrews 11:31), we can conclude that she had a role to play in the salvation and redemption of mankind. On the inscription under her bust in the trophy case in heaven is not Rahab the Harlot, but Rahab the Redeemed.

Only God, through the Holy Spirit, can transform lives in such a dramatic way and change the narratives of our lives. Let us pray daily that the Spirit will do what only He can; namely turn treason into a testimony. ■■

— DANNY R. CHANDLER

GETTING MY ATTENTION

"'For my thoughts are not your thoughts, neither are your ways my ways,' declares the Lord. 'As the heavens are higher than the earth, so are my ways higher than your ways and my thoughts than your thoughts'" (Isaiah 55:8-9 NIV).

For several years the Holy Spirit had been telling me I needed to get back to church. However, my life as a flight attendant was busy, so I ignored His voice. He decided to get my attention in a most unusual way.

One winter morning in New York, it had snowed so badly that the news encouraged people to stay inside unless absolutely necessary. I decided to go to my yoga class, which meant taking the subway. While waiting for the train, I noticed I was the only person on the platform except for a well-dressed man who smiled at me. Something about him seemed disarming, and I felt positive energy radiating from him. The train arrived and we both boarded. I sat down and started going through my phone.

After a few moments I heard someone say, "Hello." I looked up and realized it was this same man, sitting across from me. We started talking, and I was struck by how easy and natural the conversation felt. After some time, he asked me if I would like to go out with him. Now, I should probably note at this point, that while I don't see color—I only see people—he was a Jamaican man with long dreadlocks, and I am a Caucasian woman from the Midwest. However, there was a "spirit" about him. I found myself saying yes and giving him my number. He then shook my hand and got off the train at his stop.

We started talking over the phone and met about a week later. During our conversations, he started talking to me about church and invited me to watch his church's services online. I watched it a few times and enjoyed it. He later invited me to church, and I went with him several times. The people were so warm and friendly, and the messages spoke to me. I could feel the Holy Spirit telling me this is where I needed to be.

I have now accepted the Sabbath, and wherever I am in my travels, I seek out an Adventist church to worship with. Who would have thought that the Holy Spirit would have gotten my attention, and brought me closer to God, through a Jamaican man with long dreadlocks, and church members who loved and accepted me? ▮▮

— KATIE MCCHESNEY

MAY 12

THE DESIRE OF MY HEART

"I have asked one thing from the Lord; it is what I really seek: that I may remain in the Lord's Temple all the days of my life, to gaze on the beauty of the Lord; and to inquire in His Temple" (Psalm 27:4 ISV).

I love music. Music stirs my emotions. There are songs that encourage me, get me ready for battle with wickedness, make me happy, fill me with joy, make me feel sorrow and more. But there are two songs that will bring tears to my eyes regardless of who sings or plays them. One is my very favorite hymn, "Great is Thy faithfulness" and the other is, "Take Me to the King." The former takes me to the throne room of God, and the latter tells of what I do there.

I don't know about you, but I long for the Lord. I ache for Him. My desire to dwell in His presence overwhelms me at times, and I feel like I cannot live another day when I don't feel His presence. I know He will never leave me or forsake me, and I know His Spirit is with me. I do not doubt that He loves me, but I don't trust my love for Him. So, when I get in those moods, these two songs will bring me out every single time. Through these songs, the Holy Spirit reminds me that in my weakness, He is the strongest. I may fail Him, but He will never fail me!

Lord, who lives in my heart and comforts my mind, I love You! There has never been a time You have failed to let me know that You are always with me. Even in the times when You seem so far away, You let me know that's when You are the closest to me; I am in Your presence, Lord, even though I cannot see You face to face.

With great anticipation I look toward the eastern sky with hope and longing. I'm homesick for the New Jerusalem. I want to go Home. "Lord, all my longings are before You, and my groaning is not hidden from You" (Psalm 38:9 ISV). So Abba, I pray for all who belong to You and have the same sentiment; that even though we must occupy until You come, we will be comforted by Your Holy Spirit. My daily prayer is that you would, "Take Me To The King." ▮▮

— DORRIS GRIDER

MAY 13

I AM SANCTIFIED

"Nor thieves nor the greedy nor drunkards nor slanderers nor swindlers will inherit the kingdom of God. And that is what some of you were. But you were washed, you were sanctified, you were justified in the name of the Lord Jesus Christ and by the Spirit of our God" (1 Corinthians 6:10-11 NIV).

Paul lists some traits of humanity's sinful nature and states our condemnation. He then suggests that some of us, however, were this way but are now sanctified and justified by our Savior Jesus and the Holy Spirit—Praise His Holy Name.

I recognize that without this saving power, my sinful nature would keep me far away from God. In my sinful state, I give in to my carnal thoughts that may lead to words and action unlike Jesus. Oh, but for the grace of God reaching out to me while I was yet a sinner. Even a few minutes a day in God's Word draws me to the Savior. The Holy Spirit bids me to learn from Jesus to be more like Him.

As a young Christian in the faith, I used to walk with unwarranted confidence in my holiness. I snubbed my nose at thievery, greed, drunkenness and the other perverse tendencies of humanity. "No way I am like that," I thought. By all accounts, I had such high regard for how "good" I was, that the Lord might as well take me up like Enoch. I was sure that Paul was talking about "those" people; the ones who did not do their Sabbath School lessons and only attended church occasionally. But then the Spirit spoke to me, and when I realized just how bad I was, all I could say was, "Woe is me! Lord thank you for your grace."

I sought Jesus and prayed for His Spirit to take over the thieving, greedy, drunken sinner that I was. When I stopped seeing those things in others and saw them as I compared myself to Jesus, my only example, the condemnation was clear; I was guilty too. I was guilty of stealing hours on my cell phone or tablet, or watching TV when I could have been spending with Jesus. I was greedy for self-gratification and indulgence. I was drunk on the thrill of staying in a conversation where others were gossiping. I became convicted of my sinful character, and all I can do was call on Jesus and submit to the Holy Spirit to do in me the will of the Father.

Today, I am much more aware of my true condition and much more grateful for sanctification and justification. ■

— MAGGIE FERDINAND

MAY 14

THANK YOU, HOLY SPIRIT, FOR . . . MY NEW-FOUND DIABETES?

". . . a thorn in the flesh was given to me, . . . lest I be exalted above measure" (2 Corinthians 12:7b NKJV).

The Holy Spirit is finding a unique way to save me. But did He have to love me and save me like this?

At my quarterly checkup not too long ago, actually the date was November 14, my friend and longtime doctor declared to me that based on my latest blood test results, I now had diabetes. Ironically enough, November 14 is also known as World Diabetes Day. After allowing me some time to process my new status, my doctor then began outlining some attack strategies to me for recovering from this progressive disease which affects some 400 million adults worldwide, including me.

However, the primary attack strategy that my doctor failed to outline was one that he was not trained in medical school to address. Thus, it was left to Diabetes itself to speak up. Like a U.S. Marine Corps drill sergeant, Diabetes came nose to nose with me, barking, "Well, well, new recruit: You're mine now. Welcome to boot camp. Ah, don't tell me: You thought that all your Bible-quotin', church-goin', vegetarian-meat eatin'/vegan-eatin', 10,000-steps-a-day walkin' piety would somehow exempt you from me. Well, think again! You're no different, son; just the one out of your 10 fellow Americans, one out of your seven fellow Alabamians, and one out of your four fellow 65 and older AARPers—all with diabetes. You need to kiss your 'ole self-righteous arrogance good-bye."

As much as I hate to admit it, drill sergeant Diabetes was right. First, my age-old self-righteous "Veggie Arrogance" had to be self-acknowledged, forgiven and God-managed, even before this new-found deadly disease could be addressed. My diabetes resulted from being out of balance with God's plan of the original diet, primarily water consumption, daily heart-healthy exercise, and nightly seven to nine hours of sleep. The reality is, no matter how good we think we are, or what righteousness we practice, there is always something that the Holy Spirit uses to remind us of our true condition before God: wretched, and miserable, and poor, and blind, and naked (Revelation 3:17).

Thank you, Holy Spirit, for this diabetes wake-up call, this new "thorn in my flesh." It's helping to keep me humble, dependent, and focused. ▮▮

— TIM ALLSTON

MAY 15

SALVATION DOESN'T WORK LIKE NETFLIX

"For all who are led by the Spirit of God are sons of God. For you did not receive the spirit of slavery to fall back into fear, but you have received the Spirit of adoption as sons, by whom we cry, 'Abba! Father!'" (Romans 8:14-15 ESV).

Subscription services, like Netflix, usually claim to offer customers a short timeframe in which they can experience the full glory of the service for "free." If customers like the service and want to continue enjoying the benefits it provides after the trial period has expired, then they will be charged an ongoing fee to keep the service active. Otherwise, in the absence of regular payments the service will be cut off and the benefits will cease. In this model the customer, not the provider, is responsible for maintaining the continuance of the service.

Unfortunately, this is the way many Christians believe salvation works. While many well-meaning Christians love to emphasize the freeness of salvation, in practice they seem to believe that Jesus only gives us free access to salvation, at first. Maintaining salvation and the benefits it provides is the sole responsibility of the Christian. When our trial period expires shortly after baptism, we had better keep up with our obedience payments or the Provider will strike our names off His customer list and boot us off the service for good.

This view of salvation creates a crippling fear that, sooner rather than later, some calamity from without or corruption from within will leave us morally bankrupt and unable to make the steep ongoing payments. Salvation is incredibly fragile with this view; easy to receive, yet hard to keep. But this is not at all what Scripture teaches.

Netflix and other subscription services aren't really offering anything for free. Slick marketers understand that it sounds a lot better to say, "the first 30 days are free," instead of saying, "your billing cycle will start 30 days after initial sign up." The former gives the illusion that you're getting something for nothing.

Jesus uses no such tactic. Salvation is not "free" at first and then maintained by us later. Salvation is free from start to finish. Jesus will maintain our salvation from the beginning, middle, and end of either our lives or history (Philippians 1:6).

Obedience, then, is not the means of maintenance, but the sign that we are allowing ourselves to be maintained by Jesus. The Spirit longs to free us from the fear of messing up this thing called salvation. He longs to help us see that we are God's children, made totally victorious in a Jesus who the songwriter says, "paid it all." ■

— BENSHEH MORGAN

MAY 16

ROSES DON'T NEED MY HELP TO BLOOM

"Therefore be patient, brethren, until the coming of the Lord. See how the farmer waits for the precious fruit of the earth, waiting patiently for it until it receives the early and latter rain. You also be patient. Establish your hearts, for the coming of the Lord is at hand" (James 5:7-8 NKJV).

I admit I am a control freak. I like everything to happen when I want it to happen. I often joke that everything would work perfectly if everyone would just do what I tell them to do because I am a doer. Even though I am laughing when I say it, I am not really joking.

In April, the roses in my front yard started budding. I am by no means a gardener, but I love my roses because they remind me of the roses my mom and my grandmother both had when I was a child. Their roses were beautiful, and they would decorate both homes with fresh, red roses. I wanted to do the same thing.

As my roses started budding, I noticed they stayed buds for several weeks. I was ready for my roses to bloom immediately! As I drove around my neighborhood, other people's roses were blooming, but mine were not. I would excitedly walk outside every morning expecting to see beautiful, red roses. Each morning, I was disappointed.

One morning I decided if they had not bloomed by the next morning, I was going to help them out a bit. I was going to pull the green part off to help them bloom a little faster. I figured if I did that, they would be in bloom by the time I returned from work that afternoon. The next morning they were still buds. As I reached out to touch the bud, God spoke to me. He said, "Leave them alone." I quickly snatched my hand back! God was telling me to be patient.

In my microwave mind, I wanted quick results. I wanted my roses to bloom because my neighbors had roses. What I didn't realize was that my roses belonged to God, and they would bloom when He was ready, not when I wanted them to bloom. Just like my own life, I have to learn not to rush things. We bloom when the Holy Spirit is ready for us to bloom.

Three days later, my beautiful, red roses bloomed without my assistance. ■

— DEIDRE SWOOPE

MAY 17

NOTHING!!

"For I am convinced that neither death nor life, neither angels nor demons, neither the present nor the future, nor any powers, neither height nor depth, nor anything else in all creation, will be able to separate us from the love of God that is in Christ Jesus our Lord" (Romans 8:38-39, NIV).

As part of my morning fitness routine, I walk to Planet Fitness to complete approximately 90 minutes of a workout, and then I walk back home. One day while walking back from the gym, I walked past a house that usually has a dog inside the fence. Whenever I walk past the house, this dog, when it sees me, will bark and bark, and bark some more until it cannot see me anymore.

But on this morning there was no fence holding back the dog. The dog barked, and it appeared as if the dog noticed that there wasn't a fence. When the dog saw this, it ran after me because I had already taken off running. I ran as fast as I could, but unfortunately that didn't help. I got tired. Remember, I was returning home from the gym!

When I stopped, I turned to receive my fate from the dog. I figured I'd take it like a man! The dog ran up on me, opened its mouth, and licked me! His tail was wagging excitedly as he licked my legs, happy to have caught me so he could show me some love.

The Holy Spirit spoke to me and said these words, "Monte, just as you ran because you feared the dog, many of my children are also like you were this morning—running from my love! Many of my children are running from me, scared. They are scared that I'm trying to control them. They are scared because they believe I'm asking too much of them. They are scared because they want to live their best life but not have me included! And just as that dog chased you to show you love, so will I chase you; not to scare you, but I want you to receive my love!"

So I ask you, why don't you stop running scared and let Jesus show you His love? There is no distance, no obstacles, no fear, no length that the Holy Spirit will not go for you to be able to receive His love! Nothing will stop His love for you and me. Don't run from it, receive it! ▮▮

— MONTE NEWBILL, SR.

MAY 18

NO CONDEMNATION

"There is therefore now no condemnation to them which are in Christ Jesus, who walk not after the flesh, but after the Spirit" (Romans 8:1 KJV).

Parenting is a huge responsibility. When children are small, as parents we are responsible for training, nurturing, modeling, and preparing them to love God and be productive members of society. But when something goes wrong and children rebel, the doubts about our parenting choices start to consume us.

We wonder what more we could have done or why our children chose the path they took. The reality is, at some point, in spite of all our prayers, intentions, and teachings, children grow up and make decisions for themselves. All we can do is continue to pray for them and ask the Holy Spirit to do His work in their lives so that they can come to themselves, like the prodigal son.

In the meantime, what do we do with the guilt we may be feeling if we think we have not done all that we could have as parents? This is where the Holy Spirit comes in. He invites us to release our guilt and release the pain. Guilt is meant to alert us to the fact that we have strayed from God in some way, but the remedy is not to run from Him, but run to Him. The Holy Spirit points out where we are, but He also points the way back to God.

In times when we feel guilty, the Holy Spirit invites us to surrender all to God, knowing that He knows all, and allow Him to make us whole. Like anything of value, it takes effort on our part; but our part is easier when we accept that ultimately we are only responsible for ourselves. The hard part has already been taken care of by Jesus. He died to take away our sins and free us from condemnation.

If we look at the story of the prodigal son, we do not read of the father spending time lamenting about where he went wrong or what he could have done differently. We read of him looking for his son and waiting for his son to come home. What is done is done, but there is no limit to what God can do. The same way the father did not condemn his son for his actions is the same way that God will not condemn us for our actions, if we ask for forgiveness. God stands ready to receive repentant children and remorseful parents. ▮▮

— DORRIS GRIDER

MAY 19

WE HAVE NOT ARRIVED

"Therefore, as the Holy Spirit says: today, if you will hear His voice, do not harden your hearts as in the rebellion, in the day of trial in the wilderness," (Hebrews 3:7-8).

In today's text, Paul doesn't give a gentle suggestion or mild recommendation when it comes to the condition of our hearts. He says, "Today if you hear the voice of the Holy Spirit, do not harden your hearts."

Our hearts become hardened when we get accustomed to routine. Our hearts become hardened when we are consumed with work, secular or church. Our hearts become hardened when we're easily influenced by secular world views. Our hearts become hardened when we spend too much time focused on other people. Our hearts become hardened when we have no personal time with the Lord because we're busy doing other things.

With so much attention focused outward, it's easy to neglect our spirituality and have confidence in our baptism and church membership, as if that is enough. But we have not arrived.

Part of the challenge of being committed Christians, means accepting the fact that the Spirit still has much to say to us, personally. Even after baptism, even after being voted into a leadership position, there are still blind spots in our lives that Jesus needs us to see. That means the Gentiles aren't the only ones in need of the gospel; we need it as well. But we keep ourselves hardened when we think that because we are in "the house," that we have arrived.

Even Paul recognized that neither his Damascus Road experience, or his busy schedule as an itinerant preacher, meant that he had arrived. In Philippians 3:14, Paul declares there's still something he hasn't attained. I dare say, neither have we. With all of the good doctrines and sound theology we possess, we still have not arrived. There is still character development and heart surgery that must be done in all of us.

Therefore, like Paul, I encourage you not to harden your heart. Don't believe there's nothing left for you to change. Ignore the lie that says you've learned all there is to know. Quiet the voice that says, "at least you're not where you used to be." Silence the voices that seek to keep you just where you are.

Instead, honor the voice and conviction of the Holy Spirit whom you've entrusted to prepare you for the kingdom. ▮▮

— TINA CARRIGER

MAY 20

DON'T BE DISTRACTED!

"Let your eyes look forward; fix your gaze straight ahead. Carefully consider the path for your feet, and all your ways will be established. Don't turn to the right or to the left; keep your feet away from evil" (Proverbs 4:25-27 HCSB).

One morning while walking to the gym, I was thinking about the upcoming test and homework assignments that lay before me. I was also thinking about my wife, who was deployed at the time, and my younger two sons, who were in New York with their grandparents for the fall semester. I was also thinking about my inability to find a job and earn some extra money to provide for my family.

Needless to say, all of these things consumed my mind to the point where I was not paying attention, and I almost stepped on a snake. Being deathly afraid of these creatures and the damage they can cause, I jumped back, ran away quickly, and continued to the gym.

A couple of days later, as I again walked to the gym, I was more prepared. I wasn't as consumed in thought as I was a few days earlier. This time, I was on the alert to not come across any more snakes, and it's a good thing I did. I discovered that there was, once again, a snake in my pathway.

I was about to take off running again until I noticed something strange. This snake was the same snake as before, lying in the same position, dead! What's more, this same snake that I was afraid of a few days ago was dead before I first encountered it. Something had already delivered me from this snake. I was afraid of something that could not harm me or trouble me. But why did it scare me? Because I was too distracted by other things.

So I encourage you not to be so distracted by people, places, or things in your life, that you miss your deliverance. You have been delivered from something that seems to be still present along your Christian walk. But Jesus has already been there and has crushed that serpent's head. The serpent's dead body is a reminder that Jesus is greater than anything you can and will encounter.

So, child of God, if you walk with God, and if you seek to be led by the Holy Spirit, then walk with a purpose, and don't be afraid! The devil is a defeated foe, and Jesus has the victory! ■

— MONTE NEWBILL, SR.

MAY 21

FOLLOWING THE SPIRIT WHEN HE SPEAKS THROUGH OTHERS

"For it will not be you speaking, but the Spirit of your Father speaking through you" (Matthew 10:20 NIV).

I recall I was at a stage in my life when I was ready to get married. However, based on my track record with relationships, I wanted to be sure that the Lord would lead me to the right person.

While serving as a youth pastor for a church, I invited my brother to speak for a Youth Week of Prayer. The services took place every night except for Thursday. Since there was no meeting, a friend of mine invited me to her parents' house for dinner. This young lady was someone with whom I had developed a close, platonic friendship.

During dinner, my brother, who has great discernment, talked with my friend and her parents. When my brother and I got home, he said to me, "Paul, she comes from good stock. That which thou doest, do quickly." I was shocked at his statement because we were only platonic friends. However, from that point I started to think about my friend in a new light.

A few weeks later, the church's youth choir was on a trip to Michigan, and as youth pastor, I accompanied them. I decided to take some time to visit a mentor who lived in the area, and invited my friend to come with me. During dinner my mentor spoke with us, and gently "interviewed" my friend. At the end of dinner, my mentor closed with the statement, "Paul, you have my approval. That which thou doest, do quickly." Again, I was shocked at his choice of words.

Subsequently, my friend and I began courting with the view of exploring marriage. During our courtship, my friend mentioned to her landlady that she and I were dating. My friend told me one evening that out of the blue her landlady said to her, "That which thou doest, do quickly." Three unrelated people, three different occasions, one common response.

That was the confirmation we needed. We were engaged in April and married in September. As I write this, we will celebrate our 20th wedding anniversary.

Sometimes, when we ask for the Holy Spirit to speak in our lives and guide us, He uses others—ordinary people—to communicate with us. ■

— PAUL GOODRIDGE

MAY 22

FOLLOWING THE SPIRIT WHEN HE DOES NOT MAKE SENSE

"'For my thoughts are not your thoughts, neither are your ways my ways,' saith the Lord. 'For as the heavens are higher than the earth, so are my ways higher than your ways, and my thoughts than your thoughts'"
(Isaiah 55:8-9 KJV).

Have you ever been impressed by the Holy Spirit to do something that contradicts everything that you thought would be the case, according to your own plan? How willing are you to listen to the Holy Spirit despite how you feel?

I was faced with this situation not too long ago when my wife came to me after her prayer time and shared that she was impressed by the Spirit to send our daughter to boarding high school, nearly 1,000 miles away from home. Having attended a boarding school myself, I was not opposed to the idea of boarding school in general. But I was unprepared for the reality that we were discussing my 14-year-old daughter leaving home in a little more than a week.

While I was shocked and apprehensive, I have learned not to doubt my wife when she has been led by the Spirit. So that evening, we spent time in prayer, we sought wise counsel from people, we consulted with our family, and finally we asked our daughter if she was willing to go. Our prayers indicated that this was the direction we should go, wise counsel confirmed that this would be a good opportunity, our family affirmed that we were making a good choice, and finally our daughter said that she would be willing to give it a try.

For the next few days we feverishly filled out applications, bought dorm room supplies, and watched as our daughter said goodbye to her friends. The next Sunday we were moving our daughter into her dorm room and meeting her roommate. As we went to our hotel room that evening, I was still wondering if we made the right choice in listening to the Holy Spirit. I received the answer the next day when, after her first day of school, we took our daughter to the store to purchase her school uniform. The first words she said to my wife and me, after getting into the car were, "Mom, Dad, thank you for sending me here. I love it." That sealed it for me and confirmed once again that God's ways are not our ways.

Don't be afraid to listen to the Spirit and follow what He says, even if it doesn't make sense, or goes against your own plans and ideas. ■

—PAUL GOODRIDGE

MAY 23

FOLLOWING THE SPIRIT WHEN IT'S INCONVENIENT

"'For I know the plans I have for you,' declares the Lord, 'plans to prosper you and not to harm you, plans to give you hope and a future'" (Jeremiah 29:11 NIV).

Yesterday, I spoke about following the Holy Spirit when it seems to contradict your own plans. Today, I want to talk about following the Holy Spirit, even when it's inconvenient.

I mentioned that my daughter attends a boarding school nearly 1,000 miles away from home. It is a great sacrifice in time and expense traveling to and from school. However, when my daughter called to share that she was scared because she was experiencing a medical challenge, I became concerned. While I have full trust in the school staff, their reassurance that they would keep an eye on her and make sure everything was okay still left me anxious. Something within me, the Holy Spirit, was telling me that I needed to drop everything and go and be with her.

The timing could not have been worse. I was not prepared to incur the financial expense of such a trip at that time; the staff assured me they would take care of her; she was scheduled to come home in a few weeks anyway; and to make matters worse, I was scheduled to be the guest speaker at a church that same weekend. This was just not a good time to listen to the Spirit. However, all those reasons were outweighed by the overwhelming impression that my wife and I needed to see her, hug her, and let her know that we were there for her.

So, we ended up hopping in the car and driving the 14 hours to see our daughter. It turned out, unbeknownst to me but not to the Spirit, that the time we spent together was one of the best we had spent in a long time. We were able to assess her medical condition for ourselves, and subsequently get her the help she needed. All this would not have occurred if I did not listen to the Holy Spirit prompting me to go, in spite of all the reasons that I could have given as to why I needed to stay.

Listening to the voice of the Spirit can not only be uncomfortable, but it can also be inconvenient. Yet, I was reminded that a perceived inconvenience on my part can easily become a blessing on God's part. He is not trying to hurt or harm us, but He wants to bless and prosper us. ▮▮

— PAUL GOODRIDGE

MAY 24

FOLLOWING THE SPIRIT WHEN IT SEEMS INAPPROPRIATE

"'Do not be afraid of their faces, for I am with you to deliver you," says the Lord.' Then the Lord put forth His hand and touched my mouth, and the Lord said to me: 'Behold, I have put My words in your mouth'" (Jeremiah 1:8-9 NKJV).

Preaching is not easy. Anyone who has spent time preparing a sermon knows that it is not uncommon to spend at least 20 hours a week or more in prayer and study. This may not seem like a difficult task, but when one has to preach week after week, it can be daunting. One wants to make sure that one's message is what the people need to hear.

I remember one occasion when I was asked to be the guest speaker for a very auspicious occasion. The expectations were high, and the pressure was on. Typically for such an event, I would spend hours praying, reading, researching, and writing a well-crafted, meaningful word, making sure that the word rightly fit the occasion. However, in this instance, the Holy Spirit had something else in mind.

Instead of having me spend hours deliberating over what I was going to say, the Holy Spirit gave me the sermon in its entirety in one fell swoop. It's like He handed me the manuscript and said, "This is what I want you to say." I was stunned; not only because this was the first time that He had "downloaded" a message at one time in its entirety without my input, but also because the message was the last thing that I would have preached for the occasion. Imagine talking about death and estate planning at a wedding! Inappropriate! Nevertheless, it was clear that this is what the Spirit wanted me to preach.

I questioned if it was really the Holy Spirit who had given me this message. I sympathized with the prophets of old when they had to preach a stern message to people who wanted to hear peace and prosperity. Nevertheless, I obeyed the Holy Spirit and spoke the message He gave me to speak. To my surprise, not only was it received well, but individuals expressed gratitude that I spoke to the issue.

Once again, I was reminded that I must follow the Holy Spirit, even when it seems inappropriate to do so. He knows what He is doing, and my job is to follow where He is already leading. ■

— PAUL GOODRIDGE

MAY 25

I CAN SEE HIM LEADING

"Then Jesus was led by the Spirit into the wilderness to be tempted by the devil" (Matthew 4:1 NIV).

Have you ever had one of those days? One of those rough days when it appears everything is going exactly the way you didn't want it to go? In those moments where is God, or even more specifically, where is the Holy Spirit?

Now I've read that the Holy Spirit is there to guide us into all truth. The Holy Spirit convicts us when we are headed in the wrong direction. The Holy Spirit reveals God's will, and even interprets our prayers because we don't really know what to say or ask for. Indeed, the Holy Spirit also gives us wisdom if we ask for it without reservation.

When I was reading the story of Jesus being tempted by the devil in the wilderness, Matthew 4:1 jumped out at me: "Then Jesus was led by the Spirit into the wilderness to be tempted by the devil." I thought to myself, "This is crazy. The Holy Spirit led Jesus into the wilderness to be tempted by the devil?"

Now I realize that there are more than enough times when I'm tempted of my own volition, but the Holy Spirit led Jesus to be tempted. That just sounded impossible at first, but then I realized that God would only cause something like this if He knew Jesus was ready to face the temptation and be successful. God had faith in Jesus, so He sent the Holy Spirit to lead Him to a place where the devil could have direct access.

The one thing we must realize is that God is always on our side. He weighs everything that happens to us before it happens. So when the unexpected and undesirable happens, God has already weighed it and has sent the Holy Spirit to not just lead us to it, but to lead us through it. It could very well be that the Holy Spirit is leading us to and through that situation because God knows that we're ready. With Him we can face it, endure it, or He will provide a way of escape.

If you're feeling like things are just not going the way you envisioned, just remember that the Holy Spirit is leading you. And if He's leading you, then through Him you will be able to handle anything that comes your way. ■■

— JASON C. NORTH

MAY 26

LESSONS FROM A WILLOW TREE

"For I will pour water on the thirsty land, and streams on the dry ground; I will pour my Spirit upon your offspring, and my blessing on your descendants. They shall spring up among the grass like willows by flowing streams. This one will say, 'I am the Lord's,' another will call on the name of Jacob, and another will write on his hand, 'The Lord's,' and name himself by the name of Israel" (Isaiah 44:3-4 ESV).

In my opinion, one of the most recognizable trees in North America is the Salix Babylonica, better known as the Weeping Willow. It generally has a short, winding truck, with branches that extend far and wide. But its most distinctive feature is its hanging, sad-looking leaves. My sister says that every time she sees one, it makes her feel sad. The weeping willow is a tree that looks like it's crying with tears overflowing. Needless to say, its appearance doesn't inspire. The name itself is evidence that someone, other than my sister, felt the same way when looking at a weeping willow.

Thus, I find it interesting that in Isaiah 44, God says that when He blesses His people, they will grow like willows by the flowing steams. What does that suggest? Reading a little about the willow, I learned some interesting facts. First, the willow is the fastest growing tree, averaging 8 to 10 feet annually. A matured willow tree is a great indicator that there's an abundance of water available nearby. Weeping willows grow best when exposed to a minimum of four hours of direct, unfiltered sunlight each day. Lastly, its bark has healing properties, such as aspirin, that deer use to relieve themselves from itches.

The spiritual applications of these facts are clear. When we surrender to God and allow His Spirit to live in us, we become like willow trees. A relationship with God causes immediate, sustained growth. When God's Spirit dwells within our lives, there is an implicit indication to others that we are planted where there's an abundance of Living Water. We grow best when we have direct, unfiltered, access to the Son each day. Lastly, when God dwells with us, we speak healing words into the spiritual lives of others.

So maybe now when we look at a willow tree, instead of feeling depressed or sad, we'll be reminded of what God intends for us. ■■

— RICHARD GONEL

MAY 27

FOCUS ON WHAT IS BEFORE YOU

"For I know the plans I have for you, declares the Lord, plans for welfare [or peace] and not for evil, to give you a future and a hope" (Jeremiah 29:11 ESV).

A husband and wife were driving on the highway and were stuck behind a reckless driver. The husband, who was driving, began to fuss and became very angry. This reckless driver in front was attempting to delay the couple from their destination with his lousy driving of shifting from lane to lane without his turn signal, and texting while driving. The couple was on a path to a destination that would bring joy, happiness, and excitement to their life and marriage. Pretty soon, the reckless driver got caught behind a semi-truck, which allowed the couple to make it around and pass this reckless driver. With this movement, they were about to drive safely and freely on the highway once more.

However, once past the reckless driver the husband looked in the rearview mirror and became upset, and began to fuss again. He started to complain about the person's driving, and he began to rethink about the experience to the point that it ruined the mood of the journey.

The driver's wife asked her husband, "Why are you upset?" The husband responded, "Because that same reckless driver from earlier is now doing foolishness behind us!"

The wife replied, "Why are you allowing something that was happening behind you to upset you now?"

Isn't this how we are? Has not God, through the Holy Spirit, brought us through something, and instead of celebrating what He has done and focusing on what's before us, we look at our past and allow those things to distract us? Instead, let us stay focused on the destination ahead of us.

There will be reckless drivers, construction sites, and possible traffic jams in our way. But all these temporary delays are not the focus of the journey. The focus is the One who is journeying with us, and the destination to where we are going. Our destination is heaven. The devil cannot stop us from receiving the blessing that God has for us, but he can cause enough issues and distractions along the way so that we miss out on enjoying the blessings God has for us.

Let God handle the pains, issues, and frustrations of our past and enjoy the journey. ▮▮

— MONTE NEWBILL, SR.

MAY 28

THE SOURCE OF POWER

"And I, brethren, when I came to you, came not with excellency of speech or of wisdom, declaring unto you the testimony of God. For I determined not to know anything among you, save Jesus Christ, and him crucified. And I was with you in weakness, and in fear, and in much trembling. And my speech and my preaching was not with enticing words of man's wisdom, but in demonstration of the Spirit and of power: That your faith should not stand in the wisdom of men, but in the power of God" (1 Corinthians 2:1-5 KJV).

There is a power that is available to each of us that is not inherent to us. God's power is available to us, not because of our own abilities, but because of His Holy Spirit who lives in us.

There is a huge difference between the power that comes as a result of our own strength, skills, and abilities and the power that comes as a result of the presence and work of the Holy Spirit. Whatever good we do or whatever success we achieve in working on behalf of God is not as a result of our eloquence or education, but our embracing of the Holy Spirit's power in us and through us. Too often we try work under the strength of our own capabilities only to find that they come up short. Instead, we are invited to allow the Spirit of God to move and work in us so that we can live differently, and so that He can make the necessary changes in our lives.

However, this invitation to allow the Holy Spirit to do His work in our lives should be accepted daily. It should be a daily practice to surrender our will, our strength, and our lives to Christ so that the Spirit can work for us, in us, and through us. What the Holy Spirit does for us and what God accomplishes in us is only good for that day. We need a fresh outpouring of the Spirit so that He can do a new thing for us each day. Just like the Israelites in the wilderness had to have a fresh outpouring of manna each day to survive, so we must also have a fresh outpouring of the Spirit to survive.

If we would remember that the power we have is not inherent in us but appropriated to us by the Spirit, then we would find ourselves more apt to depend on the Spirit and more willing to be led by Him.

Let us begin today to ask for a daily outpouring of the Holy Spirit in our lives. ■

— KEE'LAUN CRUM

MAY 29

THE PEOPLE WHO HARNESS THE WIND

"The wind blows wherever it pleases. You hear its sound, but you cannot tell where it comes from or where it is going. So it is with everyone born of the Spirit" (John 3:8 NIV).

The 2019 film titled, The Boy Who Harnessed the Wind, tells the true, and miraculous story of a 13-year-old boy by the name of William Kamkwamba. He lived in a very poor village in Kasungu, Malawi. Kamkwamba came from a family of farmers.

In 2001, his country was ravaged by drought and famine. The famine caused him to become malnourished, and also unable to afford his school fees. So he dropped out of school. Nevertheless, he had an insatiable thirst for knowledge. He was self-determined, and went on his own to the local library where he read books about science.

As he read, he found a book titled, Using Energy. On the front cover he saw a picture of windmills. He found that the book talked about how windmills power irrigation systems. This inspired him that he could use wind energy to build a new irrigation system for his village, and combat the drought and famine.

Kamkwamba went to a scrap yard and collected spare parts needed for his very first windmill. He improved his invention until it caught international attention. His experiences led him to write a book and speak internationally, including as a featured guest of a TEDGlobal conference.

When he spoke at the TEDGlobal conference, Kamkwamba impressed venture capitalists to fund his education to Dartmouth. He received his bachelor's degree in 2014. Since then, he has built two other wind turbines and a solar-powered water pump that supplies drinking water to his village. Kamkwamba's story is an inspiring and miraculous one that reminds us of a very deep lesson found in Scripture.

Jesus told Nicodemus that, "The wind blows wherever it pleases. You hear its sound, but you cannot tell where it comes from or where it is going. So it is with everyone born of the Spirit" (John 3:8 NIV). Without the movement of the Holy Spirit in our lives, our hearts will be characterized by drought and famine; lifeless, barren and destitute. However, the Spirit of God is always moving. We just need God's grace to build us up and position us just right so that we can harness the power of the wind.

There is no power in us. The power is all in the wind. God's Spirit wants to empower the broken, spare parts of our lives to produce fruit for the glory of God. May the Holy Spirit never stop blowing life into lives. ▮▮

— CHRISTOPHER C. THOMPSON

MAY 30

THE SPIRIT KNOWS

"Likewise the Spirit also helps in our weaknesses. For we do not know what we should pray for as we ought, but the Spirit Himself makes intercession for us with groanings which cannot be uttered" (Romans 8:26 NKJV).

Memorial Day for me is a time to reflect upon the goodness of the Holy Spirit in knowing what we need in our time of need. I have never served in the military, but two of my brothers and my nephew, Stephen, have.

Several years ago I traveled to England with my husband for his father's funeral. We decided to also take some time to visit Stephen, who was stationed in England with the Air Force. Stephen and I spoke at length on the phone making plans for our time together on the base the following day. Stephen was an airplane mechanic, and as we closed the conversation, I jokingly asked if I could take a picture sitting in the cockpit of one of the jets.

"I'll see what I can do Aunty Ellen," he jokingly responded, and we both laughed. I said, "I love you," and he said, "I love you too! See you tomorrow."

The next day, my husband, his best friend and I arrived at the base and were told to wait to be escorted in. I was so excited about the next few hours with Stephen. However, my excitement slowly turned to confusion. We were escorted to a room where an officer and the chaplain for the base met us. I did not understand why Stephen was not there, and why he was taking so long to meet us. Finally, I heard what the officer and chaplain were trying to explain: there was an accident and Stephen had died. I was filled with complete shock, disbelief, and sadness all at the same time.

I thank the Holy Spirit for keeping me together in the midst of that horrible experience. He knew what I was walking into and filled me with His peace, even while feeling such pain. He gave me the opportunity to connect with my nephew before he died, and I was able to hear first-hand and see how he lived, and the positive impact he had on those around him. The Spirit was actively working quietly behind the scenes, preparing me for what I would face and giving us the strength to face it.

I look forward to seeing Stephen again when our Lord returns, where Stephen and other servicemen and women will be united with their loved ones. ▮▮

— ELLENGOLD GOODRIDGE

MAY 31

THE SPIRIT GIVES PEACE

"Do not be anxious about anything, but in every situation, by prayer and petition, with thanksgiving, present your requests to God. And the peace of God, which transcends all understanding, will guard your hearts and your minds in Christ Jesus" (Philippians 4:6-7 NIV).

Anybody who knows me knows that I love playing volleyball. Any opportunity I get to play—indoors, outdoors, or on a beach—I am there. It has to be something very significant to prevent me from playing the sport I love.

Over a period of a few weeks, when I was experiencing fatigue, a loss of appetite, and excruciating pain in my abdomen, I was forced to step away from the court and into a clinic. Once there, I was evaluated, given antibiotics, and sent home. The antibiotics did not help, and after several visits back to the clinic and emergency room, I was finally told there was a lump in my kidneys. I was told that they had to perform a biopsy to see if it was benign or malignant

When the results came back, on January 16, 2019, I was told I had lymphoma. The news was devastating. I thought, "This is it. I'm going to die." The doctor tried to reassure me, saying that it was very treatable and that I only needed to do chemotherapy for six months, or chemotherapy and radiation. However, I still felt scared and fearful of the unknown.

Later when I got home, I told myself that I was going to fully trust God to get me though this. "God brought me to it," I said, "and He will bring me through it. I am not going to be negative about it." It was at that moment that God gave me peace and calmness in my spirit.

I started treatment in January 2019. During my course of treatments, I had no major side effects except for losing my hair. With every treatment, I felt at total peace and ease with God. I was originally scheduled for six months of treatment, but after five months the doctors found that I was in full remission. Over the following months, I used volleyball as my rehab to regain my strength.

Now I am stronger than ever, and thanking God for every day of life. I am also grateful to the Holy Spirit for the peace that He gave in the midst of my storm. ∎

— MITCH MARTIN

JUNE

BIBLICAL HEROES OF PUBLIC AFFAIRS AND SOCIAL JUSTICE

Should Christians weigh in on issues of injustice and inequality, or should we should leave all of those issues to civic leaders and politicians? What does it mean to be engaged or responsive to public affairs or social justice issues in our neighborhoods, our communities, our nation, and in society in general?

This month, some we will be reminded and some will discover that throughout Biblical history God was very concerned about injustice. God sometimes intentionally brought up leaders to deal, not only with the spiritual sins of the society, but with moral and ethical sins of the society. The call to be voices for freedom, justice, righteousness, fairness, and equality rang out during the Old Testament and New Testament.

You will have a chance to read about biblical heroes of public affairs and social justice. You will be able to learn what these heroes did to make an impact in their society, and how they accomplished these tasks with the Lord clearly on their side. ▮▮

— CRYSTON JOSIAH
Director of Public Affairs and Religious Liberty,
Central States Conference of Seventh-day Adventists

JUNE 1

WHERE ARE THE SHAMMAHS?

"And after him was Shammah the son of Agee the Hararite. The Philistines had gathered together into a troop where there was a piece of ground full of lentils. So the people fled from the Philistines. But he stationed himself in the middle of the field, defended it, and killed the Philistines. So the Lord brought about a great victory" (2 Samuel 23:11-12 NKJV).

Shammah was one of King David's fearless bodyguards. His story helps us to see that there is a time to take a stand and a time to fight, even when others are running away.

The Philistines came against Israel for only two reasons: 1) To inflict casualties; and 2) to destroy the crops, which was the very thing Israel had worked so hard for and hoped to enjoy. The Philistines knew that if they could wound their enemies and bring them to a place of hunger, they would be easily defeated and enslaved.

The same is true concerning our enemy, the devil. He attacks us so that he might weaken us, making it easier to enslave us to his will. His intent is to not only rob us of our family, health and happiness, but also of our life's vision, desire, purpose, voice, destiny, and our calling in Christ.

Observing the cowardly plans of the enemy and seeing the people that were working the fields running away, Shammah was willing to stand his ground and defend the lentil patch. Though it appears to be strange, Shammah had courage to fight because he knew that without food, an entire community would perish.

Shammah stood in the middle of the field, defended it, slew the enemies of God's people, and experienced a time of conquest! Just as God gave Shammah the victory over his enemies, God will give us the victory over every physical and spiritual battle we will face in this life.

Where are the Shammahs who will stand up and fight, not only for the things of God, but also for that which is right and important? Where are the Shammahs who are not just going to talk about the poverty, the racial profiling, the high crime rate, and the failing education system in some of our neighborhoods, but are going to do something about it? Where are the Shammahs who are courageous enough to stand up and speak out against bullying, harassment, violence and victimization? Where are the Shammahs who are going to stand until we, as a country, overcome the darkness of despair? Where are the Shammahs who will continue to stand until we cross the finish line of justice and equality?

I challenge you to be like Shammah today. ■

— CLAVAL HUNTER

JUNE 2

REPROOF WITH HOPE

"The Lord sent Nathan to David" (2 Samuel 12:1 NKJV).

With every key stroke and quarry, individuals are defining themselves to Google, Yahoo, Bing, and whoever else is taking notes. In an era of technological transparency, lives of high-profile individuals are being spectated by the masses. What was once done in secret can no longer be hidden, and the characters of once perfect strangers are articulated for all to see.

It's easy to feel shock and disbelief when Twitter headlines roar with hateful rhetoric and scandal. It is just as easy to retreat from publicly giving disciplinary criticism to high-profile individuals. The fear of chastisement and being defined as radical opposition, or even the "enemy," keeps the majority silent. However, as disciples of Christ we are to "not be ashamed of the gospel" (Romans 1:16) and "open our mouths" (Proverbs 31:9) when witnessing the sins of our generation.

As a faithful steward, after David's diabolic behavior was revealed to him, Nathan, the prophet, felt obligated to be a mouthpiece for justice to a leader in need of guidance and correction.

In confidence, and standing before the man who had killed one of his most faithful subjects to cover his sins, Nathan bore the totality of King David's shame. It was at this moment when David could not depart from the reality that his sins were ever present before the all-seeing and all-knowing God, to whom he owed his life and luxury.

As followers of Christ we are to "speak the truth in love" (Ephesians 4:15) so that the reception of our rebuke or correction draws men and women closer to a loving and repentant relationship with Christ.

After Nathan's intervention, David repented and once again sought the Lord's favor in all he would do as Israel's king. (See Psalms 101.) Albeit David's repentance may or may not be the resolve of all to whom are revealed their shame, but nevertheless, like Nathan, we are to be bearers of truth to those who have lost their way.

Prayerfully, reproof will lead others to repentance, and in turn, the same forgiveness God extended to the once reprobate ruler, David.

Scripture suggests in Matthew 25:40, that in withholding truth and correction in the sight of injustice, it is not only an act of grievance against our "brothers and sisters," but much more our Lord and Savior Jesus Christ. For it is in how we treat others in our realm of influence, that reflects whom the master of our hearts and lives truly is. ▮▮

— JONATHAN GREEN

A SHE-RO FOR JUSTICE

"For if you remain silent at this time, relief and deliverance for the Jews will arise from another place, but you and your father's family will perish. And who knows but that you have come to your royal position for such a time as this?" (Esther 4:14 NIV).

The Dilemma: Maybe it was that woman's intuition that everything isn't right? Like my mama and sugar mama awaking from their slumber to pray for my safe travel from prayer meeting. (They were unaware that I had collided with a coyote in the back roads of West Texas.)

The Investigation: As another dangerous conspiracy against the Jewish nation developed, Esther, who has been undercover in the palace, must intervene as she had before, or suffer the collateral damage of her silence. Similarly, all who sit on the sidelines today, while racist remarks and sexist suggestions fly, will face their day of reaping.

The Solution: Well, I am here to remind somebody who is in their own dilemma that God not only knows the dilemma, but He also knows the means of deliverance. It was not by accident that Esther was in the palace. The same God, who spared her life when her parents died, is the same God who moved her cousin to adopt and nurture her. The same God, who caused her to be pleasing to the king, is the same God who used her to expose the bigotry and hatred of a high official who made himself an enemy of the Lord. And the trap that he set would result in his and his family's demise!

Be of good cheer! Those who contend with us, God will contend with. God must have the last word! ■

— CHARLES RAY OSBORNE, III

JUNE 4

ABEL, "THE FIRST HERO"

"And in the process of time it came to pass that Cain brought an offering of the fruit of the ground to the Lord. Abel also brought of the firstborn of his flock and of their fat. And the Lord respected Abel and his offering, but He did not respect Cain and his offering. And Cain was very angry and his countenance fell" (Genesis 4:3-5 NKJV).

In the nascent, post-Edenic society, the fruit of sin was deteriorating the good relations of the Adamic family. There were problems between the eldest son against the youngest. That post-Edenic society was already experiencing problems of social injustice.

In her book, The Story of Redemption, Ellen White says that Cain and Abel had received "indications of how to worship their Creator" (White, 1947, p. 541). Abel had the right to worship his God in the way he wanted to—which was in the way God had directed. But his older brother, Cain, did not tolerate his faithfulness. Cain was arrogant, angry and disgusted by Abel. He discriminated against, and persecuted him for faithfully worshiping his Creator (Genesis 4:4-5).

Cain's hatred grew towards his younger brother until one day he invited him to the field and killed him there. (Genesis 4:8). That was an unfair act, the injustice of killing an innocent person. According to the New Hispanic International Version, by that act, God told Cain that "from the earth, your brother's blood demands 'justice,'" because injustice is the repression of the rights of others, and all injustice is subjected to justice and punishment. The Contemporary English Version (CEV) says that God asked Cain, "Why have you done this terrible thing? You killed your own brother, and his blood flows onto the ground. Now his blood is calling out for me to punish you" (Genesis 4:10).

That was the first murder against the freedom to worship, and it was an act of social injustice. But the righteous God of Abel, who looks at all human injustice, sought Cain and asked him "where is your brother?" Cain, with a guilty and intolerant conscience replied, "I am perhaps my brother's guardian?" Then God did him justice (Genesis 4: 9, 11-12).

Thus began the story of the first hero on earth, "Abel the first Hero." Because a hero is "a person who is admired for his bravery, great achievements and good qualities," Abel's good qualities made him the first hero in history.

The story of Abel, "the brave hero," teaches us that always doing good things brings envy and persecution from bad people. In the silence of duty, doing good things bothers others when it affects their personal interests. But there is a God who sees everything and knows everything, who administers justice. We must faithfully fulfill our duties so we can be a hero like Abel. ■■

— TOMAS DEGYVES

JUNE 5

JESUS, RADICAL WARRIOR—PART 1

"And at this point His disciples came, and they marveled that He talked with a woman; yet no one said, 'What do You seek?' or, 'Why are You talking with her?'" (John 4:27 NKJV).

Weary from a long journey, Jesus decided to take a shortcut through Samaria. He stayed by a well while his disciples went to get something to eat. Suddenly, a woman approached the well. She had come to get a drink of water in the middle of the day. This was odd because most women came to the well in the morning or evening to avoid the blazing sun. But she came at noon to fill her water jug because she knew the women in the village would not talk to her; they would talk about her. After all, she had been married five times and the man she was currently living with was not her husband. But her sordid past did not bother Jesus; He saw a soul. So, as she drew water from the well, Jesus struck up a conversation with her.

When Jesus spoke to her, she was startled. It is hard for us to grasp the unprecedented nature of Jesus' actions through the lens of today's culture. In Jesus' time and culture, men were not allowed to speak to women. The division between sexes was so strong that every day a good Jewish man would repeat the same prayer: "God, I thank you that I am not a Gentile or a woman." This tradition of separation between the sexes still has a stronghold in Jewish culture. In an Orthodox synagogue, males and females still don't sit together.

Jesus' actions were so radical that when the disciples saw Him speaking to a woman, they were shocked. They could not believe their eyes. By speaking to this woman, Jesus completely disregarded the unjust parts of His culture. He would not side with oppression or discrimination. He did not treat this woman as a second-class citizen. He spoke to her and treated her with love and grace.

What about us? Are we willing to be radical like Jesus? Are we willing to challenge the unjust elements of our culture? Are we willing to stand with the least of these, including immigrants, the poor, and women? Are we willing to look past circumstances and culture to see the hurting and lonely?

If we are to be like Jesus, the radical warrior, we must be willing to stand radically against the unjust norms of our society. We must stand with Jesus and advocate for liberty and justice for all. ■■

— TREVOR BARNES

JESUS, RADICAL WARRIOR—PART 2

"Then the woman of Samaria said to Him, 'How is it that You, being a Jew, ask a drink from me, a Samaritan woman? For Jews have no dealings with Samaritans'" (John 4:9 NKJV).

Human prejudice tends to form walls of separation between people groups. We see this from Jewish bondage in Egypt, to the ethnic fighting between the Bosnians and Croatians.

Jesus faced the racial barrier in John, Chapter 4. Here we discover that Jews and Samaritans did not deal with each other because Samaritans were a mixed race that Jews would not acknowledge. In order to keep the two people apart, a Jim Crow-like system was developed. There was a Jewish area and a Samaritan area, and it was unlawful for the two groups to interact.

This is not unlike cities across the United States. City planners strategically carved out areas for certain people groups. The results of redlining and gentrification are undeniable. It is not a coincidence that the south side of Chicago is predominantly made up of people of color. It is not by chance that there is a stark contrast, between North County and West County St. Louis. In New York City and Washington, D.C., dilapidated neighborhoods suddenly see increased funding when the population demographics change. The tradition of separation is a deeply held value within human culture.

Many "good Christians" believe that they have not given into the ways of the world because they don't eat meat, go to the club, or drink alcohol. They fail to see that when we allow ethnic and cultural separation, we are complicit in lifting the banners of evil because we put human culture above the standards of God's kingdom.

But notice Jesus; He completely disregards the culture of His day. He broke down cultural walls by speaking to a Samaritan. He did it publicly and purposefully. Jesus wanted us to understand that all people should be treated with love and respect.

Jesus rejected unjust human tradition because He embraced a higher tradition. He lived by the principles of God's Kingdom. In God's kingdom, there is no separation of race, class, or culture. We are all one in Jesus. God's design is to take us back to the radical oneness of Eden, where there is no wall of racial, national, or ethnic separation. Through the power of the new Adam, the human race has been reunited.

Today, God is looking for radical people who are willing to follow in the steps of Jesus. People who live by the standard of radical acceptance taught in the Kingdom of God. It is time to abandon the broken human tradition of separation based on the ways of the world, and to embrace the unity of the kingdom of God. ■

— TREVOR BARNES

UNLIKELY CHAMPIONS OF SOCIAL JUSTICE

"Break off your sins by practicing righteousness, and your iniquities by showing mercy to the oppressed, that there may perhaps be a lengthening of your prosperity" (Daniel 4:27 ESV).

Nebuchadnezzar, King of Babylon, might seem to be an unlikely champion of social justice. Like Abraham Lincoln who started as a selfish politician, Nebuchadnezzar began his kingship as a proud, egotistical leader.

At first, it was difficult for Nebuchadnezzar to accept that Yahweh, the God of Israel, was the true God, since Babylon conquered Yahweh's nation. But through Israel's captivity, God was trying to reach him. Yahweh did not only want to show Nebuchadnezzar that He was God of all, but that humanity was a part of His family and created in His image. God wanted Nebuchadnezzar to realize that He sets people in places of leadership to take care of humanity, especially the oppressed. God went to great lengths to reach Nebuchadnezzar. He sent him dreams and revealed Himself visibly in a fiery furnace. (See Daniel 3:8-18.)

Nebuchadnezzar's last recorded dream was of a great tree that supplied shelter and food for the animals. It was exalted until a holy watcher from heaven cut it down, leaving only the stump and its roots. Daniel revealed that Nebuchadnezzar was that tree, and if he failed to acknowledge Yahweh as the true God, and his stewardship of the oppressed, he would be humbled for seven years.

History records that Nebuchadnezzar rejected the word of God and suffered seven years of schizophrenia, acting and living like an animal "with the beasts of the field" (Daniel 4:32). After seven years, Nebuchadnezzar "blessed the Most High, and praised and honored him who lives forever" (Daniel 4:34 NKJV). The Scripture implies that Nebuchadnezzar lived the remainder of his life serving the true God. Like Lincoln, who ended his life as a proponent of social justice, Nebuchadnezzar ended his life as a champion of social justice.

As Christians, we are called to leadership. This calling directs us to care for the marginalized and despondent. Like Lincoln and Nebuchadnezzar, we sometimes selfishly overlook those who need us most. Yahweh works in the good and bad to lead us to an understanding of His Lordship, and our responsibility to the oppressed.

Today, let's take on our calling by helping someone in our circle of influence who needs our help. ▮▮

— GARY COLLINS

JUNE 8

WOMEN OF INTEGRITY

"Then the king of Egypt spoke to the Hebrew midwives, of whom the name of one was Shiphrah and the name of the other Puah; and he said, 'When you do the duties of a midwife for the Hebrew women, and see them on the birthstools, if it is a son, then you shall kill him; but if it is a daughter, then she shall live.' But the midwives feared God, and did not do as the king of Egypt commanded them, but saved the male children alive" (Exodus 1:15-17 NKJV).

In my mind's eye I can imagine how it might have gone. The staff entered the building to clock in for their daily shift; each person grabbing their timecards from the rack near the time clock and inserting them into the small opening at the top of the machine. An internal mechanism triggered the stamp to move forward, stamping the time in a green box on the card. It would be another long day; the Hebrew population was growing rapidly, creating a need for more and more overtime for the midwifery division.

This meant long days and shorter nights for Shiphrah and Puah. Surely, they were exhausted. They loved their jobs and the joy that each childbirth brought to a Hebrew home, but with every birth the king seemed to be more unhappy. The day had its own challenges, but the king decided to add one more.

"Shiphrah and Puah I need to see you in my office before you report to your first home for duty," the Kind demanded.

The two made their way out of the break room and up to his office. He sat behind his desk; a shadow seemed to be cast solely on his side of the office. He asked no questions, just gave a directive. No room for conversation, just an expectation of obedience.

"From this point on, if a Hebrew woman gives birth to a male child, I want you to kill it! That'll be it for today, close my door behind you!"

As they left the office, I imagine they considered the impact that this request from their superior would have on their families. Failure to comply could cost them their jobs, or worse, their lives. But more than their lives or their jobs, was their concern for doing the will of God. So, they disregarded the orders of the king and did what was right.

This same Spirit was in Harriet Tubman as she ushered many slaves from the bondage of the American South to the freedom of the American North. This same Spirit was in Rosa Parks as she refused to be forced to move to the back of the bus simply because of the color of her skin. This same Spirit was in Viola Liuzzo as she helped shuttle black demonstrators between Selma and Montgomery, Alabama. She was eventually shot to death by the Ku Klux Klan on March 26, 1965.

The Spirit of God propelled these women, in the face of unjust laws, to stand as women of integrity.

May this same Spirit continue to be present, today, that we may fear God more than man and seek to do right, not the wrong. May this world be a better place, and no longer a safe haven for those who choose to do wickedness. ▮▮

— KEITH HACKLE, JR.

JUNE 9

NO INNOCENT BYSTANDER

"For the slaughter and violence done to your brother Jacob, shame shall cover you, and you shall be cut off forever. On the day that you stood aside, on the day that strangers carried off his wealth, and foreigners entered his gates and cast lots for Jerusalem, you also were like one of them" (Obadiah 1:10-11, MEV).

He'd recommended a truce. That morning as Jacob tried to squelch his brother's anger by giving him an enormous gift of cattle, Esau explained that an apology was not necessary; that the two should let bygones be bygones.

However, history proves that Esau was not completely over the situation. There was still a bit of uneasiness, a portion of hostility that remained. A feeling of, "I may not get you for what you've done, but you will reap what you've sown and you will get what you deserve," must have lingered in his psyche, and it was passed down through the family tree.

So when the children of Israel found themselves being raided by bandits and taken captive by enemies, the people of Edom, decedents of Esau, watched and did nothing. They did not return evil for evil, but they did nothing to prevent evil from prevailing.

This was not the first time Edom had turned their back on Israel. In Numbers 20, as the Israelites were traveling to the Promised Land, they were denied passage through Edom: "...and they came out to confront the Israelites with a large army and a strong hand" (Numbers 20:20)

A similar story of refusing to help is told by Jesus in Luke 10. Before the action of the caring Samaritan, there were individuals, considered more noble, who denied the wounded man the assistance they could have provided. Hands up and eyes down, they scurried around the wounded, seeing the need but refusing to speak out; but not the Samaritan.

This same Jesus commands us as followers, "and just as you want men to do to you, you also do to them likewise" (Luke 6:31 NKJV). The people of the day had too often ignored the needs of others at the expense of gratifying their own cravings leaving many to suffer, if not die, in the street like dogs. ■

— KEITH HACKLE, JR.

NO INNOCENT BYSTANDER – PART 2

"For the slaughter and violence done to your brother Jacob, shame shall cover you, and you shall be cut off forever. On the day that you stood aside, on the day that strangers carried off his wealth, and foreigners entered his gates and cast lots for Jerusalem, you too were like one of them" (Obadiah 1:10-11 MEV).

In more modern times, similar events of refusals to help include, but are not limited to: A high-school wrestler being told if he doesn't cut his hair, he will have to forfeit a match; a father of two being told if he doesn't pay rent, he's going to be evicted and sued while the landlord neglects to repair the rat-infested dwelling; a sitting President of the United States fat shaming a perceived protestor who was actually a supporter; and an owner of a professional sports team using derogatory language toward his players, with no castigation.

When we stand back and watch, we are just as guilty as the offenders. When we patronize organizations and individuals that intentionally oppress others, we stand with the oppressor in solidarity. When we remain mum to the injustices of the world, we are no innocent bystanders. We are not blameless; we are culpable.

Stinging are the words of the author, Ellen White, in her book, *Testimonies for the Church, Vol. 4*: "We are just as accountable for evils that we might have checked in others, by reproof, by warning, by exercise of parental or pastoral authority, as if we were guilty of the acts ourselves" (White, p. 516).

The world needs no more people to stand by and watch, recording for "likes" on social media. The world needs people to speak out and to stand up. The world needs no innocent bystanders; the world needs people of action. Even when the issue is beyond your financial ability, your physical ability or your mental capacity, there is always something you can do. You contain the most powerful antidote for any problem; inside of you is the answer to all of the world's problems— you have the power of prayer!

It is believed that Confucius once stated, "The man who moves a mountain begins by carrying away small stones." By doing what little we can, where we can, we help the Samaritan become a tangible character in the areas where God has called us to serve. ■

— KEITH HACKLE, JR.

JUNE 11

AGAINST ALL ODDS

"And Noah did according to all that the Lord commanded him" (Genesis 7:5 NKJV).

One of the things I enjoyed doing when I was much younger was standing in the doorway, watching the rain pour down. The feel of the rain and wind blowing, and seeing the sky light up with lighting and hearing the loud thunder, was chilling, thrilling, and even relaxing.

It had never rained in the history of man before the flood. This concept of rain was new to man but not so new to God. Yet God told Noah He was going to flood the earth with rain. Genesis 7:5 teaches us that Noah moved with faith, obeying God's Word to build an ark to escape the coming dreadful flood and destruction of all life upon the earth.

Knowing that Noah was a preacher proclaiming God's truth (2 Peter 2:5) in some form to the people of his day, and given his godly character, we can undertake that Noah preached about the approaching flood and the need to repent. Furthermore, providing the world with such a warning would be in keeping with the character of God. He typically gives an opportunity for repentance prior to His judgments.

Sad to say, but hardly anyone in the world is listening or responding to God anymore. Every generation is increasingly dreadful, depraved, dishonest, and devoid of God. It is fast becoming as it was in the days of Noah.

Out of all the years Noah preached, either through the spoken word or his lifestyle, only eight people went into the ark. God, at times, asks of us to do things that are unimaginable. Noah was asked to build an Ark, something that had never been seen before, heard of before, or even done before. And yet his response is the kind that we should wisely imitate:

• Noah responded with haste. Noah didn't waste time second-guessing what he should do. He went right to work.

• Noah responded with humility. Noah's lifestyle was that of a just man, so much so that he found grace in the eyes of God.

• Noah responded with heaven's blessings. Noah and his family were saved through obedience to his God.

Although the odds were against Noah, he pressed on in obedience. "For yet a little while, and he that shall come will come, and will not tarry" (Hebrews 10:37 KJV). ▮▮

— JOHNATHAN B. FIELDS, JR.

JUNE 12

STICK 'EM UP!

"And so it was, when Moses held up his hand, that Israel prevailed; and when he let down his hand, Amalek prevailed" (Exodus 17:11 NKJV).

There are three "firsts" that are found in the Israelites' victory over the Amalekites:

- The first mention of Joshua;
- The first mention of the Amalekites; and
- The first battle that Israel fought.

The children of Israel faced many hardships as they traveled through the wilderness. They were at first pursued by the Egyptians. They were troubled time and time again by a lack of food and water. They faced difficulties of living and traveling through a hot and dry desert.

God uses hardship to teach and strengthen His people. All of the trials that Israel faced are typical of the struggles and difficulties that we, the New Testament church, must face and learn from. As

1 Corinthians 10:11 reminds us, "Now all these things happened to them as examples, and they were written for our admonition, upon whom the ends of the ages have come" (NKJV).

Amalek's attack against the children of Israel did not happen after they arrived in Rephidim. Instead, it happened as they were arriving. Amalek attacked Israel when they were totally unprepared. They were unprepared physically—they were weary and thirsty; they were unprepared spiritually—they'd just finished complaining.

Moses told Joshua to choose some men and go out to fight the Amalekites. This is the earliest notice of a young warrior destined to play a prominent part in the history of Israel. While Moses, Aaron and Hur were working part one of the plan (faith), Joshua and a few good men were working part two of the plan (works). Then, Moses stood on a hill, with the rod of Jehovah in his hand. This was the same rod used to bring the plagues upon Egypt. This rod symbolized that God was with them.

Moses held the rod high so the Israelites could fight by faith, looking to the mighty arm of Jehovah fighting for them. When the rod was lowered and out of view, the Amalekites prevailed. So, Aaron and Hur had to assist Moses. They held up his arms so the rod could remain visible. While it was visible, the Israelites prevailed.

Moses reminds us that the battle is not ours; it truly is, and belongs, to the Lord. There is a war going on and we need some folks to "stick 'em up." This isn't the time to rest my friend. It's time to stick 'em up. ■

—JOHNATHAN B. FIELDS, JR.,

JUNE 13

EXODUS: A HEART OF COMPASSION PART 1

"Now it came to pass in those days, when Moses was grown, that he went out to his brethren and looked at their burdens. And he saw an Egyptian beating a Hebrew, one of his brethren. So he looked this way and that way, and when he saw no one, he killed the Egyptian and hid him in the sand" (Exodus 2:11-12 NKJV).

It is clear and apparent that the world we are living in today has a tremendous lack of compassion; hearts have indeed become cold. Jesus Himself prophesied that because iniquity shall abound, the love of many shall wax cold (Matthew 24:12).

Little more than 50 years ago, the U.S.—which in its very Constitution declared that "all men are created equal"—had to pass the Civil Rights Act, because of the way Blacks were treated. But how many of us recognize that laws can never change the heart? Why are we surprised by the vitriol and hatred that exudes from some political leaders and television ads that we see during political campaigns? Why are so many surprised and shocked by the rhetoric of some who are in the highest offices of our land, and the millions who have cheered and voted in the same light? It is clear that laws can never change the heart. Only God can change the heart.

Violence among civilians, violence among the youth, and even violence towards civilians from those sworn to protect and serve remind us that there must be a "better day after 'while." We live in a "soon ah will be done-a with the troubles of the world, I'm going home to live with God" frame of mind. However, this phenomenon is not new in earth's history.

Back in the land of Egypt, at the time described in our passage of study, Moses lived in a world of slavery, oppression, and genocide. Even in the midst of this Egyptian world, God had a plan to raise up a man, a leader, who had a heart of compassion. What is a heart of compassion? Compassion means more than just "feeling sorry for." Anyone can feel sorry for someone. A true heart of compassion moves one to action.

"Moses had supposed that his education in the wisdom of Egypt fully qualified him to lead Israel from bondage. Was he not learned in all those things necessary for a general of armies? Had he not had the advantages of the best schools in the land? Yes, he felt that he was able to deliver his people. He set about his work by trying to gain their favor by redressing their wrongs" (*Counsels to Parents, Teachers, and Students*, Ellen G. White). Scholars believe that Moses was probably learned in all the subjects: science, anatomy and physiology, math, languages, physics, astronomy, martial arts, military strategy, and every possible line of study, so that he would eventually become one of the Pharaohs of Egypt. ▮▮

— CRYSTON JOSIAH

JUNE 14

FROM EX-CON TO EXODUS: A HEART OF COMPASSION PART 2

"Now it came to pass in those days, when Moses was grown, that he went out to his brethren an looked at their burdens. And he saw an Egyptian beating a Hebrew, one of his brethren. So he looked this way and that way, and when he saw no one, he killed the Egyptian and hid him in the sand" (Exodus 2:11-12 NKJV).

There are at least three principles that we can learn from Moses' heart of compassion. Today, we'll look at the first one:

1. Identify with the Oppressed.

Even though Moses lived in luxury, even though he had all of the amenities of the finest things in Egypt—clothes, toys, education, girlfriends—he still identified with his people who were being oppressed. You see, just because you aren't hungry or thirsty, or naked or homeless, doesn't mean that you cannot sympathize with those who are hungry or thirsty, or naked or homeless. A heart of compassion says, "just because I'm not being affected doesn't mean that I can't identify with those who are affected." The gospel group, The Winans, sang a song years ago that says, "when you cry, makes me cry, don't you know you'll never cry alone."

Moses clearly identified with the oppressed, but because he wasn't fully converted he didn't yet know how to channel that compassion. He probably didn't wake up that morning with the intent to kill anyone. But he had grown sick and tired of being sick and tired, and looking at the burdens placed on his brethren. So with his martial arts training, he makes quick work of the Egyptian.

Is it possible that Moses' princess mom taught him about compassion? Exodus 2:6 says, "And when she opened it (the basket), she saw the child, and behold the baby wept. So she had compassion on him, and said, "This is one of the Hebrews' children" (NKJV).

As you pause to read Exodus 2:14-15, Moses has now become an ex-convict and fugitive from the law. It is clear that our decisions have consequences. Adam couldn't resist his fine wife, Eve. Abraham couldn't resist his handmaiden, Hagar. Jacob couldn't stop lying to his daddy and brother. David couldn't look away from another man's wife taking a shower. Many others can't control alcohol and drugs, sex and lust. They end up way outside the will of God, thus losing jobs, money, fame, and even sadly risk losing their souls. Moses is an ex-con on the run from the EBI—Egyptian Bureau of Investigation. This good man with a heart of compassion is now wanted for manslaughter. ■

— CRYSTON JOSIAH

JUNE 15

FROM EX-CON TO EXODUS: A HEART OF COMPASSION PART 3

"And Moses was learned in all the wisdom of the Egyptians, and was mighty in word and deeds. Now when he was 40 years old, it came into his heart to visit his brethren, the children of Israel. And seeing one of them suffer wrong, he defended and avenged him who was oppressed, and struck down the Egyptian" (Acts 7:22-24 NKJV).

Moses fled Egypt to save his life. He ended up in the Midian desert where he encountered another event of oppression that tapped into his heart of compassion. This event illuminates the second principle we can learn:

2. Inaction is not an Option

In Exodus 2:16-17, Moses defended seven women who were mistreated by the shepherds at a well; he not only defends them, but drew their water and watered their flock.

When you have a heart of compassion, inaction is never an option. Do you ever wonder how someone can know that someone else is in need, have the capacity to help, and still not help? Do you ever wonder how someone can see a crime, recognize the perpetrator and say nothing to the authorities because they don't want to be a "snitch"? That is a heart that lacks compassion.

As the story continues in Exodus 2:18-21, the girls returned home to their father, Reuel, earlier than planned. They described Moses as an Egyptian deliverer. They shared with their father how he had delivered them, drew the water, and watered all of the flocks. Highly impressed by the character of the man his daughters described, Reuel sent for Moses and rewarded him with one of his own daughters, Zipporah, as his wife. What a reward! The couple eventually had a son, whom they called Gershom, because Moses said, "I have been a stranger in a foreign land." This brings us to the third principle of Moses' story:

3. Recognize that you are a foreigner.

"I'm just a poor wayfaring stranger, traveling through this world of woe" (*Christian Songster*, 1858). Moses' son, Gershom, isn't so named because Moses was a stranger in Midian, but because Moses recognized that he was a stranger in Egypt. How could he be a stranger in a place where he was raised? Because his body grew up in Egypt as an Egyptian, but Moses was always a child of God, an Israelite, also from the tribe of Levi. Moses may have grown up in the White House, Pharaoh's palace, but his heart was always in the outhouse, with his people. He never forgot the God of his father, Amram, and his mother, Jochebed. ■■

— CRYSTON JOSIAH

FROM EX-CON TO EXODUS: A HEART OF COMPASSION PART 4

We are strangers in this world (remember the name of Moses' son, Gershom), because God has put enmity between His seed and the seed of the prince of darkness. We may be in the world but should never be of this world. Young and elderly people alike, please hear me: live, not for now, but for eternity. Paul, in Hebrews 11:10 says, regarding Abraham, "For he waited for the city which has foundations, whose builder and maker is God" (NKJV).

If we resist the devil, he will flee. That means, resist the urges to do what you want to do, succumbing to your flesh. Resist the entertainment of the world. I can't tell you the last time I've watched the Grammy's, or even the Super Bowl half-time shows, which desensitize our morals. Enmity between God's children and Satan's children is waning down. Good seems evil, and evil is received as good.

But as we close this four-part devotional journey, don't miss this: after we've identified with the oppressed; after we've realized that inaction is not an option; and once we recognize that we are foreigners; let's remember never to write anyone off. Why? Because Moses was an ex-con and murderer who deserved the death penalty, but God didn't write him off.

On the contrary, Moses went back 40 years later and led his people, God's people, out of slavery and oppression. He baptized them, all million plus, in the Red Sea. He pastored them for 40 years through a wilderness. He received the first written character of God, the Ten Commandments. He ate food from heaven—manna—and drank water from a rock.

Yet, because he disobeyed God, he suffered the earthly consequence of never making it in to Canaan, the Promised Land. He never did eat the pomegranates, grapes, and the milk and honey of Canaan.

But don't write him off, because God disputed with the devil for the body of Moses and took him to Heavenly Canaan. And when Jesus needed someone that had been there, done that, with the scars to prove it; when Jesus needed someone to encourage Him to suffer and endure His affliction, not with, but for the people of God; when Jesus needed someone to tell Him, weeping endures for a night but joy will come early on Sunday morning; God didn't send Gabriel this time. God didn't even send the Holy Spirit on this assignment. God sent Elijah, and God sent Moses, the ex-con. ■

— CRYSTON JOSIAH

JUNE 17

NEHEMIAH'S CHOIR

"I led the leaders of Judah to the top of the wall and organized two large choirs to give thanks. The two choirs that were giving thanks then proceeded to the Temple of God, where they took their places. So did I, together with the group of leaders who were with me. (Nehemiah 12:31a & 40, NLT).

Nehemiah is the Bible's great wall builder. The Bible tells us how he prayerfully led his people to get justice by seeking permission from the king, fundraising, organizing, and encouraging the people to know the importance of rebuilding and repairing the walls of Jerusalem.

Remember what the enemy said about the wall? ""That stone wall would collapse if even a fox walked along the top of it!" (Nehemiah 4:3). What we have now are two large choirs marching and singing on the wall. Who has the last word? God! The wall itself is a testimony of the providence of God. Who can thwart God's will?

Even the enemies had to confess, when the wall was completed in a short 52 days, "When our enemies and the surrounding nations heard about it, they were frightened and humiliated. They realized this work had been done with the help of our God" (Nehemiah 6:16).

After this victory, Nehemiah commands the organization of two grand choirs. The details of the processions—how they organized themselves and where they walked to—are less important than the spirit in which these were done. The people are happily singing and making music to God for what they see. And what are they seeing? The fully restored city of Jerusalem! The act of God!

Every generation is blessed with wall builders to work on that which is broken, and replant that which the locusts have eaten (Joel 2:25). It is our duty to listen and be willing to be led. Even the choirs that Nehemiah appointed had to be conducted by Jezrahiah (Nehemiah12:42).

The Levite singers, the priests, the leaders and officials, the musicians from both choirs, plus all the rest—particularly the women and children mentioned, likely because they were not in the procession—followed joyfully. Together as one people, they praised God in the house of God!

If we have a hard time worshipping God, it is because we are not seeing the character and the acts of God in our lives. If we are oblivious to who He is and what He has done or is doing, then we have nothing to sing about. ▮▮

— LEAKEY NYABERI

JUNE 18

ESTHER PRAYED!

"Go, gather together all the Jews who are in Susa, and fast for me...When this is done, I will go to the king, even though it is against the law. And if I perish, I perish" (Esther 4:16 NIV).

Haman, the evil high official to King Xerxes, hatched a plot to kill the Jewish race in Susa and the entire empire. The king sanctioned the move after taking in Haman's fake gossip that a certain people scattered across the empire "do not obey the king's laws and that it's not in the king's best interest to tolerate them" (Esther 3:8 NIV).

The king did not take time to verify the charge and ask who these "certain people" were. The Jews were not recent immigrants. They had been around for over 70 years doing honest jobs and paying the taxes. But no attempt to find out the truth was made. King Xerxes did not even consider the consequences of such a move. What will a civil war or a racial and ethnic cleansing do to his kingdom? How will the rest of the minority races see this? When will their turn to be killed come? Instead, the king took out his signet ring and gave it to Haman, practically giving him a "blank check" to do what he wanted.

Orders were written in the various languages to be sent to all the provinces, telling the people that on the 13th day of the 12th month, they could "destroy, kill and annihilate all the Jews... and plunder their goods" (Esther 3:13 NIV) Legalized looting! The funny thing is that Haman gave himself 11 months to commit this injustice!

Paul says in 1 Corinthians 3:19-20, "For the wisdom of this world is foolishness in God's sight. As it is written: 'He catches the wise in their craftiness'; and again, 'The Lord knows that the thoughts of the wise are futile'" (NIV). Before a sovereign God in whom we trust, we don't need to be afraid of evil men in their plots against us.

God had positioned Esther in the palace "for such a time like this" (Esther 4:4-11). She ordered prayer and fasting when Mordecai presented the evidence! This one act of prayer then action made a difference in human history. If you take Esther out, there is no Jewish nation and, therefore, no Jesus Christ. Esther's answered prayers preserved salvation's plans.

How willing are you to stand against injustice through prayer? ▮▮

—LEAKEY NYABERI

JUNE 19

A BODY IN THE ROAD

"But he, wanting to justify himself, said to Jesus, 'And who is my neighbor?'" (Luke 10:29 NKJV).

Jesus shares a story about a man traveling from Jerusalem to Jericho, possibly a trader of goods and services, who is assaulted. He is stripped naked, beaten, relieved of his possessions, and left to bleed to death in the road. Jesus says that eventually a priest, a holy man, by chance comes upon this grisly scene and sees the body in the road.

This unfortunate soul is naked (no clothes to identify where in the greater Palestine region he might be from); he is unconscious (thus unable to speak as the dialect or language could have helped identify him); and his features are bloodied (making him unidentifiable).

The priest realizes that if he stops to render aid, not only might he fall victim to the same highwaymen, but he would be ceremoniously unclean. This would render him unable to serve in the temple, eat of the tithes, and cause him to have to go through a series of rituals to make himself pure again. So, he passes on by.

Next, Jesus says a Levite, the custodian of the temple, happens upon the scene. It is believed by some scholars that Levities, at this time, carried portions of the offerings with them to be distributed amongst the orphans and widows. Not wanting to be robbed himself, as his job was to safeguard the funds—after all the bandits might still be in the area—he hastens on by as well.

Which brings Jesus to the next individual—a Samaritan, considered to be an infidel by the Jews. He is a trader and is flush with funds and goods. He comes upon the body in the road. While he also practiced ceremonial purity, and touching this man would require time at Mt. Gerizim to purify himself, he does not ignore the body in the road. Jesus says he took water and wine (both, by the way, are used in the religious ceremonies on the altar of God in both places of worship) and begins to start the healing process on the wounds. Taking the wounded man to a hotel, the Samaritan pays for his keep until the man regains his strength and health.

Jesus concludes the story by asking who was the neighbor.

Friends, every week we encounter bodies in the road. No, they may not be beaten and bloody, but they are hungry, homeless, and unable to take care of their most personal needs. Every week we encounter bodies in the road; strangers and aliens in a foreign land, who are in danger of predators and government agents looking to take advantage of their situation. Jesus told us this story to remind us that we cannot just step over the bodies in the road; they are our neighbors. ▮▮

— HAROLD ALLISON

JUNE 20

ISAIAH: THE SABBATH AND SOCIAL JUSTICE

Is this not the fast that I have chosen: To loose the bonds of wickedness, to undo the heavy burdens, to let the oppressed go free, and that you break every yoke? Is it not to share your bread with the hungry, and that you bring to your house the poor who are cast out; when you see the naked, that you cover him, and not hide yourself from your own flesh?" (Isaiah 58:6-7 NKJV).

For many years I read Isaiah 58 and never considered the connection between the Sabbath and social justice. However, one must ask the question, why does Isaiah end one of the most prolific social-justice chapters in the Bible by explaining the proper way to worship on the Sabbath?

The answer is simple. The Sabbath plays a crucial role in our relationships with others. Isaiah added the Sabbath to his social justice exhortation, because the distortion of the Holy day is linked to the unfair treatment of people. When we don't rest from our self-interests, we begin to oppress others and view them as objects to be used for our personal gain. The Sabbath causes us to pause and reflect on Jesus who lives not for Himself, but for those whom He loves. When delighting in God in this way, a transformation takes place in us and we begin to see our neighbors as people to love, not exploit.

Jesus certainly viewed the Sabbath He created in this way. When He saw how the underprivileged were burdened with the yoke of oppression, He said, "Come to me, all you who are weary and burdened, and I will give you rest" (Matthew 11:28 NIV).

The question for us is, do we have the same understanding of the Sabbath as Jesus and Isaiah?

We need a renewed understanding of the Sabbath, because it is well documented that the church today has a history of mistreating people, just as the "church" did in the time of Isaiah. Should we wonder why young adults and new converts aren't staying in the church? Should we wonder why tithe is down and baptisms low? It is evident that God's light is not shining on us, because He refuses to participate in our system of oppression.

Nevertheless despite our failures, if we decide as a community to delight in Him on the Sabbath and right our social wrongs, we can be assured that our 'light will break forth like the dawn, our healing will quickly appear' and we will be "fed with the heritage of Jacob" (Isaiah 58:8 & 14b NIV).

Therefore, let us answer the call to be mouthpieces like Isaiah and cry aloud for social justice. Let us champion the cause for the less fortunate. Isaiah answered the call in his day. Will you answer God's call today? ■

— BRIAN IRBY

THE SON OF MAN'S JUSTICE SYSTEM

"When the Son of Man comes in His glory, and all the holy angels with Him, then He will sit on the throne of His glory. All the nations will be gathered before Him, and He will separate them one from another, as a shepherd divides his sheep from the goats" (Matthew 25:31-32 NKJV).

In the Middle East, specifically Palestine, where Jesus did most of His ministry, sheep and goats looked exactly alike. They could easily be mistaken for each other. In this Gospel narrative we get a glimpse of the Divine process of the separation of sheep and goats, and we will observe how the justice system of the Son of Man really works.

First, Jesus refers to Himself as the Son of Man, who will come in all of His glory with holy angels and will be sitting on a throne. As we are tossed, turned and troubled by the present American justice system, Jesus, in effect, says, "I got this." As a matter of fact, this isn't the first time He refers to Himself as, the Son of Man.

In John 5:26-27 Jesus declared, "For as the Father has life in Himself, so He has granted the Son to have life in Himself, and has given Him authority to execute judgment also, because He is the Son of Man" (NKJV). We should all be grateful that not only is Jesus our Savior, Redeemer, and Friend, but He is also our Judge. And when you know the Judge, then you know that everything will be alright.

Second, the Son of Man separated the sheep from the goats based on how they responded to those who were hungry, thirsty, naked, sick, incarcerated, or strangers. But we must recognize not just what separated the sheep from the goats, but what did not separate the sheep from the goats.

The separation was not based on theology, the study of God. It was not based on their knowledge of signs and seasons, or preaching in His name, or on understanding all of the biblical prophecies. But the separation occurred based on practical actions, and social and relational actions of care and concern towards humanity—in particular, the least of these.

Last, but certainly not least, the motives of the sheep are pure. The sheep are so driven to make a difference in their society and be helpers to all those in need, that they are totally unaware and oblivious that they are ministering to Jesus Himself. Jesus literally had to tell them (Verse 40), "...everything you did for the least of these, you did for me." The attitude of the righteous toward those who are in need, becomes the clincher for the King.

May we seek, by God's grace, to model our lives after the sheep, so we may hear the words from the Son of Man, "Come, ye blessed of my Father, inherit the kingdom prepared for you from the foundation of the world" (Matthew 25:34 KJV). ▮▮

— CRYSTON JOSIAH

DORCUS – NOT JUST ABOUT GIVING AWAY CLOTHES PART 1

"Now there was at Joppa a certain disciple named Tabitha, which by interpretation is called Dorcas: this woman was full of good works and almsdeeds which she did" (Acts 9:36 KJV).

If all were fair, would there be a need for social justice? People don't seek social justice unless a need has not been met or a service has been withheld without a legal explanation. Unfortunately, people who seek justice, without success—whether it be freedom or a simple basic need—grow weary in trying to reach for it. So, the people settle or give up. So much for "liberty and justice for all"!

Fortunately, there are those who recognize the inequality, see the need, and instead of walking away from it as if to say, it's not my problem, they do something about it.

Acts 9:36 speaks of such an individual. "Now there was at Joppa a certain disciple named Tabitha, which by interpretation is called Dorcas: this woman was full of good works and alms deeds which she did" Acts 9:36 (KJV).

The Bible doesn't say much about Dorcas beyond her being a disciple who served others. But if we look further in the book, Welfare Ministries, the author writes, "In Joppa, there was Dorcus, whose skillful fingers were more active than her tongue. She knew who needed comfortable clothing and who needed sympathy, and she freely ministered to the wants of both classes" (White, 1952, p.142). Fingers faster than her tongue—she was more about action than talking about action. Dorcas was a disciple of Christ.

Yes, she was a woman. You can close your mouth now, it's a fact. You find her in the book of Acts, which means she had to be around to catch the Pentecost power! Catching the power was not just "a sit and let it sweep over you" event; it was a "I've got the power and I've got get up to use it" event. ▮▮

— TONYA L. ANDERSON.

JUNE 23

DORCUS – NOT JUST ABOUT GIVING AWAY CLOTHES PART 2

"Now there was at Joppa a certain disciple named Tabitha, which by interpretation is called Dorcas: this woman was full of good works and almsdeeds which she did" (Acts 9:36 KJV).

Sister Dorcas had compassion as she served those who were less fortunate. She also had commitment to help the less fortunate find the resources they needed to provide for themselves.

The Bible doesn't say that Dorcus represented people in a court of law; or went with the people to sit in the Office of Social Services all day, to hear "No" as the answer to a simple question of survival. It doesn't mean it didn't happen. What we do know is that Dorcus served as only she could to those who were being overlooked.

Sometimes social justice is about pointing people in the right direction. There is a saying that goes, "You have not because you ask not." There are times when people don't know whom to ask, what to ask for, or where to go to have their needs met. We, as Christians, need to be that arrow that points them in the right direction, not the broom that sweeps them aside.

Social justice isn't a "let me see" activity. It requires us to step out of our comfort zone to give someone a "hand up," or maybe even "stand in the gap" for the person until they can stand on their own.

The needs of people vary. It may be money or a moment of your time; food or a friendly smile; advice or an advocate. Or it could be just an introduction to, or reminder of, Jesus Christ the Supreme Advocate. People wept when Dorcus died. Would they weep for you?

When you think about it, social justice is actually another term for the "golden rule": "In everything, therefore, treat people the same way you want them to treat you, for this is the Law and the Prophets" (Matthew 7:12 NASB). ■

— TONYA L. ANDERSON

JUNE 24

SILENCE IS NOT CONSENT—PART 1

The Sarai, Abram's wife, took Hagar her maid, the Egyptian, and gave her to her husband Abram to be his wife...So he went in to Hagar, and she conceived. And when she saw that she had conceived, her mistress became despised in her eyes" (Genesis 16:3-4 NKJV).

In Chapter 16 of Genesis, we are 10 years removed from the Egyptian experience of Chapter 12, where Abram encourages Sarai to lie, and Hagar is given to Abram's family as a gift from the Pharaoh. For 10 years Hagar has remained virtually anonymous in Abram's home simply because she was a foreign servant or slave—that is until the problem is introduced.

For 10 years, Abram and Sarai have been expecting to have a son. Ten years before, God had made that promise! But after ten years passed, their greatest pain was the fact that Sarai still had not produced any children. After ten years, there is still there no pregnancy, and God is silent. And when God is silent, Abram and Sarai begin to doubt God.

Abram and Sarai decide to follow after the flesh, instead of following God in faith. The problem is that Sarai cannot conceive. Sarai can't have children, and unfortunately a woman or a wife who was unable to produce children, especially male children, was regarded as a misfortune. This leads to the proposal found in Genesis 16:2-3.

Sarah gets an idea and tells Abraham that even though she cannot provide him with a son, since Hagar belongs to her, Hagar could! Sarah convinces Abraham that this was their only option. Sarah proposes a human idea that pointed to Hagar as the solution, and not to God. So, after 10 years of living in the land, Abraham takes Hagar as his second wife.

When God is silent in your life, do you wait on the Lord? Or do you look for another alternative solution; maybe find a "Hagar?" Many times a "Hagar" is introduced—some worldly measure is embraced—and although it may get results, there are always negative consequences.

Sarah convinces Abraham to agree to this proposal. Although it involves Hagar, never once is Hagar consulted for her opinion. This happens because Hagar is a slave. She has no choice in the matter.

Hagar is then mistreated and reacts naturally by running away!

I'd like to suggest to you that when God is silent, and a test comes, as children of God, He wants us to act godly, not naturally! ▮▮

— KELBY D. MCCOTTRY

JUNE 25

SILENCE IS NOT CONSENT—PART 2

"And He said, 'Hagar, Sarai's maid, where have you come from, and where are you going?' She said, 'I am fleeing from the presence of my mistress Sarai'" Genesis 16:8 NKJV).

As Hagar is running away, God stops her and with loving tenderness, identifies Hagar by her name and proper title: "Hagar—Sarah's servant," not, "Hagar—Abram's wife!" Then God presents her with two questions: "Where have you come from?" and "Where are you going?"

Hagar doesn't have a good answer to that last question. Her life is in such chaos that she really doesn't know. She may be on a road that leads to Egypt, but the truth is, she has no idea what's she going to do even if she gets there! But she can answer the first question.

"I'm running from my problems" she says. "I'm getting as far away from Sarah as I can!"

Very seldom is running away from something ever the answer. Many times, whenever you get where you are running to, the problem you were running from is already there ahead of you. The Lord does two things for Hagar in Genesis 16: He instructs her, and He encourages her. The instruction is to stop running. God tells Hagar to "Go back to your mistress and submit to her" (Genesis 16:9 NIV).

I'm pretty sure that was not what Hagar wanted to hear. "Hagar, I know that it doesn't seem fair. The very people who should know better have not treated you right. But can you trust Me enough to go back and stay in My will?"

The good news is that Hagar obeys. When she agrees to go back, God encourages and strengthens her by making her some promises; telling her what He will do for her. "I will so increase your descendants that they will be too numerous to count...and you will have a son. You shall name him Ishmael, for the LORD has heard of your misery" (Genesis 16:10-11 NIV).

Today, maybe like Hagar, you have been running away from God. Maybe like Hagar, you feel like giving up. But I want to remind you that God has heard your misery! Today, God says, "Stop running! Don't give up! Learn how to wait!

For Hagar, going back to Egypt—the things that were comfortable—was not an option. Each one of us should be able to see ourselves in Hagar. If we are to be true followers of Christ, then unlike Sarai, we must refuse to get rid of, or discard those, who are suffering. Unlike Abram, we can't just wash our hands of the situation either.

We are called to identify with the ones who suffer, because Jesus not only identified with suffering, He took the burden upon Himself for our sakes.

As Hagar's story unfolds, we can see that despite her trials Hagar was never alone. The fact that God showed up to console Hagar, demonstrates the magnitude of God's mercy. God loves all people and is nondiscriminatory with us. Here, God maintains His promises to Abram, and at the same time, takes care of Hagar.

Today, He wants to take care of you too. ■

—KELBY D. McCOTTRY

JUNE 26

BE JUSTICE

"Now the birth of Jesus Christ took place in this way. When his mother Mary had been betrothed to Joseph, before they came together she was found to be with child from the Holy Spirit. And her husband Joseph, being a just man and unwilling to put her to shame, resolved to divorce her quietly" (Matthew 1:18-19 ESV).

I know what you're thinking. What does the story of Jesus' birth have to do with social justice? Well, let's take a look.

The story is that Mary, whom the Bible refers to as pure, is engaged to Joseph. According to Jewish custom an engagement was as good as a present day wedding. The marriage, which was arranged, would begin with a year of espousal and end with a feast and the subsequent consummation. The only way to break off this engagement was by a legal bill of divorce.

According to Luke, during this year of espousal Mary goes away to visit her cousin Elizabeth (Luke 1:54), and after three months comes back pregnant. To make matters even worse, she claims that God did it. What a scandal! Based on Jewish law at the time, the punishment for her pregnancy out of wedlock was stoning. And while the Roman government had taken the death sentence from the hands of the Jews, the stoning of Stephen and crucifixion of Jesus proves that you only have to get the crowd angry enough. Mary is in trouble.

On the other side of the story is Joseph, the son of Jacob, her betrothed and the man legally responsible for her. Can you imagine the position that he is in? By law his wife must be handed over to the authorities and justice be exacted. On the other, he could also argue that the law was unjust to begin with, as it subjugated her on the basis of gender and social standing. It is apparent from the text that there was pressure to make an example of her. Joseph is conflicted, but he has to do something.

Matthew breaks the tension with this detail, "Joseph being a just man and unwilling to put her to shame, resolved to divorce her quietly" (Matthew 1:10 ESV). He does not allow the crowd to dictate his social stance, nor does he take to the streets to protest his position. Instead, he guards her innocence, even though he doesn't seem to believe her story, as he does decide to divorce her. And what drives his decision making? He is a "just man." In the Greek, it is better translated as, "righteous or a person determined to do what is right." Joseph did the right thing. And, it wasn't because it was popular, but because that's who he was.

How often we allow for society, the current political correctness, or the crowd to dictate our stance on social topics, or who and what we advocate for. How we stand for justice should not simply be predicated on the current cause of the day, nor should it be based on any personal gain, whether that be popularity or otherwise. Our stance should flow from who we are; not simply social justice advocates, but just people in tune with a just God. ■

—KORY P. DOUGLAS.

JUST LIKE A THIEF

"One of the criminals who were hanged there was hurling abuse at Him, saying, 'Are You not the Christ? Save Yourself and us!' But the other answered, and rebuking him, said, 'Do you not even fear God, since you are under the same sentence of condemnation? And we indeed are suffering justly, for we are receiving what we deserve for our deeds; but this man has done nothing wrong'" (Luke 23:39-41 NASB).

I wonder if the man we have come to call, "the thief on the cross," would have pictured his life turning out the way it did. We are given little information about him, or what he has done to deserve to be hanging next to Jesus that day. He could have been the vilest of criminals, a petty thief, or just caught in the wrong place at the wrong time. What we do know is that on that day, he found himself hanging next to the Son of God on a day foreordained in eternity to be the day that humanity would be rescued from the death grip of sin.

The Gospel writers do not share with us at what point the two thieves are aligned with Jesus. Here is what we do know: While Luke portrays the thief on the cross as coming to the rescue of Jesus, Matthew lets us know in his gospel (24:44) that both thieves have, to this point, taken part with the crowd in the verbal assaults of the Messiah.

That's right. The same thief, who we praise for stepping up to defend the innocent Christ and to seek out his place in the kingdom, just prior to that was part of the problem. Up until that point, he was just as guilty as the crowd that cried, "Crucify him," the religious leaders who sought his death, and those that carried out Jesus' death sentence.

But here is the lesson we learn from the thief on the cross; in order for us to truly act justly, we must admit our own guilt. We must come to the same conclusion that the thief came to; that there is only one innocent, and that is Jesus. This is not an easy task, as sometimes we are so focused on the guilt of others that we forget who we are and what we've done. However, the reality is that, "all have sinned and fall short of the glory of God" (Romans 3:23, NASB).

For this reason, the task of owning up to our guilt can only come as it came for the thief on the cross; as we focus on the Jesus. As the thief listened to Jesus' words on the cross—how He prayed forgiveness for His persecutors and spoke to His father—his heart was moved. He felt the overwhelming conviction to confess his own sin.

"We indeed are suffering justly, for we are receiving what we deserve for our deeds; but this man has done nothing wrong," the thief says. Admitting his guilt, the thief also vindicates the innocent Christ.

Jesus responds in kind, "Truly I say to you, today you shall be with Me in Paradise" (Luke 23:43 NASB). With his handful of some of his last words, the thief himself is justified. ▮▮

— KORY P. DOUGLAS

JUNE 28

HER NAME IS RAHAB AND SHE IS A HERO—PART 1

"Now Joshua the son of Nun sent out two men from Acadia Grove to spy secretly, saying, 'Go, view the land, especially Jericho.' So they went, and came to the house of a harlot named Rahab, and lodged there. And it was told the king of Jericho, saying, 'Behold, men have come here tonight from the children of Israel to search out the country'" (Joshua 2:1-2 NKJV).

Many of us know the story of Joshua and the battle of Jericho, where God ushers the Israelite people into the Promised Land. This miracle would not have happened without the heroic work of a social justice warrior named Rahab.

Rahab worked as a prostitute in the city of Jericho. One can only imagine the immoral things that have taken place within the walls of her house. Imagine the faint scent of incense, mixed with the sour stench of human flesh wafting through the corridors. Imagine her floor creaking, crying out tales of unwanted advances and unfulfilled encounters. If her walls could talk, surely they would tell of nights awake, heavy hearts, and tired tears.

One day two men show up at her door, and she lets them in. This is probably not the first time strange men have shown up at her door, and probably not the first time she has let men in her house for a risky rendezvous. However, these men—and the nature of this risk—are a little different.

The men are Israelite spies, sent to survey the land. They tell her because of her kindness she will be spared when God destroys the city. All Rahab and her family has to do is stay within the walls of her house. The walls of her home, which were once a place of suffering sensuality, now becomes the place of her survival. Rahab is protected inside of the walls, proving that God can rewrite the narrative about the place that you are in.

Sometimes fighting for social justice can be exhausting, especially if you are a victim of the oppression that you are fighting against. It can seem as if you will be stuck in the place where you are, perpetually, because God doesn't always change the place immediately. Instead, God will change how you view what you see, so you can recognize that God can use the place that has been meant for evil for your good.

The walls of oppression were meant to restrict you, but God can use them to retain you. Now, these walls do not confine you, incarcerate you, insulate you, shut you up, box you in, lock you up, pen you in, cage you, coop you, hedge you, or corral you. Instead, you can be loosed and liberated in Jesus name. Just like Rahab you can be set free. ▮▮

— MARCUS LARIVAUX

HER NAME IS RAHAB AND SHE IS A HERO—PART 2

"Then the woman took the two men and hid them. So she said, 'Yes, the men came to me, but I did not know where they were from. And it happened as the gate was being shut, when it was dark, that the men went out. Where the men went I do not know; pursue them quickly, for you may overtake them'" (Joshua 2:4-5 NKJV).

Yesterday we spoke about Rahab the hero. In her story, two men show up at her door and she hides them on her roof. Rahab even lies to the King of Jericho in order to save them. This lie makes it possible for her and her family to be rescued, and eventually for Rahab to become a part of the lineage of Jesus Christ. So is her lie heroic?

We understand that the Bible is not encouraging us to lie in order to get what we want. Knowing this, perhaps this text is not prescriptive of how we should behave, but descriptive of what happens when we perpetuate systems of oppression in society.

Rahab wants out of her old life; she's stuck in a system that creates a situation where she has to sell her body for survival. In order to get out she must choose between lying and having an opportunity for a new life, or telling the truth and remaining oppressed. She must choose between social salvation and soul salvation. But what if soul salvation without social salvation is no salvation at all? What if the "right" choice is also the "immoral" choice because society has made morality a luxury and not a necessity?

Say you are a single mother of three kids who haven't eaten in three days. You have tried all you know to find a way to feed them but you have failed. Then, someone offers you money for sex. Would you consider prostituting your body in order to feed your children? Is it possible to have a "right" but immoral choice?

I don't have the answers to these questions. What I know is when you perpetuate systems of oppression, like the ones that Rahab faced, you create ethical conundrums and construct moral quandaries. That's why we ought to protect the marginalized and neglected in our society. It is our responsibility to fight for the right of every person's access to jobs with decent wages, good education, healthy food, and a place to live.

God has called us to honor the integrity of every human's rights, and to speak truth to power wherever injustice rears its ugly head. Rahab waged war against the system that had oppressed her and her family, and by doing so she became a hero of social justice.

It's time for you to do the same. ■■

— MARCUS LARIVAUX

JUNE 30

GOD IS UNORTHODOX: DEBORAH AND JAEL

"Sisera, who had 900 iron chariots, ruthlessly oppressed the Israelites for twenty years. Then the people of Israel cried out to the Lord for help" (Judges 4:3 NLT).

Even though Judges 4 begins with the children of Israel doing evil in the sight of the Lord, yet again, when they cried out to God—who is compassionate, long-suffering, and abundant in mercy and grace—He heard their petition and answered their cries. However, He answered in a way that He never had before, and He chose a type of person that He had never chosen before to task with delivering His people.

In the book of Judges, all the judges up to this point were men. They were all mighty men of valor and strength; warriors who had battled against Israel's surrounding enemies. But because God is unorthodox and can choose whomever He wants, and can use whomever He wants, He finds a man named Lappidoth; but He doesn't call him. God calls his wife, Deborah, to be a judge and deliverer of His people.

Deborah not only was a prophetess of God—a spiritual leader who shared the Word of God to His people—she was also the Chief Justice of the Israeli Supreme Court. She was a preacher, prophet, and judge all wrapped up in one (think Dr. Hyveth Williams, Ellen White, and Judge Ruth Bader-Ginsburg).

God uses Deborah to prophesy to Barak, son of Abinoam, letting him know that if he could simply assemble 10,000 warriors from the tribes of Naphtali and Zebulun at Mount Tabor, God would give them victory over the mighty army of Sisera, with their iron chariots. Deborah is such a spiritual and powerful leader, that Barak says that he will only go if she goes. Deborah responds with a powerful statement that should also resonate with us today.

"'Very well,' she replied, 'I will go with you. But you will receive no honor in this venture, for the Lord's victory over Sisera will be at the hands of a woman'" (Judges 4:9 NLT).

Towards the end of the battle, this statement becomes a reality when Sisera is killed by Jael, who drives a tent peg through his temple.

God used Deborah and Jael, women, to deliver His children from oppression. And God can use you to deliver His people today, as well. All God needs is willing hearts and hands, and you, too, can be a hero for social justice right where you are. ■

— CRYSTON JOSIAH

JULY

BIBLICAL HEROES OF CONSCIENCE AND RELIGIOUS LIBERTY

For the month of July, we invite you to pull back the curtains of the old and new testaments and join us on a journey of discovery as we explore the theme, "Bible Heroes of Conscience and Religious Liberty."

And as you venture into the personal space of each character's story you will find them at different intersections of life. These junctures are where conscience and belief in God, on the one hand, will often come into conflict with the realities of choice and destiny on the other.

Observe how each dared to face and weather the fierce headwinds of social and religious oppression, while standing as a wall of partition, accountability, and protection for those unable to do so for themselves.

We pray these stories will do more than just inform you. We hope they will challenge, change and inspire you. And having done that, the God of these Bible Heroes of Conscience and Religious Liberty will secure His place in your own personal story empowering you, like them, to rise, go out and do the same. ▮▮

— KINGSLEY O. PALMER
Director of Public Affairs and Religious Liberty,
Arizona Conference of Seventh-day Adventists

JULY 1

COURAGEOUS MIDWIVES IN EGYPTIAN BONDAGE

"But because the midwives feared God, they refused to obey the king's orders. They allowed the boys to live, too" (Exodus 1:17 NLT).

What do you do to prevent genocide in a place where you yourself are enslaved? How do you respond to direct orders from a deranged king to literally kill all the Hebrew boys when they are born, but not the girls? This is the dilemma in which Shiphrah and Puah find themselves as Hebrew midwives in Egypt.

Pharaoh began pedaling two false narratives to his people that led to this ungodly and violent decree. First, he told the Egyptians that the people of Israel were mightier than them, which was a statistical lie based on the current Egyptian population at that time. Pharaoh desired to create a fear of control in his people, to carry forward his plans to oppress the Hebrews. Second, Pharaoh told his people that the Hebrews would join their enemies and fight against them. This was to create a fear of survival amongst the Egyptians, even though the Israelites had no plans to fight against them.

Subsequently, the fears of control and survival tactics worked. Not only did the Egyptians make the Israelites work harder, but now a form of genocide, in the mass murders of all male Hebrew babies, is declared. What a sad commentary that when fears are stoked, people and leaders will do anything to oppress those who are different.

Doesn't this scenario remind us of the realities of life in America?

Even today in 2021, while the black population stands at 12.9 percent of the total population, the narrative of the fear of losing control still exists. The narrative that minorities will take all of the jobs, and somehow take over "our" entire nation are not only lies, but is not possible just based on raw numbers. It is the same spirit of Pharaoh that we are seeing made manifest in our lifetime.

But look at God. Pharaoh ran into the wrong sisters, who defied and disobeyed his plan of genocide by gender. "Note the irony: a powerful but nameless Pharaoh speaks directly to Israelite midwives. While he fears males, it is really two women who oppose him and foil his plan" (*Andrews Study Bible*, Andrews University Press, 2010, p. 74).

God gave Shiphrah and Puah the words to say that not only saved the lives of hundreds, yeah thousands of Hebrew baby boys, but saved their own lives as well. "It's above me now" was the essence of their refrain. And instead of decreasing, the Bible declares that "the people multiplied, and waxed very mightily" (Exodus 1:20 KJV). ▮▮

— CRYSTON JOSIAH

JULY 2

THE FIVE DAUGHTERS OF ZELOPHEPAD

"Why should the name of our father be done away from among his family, because he hath no son? Give unto us therefore a possession among the brethren of our father" (Numbers 27:4 KJV).

As Israel approached the end of their 40-year wilderness experience, it was time for the long-awaited tribal distribution of the Promised Land. Mahlah, Noa, Hoglah, Milcah, and Tirzah, the five daughters and only children of Zelophepad, came to the realization that since their father was dead they would be excluded from their family's inheritance. This would leave them with no home and no place in their community because they had no male siblings. This was understood to be not only the law of the land, but also directions from God.

The five sisters, not losing hope or courage, took their concern to the Tent of Meeting before Moses, Eleazar the priest, and other leaders. They asked the leaders to honor and restore their father's name and give them their father's portion. Moses, not sure of how to handle this unusual request, took their case before God, seeking wisdom and courage to do the right thing. God not only says that the daughters are right in their request, but permanently changes the inheritance law. (See Numbers 27:7.)

These five fatherless, husbandless, courageous superheroes dared to speak up and ask for justice for themselves, and for those who would come after them. In the times in which we live, there are three take aways from this story which serve as a message of hope for those who face obstacles.

1. Show up—the sisters dared to challenge the social destiny imposed on them and participated early in the discussion before implementation. They did not wait to see what would happen and then complain after the fact.

2. Stand up—they dared to stand up for what they believed was right even though what they were asking was contrary to prevailing laws and customs. In the Talmud, the five sisters are called wise, astute interpreters of the law, and pious for their faith that God would be fair. They knew the law and their history, they prepared a compelling argument, and they engaged effectively.

3. Speak up—the sisters were not afraid to speak up against systemic and ingrained laws and traditions that they considered inadequate for their circumstances. They spoke up for themselves and for others who would come after them, and changed the inheritance laws forever. Like the five daughters, we can speak up and walk away with change.

Every situation in life has purpose in the hands of God. Let us allow God to use us to help those who have less voice and privilege. Let us remember that in God's kingdom, our Promised Land, all are welcome and no one is excluded. ▮▮

— EILEEN KNIGHT WHITE

JULY 3

EQUAL VALUE

"And the men answered her, 'Our life for yours, if ye utter not this our business. And it shall be, when the LORD hath given us the land, that we will deal kindly and truly with thee'" (Joshua 2:14 KJV).

I'm often saddened when I turn on the news and hear those who are not Christian talk about what experiences they have had with those who follow Christ. These experiences and ordeals are challenging enough and often downright horrible. Whether it is violence done in Jesus' name or discrimination supported by Jesus' followers, or the less fortunate being ignored by those who claim to be like Jesus, the reports come in time and time again. To be sure, some are unfair.

However, I'm also certain that some of those testimonies are true. For a church that is attempting to show the world a clear picture of who God is, a tainted witness is a problem.

Have we ever stopped to think about what kind of God we are showing the world? When I was learning how to cook, my sister-in-law, Kendra—herself a chef—taught me that presentation matters.

The ingredients are important, and the food has to be cooked properly in order to be enjoyed. However, if the food is not presented in a way that is appealing, even the most easy-going customer will find the meal difficult to enjoy.

Maybe our biggest problem is how we present who God is and His gospel.

I doubt that Rahab had ever met Israelites before the day she met those two spies; but she knew a little about their God. She had heard the stories about the miracles and their legend, yet she was willing to learn more.

I believe that there is one additional, often overlooked idea within the story, though. The biblical account of Rahab's interaction with the two Israelite spies is interesting, instructive and simple, yet profound.

Rahab was a foreigner, a woman and a prostitute; yet they treated her like she was valuable.

Think about it. The Israelite spies made this foreign prostitute a promise they didn't have to keep, yet, they kept it. Despite her differences, the spies treated her like she was valuable. There's a lesson there for all of us.

When we think of rights that need to be protected, do we think only of the rights of those who look or sound, believe or behave like us? Or because they so are different, we don't fight for their rights like ours.

The followers of Jesus should seek justice for everyone! Even the Rahab's of this world. Why? Because God loves and values them. ▮▮

— GAMAL ALEXANDER

JULY 4

JUSTICE ROLL CALL

"Blessed are those who keep justice, and he who does righteousness at all times!" (Psalm 106:3 NKJV).

Do you remember sitting in a classroom listening to the teacher doing roll call? I've always wondered why it was necessary to confirm our presence, even if at times the teacher saw us coming into the classroom.

Roll call does more than confirm that we are physically in the room. Uttering out loud that we are present psychologically includes us as members of the classroom community, and makes us accountable to participate.

The reason behind this is obvious: There is a difference between presence and participation.

Come let us delve into the manner of how we respond to God's roll call for those who are willing to participate in fighting injustices, by comparing two biblical characters' response to their respective situations.

The first character is found in Judges Chapters 4 and 5. Barak was summoned by God, via then Israelite prophetess leader Deborah, to go and fight the oppressive Canaanite government.

It's evidenced in these chapters that God cannot remain a spectator or just an outside observer when it comes to injustice. However, the Omnipotent God, instead of fixing things on His own, is looking for participation from His people. But notice how Barak answers the call:

"And Barak said to her (Deborah), 'If you will go with me, then I will go; but if you will not go with me, I will not go!'" (Judges 4:8 NKJV).

Although this periscope does not tell us the reason behind Barak's response, it undoubtedly shows us that his willingness to be a part of God's plan to end injustice was only conditional, partial and not absolute. As a result of this inadequate reaction, God had no problem choosing another willing participant to finish the job.

On the other hand, Nehemiah's response to the injustice during his time is completely different. During the post-exilic era, this prophet couldn't remain silent when the Jewish nobles and officials were treating the less fortunate unfairly. Consider Nehemiah 5:6-8:

"When I heard their outcry and these charges, (1) I was very angry. (2) I pondered them in my mind and (3) then accused the nobles and officials…" (NIV).

The prophet's, (1) anger, delineates the fact that unfairness is unacceptable, and injustice is intolerable. Nevertheless, acting with anger is not recommended.

Nehemiah, (2) took some time to think, analyze and reflect on the situation and then, (3) protested by publicly accusing the perpetrators. He did this because no matter how important individuals were, they were expected to act for the benefit of the group.

So the question is: When God will do His justice roll call, will you be a present bystander, or will you participate in His plan to bring good news to the afflicted, to bind up the brokenhearted, to proclaim liberty to captives and freedom to prisoners? ■

— H. NEAT RANDRIAMIALISON

JULY 5

FROM BITTER TO BETTER

"And she said unto them, 'Call me not Naomi, call me Mara: for the Almighty has dealt very bitterly with me'" (Ruth 1:20 KJV).

The story of Ruth is a biblical non-starter. First of all, she's a descendant of Lot! (Remember Sodom and Gomorrah?) She's born into a land of idolatry called Moab. Ruth then marries into a Hebrew family and shortly after, she, her sister- in-law and mother-in-law all become widows. But now here's the rest of the story.

Ruth accepts her late husband's faith, experiences God for herself, and her former lifestyle is changed. Naomi, with nothing to gain from the loss by staying, decides to return to her homeland. Ruth refuses to let her go alone; she insists on going too.

Now why would any foreigner—"someone different" with no other family connections—clothed in their right mind, choose to visit or live in Canaan of all places? Did it not belong exclusively to God's chosen people, the Hebrews?

They were already known for their hostile treatment of foreigners and other immigrants. Ruth knew that a decision like that would take a great deal of faith, courage and sacrifice. Her love for God and that for Naomi, her elderly mother-in-law, and her concern for Naomi's welfare was far more important to Ruth than staying home and doing nothing.

The story ends with Ruth meeting and marrying Boaz, Naomi's kinsman redeemer. Sometime later, Naomi's empty arms are filled holding her grandson, Obed, to love and nurture (can't you see her kissing the baby on its cheeks and singing stories to him?).

Later, Ruth is listed several times in the New Testament as one of the ancestral mothers of Jesus Christ, our own Kinsman Redeemer.

So, what can we learn from this story?

1. Ruth's devotion and caregiving for her late husband's mother, and the unfolding of God's providence for her life enriches our admiration of the inclusivity of our God.

2. Ruth's story showcases the unconditional love of God for the "foreigner"—the immigrant, the disenfranchised, the poor, the LGBTQ community— and our need for interfaith ministry and compassionate interaction with the human race without regard to gender, or anything that would build a wall to exclude any people.

3. Finally, it also broadens our desire to fulfill God's will in our lives as His hands and mouths, to seek those who are lost and reach others with genuine love for God, regardless of who they are or where they came from with no strings attached.

Jesus Christ our Kinsman-Redeemer is ready to move you from "something bitter" to a life that is lived for "something better" that God has in mind for you. ■

— WANDA FLOWERS

JULY 6

ABIGAIL TAKES A RISK

"Then David accepted from her hand what she had brought him and said, 'Go home in peace. I have heard your words and granted your request'" (I Samuel 25:35 NIV).

The narrator of 1 Samuel presented a drastic contrast between the two husbands of Abigail. Nabal was powerful and rich, but others considered him foolish and mean. David was also powerful, but he heeded the guidance of his God. When Abigail heard Nabal had insulted David, she acted quickly behind his back and saved her entire household from harm by using good judgement. From the story, we know Abigail was wise, decisive, brave, and loyal. She knew exactly what she needed to do when she found out David was ready to get violent.

With loads of food, Abigail went to meet David. She fell at his feet and said: "Pardon your servant, my lord, and let me speak to you; hear what your servant has to say. Please pay no attention, my lord, to that wicked man Nabal. He is just like his name—his name means Fool, and folly goes with him. And as for me, your servant, I did not see the men my lord sent. And now, my lord, as surely as the Lord your God lives and as you live, since the Lord has kept you from bloodshed and from avenging yourself with your own hands, may your enemies and all who are intent on harming my lord be like Nabal. And let this gift, which your servant has brought to my lord, be given to the men who follow you" (1 Samuel 25:24-27 NIV).

So, did our Bible heroine take a risk or was it just good judgement?

Recent biblical scholars hold an expanded view of women's risk-taking nature by looking into our first mother, Eve. Besides being nurturers and supporters, women are created to be the seekers of knowledge and testers of limits. Eve accepted Satan's offer and willfully disconnected from God, but God did not stop blessing women and men with spiritual gifts.

Among those divine gifts, inquisitiveness and wisdom are to be affirmed. Women's voices can benefit our society in a very significant way when they are connected to the Spirit of God. As a woman, I have learned to trust my inner guide led by the Holy Spirit, first by having a steady connection with God, and then not relying on my own understanding.

May we ask God to turn our knowledge and understanding into wisdom. It's never a risk when we let God lead. ■■

— ANGELA H. LI

JULY 7

SPEAKING UP FOR JUSTICE

"Speak up for those who cannot speak for themselves, for the rights of all who are destitute. Speak up and judge fairly; defend the rights of the poor and needy" (Proverbs 31:8-9 NIV).

At the outset, it had all of the makings of a parable drawn from the prophet's imagination. But as Nathan, the man of God, began fleshing out his narrative, the understanding came quickly that the story of cruelty being told bore the foul odor of injustice, while being fully qualified as front page news.

"There were two men in one city, one rich and the other poor" (2 Samuel 12:1). The rich man had an abundance of flocks and herds. Meanwhile, the poor man was the owner of one, solitary animal—a little ewe lamb. The poor man loved that lamb, raising it like one of his children. Two men, whose worlds collided on the day a traveler visited the rich man.

Social customs would have assured the traveler of a meal at the rich man's table. However, unwilling to sacrifice one of his own animals, the wealthy host ordered his servants to seize and cook the poor man's only lamb. As he listened, David, King of Israel, was determined that the ugly face of injustice would not be allowed to parade unpunished.

Hearing of the poor man's loss, the king was furious. This was wickedness worthy of death. Self-assured of a conviction and a sentence of death, the king determined that prior to being put to death the rich man must make restitution. Four lambs were to replace the one.

King David demanded the name of the one guilty of committing such a shamefully selfish act. Nathan's stunning reply was like a two-by-four between the king's eyes. "You are the man." David's secret affair with Bathsheba, and the cover up leading to the death of her husband, had only seemed like a secret. God had seen it all. In that moment, Nathan became a hero of justice, speaking out against royal injustice.

Ever since 9-11, the watch words for America have been, "See something, say something." It's not a new concept, however. From the beginning, whenever injustice presented itself, God has seen and He has spoken. In many cases, God has spoken through men and women He has compelled to speak up against the wrongs of an unjust society. Nathan, like other heroes standing against injustice, understood the need of Proverbs 31:8-9; to speak up for those with no voice, and to defend the rights of the oppressed. Likewise, they embrace the admonition in Isaiah 1:17 to defend the oppressed, and to seek justice.

No matter how secret, injustice cannot be allowed to victimize in silence. Because of His great love for us, God chooses not to remain silent, forever. He will speak up and righteousness will prevail. ■

— DONALD L. McPHAULL

A KID IN A CAGE

"Now bands of raiders from Aram had gone out and had taken captive a young girl from Israel, and she served Naaman's wife. She said to her mistress, 'If only my master would see the prophet who is in Samaria! He would cure him of his leprosy'" (2 Kings 5:2-3 NIV).

Her story is only 47 words long. Her name is unknown. Her age is about seven years old. She's lost the innocence of playing. She's not advancing her dreams. She's been snatched from the protection of her parents' arms and now lives in captivity, confined to a cage.

2 Kings 5 shares that while the girl is encaged, she finds out that the man whose holding her captive has become terminally ill. For some reason, this caged girl becomes more concerned about her captor's illness rather than her own life. She takes a risk in speaking about the power of God regarding his sickness.

What seems like a bad situation is actually God allowing two unlikely people to have their paths cross in an untimely interruption, so that it can become the canvas for His divine appointment to take place!

This kid in a cage teaches us that we should "share what we know." Clearly, this young girl didn't have any medical knowledge or specialties in dealing with a deadly disease. She's not a dermatologist—but she didn't concern herself with what she didn't know or have within her possession; she simply shared what she knew.

This was a life and death situation. Though she could've said, "I'm just a kid in a cage, what can I do?" or seized personal justice or revenge and let her captor die, she chose to love, and seized grace. She shared what she knew!

This kid in a cage also teaches us to "touch people within our circles of influence." She didn't wait for a large crowed to be present before stepping up and saying something. In fact, she didn't even wait to be asked. She shared what she knew with the people with whom she had daily contact, her captors.

She had every reason to be distracted and consumed with grief over her less than ideal circumstances. Yet, she realized that the mission was bigger than the misfortunes of her captivity. This kid in a cage was able to stay attuned to God's purposes for her life and for her captor's lives, and point them to a relationship with God.

As a result of her testifying to those she had contact with, her captor not only received full healing from God, but the entire household came into a knowledge and relationship with God. ■■

— CHANDRA NUNES

NAAMAN—LESSONS FROM A LEPER

"But may the Lord forgive your servant for this one thing: When my master enters the temple of Rimmon to bow down and he is leaning on my arm and I have to bow there also—when I bow down in the temple of Rimmon, may the Lord forgive your servant for this" (2 Kings 5:18 NIV).

The story of Naaman is a story of contrasts. Naaman is described as a great man; he is a military man; he is an accomplished man; but, he is a leper! One could wonder why this story was chosen by our Creator for our learning. Look at the lessons of contrast in the story, and ultimately the issue of freedom of conscience.

Naaman served the King of Syria but his king had no power to heal him. His king was not able to direct him to the god of Syria for healing. However, a slave girl who had no position knew the true G_d and his prophet, and informed Naaman's wife of the G_d of Israel and his prophet.

Naaman went to Israel. He was accustomed to being treated based on his status and his accomplishments; the prophet did not even come out to greet him. Simple instructions were given: go and dip in the dirty Jordan River seven times. Naaman was insulted at such a suggestion, but G_d's redemption is not only in the result; it is in the methodology. Naaman contrasted the Jordan River to that of the clean rivers in Damascus and wondered to himself if those rivers were not better?

Naaman heeded the instruction, dipped seven times, and was healed. Naaman was so overcome with gratitude that he offered to pay the prophet, but the prophet declined. However, Elisha's servant, Gehazi, desired Naaman's wealth. Here was another contrast: an unbeliever willing to give all he had and a believer willing to give up his G_d for the wealth of the unbeliever.

There is one more lesson from this leper, a greater lesson.

Naaman's conscience was awakened. The manner in which he was healed quickened his mind to see beyond his wealth and beyond his status. He needed to know he had peace with G_d.

Naaman was troubled in his mind. He realized that his required duties to the Syrian king placed him in direct conflict with the G_d of Israel. He was concerned that when the king genuflected before his idol god that he, too, would have to bow before the idol. He needed to know what to do. How could he do this against the G_d who just healed him?

The prophet spoke three simple words: "Go in peace." These three words honored Naaman's conscientious understanding of worship. These three words upheld the healing miracle, and at the same time respected his reality.

Elisha could have instructed him to stay in Israel. He could have told Naaman that Israel was the true representative of Jehovah. Instead, he uttered three words that reverberate through the annals of history as an indicator of how we are to treat those who come to a knowledge of G_d and whom G_d heals: "Go in Peace."

May you experience peace in your mind this day. ■

— LANSTON SYLVESTER

JULY 10

IF MY PEOPLE

"If My people who are called by My name will humble themselves, and pray and seek My face and turn from their wicked ways, then I will hear from heaven and will forgive their sin and heal their land" (2 Chronicles 7:14 NKJV).

I remember the embarrassment at the first day of school when my five-syllable, Eastern European last name would be slaughtered like an animal for the kill. I just wanted to put my head in the sand and have someone else say, "Present." Everything my last name represented, where my family had come from, meant nothing to these foreigners with last names like "Smith," "Cunningham," and "Williams." To make matters worse, early on in my school days I did not bring a positive reputation to our family name.

The people of Israel had found themselves identified with a name they had not made a positive reputation for, either. Going forward they could either represent the name well or compromise the reputation further. King David, as well, was known to have dishonored the pure name of God by bloodshed and would not be allowed to build a temple for God. His son, Solomon, ended up completing the temple.

When Solomon finished, he fervently sought God's blessing and approval for what he had done on behalf of himself and his wayward people. God responded to him in our text for today: "If My people who are called by My name will humble themselves, and pray and seek My face and turn from their wicked ways, then I will hear from heaven and will forgive their sin and heal their land." Two beautiful images emerge, regardless of Israel's poor past choices.

First, they were still God's people and, second, God promised a way out of their challenging situation. Yet this blessing was contingent upon their submission to Him. In this next generation, God wanted a different weapon to be used called humility and prayer, and a people who relied upon Him, not their swords. God wants this weapon for His future church too.

You might find yourself in a painful place in life, embarrassed of the name you've made for yourself, scared for what is to come, or unsure if God will and can do anything to help in the circumstances in which you find yourself. At this point you can do one of two things; force your way to make a name for yourself, and rely on your own wisdom and scheming.

Or, you can choose a weapon that unleashes the power of God on your behalf by submitting your way to God in humility, through prayer (i.e. acknowledging you cannot do this alone), and repenting of your missteps of the past.

God wants to make an impact in your life like He did in Israel's. Will you humble yourself today, seek Him in prayer, and repent? Violence will not bring glory to God's name, but a people who seek His blessing and might by spiritual warfare will create a powerful legacy (John 13:35); one in which there is no embarrassment. ■■

— FILIP MILOSAVLJEVIĆ

JULY 11

THE WOMAN WHO TURNS GENOCIDE INTO SUICIDE

"'Look! The gallows, fifty cubits high, which Haman made for Mordecai, who spoke good on the king's behalf, is standing at the house of Haman.' Then the king said, 'Hang him on it!'" (Esther 7:9 NKJV).

How could it be that a book in the Bible, that doesn't even mention God by name, could be a modern-day Netflix miniseries? The literary genius of this book—with its setting, plot, dramatic irony and breath-taking climax— reads like a New York Times best seller!

How is it that a book written in a male dominated society could feature a woman as its heroine? How is this possible? It is only possible because this book is inspired by the unmentioned, the uncaused Cause, God!

The book of Esther is set in the capitol city of Susa in Persia during the Jewish exile, and explains the origin of the Jewish celebration of Purim.

The story begins with the Persian King Xerxes hosting a banquet for his nobles and officials. Everything is going fine until the inebriated Xerxes decides he wants to show off his gorgeous wife, Queen Vashti. The drama begins when Queen Vashti refuses to attend the drunken rabble!

This act of independence, but good judgement, is deemed defiant, rebellious and an endangerment to the stability of the kingdom because Queen Vashti was willing to speak truth to power and was unwilling to be displayed as some trophy wife. She was summarily dismissed as queen and immediately a search began to find a beautiful young virgin to replace her.

Vashti serves as the unsung hero of this portion of the narrative, setting the stage for our ultimate heroine. Esther is selected as the next queen after winning a national beauty contest. The plot thickens and takes an ominous turn.

Fast forward. Xerxes' highest ranking nobleman, Haman, has a run in with Mordecai. Mordecai refuses to bow and pay him homage. This is offensive to Haman. Once he discovers that Mordecai is a Jew, Haman decides he will engage in genocide and annihilate the entire Jewish race!

Once Haman's plan is discovered by Mordecai, Esther, who no one knows as a Jew, is called upon to deliver her people.

In a twist of fate, Esther makes a request of Xerxes to save her people. Xerxes discovers that his wife is a Jewess and Haman finds out he was planning to destroy the queen's race!

The very pole that Haman planned to impale Mordecai on was the one he was impaled on. Although God is never mentioned, God used a woman who turned genocide into suicide. ▮▮

— JONATHAN SMITH

JULY 12

GOD, DO SOMETHING!

"Then Job arose, rent his mantle, and shaved his head, then fell down on the ground, and worshipped" (Job 1:20 KJV).

When we first meet Job, the protagonist, he is far from suffering. Job was a perfect and upright man who feared God. He was one of God's Heroes. He was the richest man in the whole land. In an instant, Job lost everything.

Through all this Job never sinned (Job 1:21; Job 2:10). In Job 1:21 he said, "The Lord gave, and the Lord has taken away; blessed be the name of the Lord" (NKJV).

This story pits the faulty theology of the antagonist, Satan, against the flawed theology of the protagonist, Job. By the time we reach the end of Job's story we discover that neither theology is adequate for salvation.

The devil's theology said Job was faithful because he was blessed. What a testimony from the devil. Job's theology said his blessings were the fruit of his faithfulness. The devil's strategy suggested to God that a breach in Job's blessings would yield a breach in his devotion to God.

While Job's theology survived suffering, it could not survive the cognitive dissonance brought on by physiological, psychological, sociological, and theological perspectives. Job reasoned, sooner than later, that God should be doing something about his dilemma to bring deliverance. Like Job, we are often anxious for God to do something about sin, especially when it affects us.

The story is further complicated by Job's Facebook friends, Eliphaz, Bildad and Zophar. They subscribed to the doctrine of "Religious Privilege"—God blesses the righteous and afflicts the wicked. Their counsel, while logical, was not spiritual. Sound counsel came from Job's friend, Elihu, who said, "God is trying to teach you something." Although, this was sound counsel, it was not profitable for Job. I would simply interject, here, that Jesus suffered greater than anyone and He was without sin, which contradicts the friends' doctrine.

One researcher at Cambridge University in the UK stated, "It doesn't matter in what order the letters in a word are, the only important thing is that the first and last letter be in the right place. The rest can be a total mess if you can still read it without problem."

I'd like to suggest to you that the Christian who starts his or her day off with God and ends it with God, has victory throughout the day regardless of the chaos the enemy plans in between.

Humility taught Job that God has a purpose in whatever He allows in our lives. Our value is determined by the owner, and that owner is God! Although we may not always understand it, God is always doing something good! ■

— VIRGIL S. CHILDS

JULY 13

THE TYRANT SHALL BE NO MORE!

"The tyrant shall be no more...all those alert to do evil shall be cut off—those who...deny justice to the one in the right" (Isaiah 29:20-21 NRSV).

No matter your origin or background, the prophet Isaiah ignites a potpourri of emotions in his book. Isaiah's entire work is a capstone; a treasure trove for conscience and religious liberty fighters. Justice and judgment—next to mercy and compassion—are probably the biggest themes in Isaiah. So it's no coincidence that the interpretations, applications, and theological commentaries people walk away with are equally controversial and compelling.

Nevertheless, Isaiah's words are not only an indictment on passivity and inaction, but they are also poetic, powerful and prophetic. We see echoes of Isaiah's pathos captured in the sentiments of patriarchs and modern day monarchs, particularly the great Emperor Haile Selassie I who said, "Throughout history, it has been the inaction of those who could have acted; the indifference of those who should have known better; the silence of the voice of justice when it mattered most; that has made it possible for evil to triumph."

Isaiah's message transcends time, culture, status and ethnicity. It really does not matter if the tyrant is the Assyrian King Sennacherib, a German chancellor, an American president, or an African despot—no justice no peace.

While not all people groups experience the same sense of desperation and injustice, if members of your family were pillaged, raped, shackled and chained together for three months in a dungeon under a church chapel waiting for another two months to be shipped across an ocean, you would not only desire justice, you would crave it like a man buried alive.

Isaiah offers refreshing, resounding hope to the cries for justice, coming from: tent cities in California; wars around the world; and the relentless, systemic violence in suburbia. He offers hope to the one in three women who are beaten or sextorted, or otherwise abused. He offers hope to child abuse victims, victims of child marriage, or victims of female genital mutilation. He offers hope to families living with intermittent, excruciating memories and current episodes of racism and atrocities in the "land of the free and home of the brave."

Isaiah promises "the tyrant shall be no more." There's hope for the hopeless and rest for the weary (Isaiah 11:1-9). Whatever your tyrant, it shall be no more!

Personalize this promise today: My _ _ _ _ _ _ shall be no more! ▮▮

— RUSSELL S. LEWARS

JULY 14

THE RELUCTANT SUPERHERO

"'For I know the thoughts that I think toward you,' saith the LORD, 'thoughts of peace, and not of evil, to give you an expected end'" (Jeremiah 29:11 KJV).

There are times in our lives when it is clear that God wants us to represent Him. Many of us, due to our fears or our want for privacy, fail to do God's will. Whenever I am asked to do a certain task, I prefer to have a clear idea of what the outcome will be.

When I was in high school and my track coach would tell us to start running, I would often ask how far and for how long. Without these demarcations, I would feel reluctance rather than motivation as it seemed I would be running an unspecified distance.

Nestled in the Old Testament of the Bible, we find a reluctant superhero that had the prophetic superpower of discerning God's call and direction. In the book of Jonah, we see a man that God had directed to go to Nineveh—a rebellious, abhorrent city—and implore them to turn away from their wickedness to save them from certain destruction.

While Jonah fully understood the will of God, he didn't see how it made sense to waste his time trying to save a city that was, in his opinion, too far gone. Instead of running towards the destination God had set for him, he chose to run away.

Jonah decided to hide on a ship headed in the opposite direction, when a violent storm suddenly appeared, instilling fear in the ship's crew members. It was at this moment that Jonah's spiritual superpowers of discernment kicked in as he quickly realized the storm was from God. Questioning why he'd even attempted to hide from God, he told the crew to do the only thing that would get rid of the storm—throw him overboard.

Three days after getting swallowed by a whale and being delivered to the shores of the mission field, Jonah finally submitted to the will of God. To his surprise the people of Nineveh were very receptive.

Each and every one of us has been given God-ordained superpowers that, under the guidance of the Holy Spirit, should be used in promoting God's cause. We will never reach our full potential unless we activate those powers and use them for His glory.

So the next time God tells you to run, don't ask Him how far or how long, and don't doubt His judgement by running the other way. Just follow His will, trusting that He knows where you need to be, and use your superpowers for Him. ■

— ONEIL MADDEN

JULY 15

RISKY BUSINESS!

"So the king told Ebed-Melech, 'Take thirty of my men with you, and pull Jeremiah out of the cistern before he dies'" (Jeremiah 38:10 NIV).

You may have heard it said, "Show me your friends and I'll tell you who you are."

Now ask yourself: What business would any high ranking, foreign diplomat assigned on a special mission to a nation in demise, and so close to annihilation, have in common with someone viewed as public enemy number one? And would it be wise to associate yourself with this, so called, God-sent messenger spouting an inconvenient truth filled with doom and damnation upon his own people?

Here is the story of two very different individuals, namely the prophet Jeremiah and an Ethiopian official called Ebed-Melech. Their paths cross and destinies entwine in a saga of moral necessity versus political vice and intrigue.

God had reached His limit with Judah's relentless idolatry and immoral decline, especially those in Jerusalem, the nation's capital, under the rule of King Zedekiah. He declared judgment upon the city and its people to destroy it using Babylon. And Jeremiah is sent to tell them.

In Jeremiah 38:1-5, Jeremiah is placed under house arrest in King Zedekiah's palace, yet he continues to share God's message with the people. However, a spy overhears what is said, reports it to the king, and a death warrant for treason is issued.

Privately, Zedekiah respects Jeremiah, yet he lacks the moral and intestinal fortitude to stop his men from doing what they desire. Political necessity and survival mean more to the king than to trust and depend on God.

Zedekiah washes his hands, but allows Jeremiah to be taken out of prison, thrown down into a deep cesspool of rising mud, and left to suffocate and die.

Enter Ebed-Melech. He hears of the plan and is deeply moved to do something to help Jeremiah, but there was one major problem. Policy dictates that diplomats who interfere in another country's affairs without permission could face dismissal, disgrace or even death itself.

Ebed-Melech recognizes the stakes are high and he has much to lose if he intervenes. Now reflecting upon his own life and Jeremiah's, he realizes the prophet's life is much like his own—filled with loneliness, rejection, and pain in order to serve others.

Ebed-Melech's makes up his mind. Quietly he goes and intercedes with the king to save Jeremiah's life, and succeeds. God delivers both Jeremiah and Ebed-Melech, to live out their days in peace (Jeremiah 39:11-18).

Risky business God's way means daring to stand for God and to speak inconvenient truth to power on behalf of the powerless; to suffer, giving voice to those who are silenced right now, or wherever your next assignment takes you. ■

— KINGSLEY O. PALMER

JULY 16

SILENCE IS NOT AN OPTION!

"'So I sought for a man among them who would make a wall, and stand in the gap before Me on behalf of the land, that I should not destroy it; but I found no one. Therefore, I have poured out My indignation on them; I have consumed them with the fire of My wrath; and I have recompensed their deeds on their own heads,' says the Lord God" (Ezekiel 22:30-31 NKJV).

This is what the prophet Ezekiel said in Ezekiel 22:26-29 concerning the religious and government leaders of his day.

God says I am angry because your priests are violating my laws and desecrating my holy day. Your politicians have become like wolves prowling, killing, and taking whatever they want. And your preachers are covering up for the politicians by pretending to have received visions and revelations. They say that this is what God says when He has not said a thing. And when leadership becomes corrupt and widespread, it is the poor and needy who are left abused (MBV).

Priests: These men were responsible for instruction in the law and guarding the holiness and purity of the temple. They were to make a clear distinction between holy and worldly, the clean and unclean. Instead the priests violated the laws of God, distorted the line between the holy and the profane, with blinded eyes to defiling the Sabbath. Yet the prophet warned them, "Silence is not an option!"

Government Officials: "Officials" is used in this context by Ezekiel to refer to those appointed as government officials rather than nobility. These officials were compared to wolves attacking and tearing their prey. They were supposed to serve the people, but instead had made them their victims. Silence is not an option.

Prophets: These spokesmen were to serve as the moral and spiritual conscience of the nation. Instead of preaching against sin, they gave false prophecies and lying divinations; they whitewashed sin in general. In the face of the impending destruction of Jerusalem and fall of Judah, they continued to preach peace and safety. And Ezekiel warned them that God's "Silence was not an option."

People of the Land: What kind of society would such leadership produce? It should come as no surprise that it was filled extortionists, robbers and oppressors. They were inhospitable to strangers while protecting those who subverted justice. Their society was a showcase of violence, greed, and indifference to the poor, the weak and the suffering, with a general apathy towards God's Word. The lack of discipline in the homes, and sexual indiscretions became commonplace; a general lack of moral restraint became the order of the day.

In conclusion, I would like to repeat the words of a prominent leader in the nation's capital, Rear Admiral, Dr. Barry Black, chaplain to the U.S. Senate, in a recent address to Senators. He stated, "Silence is not an option. All of us are accountable to Jehovah and we will reap what we sow," as he referenced the prophet Ezekiel.

To paraphrase Edmund Burke, all that is needed for evil to prevail is for good men and women to do or say nothing. Will silence still be your option? ■

— DONALD MCLEOD

JULY 17

GOD'S HEROES

"Shadrach, Meshach, and Abed-Nego answered and said to the king, 'O Nebuchadnezzar, we have no need to answer you in this matter... our God whom we serve is able to deliver us from the burning fiery furnace, and He will deliver us from your hand, O king. But if not, let it be known to you, O king, that we do not serve your gods, nor will we worship the gold image which you have set up" (Daniel 3:16-18 NKJV).

They are "stand out" famous in biblical literature. Every preacher and Bible teacher has preached or taught from this story, found in Daniel 3.

Their faithfulness, loyalty and commitment to God is legendary.

Shadrach, Meshach and Abednego (SMA) were heroes for God.

From the beginning of the book of Daniel, they are in the forefront. Along with Daniel, they made a quartet of quantum holiness.

Captured and brought to the king's court to be educated and trained in the culture of Babylon, the four of them made a decision not to eat from the king's table. Undoubtedly, it included unclean food and items offered to idols. They chose to eat a vegetarian or plant-based diet.

Later, a death decree was announced because the wise men of the kingdom could not recount and interpret King Nebuchadnezzar's dream. Daniel begged their supervisor to take them to the King. Daniel asked for time, which was granted. Having pre-established access to Yahweh through their prayer life, recorded in Daniel 1, they prayed and God answered by revealing the dream and its interpretation.

On the Plains of Dura, Nebuchadnezzar assembled all the government officials before a 90-foot tall statue. Many expositors believe the head of this statue resembled the king. He wanted the worship of the people, and this was to be demonstrated by their bowing down to the statue of him when the music played.

Music played; people bowed down, all except SMA. They didn't bow to the music, and stood out like a sore thumb. A proverb says, "the nail that stands out gets pounded down." God's boys were about to be pounded.

"Ratted out" by others participating that day, they were summoned to the king. When questioned, they admitted they had disobeyed the royal orders. Nebuchadnezzar offered them a second chance. They declined his offer, stating their trust in God. Enraged, the king ordered the furnace to be heated seven times hotter than normal.

The showdown was on. Nebuchadnezzar had them thrown into the furnace. It was so hot, the men who tied them up and threw them into the furnace perished by its heat.

But, the Son of God showed up and chilled the fire, preserving them completely. The only thing that burned was the ropes binding the three Hebrew boys! More than amazing, it was miraculous. As a result, King Nebuchadnezzar exalted the God of SMA!

Here are the take-aways from this event:

- First: Faithfulness in small things prepares us for faithfulness in large things.
- Second: When the "chips are down," God shows up and shows out.
- Third: This was miraculous; and the miraculous always leads to someone's conversion.

We can be heroes for God by being faithful to Him, no matter what. ▮

— RICARDO GRAHAM

JULY 18

AMOS: GOD'S MESSENGER FOR A SPECIAL TIME

"The words of Amos, who was among the sheepbreeders of Tekoa, which he saw concerning Israel in the days of Uzziah king of Judah, and in the days of Jeroboam the son of Joash, king of Israel" (Amos 1:1 NKJV).

Amos was one of God's most prolific messengers. Although considered a minor prophet, he had a jealous passion for God's reputation for being gracious, merciful, fair and equitable with all people. Amos valued it and had much to say about oppression and the condition of the poor in Israel.

During his time, there were at least three major areas of concern that deeply bothered God's special messenger the most: 1) the nature of who God is; 2) the individual's role and relationship to God and what was expected; and 3) the role and function of a system charged with the responsibility for taking care of its people.

Through the wilderness years, Israel already knew how God had constantly provided for their every need, and who had protected and guided them through their 40 years of wandering till they crossed over into the Promised Land.

Long before they had arrived, God, in the books of Exodus, Numbers and Leviticus, had given them specific laws and instructions on how Israel was to honor Him as their Creator, and how to treat others.

Yet upon entering the land of milk and honey, Israel soon forgot where they had come from and what the God of Righteousness had brought them through. By the time Amos arrives he finds it hard to see the difference between God's so called, "Chosen People" from other nations around them. Amos, God's special messenger, is filled with righteous indignation, and being a former sheep herder and farmer, he declares in Amos 7:14, "I am not a prophet or the son of a prophet." Amos begins to deliver God's special message in the only way he knows how—the unfiltered truth to the masses, with no exceptions.

In reading the book of Amos it's hard not see how much the Lord is deeply grieved when nations deal treacherously with each other, or how they treat the weak and helpless in their societies who are crushed by the cruel and the powerful.

Nowhere in the book of Amos does the Lord ever accuse poverty for being the fault of the poor. This kind of behavior was offensive to Him. Yet greed and poverty forced people in Amos' time to sell themselves and their children into slavery, many of whose wealth had been built off the backs of the poor. If the Lord can show compassion for the widow and the afflicted, should He expect any less from His own people?

Elements of social injustices found in Amos can also be viewed from a universal prospective today. In Amos 5:24 he declares, "Let justice roll on like a river,[and] righteousness like a never-failing stream" (NIV).

Will you be that Amos for the 21st century who will, "Cry aloud and spare not?" ▮▮

— ERNEST LEWIS

JULY 19

WHAT DOES THE LORD REQUIRE?

"He hath shewed thee, O man, what is good; and what doth the Lord require of thee, but to do justly, and to love mercy, and to walk humbly with thy God?" (Micah 6:8 KJV).

The prophet Micah is not one that we hear a lot about. He is called one of the Minor Prophets, but he has a major message. When you study his book, you'll discover that Micah lived during the 8th century, according to the names of the kings recorded in this book. He is obviously a contemporary of both Amos and the prophet Isaiah.

Micah finds himself embroiled in a heated conflict between an angry God and an alienated and disenfranchised people. God was upset with His people because they had rejected His ordinances and were walking away with their backs facing Him. Now, the nation was suffering because of their disobedience and defiance.

The contextual setting of the book of Micah is that of a court room. God summons His people, as it were, to come into the court of law, and says, "State your case against me, because I certainly have a complaint against you" (Micah 6:1-2 paraphrased). It appears they were suing one another for breach of promise.

Again, God summons them and asks, "What have I done? Tell the world what you have against Me" (Micah 6:3 paraphrased).

God wants to know: Have I not done all that I know to do for you? Now look at yourselves walking in disregard, to become a recalcitrant people. You care more about yourUpon reading the sixth chapter of the book of Micah, he enumerates all the things God has done for His people. Then he records the people's response upon hearing how God cared for them, delivered them, protected them, and loved them.

Micah reminds them how God has been merciful to, and even forgiven, them. They respond by asking, "What offering should I bring when I bow down to worship the Lord God Most High? Should I try to please him by sacrificing calves a year old? Will thousands of sheep or rivers of olive oil make God satisfied with me?" Micah responds with these simple words: "The Lord God has told you what is right and what He demands: See that justice is done, let mercy be your first concern, and humbly obey your God" (Micah 6: 6-8 CEV) ▮▮.

— ROYAL HARRISON

JULY 20

RELENTLESS FAITH

"She replied, "That's true, Lord, but even dogs are allowed to eat the scraps that fall beneath their masters' table." " (Matthew 15:27, NLT).

As I write this piece, I cannot forget the look on my mother's face that my brothers and I witnessed the day our father deserted us. It was a day consumed with tears of pain and anxiety. Now she stood to lose everything her worn out immigrant hands had worked so hard to provide.

The prospect of being homeless with three kids and no roof over our heads meant losing us too. After mom finished praying, I looked into her eyes once more and saw unrelenting resolve and a steel-like stubbornness. For her to lose a battle without a fight was no longer an option.

The law of averages states that everything will work itself out in the short term. That was not true for my mother. It took some time, yet her faith never wavered. That law may apply to those who live a trouble free life, but not to those whose existence by itself is challenged every day.

Our hero's story is recorded in Matthew 15:21-28 and Mark 7:24-30, where things begin to go south, quickly.

In ancient times, Tyre and Sidon were bustling, prosperous, hedonistic cities, and once the epicenter of world's trade and commerce. At the time of the story, a Canaanite woman's birth, gender and ethnicity were not only a problem, but considered by many to be a curse.

The city's health care system was too expensive and well beyond her means. When the leaders from her own religious community were powerless to heal her daughter, her faith in them disappeared. Upon hearing that Jesus was in her neighborhood and had incredible powers to heal, this desperate woman set off to find Him.

Imagine entering a medical establishment expecting to get help, but as soon as they see you coming, see who you are or how you look, you're ignored. Your zip code tells your story and they already know what to do next.

She approaches and petitions Jesus, but is treated as if she is invisible or non-existent. That is bad enough. But the "dog and crumbs insult" she can't let pass. Relentless faith will not let her.

Ignoring the ignorant public, this woman looks directly into the face of Jesus. This Canaanite sister then delivers her Oscar-winning comeback, as she stands her ground, defends her dignity, and lets Jesus know crumbs or no crumbs, this dog's child is going to be healed today.

"And I am telling you, I'm not leaving," without your blessing. Do you have a problem Lovingly, Jesus not only grants this woman's request, but publicly recognizes and affirms her humanity.

In this encounter, Jesus goes out of the way to show His followers what relentless faith, looks like, feels like and does.

Now the question for you is, how relentless will your faith be in times of life's most difficult and impending trials? ■■

— KOFI OLIVER

JULY 21

WHAT'S IN A NAME?

"And the King will say, 'I tell you the truth, when you did it to one of the least of these my brothers and sisters, you were doing it to me!'" (Matthew 25:40 NLT).

An "Adventist" is someone who seeks to live life in expectation of the Second Coming of Christ.

It is easy to ponder, deliberate, and even applaud this, but in today's text, Jesus lets the disciples know that this is what He expects of all believers (Adventists). Jesus gives a lesson regarding his next Advent, with a picture of sheep and goats, saying that currently we are all in the pen together, but there will come a time of separation.

This separation is for three reasons: the first is for the purpose of inheritance. "Then the King will say to those on His right hand, 'Come, you blessed of My Father, inherit the kingdom prepared for you from the foundation of the world'" (Matthew 25:34, NKJV). Later in Verse 40, we see that when we show love in advocating for others, God is going to reward us for it at the Second Coming.

The next reason for separation is punishment for inactivity. In Verses 41-46, we see that when we don't live our lives for someone else's progress, promotion, or benefit, God is not pleased and there will be punishment. Sometimes we think we're O.K. just learning about, and loving Jesus. But Jesus says we must do something for the least of these or else we'll be in for a rude awakening.

Finally, separation will be based on the principle of inclusion. Jesus says, "'I tell you the truth, when you did it to one of the least of these my brothers and sisters, you were doing it to me!'" (Matthew 25:40). When we advocate for justice for the least—the last, the left out, the left behind—we are doing for "His" brothers and sisters. These are not just some unfortunate individuals, but those who are included as part of "His" family.

For those who have an issue advocating for others or even looking down on those who need advocates, they will have to change the trajectory of their outlook. Those people are Jesus' brothers and sisters. Those affected by the prison industrial complex, income inequality, unaffordable housing—injustice of any kind, are not just people "down and out on their luck," but family members that Jesus has entrusted to our care.

An "Adventist" is someone who seeks to live life in light of the fact that Jesus is coming back. I hope to live in such a way that I can receive that inheritance; in a way that I won't be accused of inactivity; and in such a way that Christ can say I was inclusive. ■■

— MARK L. HOWARD

JULY 22

THE GREAT CONFESSION

"So, when the centurion and those with him, who were guarding Jesus, saw the earthquake and the things that had happened, they feared greatly, saying, 'Truly this was the Son of God!'" (Matthew 27:54 NKJV).

It had been a long day for the Roman officer in charge of crucifixions, a centurion and a seasoned man in the trade. Everything about this crucifixion was different. The detained was accused of calling himself the Son of God, a claim worthy of the death penalty.

The centurion knew his job was to execute the criminal, not to decide if he was guilty or innocent, but things did not align as in other executions. Even the trial seemed sloppy and in a hurry. One of the most wanted criminals, Barabbas, was actually set free in exchange for this man?

Also, the convict did not behave like one. When one of centurion's soldiers was wounded by one of the disciples, the convict—just a suspect then—performed a miracle surgery, replacing the ear.

They ridiculed this convict, and spat in His face. They slapped Him around; crowned Him with a crown of thorns to hurt him, and made fun of Him. All He did was pray for them, that their sins of ignorance would not be counted against them.

Suddenly, things got a little crazier. The man was not supposed to die so soon. Crucifixions were meant to be long, shameful and painful deaths. But after this convict dies, what happened next shook him to his core.

The sun went dark, followed by a bad earthquake. And as if that was not enough, people started popping out of the cemetery! Yes, the convict dies but people are resurrected from the graves at the same time!

Unable to contain himself and his emotions, and from the depths of his soul, the centurion confirmed and responded to the question in everybody's mind: "This truly was the Son of God!"

We don't know what happened next. All we know is that against all odds, and against popular demand, he confessed this, the greatest truth of all time.

What about you? Are you confessing that Jesus is the Son of God, at the risk of losing everything? Are you confessing that Jesus is the Son of God to a politically divided nation, as you seek reconciliation? Are you confessing that Jesus is the Son of God as you advocate to close the gap that separates us in a socially and racially divided nation?

Are you confessing that Jesus is the Son of God as you work to eradicate systems of oppression designed to keep the poor, poorer and the rich, richer?

Are you confessing that Jesus is the Son of God as you reconstruct a meta-narrative that highlights the Son of God as the real Commander-in-Chief? A meta-narrative where our own stories intertwine with each other, making us brothers and sisters of equal value despite of our differences?

Our wounded world awaits the revelation of the children of God in their willingness to confess with actions that Jesus is the Son of God, indeed. ▮▮

— CARLOS A. CAMACHO

JOHN THE BAPTIST VS. HEROD

"'And you, child, will be called the prophet of the Highest; For you will go before the face of the Lord to prepare His ways, to give knowledge of salvation to His people'" (Luke 1:76-77 NKJV).

John the Baptist was a child of promise, born to Zechariah (a priest) and Elizabeth (barren for many years). His parents recognized the calling of God in their son's life even before his birth (Luke 1:76-77). John, Jesus' cousin, lived in the desert, ate locusts and wild honey, and wore clothes made from camel's hair—certainly not a fashion statement. His objective in life was to point people to Jesus: "The voice of one crying in the wilderness: 'Prepare the way for the Lord....'" (Isaiah 40:3). John had the privilege of launching Jesus' ministry by baptizing Him in the Jordan River.

Herod Antipas was the son of Herod the Great; yes, the same Herod the Great who ordered the death of all male babies after Jesus' birth. Herod's family was Edomite; they were converts to Judaism, and clever politicians. They solidified their political position by marrying Jewish royalty and befriending the Romans.

Herod Antipas eventually married Herodias, his half-brother's wife. They married after each divorced their spouses, against Jewish law (Leviticus 20:21). John, without holding back, challenged the legitimacy of the marriage with these words, "It is not lawful for you to have her" (Matthew 14:4). Mark 6:20 records that Antipas feared John, knowing he was a just man, and trying to protect John from his wife, Herodias, put him in jail.

On Herod's birthday, Herodias' daughter danced for him and his guests. Herod was so pleased that he swore he would give her anything she asked, up to half his kingdom. That must have been the greatest dance of all time. How foolish this hasty promise proved to be. The head of John the Baptist on a platter was her request after consulting with her mother. Because Herod valued the opinion of his guests more than his duty and obedience to God, he missed the prodding of God on his heart, and ordered John's execution.

What a contrasting character comparison—John pleased God and Herod pleased man. John lived a simple life; his only distraction came from the beauty of God's nature. Herod lived in the splendor of court life, where the intrigue of politics, backroom deals, and compromise were the norm.

Following the Lord and His word faithfully doesn't ensure peace in life, and as in John's case, it may even lead to death. John completed his life's task, pointing others to Jesus. As a result, he was heralded by Jesus as being a man of greatness (Matthew 11:11). Wow!

I want Jesus to say the same about me. Join me in saying yes to the calling of God in our lives, and pointing others to Him. ▮▮

— SONIA BARKSDALE

JULY 24

BUT DR. LUKE, YOU'RE NOT JEWISH

"He unrolled the scroll and found the place where it was written, 'The Spirit of the Lord is upon me, because he has anointed me to proclaim good news to the poor. He has sent me to proclaim liberty to the captives and recovering of sight to the blind, to set at liberty those who are oppressed, to proclaim the year of the Lord's favor'" (Luke 4:17-19 ESV).

I am grateful we are given four different perspectives on the "greatest story ever told." While I appreciate each of the "Gospel according to-s," Luke is perhaps my favorite version of the Jesus story.

One reason I adore Luke's Gospel account of Jesus is that he told the Jesus story after doing careful research. "It seemed good to me also," Luke writes at the beginning of his Gospel, "having followed all things closely for some time past, to write an orderly account for you, most excellent Theophilus, that you may have certainty concerning the things you have been taught" (Luke 1:3-4, ESV).

When I consider the fact that Dr. Luke was a gentile (an outsider), this feature of his gospel is even more intriguing; because perhaps Luke's version of the Jesus story is the most diverse. It features some of the most dramatic stories of God's love for the outsider, in all of Scripture. Through God's leading, Luke curated these wonderful examples of God's radical inclusion in his gospel (as well as in his sequel, the Acts of the Apostles).

One of the best examples of God's love for the outsider comes toward the beginning of Luke's Gospel, where he sets his readers up for what lays ahead in the Jesus story.

In Luke 4:16-30, Jesus visits his hometown on a Sabbath day and proclaims the Gospel in his childhood synagogue. In many ways, this "Spirit's manifesto" is a summary of Luke's entire Gospel. Often referred to as "the Gospel to the Gentiles," Luke demonstrates the radical inclusiveness of God's in-breaking Kingdom, inaugurated by Jesus.

The story provides a rich biblical and theological framework for our missional activities today. Dr. Luke's point? We must never become comfortable with our understanding of where God is at work in the world. The Spirit of Jesus is always out ahead of us, waiting to reveal His Kingdom to us in new places and in new ways, with new faces. Will you have the eyes and heart to see where God is at work around you today? May it be so! ▮▮

— JEFFREY GANG

JULY 25

PRAY FOR JUSTICE

"Then Jesus told his disciples a parable to show them that they should always pray and not give up" (Luke 18:1 NIV).

In Luke 18:1-8, the names of the woman and her adversary in this parable are not revealed, and the painful injustice she suffered is not identified, but her cause is clear; "Grant me justice." This woman's cause is the cause of Breonna Taylor, Tamir Rice, George Floyd, and countless other people whose names we do not know, but we know their cause; "Give me justice."

Sadly, the judge in this parable was unjust. "For some time he refused" to give her justice (Luke 18:4 NIV). By refusing to give her justice, he was working against her and violating her rights. Justice is a birthright given by God to every person. It is one of the inalienable rights guaranteed in the Preamble of the United States Constitution. Therefore, we must give justice—restore it swiftly every time it is violated.

Injustice is sin—the violent breaking not only of laws and statutes, but also the violent breaking of God, a person, a people, and humanity. It is a violent spiritual, moral, and psychological breaking of the victim and the victimizer. Christ on the cross is the ultimate manifestation of man's injustice toward his fellowmen and violence against God. Upon the cruel cross He was nailed, and died; the just for the unjust, that He might bring us back to God when we repent.

We know that injustice is deeply hurtful, and the damage is long lasting. Relief from the pain and healing from the damage will not take place until justice is served. That is why God requires it from all, for all.

This woman in the parable is introduced to us by Jesus as an example, because she stood up and fought back non-violently for justice until she got it. She showed up and protested non-violently to the judge against the injustice that hurt, damaged, and diminished her humanity. Finally, the judge gave her justice because her non-violent fight wore him down.

What was the secret to this woman's successful fight in finally getting justice? The secret strategy to her success was patient faith, non-violent protest, and persistent prayer. She fought for justice because it was the right thing to do for herself, her enemy, her community, and the judge.

From the example of this woman, Jesus encourages us to "pray always and not give up." Why prayer? In our non-violent fight for justice, prayer not only brings results, it also reminds us that God is with us in our fight—for justice. ▮▮

— JAMES E. SCARBOROUGH

JULY 26

LESSONS FROM PETER'S DENIAL

"Peter replied, 'Man, I don't know what you're talking about!' Just as he was speaking, the rooster crowed" (Luke 22:60 NIV).

In Luke 22:54-62, we read the account of a very sad but pivotal moment in Peter's life. He blatantly denies Jesus Christ, his Lord and Savior. This was the turning point in his life and relationship with Christ.

Up until this point, Peter was unaware of his capability of denying Jesus. This denial revealed that Peter's connection to Christ was based on the works he had done for Christ and his devotion to the ministry, but not on Christ alone and His merits demonstrated on the cross.

What can we learn from Peter's denial? In Peter's case, and ours today, such a denial indicates that "sin lies at the door." This is the type of malady that goes to the core and is not easily detected without a dramatic encounter with one's self and God.

As Peter did and his denial showed, perhaps we have based our relationship with Christ, and its validity, on three things: The correct doctrine (intellectualism), emotionalism (enthusiasm about the Gospel), and activism (doing great things for God). These things are not bad in and of themselves, but become a cover up to what God needs to do in us.

We need to know how God sees us, and who we are as sinners. Jesus had warned Peter that he would deny Him before the rooster crowed. Peter could not fathom such. We can Thank God, He will not leave us in this condition. In Luke 22:61, when Christ turned and looked at Peter, his heart was broken and a contrite spirit filled him with bitter tears and sorrow, and repentance of sin. This was the moment Peter became a changed man. Nothing he did meant anything, except his total surrender to Christ and Him only.

He now becomes an agent of change. He has the power and wisdom to live for Christ. Thus, we see a man that is growing in grace; who becomes a genuine hero of conscience and religious liberty.

See him, in Acts 11:18, champion the inclusion of the Gentiles becoming followers of Christ. In Romans 3:22-24, he fights against the impartiality of the grace of God—it is available to all—all have a right to the tree of life.

In Acts 8:14-24, Peter demonstrates his conversion from racial prejudice. Galatians 4:11-14 tells how he instructs the new believers that it is not necessary to return to the repressive teachings of the Mosaic Laws. In Galatians 3:28, he denounces physical and spiritual slavery.

Just as Peter found oneness with Christ, we must discover our deepest need—to know God, and rest in Him alone. Then God will equip us to serve our fellowman (woman) in protecting their human rights and promoting equality for all. ∎

— EDWIN F. BROWN

TEARING DOWN WALLS!

"And many of the Samaritans of that city believed on him for the saying of the woman, which testified, He told me all that I ever did" (John 4:39 KJV).

One of the greatest champions of conscience who ever lived is an anonymous Samaritan woman. Years before Paul would write about how Christ demolished the dividing wall between Jews and Gentiles, and how in Christ there is neither male nor female, but all are one, there was the woman at the well.

John records, in Chapter 4 of his Gospel, how Jesus, a Jewish man, is alone at midday at a well with a Samaritan woman. For our benefit, John reminds us that Jews and Samaritans had no dealings with one another. In fact, they hated each other. Each believed their religion was the true one, and the other, false.

Before the woman can do the honorable thing and depart, Jesus asks her for some water. She is astonished. Rather than comply meekly, she is startled out of her subservience, and engages Jesus in conversation. He offers her "living water." This is a biblical expression, dating back to Moses calling forth living water from the rock. The woman is intrigued, and perceives Jesus is a prophet. She questions Jesus about whose religion is true. This leads to Jesus stating directly that He is the Messiah.

Their encounter is interrupted by the disciples, none of whom has the audacity to chastise Jesus for speaking to a Samaritan woman, and doing so while alone, at that! But what follows is even more remarkable: the woman returns to her village, and preaches the good news of Jesus, the Messiah. Jesus is invited to stay, and for two days Jesus and His disciples enjoy the hospitality of the Samaritans. After meeting Jesus and hearing Him for themselves, many Samaritans came to believe that Jesus was, "indeed the Savior of the world!" (Luke 4:42 KJV).

This anonymous Samaritan woman became an early gospel evangelist, but also a champion of conscience. How so? Because liberty of conscience is an essential part of the gospel itself, since Christ forces no one to believe, but freely offers grace to all. This Samaritan woman stands as a testament to the fact that even those who regarded the Jews as enemies, could overcome bias and hatred and believe in Jesus. This solitary Samaritan tore down barriers of race and gender, that society has sought to maintain for centuries ever since.

God blessed this Samaritan woman. God help us to be inspired to tear down our walls so that all may believe that Jesus is, indeed, the Savior of the world. ▮▮

—ALAN REINACH

JULY 28

LOUD ACTION, QUIET WORDS

"Joseph, a Levite from Cyprus, whom the apostles called, Barnabas (which means "son of encouragement"), sold a field he owned and brought the money and put it at the apostles' feet" (Acts 4:36-37 NIV).

His wife, if he had one, probably threw Barnabas a pillow, closed the bedroom curtains and shut the door, suggesting he sleep on the roof after deciding to sell some of the family property to support the new group who were followers of Christ. His wife tried in vain to reason with him, and wondered what was wrong with him.

Jewish law didn't demand such extremes; a tenth was all that was required to be a good Sadducee, Pharisee or Scribe. Perhaps a few thank offerings on feast days and to remember those crying, "alms for the poor." So, "why are you making this heroic spectacle?" his wife could've asked. "Why are you giving your inheritance away and leaving your sons with nothing? To a Jew, selling land was a sign of debt owed and ensuing poverty. But Barnabas' heart was fixed; his decision was final.

The four Gospels do not provide insight into the developing character of Barnabas, or his motivation to love and encourage the early church with this more than generous offering. Yet, after being introduced to the Son of encouragement, Barnabas is chronicled 32 more times.

Whatever sparked his love for God and people took him on a life-long journey of standing up for social justice in incredible ways.

Barnabas was a Levite from Cyprus, a large wealthy island in the Mediterranean. His native tribe, the Levites, was part of the second tier of priests, and apparently not big talkers. The only quoted words of Barnabas in the Bible are attributed to both he and Paul, in Acts 13:46. (Whenever Paul spoke, it was Barnabas who did the follow up.)

Barnabas was a man of action, intent on social justice. Upon meeting Saul, who later became Paul, the apostle recognized Saul's authentic conversion and asset to "the Way." So Barnabas boldly took him to meet the apostles. Barnabas was more intrigued by Saul's present than his past. Surprisingly, Barnabas became Saul's personal mentor

As a matter of fact, Barnabas was often sent to encourage congregations to deliver gifts to the elders, and to plant churches. Barnabas and Saul's ministry had a tremendous impact on the spreading of the Gospel.

Barnabas' lifelong service to God and people may be over shadowed when compared to Peter, James, John or even Paul. But his bold faith, extreme generosity, and life of service to the Gentiles, to the downtrodden, and to the believing Jews, is a powerful demonstration of Christian love and practical social consciousness. Barnabas, son of encouragement, truly lived up to his name. ■

— SALI BUTLER

JULY 29

ISSUE SETTLED—PART 1

"Then Peter opened his mouth and said: 'In truth I perceive that God shows no partiality. But in every nation whoever fears Him and works righteousness is accepted by Him'" (Acts 10:34-35 NKJV).

As I think about Peter's conversion experience and that of many Christians today, it seems like the same "soup warmed over." We seem to have made positive gains against racial inequalities and social justice issues, only to be confronted by the harsh realities that we've only kicked the can down the road a bit, leaving much yet to be done in our hearts.

Peter's issue with the clean and unclean is still an issue today, isn't it? You would have thought that by the time we arrived at Acts 10 and 11, Peter would have already settled the issue that all men and women were created equal in the eyes of God. The same God, Jesus, served notice previously.

"Simon, Simon! Indeed, Satan has asked for you, that he may sift you as wheat. But I have prayed for you, that your faith should not fail, and when you have returned to Me, strengthen your brethren" (Luke 22:31-32 NKJV). What was missing in Peter's conversion experience was his need to overcome prejudice for others.

After Peter sliced off the ear of one of the soldiers sent to arrest Jesus, only to have a Jesus restore it, he could have learned the truth of the matter. One would think that being forgiven by Jesus for lying that he even knew Him, would have motivated Peter to forgive the Romans. I mean friend, Jesus made you the leader of His church with an assignment: "If you love Me Simon, feed My lambs who need to be fed and My sheep who need to be watched and guided. You don't get to pick and choose, Peter, who are the lambs and the sheep" (John 21:15-17 paraphrased),

Yes, Simon Peter has put his knife away, hopefully, and isn't cursing as he once did. He still has some racism issues in his heart against Romans that need to be dealt with if he's to become the true leader of others.

In Acts, Chapter 10, Peter is challenged by God to confront the racism that still existed in his heart.

The Lord used a sheet of unclean animals in a time of hunger for Peter, to get his attention and immediately Peter determines that there's more to this vision than might be imagined at first glance.

Someone rightfully said, "confession is good for the soul," and in Acts 10:28 Peter confesses the biases the Jews had for anyone outside of themselves. "You know how unlawful it is for a Jewish man to keep company with or go to one of another nation. But God has shown me that I should not call any man common or unclean" (NKJV).

It is difficult, friends of mine, to strengthen the brethren when you are struggling with your own personal racism. Peter goes on to settle the issue in his heart, with God's help, that all human beings are created equal in the eyes of God. ▮▮

— WILLIE JOHNSON, JR.

ISSUE SETTLED—PART 2

"And since God gave these Gentiles the same gift he gave us when we believed in the Lord Jesus Christ, who was I to stand in God's way?" (Acts 11:17 NLT).

The year was 1992, my second year at Southwest Adventist College as a theology major, when I decided to resurrect my literature evangelism ministry in Keene, Texas and surrounding areas.

I felt led by God to canvass a mobile home park, and I knocked on the door of a gentleman named Robert, several times. Once he opened his door, there stood before me a Charles Manson look-alike in the flesh.

The demonic and hateful look on Robert's face suggested that perhaps he really was either the lead actor in "Helter Skelter," or Manson himself had escaped and I just wasn't aware of it. He just stared at me until his wife and son walked into the room, smiling, and began talking with me. What a relief that was for sure!

Robert's wife invited me in and I soon discovered that God was contending with Satan for the soul of her racist husband and his family. Without saying a thing Robert began to weep uncontrollably, and after what seemed like an eternity, he told me his story of all the evil things he had done to people of color. He had burned crosses in the yards of black people and their churches, and many other hateful things. He was raised Seventh-day Adventist, which means nothing if you haven't settled the issue of racism in your own heart.

I prayed for Robert and his family, as his wife joined him in tears of both remorse and joy. He is now a baptized deacon in the church into which he was born and raised, and we are brothers in Christ who love each other to this day. He finally settled the issue in his heart.

Our featured texts, Acts 10:34-35 and Acts 11:17, point out three things that are relevant in our battle against racism and social justice today, among Christians:

1. God shows no partiality towards people. Paul states as much in Acts 17:26: "And He has made from one blood every nation of men to dwell upon all the face of the earth, and has determined their pre-appointed times and the boundaries of their dwelling" (NKJV). James, one of the leaders of the church in Jerusalem, points this out as well in James 2:1-13.

2. The Lord Jesus accepts anyone who fears Him and is willing to be born again by way of the indwelling of Jesus leading them to righteous living.

3. You have to take a stand when it comes to racism and social justice issues. Peter defines God's grace in Acts 11:17; "If therefore God gave them the same gift as He gave us when we believed on the Lord Jesus Christ, who was I that I could withstand God?" (NKJV).

Have you settled the issue in your heart? ■

— WILLIE JOHNSON, JR.

JULY 31

HERO OR VILLAIN?

"There is neither Jew nor gentile, neither slave nor free, nor is there male and female, for you are all one in Christ Jesus" (Galatians 3:28 NIV).

The satisfaction in Saul's smile at the news of the increased numbers imprisoned, contrasted with the inverse torment on Steven's battered face. Saul had brought justice for the purity of his Jewish elite traditions. His eyes glanced at the spurted blood from a stone that found its target on Steven's head. Meanwhile, hiding Christian neighbors, hearing screams from next door, crouched and shrank a little lower in fright, wondering when the soldiers would find and chain them. The laws of Moses and the Jewish race, and its future, were again protected from gentile contamination.

Gamaliel, Saul's teacher at the foremost Jewish "seminary," would have praised him for his zeal, and his strict adherence to the laws and precepts. Jews were the chosen people, favored above others, right, and therefore entitled to persecute, chastise, and even kill others who deviated from their teachings. Eradicating the Christians, Saul was a hero to the Jewish elite. But to the new Christian minority, he was a villain. With love and reason extinguished by his fanaticism, it took no less than Divine intervention to change his attitude. Then he became a villain to the Jews.

For the early Christians, Saul became a renovated hero, receiving the same fanatical barbarism that he meted out to others. For then, as Paul, he preached with equal zeal and conviction, that there was 'neither Jew nor gentile, neither bond nor free." His bashed face bled, his mauled limbs dangled, his clothes were torn by lashes, and he limped from harsh beatings inflicted on his feet. He emerged a scoundrel to the Jews, but a hero for the Christians.

As you anticipate the day ahead of you, do you see heroes or scoundrels in your pathway? Might you need protection, or might you be the hero or even the villain? Are you identified with a specific group: more educated, less educated; abused, abuser; ordained men, un-ordained women; oppressor, oppressed; straight, gay; conference, regional conference; conservative, liberal; foodie, vegan?

Perhaps today, we are called onto the nearby path: to choose between being the hero or the scoundrel for our health, our cultivated inner power, our rest, or our own replenishment from Jesus' forgiving and non-judgmental love. This could extend through us to all groups, assisting them, restraining them, modifying ourselves, and sacrificing ourselves when necessary.

Today, God is with you, no matter what your circumstance or choice. ■

— JOY ALEXANDER

AUGUST

THE PARABLES OF JESUS

This month you will take a tour of the parables of Jesus. Each author thinks of, and expresses their concept of the meaning of the parable. They also often highlight social justice implications of the meaning of the parable.

If we considered a theme for this month, it would be to invest time with Jesus. While this theme is not explicit in each devotional, it is implicit as a backdrop for the thought of the day.

The second coming of Jesus is nearer than it has even been. Recent occurrences demonstrate the truth that the final movements will be rapid ones. No one knows the day or the hour of Jesus' return, but we know He is coming soon!

As you read the devotionals for this month, I challenge you to reflect on your relationship with Jesus. Consider the practical meaning of His words. Determine how you will incorporate them into your life and lifestyle until He returns to take us all home for eternal fellowship with God. ▮▮

— JACKSON M. DOGGETTE, JR.
Director of Public Affairs and Religious Liberty,
Allegheny East Conference of Seventh-day Adventists

AUGUST 1

CHOICES AND CONSEQUENCES

"There was a man who had two sons. He went to the first and said, 'Son, go and work today in the vineyard.' 'I will not,' he answered, but later he changed his mind and went. The father went to the other son and said the same thing. He answered, 'I will, sir,' but he did not go" (Matthew 21:28-30 NIV).

In life we are all faced with choices each day the Lord our God wakes us up. Choices like what to eat, how to dress, and our attitude for the day, along with many other choices.

The three areas that are of vital importance to counsel with God about are:

1. The God you serve. Many claim to be Christian. But many, in reality, based upon their conversations, actions, thoughts, and choices reveal their true character without their spiritual awareness. Negotiable integrity and behavior wavers under popular opinion.

The God of heaven would have each of us represent Him fully and to the best of our ability. Prayers should go up every day seeking God's approval for the day's schedule. Map out your plans, submit them to God and allow Him to change whatever is necessary for your journey to the Promised Land.

2. The career you choose. The occupation we choose should be based upon the gifts God has placed in us for His glory. Evaluate your talents and gifts, and bathe them in prayer and commitment to the Lord Jesus Christ at the beginning of each day. Seek His guidance and the counsel of spiritual men and women of character who will be honest and forthright with you.

Many have chosen careers because of the paycheck. They may be traveling the burdensome highway of unhappiness that heaven records. God never meant for us to live that way. Parents, don't choose your child's career based on what you think. Seek God's counsel and truthfully observe their gifts and talents. God has given gifts to all, and when employed for His glory, this is where happiness, contentment and satisfaction are found. It will feel as if this is not work at all, and will give God the glory for the great things He has done.

3. The life partner you marry. Choosing a life partner is the most impactful decision you can make. Many are deceived by lust that masks as love. God seems so far away, not within reach, and deaf to our prayers. We sometimes rationalize our way into these arrangements. We have rationed out lies to ourselves.

God's grace is sufficient for each of us. He specializes in fixing broken vessels. Go to Him in prayer and seek His wisdom, counsel and strength to live according to His will, way and word. God is still in the blessing business and working miracles every day. My favorite writer says God has a thousand ways to bless us we know not of. You control your choices but not the consequences. Choose wisely. ▮▮

— CARLOS MCCONICO

AUGUST 2

IN PURSUIT

"Then Jesus told them this parable: 'Suppose one of you has a hundred sheep and loses one of them. Doesn't he leave the ninety-nine in the open country and go after the lost sheep until he finds it?'" (Luke 15:3-4 NIV).

My second daughter had just turned two months old when I decided to take her to a portrait studio. Also in tow was my other daughter, who was just shy of being two. As we sat in the waiting area, it became clear to me that keeping my toddler still would be a challenge. She repeatedly darted out of the studio into the "wonderland" of the adjoining department store, and each time I guided her back inside.

Soon it was time for our photo session. I quickly became occupied with outfit changes and conjuring up cute baby giggles. Before I knew it, my toddler was nowhere in sight. My child was lost! I was flooded with the fear of her being abducted, and devastated at the thought of how overwhelmed she must be.

After saying a prayer and frantically searching, I heard an announcement over the loud speaker about a lost child at the customer service desk. As I made my way to her, I saw her little face brighten as she saw me approaching and ran toward my welcoming arms. She was found!

Similarly, in the parable of the lost sheep, the shepherd lost one of his own. I imagine the love for his sheep was comparable to that of a parent and child, and the pursuit of the missing member was instinctual.

Jesus shared this story as a lesson to the Pharisees who challenged his relationship with sinners. How could He fraternize with people who did not believe or practice as they did? Jesus, however, hoped to illustrate that just because individuals may have lost their way or may not have come to know the truth, does not mean they deserve to be avoided or discarded. Instead of shunning sinners, Christianity should activate a desire to see everyone return to the arms of safety.

The same counsel applies to us today. We can be quick to judge, disparaging others for their poor choices. In some ways, we can encourage them to stay lost by our judgmental actions toward them. However, we see when the shepherd was reunited with his sheep, he did not flog it to teach it a lesson, but rejoiced; just as I did when I found my lost daughter.

Praise God that He loves us so much, He believes we are worth pursuing, and desires for each of us to be saved. May we strive to treat our fellow man in the same manner—worthy of pursuit. ▮▮

— LATASHA HEWITT

AUGUST 3

THE RICH FOOL

"This is how it will be with whoever stores up things for themselves but is not rich toward God" (Luke 12:21 NIV).

The parable of the rich fool (Luke 12:15-21) was used by Jesus to broaden His response to a request that had been made of Him. One of His hearers, whose brother refused to share with him the inheritance from their father, asked Jesus to tell his brother give him his rightful share of what had been bequeathed to them (Luke 12:13).

Jesus immediately recognized the real problem was greed and warned against it. He pointed out that the value of one's life cannot be measured solely by the abundance of one's possessions (Luke 12:15). He then proceeded to expand on His assertion regarding the folly and meaninglessness of the selfish quest for material things, even at the expense of one's "brother" and without due concern for his needs. Jesus did this by telling the parable of the rich fool.

This rich farmer, the beneficiary of the iniquitous inequities of a cruel and oppressive socio-economic system, built his riches on the hard work of poorly-paid laborers. He appears bereft of any concern for the plight of the less fortunate, much less any inclination to address it. He represents those who live with the mindset that when you have more than you need, don't think to share it with those in need; just store it up for yourself. Such persons have no desire to share the "inheritance" they have received from the Father with their needy brothers and sisters.

While the parable shows this man's folly in pursuing material wealth without displaying any concern for the needs of others, the Bible speaks of another very rich man who used his wealth to help those in need.

The patriarch Job addressed the needs of the poor, the fatherless, the widows, the helpless, the perishing, the blind, and the lame (Job 29:12-16). He also sought to find out about other needy situations of which he was not aware (Job 28:16). He went even further, working toward eradicating socially-entrenched mistreatment: "I broke the fangs of the wicked and snatched the victims from their teeth" (Job 29:17 NIV).

In the parable of the rich fool, Jesus teaches the folly of the acquisition of wealth to satisfy selfish greed. In contrast, the life of Job exemplifies the selfless use of one's material resources to meet the needs of others. The call to this way of living was a prominent feature of the teachings of Jesus (Matthew 25:31-35). ■

— ORLANDO MONCRIEFFE

AUGUST 4

THE PARABLE OF THE TALENTS

"For to everyone who has, more will be given, and he will have abundance; but from him who does not have, even what he has will be taken away. And cast the unprofitable servant into the outer darkness. There will be weeping and gnashing of teeth" (Matthew 25:29-30 NKJV).

Talent is a natural endowment or special ability of a person. The Bible is clear that human beings are created in the image of God (Genesis 1:27). At birth we are endowed with certain natural abilities or, more precisely, talents that can be used to glorify God and serve others. God gives talents to everyone regardless of a person's belief in Him. There are times God desires to endow certain individuals with certain talents (Exodus 31:1-6).

While a person is born with natural talents, spiritual gifts, on the other hand, are given to all believers by the Holy Spirit. This happens when believers accept Jesus as their personal Savior and place their faith in Christ for the forgiveness of their sins (Romans 12:3, 6; 1Corinthians 12:11; 28-30; Ephesians 4:7-12).

In one of His "Kingdom sayings," Jesus spoke about the parable of the talents (Matthew25:14-30). A man was traveling to a far country and called his own servants and delivered his goods to them. He gave one five talents, another two talents, and to another one talent, according to their abilities. Then he immediately went on a journey.

When the man returned from his journey to settle accounts with them. The one who had received five talents worked with it and doubled it. And likewise, the one who received two talents gained two also. Both of them received the same commendation from the Lord (Matthew 25: 21-23). But the one who had received one talent dug up the ground and hid his talent in it. He brought the talent to the master and explained why he decided not to work with it (Matthew 25:24-25). His master described him as a lazy servant, took his talent away from him, and gave it to the one who had ten talents (Matthew 25:26-28).

I have learned several lessons from the parable of the talents:

- God gives talents to individuals according to their abilities, and those talents should be appreciated.
- You should make every effort to identify your talents and make the maximum use of them.
- God did not give talents to individuals for selfish gains, but for the benefits of others and for His glory.
- If you fail to use and develop your talent, it is wasted, and you become unprofitable.
- On the day of reckoning, you should be ready to give an account to God on how you used your talents.
- If you are able to give a good account to God of how you used your talent, you will have great reward (Matthew 25:21, 23).
- If you are unable to give a profitable account to God of how you used your talent, you lose the talent and suffer punishment for the unwise decision you made (Matthew 25:30). ■

— AMOFAH A. ASAMOAH

AUGUST 5

CAN I SPEAK TO THE MANAGER?

"So the last will be first, and the first last. For many are called, but few chosen" (Matthew 20:16 NKJV).

"What do you mean only one denarius? Do you know how long I've worked today? You saw me. I was here before the sun rose, back bent over, lifting these vases, tilling the soil, pressing the grapes, and feeling the excruciating heat of the sun on my body. No, I want to speak to the manager! I know what I deserve!" said a man we'll call "Richard," the laborer, as he argued with the Steward to collect his day's wages. Conveniently, the Manager walks in.

"What seems to be the problem?" He asks. Richard hurriedly repeats his concern (Matthew 20:1-12).

The Manager and Richard hold a deeply rooted, yet ever-transforming conversation. The honesty from Richard provokes the reader to wonder, who holds the authority to decide "wage distributions"? Where does my heart lie in this matter, and why does Jesus promote this revolutionary new world order on societal and economic equity?

Like the example of Richard, the increased time spent working in the vineyard may create feelings of entitlement and/or ownership. The increase of laborers as the day prolongs does not decrease your value in the vineyard. Instead, it promotes an environment of similar vision towards a common goal; salvation for all. The Manager provides the resources, thus, He is the one to decide how, how much, and to whom the daily "denarius'" are distributed.

The parable brings to light the heart motives of the laborers; are my actions of service for personal reward or for the collective good? The Manager asks, "Is your eye evil because I am good?" (Matthew 20:15). Do I advance in church and public affairs for a heightened view of self and progress to the next higher class? Or, do I faithfully serve in my current sphere of influence with a purity of heart?

As the Manager asks about our dissatisfaction with our pay, He simultaneously unveils where our eyes are placed and breaks down the promotion of an earthly, spiritual, classist hierarchy. No longer can we perpetuate an ideology that rewards "if I do more works, I get more benefits."

Thus, by paying the last first, and the first last, socially, the Master pinpoints that all are equal in His sight. Economically, we are all beneficiaries of the large price Christ paid for us on the cross. The Manager states that it was never by our works; it was never by our selfish intentions to run up the social and economic ladder as quickly as possible; it was never about the quantity of the denarius; and it was never by disregarding those "standing idly." It was always because God knew us before we knew ourselves, graced us with Himself and His abundant resources, and transformed us to become laborers who serve with a pure heart and a willing spirit.

So yes, we can speak to the Manager, but are we ready to receive His answer? ▮▮

— CHINYERE ERONDU

THE PARABLE OF THE SOWER AND JUSTICE

"Then he told them many things in parables, saying: 'A farmer went out to sow his seed'" (Matthew 13:5 NIV).

The parable of the Sower is one of the most popular parables of Jesus, recorded in three of the Gospels (Matthew 13:1-23; Mark 4:1-20; Luke 8:4-15). It is considered one of Jesus' longest parables.

Although the parable might seem very simple to us, when Jesus told it to the disciples, they asked, "why do you speak to us in parables?" And Jesus responded saying He spoke in parables that the spiritually blind, hard of hearing, hard-hearted and unrepentant might not be able to see, hear or understand and ultimately be saved (Matthew 13:10-17).

Some individuals reject the Word of God altogether. Some receive it, but soon it withers away. Others receive it, but it gets choked by the corruption in the world. They lose spiritual sensitivity and become calloused and unresponsive to the call of the Spirit. Only a few accept the Word of God and bear fruits from it.

While many commentators have spiritualized away the parable, others see in it questions of justice. For example, one might think of the issue in reference to environmental justice. People who have wholesome hearts will be doing all for the preservation of the earth, while those of the wayside soil, stony soil, and thorny soil will fail to appreciate the significance of climate change that is destroying the good earth.

Another viewpoint is from a social justice perspective. Some represent the good earth where the seed is sown to focus on the need for water purity, water conservation and issues of poverty and food scarcity. On the other hand, they categorize those who have hearts like the wayside, stony and thorny soils hearers, as having little care about soil destruction, water preservation, and air pollution.

The personal justice perspective purports that those with hearts as fertile soil will manifest love, compassion, grace, empathy, affection, and those other positive virtues that bring blessings to lives about them. While in contrast, wayside, stony, and thorny soils represent those with hearts that are selfish, lacking in compassion, grace, and empathy. Such traits result in communicating cruelty, violence, moral insensitivity, abusiveness, resentfulness, rage, and a lack of responsiveness to the critical needs of others.

The "Parable of the Sower" is about the diverse hearts of humanity, in which those with wayside hearts stand in contrast to those with the sound, healthy, and vulnerable hearts. The hard wayside, rocky, and thorny soil, or corrupt, depraved, cruel, spiteful hearts, disdain and scorn people. The good-hearted will seek to advocate, support, and affirm people.

While the parable speaks of the diverse hearts among human beings, it speaks of one seed—the Word of God. It is noteworthy that the injustices we experience in the world arise from hard, shallow or corrupt hearts, while the justice experienced come from kind hearts.

If you were asked where, on the spectrum of justice, you see yourself, what would you answer? Could you say, my heart is a good soil, or would you say, my heart is with the infertile soils? ■

— D. ROBERT KENNEDY

AUGUST 7

THE TWO DEBTORS

"There was a certain creditor who had two debtors. One owed five hundred denarii, and the other fifty. And when they had nothing with which to repay, he freely forgave them both. Tell Me, therefore, which of them will love him more? Simon answered and said, "I suppose the one whom he forgave more." And He said to him, "You have rightly judged" (Luke 7:41 NKJV).

Each guest reclined at the dinner table. The woman came by and stood at Jesus' feet and began to weep. As she wept, her tears fell on Jesus' feet, and she wiped them with her hair. Then she kissed His feet, and anointed his head with precious ointment (Luke 7:36-38). On seeing what the woman did, Simon—the Pharisee who invited Jesus to this feast at his home—became angry that Jesus accepted such courtesy from a woman with her reputation. This prompted Jesus to tell the parable of the two debtors in today's text.

Many focus on the teaching of the awesomeness of the forgiving grace of God. However, further reading of the parable reveals that Jesus challenged Simon for his neglectful behavior:

"Then He turned to the woman and said to Simon, 'Do you see this woman? I entered your house; you gave Me no water for My feet, but she has washed My feet with her tears and wiped them with the hair of her head. You gave Me no kiss, but this woman has not ceased to kiss My feet since the time I came in. You did not anoint My head with oil, but this woman has anointed My feet with fragrant oil. Therefore I say to you, her sins, which are many, are forgiven, for she loved much. But to whom little is forgiven, the same loves little'" (Luke 7:44-47 NKJV).

Jesus also challenges our debt-burdened culture. How do creditors treat those who are indebted to them? We know there is a mercilessness of creditors in our banking, mortgage, credit card, and student loan systems. Our other lending systems offer little fairness or equity to people of color and low-income communities. Understanding these inequities can cause us to manage financial strategies and resources accordingly. Knowing the median household income of blacks was $49,258, Hispanics averaged $59,486, whites averaged $68,145 and Asians averaged $81,131, according to a 2017 report by the U.S. Census Bureau, teaches us how to approach creditors and debtors.

Our best encouragement is to stay out of debt (Proverbs 22:7, 26-27). But in a credit-driven society it is hard not to create some debt, so we should search for credit systems that understand debt justice, or debt and forgiveness. We who have substance, like Simon, must learn to treat others with mercy. Those of us with little substance must avoid the loan sharks who prey upon lower income communities with their enormous interest rates. Taking advantage of others' misfortunes receives the toughest condemnations of God.

The lesson Jesus sought to teach from Simon's attitude is that we should not look down on others and take advantage of them. The lesson from the perspective of the creditor is to learn debt forgiveness. Sin is considered a debt. As God forgives us, so are we to forgive others. ■

— D. ROBERT KENNEDY

AUGUST 8

THE LOST COIN

"'Or what woman, having ten silver coins, if she loses one coin, does not light a lamp, sweep the house, and search carefully until she finds it?'" (Luke 15:8 NKJV).

The "Parable of the Lost Coin" is one among three parables in Luke 15, where Jesus spoke to illustrate the Father's concern in finding that which is lost, no matter where they are. It contrasts with the Pharisees and scribes who have no concern for the lost. In each of the three parables, there is joy in heaven every time the lost is found.

We might have lost things that might not be of value to us, but in these parables, the items were all valuable. For that which is of value, no matter the cost, there must be a great effort made to find it.

It might be that in your church there are members who have lost their first love, or they've lost a good recollection of the love of the Father. As a church, it is our responsibility to sweep the house; we must help them bring back to memory the time when they were in the shepherd's fold, the Father's house. It is time to go and seek those who, for one reason or another, are not coming to church; who were, at one time, part of the ten coins in the hand of the woman.

The lamp, which is a symbol of the Word of God, must be lit with the oil and fire of the Spirit. It is time for a revival in your church. We must light the lamp with the fire and oil of the Spirit of God.

The way we sweep the house is how we take away those things that are not benefiting our church. We must prepare the church for God's Spirit to do His work. We must sweep the house, putting away the traditions that do not benefit us in any way. As the woman was able to do a careful search, so God's church must get together in prayer, fasting, personal heart searching, and assessing our lives.

In the economy of heaven, that which was lost was of great value. There is no devaluation of that which has been purchased by the blood of the Lamb. The blood of Christ is ever valuable; it is always the most precious thing that cleanses us from sins, and it never runs out of its effectiveness.

In the parable, Christ is implying that the shepherd's responsibility is to find the sheep, the father the son, and the woman the coin.

We are to ask God to reveal to us what needs to be reformed in our lives and churches. How can we help bring back those who are lost inside and outside of our church? We need to ask God to reveal the reasons for the spiritual lethargy in our churches.

Let us notice that no matter the situation of the lost, in all three parables, there is a calling for others to come and rejoice, just like there is joy in heaven. The angels rejoice for the grace and love that have won back men's hearts to God. ■■

— FELIX M. AMPAROIS

WHO IS LYING AT YOUR GATE?

"But Abraham said, 'Son, remember that in your lifetime you received your good things, and likewise Lazarus evil things; but now he is comforted and you are tormented'" (Luke 16:25 NKJV).

At one point or another in our childhood, we have been reprimanded by our parents for misbehaving. When rebuked, we would often argue our innocence by saying, "I didn't do anything wrong!" This is how most of us measure morality. We believe we can only be held accountable for what we have done, not for what we have not done. Yet, Scripture reveals that even when we fail to act in doing the right thing, we are guilty of wrongdoing (James 4:17).

In the "Parable of the Rich Man and Lazarus," the wealthy antagonist is not guilty of being ignorant of the poor man's condition, but he is guilty of ignoring him. The rich man lived a life of luxury while Lazarus was lacking. One man was clothed in silks while the other was covered in sores. One man had a banquet table spilling over with food while the other longed for leftovers. Yet, this rich man would not help him, even though Lazarus was right at his front gate.

The rich man's problem was not a lack of knowledge, but a lack of compassion. He refused to use his privilege to clothe, comfort, and feed Lazarus. Though it is easy for us to condemn the rich man, we must ask ourselves, "Who is my Lazarus? Who have I been ignoring? Who do I have the power to help but I am not helping? Do I advocate or do I avoid? Do I cover my ears to the cries of those who "hunger and thirst for justice? (Matthew 5:6 NLT). Who is my Lazarus?"

We as a church, and especially as a nation, are guilty of ignoring those who are at our gates; the gates of our churches and our communities. We have been so blinded by our own privilege, that we have become indifferent to the suffering of others. If we continue to refuse to help the Lazaruses of our day, our faith will become futile and our holiness will be hollow. It is time for us to end our idleness, and to go liberate Lazarus.

At the eschaton, Christ will say to some, "When you refused to help the least of these… you were refusing to help me" (Matthew 25:40 NLT). Who is your Lazarus? Who is lying at your gate? There is no excuse for doing nothing. We are called to help Lazarus. ■

— ISMAEL S. WADE

AUGUST 10

PEARL OF GREAT PRICE

"'Again, the kingdom of heaven is like a merchant seeking beautiful pearls, who, when he had found one pearl of great price, went and sold all that he had and bought it'" (Matthew 13:45-46 NKJV).

The merchant searched high and low for goodly pearls. I imagine him going from city to city, from town to town, from port to port looking for something greater.

This is the same with all of mankind. We are all looking for something greater. We're never satisfied. If we put our trust in riches, we will soon find out it isn't enough. It can't satisfy us. If we put our trust in our occupation, we will soon come to the realization our occupation can't satisfy us. If we put our trust in people, we will realize they are incapable of satisfying us.

However, when this merchant, who was looking for goodly pearls, found just one pearl of great price that changed everything. Just like experiencing the unconditional love of God changes everything.

Jesus says, "He went and sold everything." This pearl was of so great value that this merchant did not have enough on him to purchase it. He could have said it costs too much, I can't afford it and walked away empty. He could have brought several pearls of lesser value, or a fake pearl that appeared to be of great value, but still would have walked away empty. But realizing the enormous value of the one pearl, this man goes and liquidates everything he owns. He sacrificed all because this great pearl was worth it.

We are the merchant who, when we find Jesus, count the cost and are willing to give up everything to follow Him.

Jesus is the merchant. We are the sons and daughters who needed to be found. When Jesus found us, He saw our great value. He went and sold everything by sacrificing Himself on the cross for us. Then, He purchased us with His own blood. ■

— KEENAN TYLER

AUGUST 11

LIVING IN THE TIME OF EXPECTANCY

"Then He spoke to them a parable: 'Look at the fig tree, and all the trees. When they are already budding, you see and know for yourselves that summer is now near'" (Luke 21:29-30 KJV).

As the disciples were leaving the temple with Jesus, they asked Jesus for a sign foretelling the destruction of Jerusalem and of the end of the world. As Jesus unfolded to them the various signs, His introduction was very revealing: "Look at the fig tree and all the trees..."

"The Fig Tree"

It takes three years for a fig tree to produce fruit. First, the fruit comes and then the leaves fill the tree indicating that the fruit is ready for picking. That is why fig trees are being studied for their ability to bring deforested land back to life. The fig tree has withstood much. It has never been in danger of extinction. It stands as a witness of fortitude. "Watch," Jesus said. We should see what Jesus showed us.

"All the Trees"

One tree can absorb as much as 48 pounds of carbon dioxide annually. One tree can produce sufficient oxygen to physically support the lives of two people. Trees cleanse the air, regulate the climate, preserve water, conserve the soil, and sustain humans and animals.

While trees have an important agricultural role in maintaining life, trees also have a historic significance and a prophetic role in preparing God's people for living in the time of expectancy! "Watch and pray," Jesus said. We should do as Jesus told us.

In *Testimonies to the Church, Vol. 9*, author Ellen White says,

"How many are studying the words of Christ? How many are deceiving their own souls and cheating themselves out of the blessings that others might secure if they would believe and obey? [Emphasis provided] Probation still lingers, and it is our privilege to lay hold of the hope set before us in the gospel. Let us repent and be converted forsaking our sins, that they may be blotted out. 'Heaven and earth shall pass away: but My words shall not pass away. And take heed to yourselves, lest at any time your hearts be overcharged with surfeiting, and drunkenness, and cares of this life, and so that day come upon you unawares. For as a snare shall it come on all them that dwell on the face of the whole earth. Watch ye therefore, and pray always, that ye may be accounted worthy to escape all these things that shall come to pass, and to stand before the Son of man'" (White, p. 268)

Bearing fruit is inherent in healthy trees. It is a legitimate expectation. The ways and means our Lord will provide for "all the trees" is that His blessings upon them will be brand new every morning, throughout every season. This will bestow that measure of faith in us to fulfill our labors before and, yes, even during the unfolding of the signs of the end. Watching and praying will yield fruit. ■

— MELVYN E. HAYDEN, JR.

AUGUST 12

TINY SEED, BIG RESULTS

"Another parable He put forth to them, saying: 'The kingdom of heaven is like a mustard seed, which a man took and sowed in his field, which indeed is the least of all the seeds; but when it is grown it is greater than the herbs and becomes a tree, so that the birds of the air come and nest in its branches'" (Matthew 13:31-33 NKJV).

There is a remarkable idiom which states, "big things come in small packages." It is beautiful to know the word of God takes this expression and unpacks the idea of just how Jesus, the storyteller, describes the concept of the Kingdom.

The kingdom of God is meant to be a system which shows growth process. It uses the illustration of the mustard seed as an example of little becoming much. This seed is considered to be one of the smallest seeds in the world. Some may consider the mustard seed to be insignificant when it is compared to other seeds, even other types of mustard seeds. The New Testament parable of the mustard seed in all three Gospels is describing the Brassica Nigra, which is a plant grown in the regions of North Africa. It was cultivated for its black and brown seeds.

Mustard seeds can grow in all types of soil, but the Brassica Nigra is best grown when the soil is warm. If the Niger species of the mustard is planted in a cold, nonproductive setting, it will wait until it gets warmer. I am intrigued with this seed simply because of its ability to wait on better conditions. The conditions of the environment must be at its best for the germination of the plant to grow and give the best product.

These seeds can hardly be seen by the eye and can be easily looked over. Jesus not only came to this earth to seek and save the lost but He came to pursue justice for the lives of those who are easily overlooked. The Master cares deeply for those who are faced with injustice, alienated and mistreated. The kingdom of God is not only for the big and lofty, but setup for those who are meek and mild. The kingdom of God is meant to bring growth and comfort to those who are less fortunate. It is a purposely designed field with great soil meant for the last to become first and the little to become much.

The kingdom of God is for the small, insignificant, and looked over. It is meant for the oppressed and the vulnerable to shine. In the event one of God's creations is being downtrodden, it is the responsibility of those seeking citizenship of this same kingdom to implement justice and fairness.

Christians, let us do our part in watering the mustard seed. ▮▮

— PATRICK G. GRAHAM

AUGUST 13

PARABLES AS A CENTRAL FEATURE OF JESUS' TEACHINGS

"And with many such parables He spoke the word to them as they were able to hear it. But without a parable He did not speak to them. And when they were alone, He explained all things to His disciples" (Mark 4:33-34 NKJV).

It's children's story time at church. There are some young people that race to get a seat, some who reluctantly make the walk to the front of the church, and still others who are carried or coerced by their parents. We push our little ones to get in the right place for the story with the hopes that the designated storyteller will share something worth listening to.

When the storyteller struggles, the children's story time seems to last for an eternity. When the storyteller does their job well, the entire congregation hangs on every word. It feels like the storyteller and the audience are in sync.

That's the power of a good children's story. It wraps the lesson into a memorable event that captivates the attention of children, while the deeper meanings are often understood by parents who look forward to the day when their young ones will "get it."

What would it have been like to fight through the crowd, searching for the perfect spot to sit and listen to Jesus? Imagine what it would have been like sitting by the Sea of Galilee and listening to Jesus paint clear pictures with His words.

Jesus is not speaking in far off tones. His stories are simple. They are relatable. He grabs artifacts from the culture that everyone would have connected with. The listeners could easily see themselves in the narratives. Sower and seeds made sense. Many in the listening crowd knew what it meant to have to decide between burying money or taking their chances with a money lender. A bridal party making extensive preparations for a wedding was part of the culture. The Scriptures teach us that whenever Jesus spoke to the people, He told them parables (stories).

So when Jesus wraps the truth of the gospel inside a story that the people would have easily understood, something amazing happens. Neural entrainment suggests that the brain wave patterns between storyteller and listener are closely in sync. Jesus wasn't just looking to entertain a crowd. His aim was to present the kingdom of God in a way that could be easily carried along as people retold the stories He shared. Jesus knew that transformative stories can help move people to action.

For those with open hearts and minds the parables of Jesus led to more questions or provided clarity. For those who didn't have an interest in going deeper, the good story was their reward. Either way the listeners were left with an easily repeatable piece of the Man called Jesus. In a world dependent on oral tradition great stories were king.

Today, stories still hold incredible weight. It should be no surprise that as we continue to share the stories of Jesus, that others will continue to be drawn to Him. ■

— PIERRE QUINN

MOMENTS OF MERCY

"'So which of these three do you think was neighbor to him who fell among the thieves?' And he said, 'He who showed mercy on him.' Then Jesus said to him, 'Go and do likewise'" (Luke 10:36-37 NKJV).

It was a beautiful day in the neighborhood; a beautiful day to have a neighbor. This day would prove to be like many others for Jesus, for there was another contestant in the crowd. An expert in the law, as the Bible designates Him, came to test Jesus. Jesus' ministry was plagued by representatives from certain religious groups who made public attempts to trap Him in battles of Old Testament rhetoric, semantics, and interpretation. Strongly opposed to the ministry of Jesus, they did not understand His message, support His mission, or affirm His methods. Their stubbornness led to bitterness, envy, hatred, and resentment.

Infiltrating the crowd, the expert in the law offered a pointed query; "And who is my neighbor?" Jesus responded with what has been popularly called the "Parable of the Good Samaritan." The masses were shocked by the parable and its implications. However, no one was more baffled than the religious expert. The parable exposed his prejudice, nearsightedness, and bias, for the last person he expected to be his neighbor was a Samaritan. Yet, the Samaritan saw what the priest and the Levite missed: a moment of mercy.

When do we miss moments of mercy?

We miss moments of mercy when we prioritize programs and positions over people. There is nothing inherently wrong with programs or positions. Prayer meeting, Sabbath school, Sabbath worship, Bible study, youth federations, and camp meetings have their place. Authentically felt needs are commonly met during these programs. However, the programs we plan and present can easily become about us. Likewise, the positions we are entrusted with can feed our egos, but empty our hearts. If we are not careful, we can wear a positional title so closely that we miss moments to practice what we profess.

We miss moments when we privatize our Christianity to our culture. Though we may not admit it, the Lord knows our hearts. We have refused opportunities to serve those outside of our preferred and comfortable cultural contexts. We have turned our eyes, leaving someone of "their own kind" to do the job. I contend that Christian maturation stretches us and pushes us beyond the boundary lines of all that comprises our cultural comfort zones, into relationships where we can show mercy.

Finally, we miss moments because we ostracize mess and mercy. Putting aside the primary reason for his own journey and setting aside his cultural differences, the Samaritan showed mercy by getting messy. Can you see him carrying the afflicted pilgrim into the nearest hotel, using his personal travel funds to pay for the room, and clothing the man in his personal wardrobe? Can you see him lifting the man's head and feeding him from his personal food supply, periodically attending to the fire to ensure the most comfortable temperature, and fasting from sleep so that a stranger would not die on his watch? That's mercy!

My friend, God wants you to maximize the moments in life that call for mercy. Will you be a neighbor? ■■

— RICHARD MARTIN

AUGUST 15

DRAGNET

"'Again, the kingdom of heaven is like a dragnet that was cast into the sea and gathered some of every kind, which, when it was full, they drew to shore; and they sat down and gathered the good into vessels, but threw the bad away. So it will be at the end of the age. The angels will come forth, separate the wicked from among the just, and cast them into the furnace of fire. There will be wailing and gnashing of teeth'" (Matthew 13:47-50 NKJV).

There He goes again! Jesus just can't stop talking about the kingdom of heaven. If there is anything I want to be known for, it's being an ambassador for the kingdom of God.

In this story, Jesus compares the kingdom of God to a net. Today, most of us associate a net with the internet, social network, or the game of basketball. But the original word, "sagene," means a dragnet. Fishermen would drop this dragnet in the sea and catch all kinds of fish. At the appropriate time, they would bring up the dragnet and inspect their catch. The good fish were kept, while the bad were thrown away. If you're not into fishing, like me, you're probably wondering, what does this teach us about the kingdom of God?

First, the kingdom of heaven is attractive. There is a magnetic pull that draws many people to Jesus. Why? Because He is the solution to every human problem. While many deride kingdom dwellers, undoubtedly, they crave the elusive peace we possess. Child of God, we have what the world is looking for, Jesus Christ! Confidently, let's share and live the amazing attributes of the King and His kingdom.

Second, the kingdom of heaven is controlled by the All-Knowing One. While the angels are tasked with separating the good from the bad fish, it is God who gives the directive. God is omniscient. He knows everything before anything. Hallelujah, God is in control! While we may detest the character and actions of the bad fish in the kingdom, it's God's job to evict them, not ours. Instead, as good fish, let's use our influence to encourage others to look to Jesus, the Author and Perfecter of our faith.

Today, I encourage you to boldly share the attractive attributes of the kingdom of God with someone who needs Jesus to turn their darkness into day, and bring the beauty of salvation in their lives. ∎

— WAYNE C. HOSTEN

AUGUST 16

TREASURE IN A FIELD

"Again, the kingdom of heaven is like treasure hidden in a field, which a man found and hid; and for joy over it he goes and sells all that he has and buys that field" (Matthew 13:44 NKJV).

When I think of a field, I find myself reminiscing about childhood and the joys of running free outside with siblings and friends. The sun is shining, birds are singing and life is great. If I think a bit harder, I can remember the scraped knees, briars poking into my skin, and unwanted mud puddles ruining my favorite shirt. The field wasn't always a place of uninhibited imagination. It often left scars and reprimands from parents because I had gone too far to be properly supervised.

Christ is with His disciples and He is reminding them the "kingdom of Heaven is like a treasure hidden in a field." The disciples know Christ is referencing the world as the field. Many would say the hidden treasure is salvation and we should do all we can to obtain it. I agree whole heartedly, and yet, I would like to invite you to observe this field from a different perspective.

What if Christ was that man and you are that hidden treasure He found in the field? Truly Christ was born, lived, died, and rose again so that He could have you, His hidden treasure.

You're not in Heaven, yet, but you know who owns the field you reside in. Life in this field is full of briars, mud pits, snakes, and unpredictable weather. There are also moments of peace and hedges of protection from the enemy.

Where did Christ find you in this world? Were you not hidden, waiting and longing to be found and hedged in with the protection of a loving Savior? Did you not feel the joy that can only come from Him sweeping over your life? Our Heavenly Father allowed Christ to redeem this wicked world so you, a treasure of God, could be found, loved and joyed over.

Take heart and know you are not living in vain. You have a Savior, who saw the treasure you are and gave everything just to have you. Will you not do the same? ■

— WHITNEY MACK

AUGUST 17

THE DOCTRINE OF LEGITIMATE EXPECTATION

"They come unto thee as the people cometh, and they sit before thee as my people, and they hear thy words, but they will not do them; for with their mouth they shew much love, but their heart goeth after their covetousness" (Ezekiel 33:31 KJV).

In administrative law there is the Doctrine of Legitimate Expectation which premises the expectation of fairness to everyone from the person in authority over them by a consistent practice demonstrated in the past.

In Matthew 25:1-13, Jesus told the parable of the ten virgins in order to expose details about the kingdom of heaven where there is equity and opportunity for all. Everyone has a legitimate expectation to be saved at His second coming. Jesus was careful with the details, because it would be those details that would expose a lesson to every generation.

The details in the symbolism define the historical and future values which will be placed on fairness by a merciful God. The virgins represent the followers of Christ. The lamps represent the Word of God, the oil is the Holy Spirit, vessels are our hearts, slumber is spiritual weariness, midnight is the darkest hour of spiritual darkness, the wedding is intimate faithfulness, and the Bridegroom represents Jesus Christ.

In the story, the ten virgins start out together toward the same legitimate expectation—meeting the Bridegroom. All carry lamps. All have oil in their lamps. All go to sleep. All understand there may be a delay (because no wedding ever starts on time). All respond to the midnight call.

As they travel together to meet the Bridegroom, some have no reserve oil in their vessels for their lamps. Jesus designates them as foolish. They profess to have a form of godliness, but deny the power thereof. They have not surrendered their lives fully to the inner working of the Holy Spirit's power, and their service and relationship to God dissipates so much that they are comfortable slumbering (and finally sleeping in the pews).

They have fooled themselves with their own self-righteousness. They have legitimate expectation to meet the Bridegroom, but they are unable to finish the work they started, and the door is shut before their arrival. Seeking the reward of relationship and faithful service, they came with a legitimate expectation saying, "Lord, Lord, open to us." But in Luke 6:46, Jesus said, "And why call ye me, Lord, Lord, and do not the things which I say?" (KJV). The foolish have sought no personal relationship with Jesus.

The wise, however, wake up with oil to finish the work of lighting the way to the marriage. They have filled the empty vessels of their old natures with the sanctifying oil of the Holy Spirit. Everyone who has that intimate relationship with Jesus has a legitimate expectation to meet the Bridegroom. ■■

— DENISE F. HAYDEN

AUGUST 18

CHARACTERISTICS OF JESUS' PARABLES—PART 1

"All these things Jesus spoke to the multitude in parables; and without a parable He did not speak to them" (Matthew 13:34 NKJV).

The parables of Jesus are rich with life-giving lessons. They are refreshing, interesting, and meaningful. Today, we are simply exploring two of the four primary characteristics of the parables, themselves.

A review of the parables of Jesus will reveal they vary in complexity and length. Sometimes, the parable is short and simple. Matthew 7:6 (NLT) simply states, "Don't waste what is holy on people who are unholy. Don't throw your pearls to pigs! They will trample the pearls, then turn and attack you." Only one verse of scripture but loaded with truth.

Matthew 13:24-32; 36-43 (NLT) represents a longer and more complex parable. Jesus' disciples heard the parable but did not understand it and asked Jesus to explain it to them. Jesus explained that parable directly and with two more parables. When he finished, He asked, "Do you understand all these things" (13:51 NLT)? When they said they understood, He added a final explanation, "… Every teacher of religious law who becomes a disciple in the kingdom of Heaven is like a homeowner who brings from his storeroom new gems of truth as well as old" (Verse 52 NLT). This is an example of a parable that is much longer and more complex.

A second characteristic of Jesus' parables is they vary in their use of metaphors, word pictures, objects and action. We can almost experience the sights as Jesus speaks of light, coins, lamps and treasure. We can almost taste a bite of good food as Jesus speaks of us as the salt of the earth. We can almost hear the sound of excited little children running to Jesus as He tells us what it takes to enter the kingdom of Heaven. Or feel the disappointment of going to a fig tree for fresh fruit to find nothing but leaves. Metaphors, word pictures, objects and action are all employed by Jesus to make His lessons more memorable and vivid.

Knowing Jesus' parables vary in complexity and length as well as in how He employs other tools adds interest, clarity, and indelible impressions.

We will explore two more characteristics of Jesus' parables in our next offering. ▮▮

— JACKSON M. DOGGETTE, JR.

AUGUST 19

CHARACTERISTICS OF JESUS' PARABLES—PART 2

"I will open my mouth in a parable" (Psalm 78:2 NJV).

Yesterday, we explored two characteristics of Jesus' parables. We learned His parables vary in complexity and length. We also learned Jesus' parables vary in their use of metaphors, word pictures, objects and action.

Today, we will learn two more characteristics of Jesus' parables. First, Jesus' parables exhibit different levels of meaning. What we mean by different levels of meaning is that some parables provide multiple lessons within a primary lesson. Examples of this characteristic can be found in the "Parable of the Good Samaritan" or the "Parable of the Lost Son."

The "Parable of the Good Samaritan" reaches its climax with the question, "Now which of these three would you say was a neighbor to the man who was attacked by bandits" (Luke 10:36 NLT)? The primary lesson is to answer the question, "Who is my neighbor?" But within that primary lesson are multiple lessons about culture, ethnicity and social interaction, to name a few.

Second, Jesus' parables often draw on human experience. The "Parable of the Yeast" (Matthew 13:33; Luke 13:20-21), the "Parable of the Lost Sheep" (Matthew 18:12-14; Luke 15:1-7), and the parable of the man who loaned money to two people (Luke 7:40-50) illustrate this point. Human experience draws people in because all humans have experiences and can relate to those that remind them of their own or introduces them to a new experience.

Jesus is genius in teaching lessons through parables that exhibit different levels of meaning and employ human experiences. We know you are being blessed through this month as you read the parables of Jesus. ■

— JACKSON M. DOGGETTE, JR.

AUGUST 20

RESPONSES TO JESUS' PARABLES

"'To those who listen to my teaching, more understanding will be given, and they will have an abundance of knowledge'" (Matthew 13:12a NLT).

There are at least three possible responses we can have to Jesus' parables. We can accept the truths they teach. We can reject the truths they teach. And we can choose to act upon what we learn from the lessons.

Examples of people accepting the truths of Jesus' parables can be found in Scripture. Matthew 13:51 is an example of people acknowledging they understand the lessons Jesus is teaching. "Do you understand all these things?" "Yes," they said, "we do" (NLT). Another example of this is found when the people were amazed by Jesus' teaching. "When Jesus had finished saying these things, the crowds were amazed at his teaching, for he taught with real authority—quite unlike their teachers of religious law" (Matthew 7:28-29 NLT). Finally, Jesus, Himself commended those who accepted His teaching. "But blessed are your eyes, because they see; and your ears, because they hear" (Matthew 13:16 NLT).

Many times, people rejected the truths Jesus was teaching. This, unfortunately, was often true of those who claimed to be God's representatives on earth.

The teachers of religious law and the leading priests wanted to arrest Jesus immediately because they realized he was telling the story against them—they were the wicked farmers. But they were afraid of the people's reaction (Luke 20:19 NLT).

Another time, Jesus exposed the rejection of those who claimed to be God's representatives on earth.

The Pharisees, who dearly loved their money, heard all this and scoffed at Him. Then He said to them, "You like to appear righteous in public, but God knows your hearts. What this world honors is detestable in the sight of God" (Luke 16:14-15 NLT).

Whether one accepts or rejects Jesus and His teachings, every parable demands action. "In the same way, let your good deeds shine out for all to see, so that everyone will praise your heavenly Father" (Matthew 5:16 NLT). "Hypocrite! First get rid of the log in your own eye; then you will see well enough to deal with the speck in your friend's eye (Matthew 7:4 NLT).

The parables of Jesus demand a response. I invite you to accept the truths they teach and order your life in line with Jesus' lessons. ▮▮

— JACKSON M. DOGGETTE, JR.

AUGUST 21

THEMES OF JESUS' PARABLES—PART 1

"Then he added, 'Every teacher of religious law who becomes a disciple in the Kingdom of Heaven is like a homeowner who brings from his storeroom new gems of truth as well as old'" (Matthew 13:52 NLT).

Jesus' parables can be categorized into themes. If you have read any of His parables, you can readily recognize some of these themes.

One of the themes is the kingdom of God. Often, the theme is introduced directly by Jesus. Mark 4:30 begins with, "Jesus said, 'How can I describe the kingdom of God? What story should I use to illustrate it'" (NLT)? There is no question that Jesus was about to describe the kingdom of God in the parable He was about to tell. Or, "Here is another illustration Jesus used: 'The Kingdom of Heaven is like a mustard seed planed in a field'" (Matthew 13:31 NLT). No one need guess what theme Jesus wanted to expound upon because He simply says it.

Sometimes, Jesus just launches into the story. The theme emerges as the story is told. We get the point when we see the situation unfold which prompted Jesus to teach through a story.

Tax collectors and other notorious sinners often came to listen to Jesus teach. This made the Pharisees and teachers of religious law complain that He was associating with such sinful people even eating with them! So Jesus told them the story found in Luke 14:1-3.

The story that emerges reveals the theme of how people enjoy a relationship with God. The theme of how to have a relationship with God is repeated in His parables of Effective Prayer (Matthew 7:7-11; Luke 11:11-13), the Lost Sheep (Matthew 18:12-14; Luke 15:1-7) and the Persistent Widow (Luke 18:1-8).

Another theme we can identify is the theme regarding right behavior. The "Good Samaritan" (Luke 10:30-37), "Building on a Solid Foundation" (Matthew 7:24-29; Luke 6:46-49), and the "Parable of the Barren Fig Tree" (Luke 13:6-9) illustrate Jesus' teachings regarding right behavior.

We will explore two more themes in tomorrow's devotional. ■

— JACKSON M. DOGGETTE, JR.

AUGUST 22

THEMES OF JESUS' PARABLES—PART 2

"The crowd was listening to everything Jesus said. And because he was nearing Jerusalem, he told them a story to correct the impression that the Kingdom of God would begin right away" (Luke 19:11 NLT).

We looked at the themes of the kingdom of God, how people enjoy a relationship with God, and the theme regarding right behavior. Today, we will look at two more themes that emerge from the parables of Jesus.

The time of the end is another interesting theme of Jesus' parables. This theme is expressed in different ways but is unmistakable. Although not directly stated, one cannot miss Jesus' intention in telling the "Parable of the Final Judgement" (Matthew 25:31-46). One group will be lost. One group will be saved. "And they will go away into eternal punishment, but the righteous will go into eternal life" (Verse 46 NLT). The same can be said of the "Parable of the Ten Bridesmaids" (Matthew 25:1-13), "So you, too, must keep watch! For you do not know the day or hour of my return" (Verse 13 NLT); and the Parable of the Three Servants (Matthew 25:14-30; Luke 19:11-27).

"Yes," the king replied, 'and to those who use well what they are given, even more will be given. But from those who do nothing, even what little they have will be taken away. And as for these enemies of mine who didn't want me to be their king—bring them in and execute them right here in front of me'" (Luke 19:26-27 NLT).

Some parables with the theme of the time of the end emphasize we must be ready for Jesus to return. Mark 13:33-37 reminds us we do not know when Jesus will return but we must be ready. "Don't let him find you sleeping when he arrives without warning. I say to you what I say to everyone: Watch for him!" (Mark 13:26-37 NLT). Luke 12:35-40 emphasizes "The servants who are ready and waiting for his return will be rewarded..." (Verse 37 NLT). So, we see different aspects of the time of the end theme in the parables of Jesus.

Finally, Jesus speaks of Himself as a theme in His parables. The "Parable of the Evil Farmers" in Matthew 21:33-46 is all about how people treat Jesus. "But when the tenant farmers saw his son coming, they said to one another, 'Here comes the heir to this estate. Come on, let's kill him and get the estate for ourselves!'" (Verse 38 NLT). How people treat Jesus was so important it was repeated in the Gospels of Mark (12:1-12) and Luke (20:9-19).

The two themes we discussed today are the time of the end and Jesus, Himself. Try to find the theme as you read the parables of Jesus. ■

— JACKSON M. DOGGETTE, JR.

AUGUST 23

UNDERSTANDING JESUS' PARABLES

"He replied, 'You are permitted to understand the secrets of the kingdom of God. But I use parables to teach the others so that the Scriptures might be fulfilled: 'When they look, they look, they won't really see. When they hear, the won't understand'" (Luke 8:10 NLT).

Parables were used by Jesus to teach lessons. But the meanings of Jesus' parables were only apparent to those whose hearts and minds were opened to receive the lesson. The meaning was intentionally hidden from those whose hearts and minds were closed to the lesson. God told Isaiah (Isaiah 6:9-10) this would be the case. Jesus, Himself, made this point to His disciples.

... "'You are permitted to understand the secrets of the Kingdom of God. But I use parables to teach the others so that the Scriptures might be fulfilled: When they look, they won't really see. When they hear, they won't understand'" (Verse 10 NLT).

The fact that Jesus was intentionally hiding the meaning of His parables is clear in Mark 4:11-13 and Luke 8:10. The reason for hiding the meaning of His parables is clear in Matthew 13:11-17 as Jesus quotes parts of Isaiah 6:9-10.

"He replied, 'You are permitted to understand the secret of the Kingdom of Heaven, but others are not. To those who listen to my teaching, more understanding will be given, and they will have an abundance of knowledge. But for those who are not listening, even what little understanding they have will be taken away from them. That is why I use these parables, for they look, but they don't really see. They hear, but they don't really listen or understand. This fulfills the prophecy of Isaiah...'" (Matthew 11-14a NLT).

Explanation was often needed even for the people whose hearts and minds were open to learn from Jesus. Jesus said, "I will speak to you in parables. I will explain things hidden since the creation of the world" (Matthew 13:35 NLT). Sometimes Jesus' disciples had to ask for explanation: "Then Peter said to Jesus, "Explain to us the parable..."" (Matthew 15:15 NLT). But whether Jesus initiated the explanation or His disciples asked for it, Jesus was always willing to make sure His lessons were understood by those who really wanted to learn and live what they learned.

We have the wonderful opportunity to learn lessons from Jesus that have been hidden from the creation of the world. Let us take every opportunity to grow in our understanding so we can live in line with Jesus' Truth. ■

— JACKSON M. DOGGETTE, JR.

AUGUST 24

DO SOMETHING!

"The master commended the dishonest manager for his shrewdness. For the sons of this world are more shrewd in dealing with their own generation than the sons of light" (Luke 16:8 ESV).

I can still hear in my ears the shout of a recent camp meeting sermon by Rear Admiral Barry C. Black (Ret.), Chaplain of the United States Senate, saying, "Do Something! Something is at least better than nothing!"

My first thought upon reflecting on this parable in Luke 16:1-8 was, "Really!" A rich owner is giving accommodations to an irresponsible steward (trustee). How can this be? Where is the justice in this trustee's action? An irresponsible trustee has wasted the owners' resources. The trustee realizes that the owner is coming to relieve him of this present responsibility as trustee of his estate because he has wasted what was not his to waste. So, he is fired.

Upon being released, the ex-trustee could have decided to do absolutely nothing. He could have wallowed around in self-pity and made excuses for his failures and blamed others. Notice the ex-trustee made no excuses and leveled no blame. Instead, his first action following his dismissal is to get some return on the rich owners' investments.

From one debtor, he gets 400 gallons instead of 800 gallons of olive oil. From another debtor, he gets 800 bushels instead of 1,000 bushels of wheat. He turns these investments over to the rich owner in hopes that he will be able to obtain future employment elsewhere. He left on a good note! With the time, talent, and influence that the trustee presently has, he does a little something. Something is at least better than nothing!

Upon further reflection, I believe, Jesus was not teaching His disciples to be dishonest like this irresponsible trustee because in the story he was fired. I realize Jesus was teaching His disciples to own up to your present failures and mistakes—do not make excuses and blame others. Instead, make wise use of the time, talent, treasure, and influence that you have now for the Lord. In doing so, you are making a wise investment in your future by your present actions. "Do something with what you have!"

Remember, don't blame and complain. Act on what time, talent, and treasure that you have today! Give it all to Jesus! And you will hear His commendation, "Well done, thou good and faithful servant. Enter into the joy of the Lord!" ▮▮

— MARCELLUS T. ROBINSON

AUGUST 25

NO HELP!

"...and no one gave him anything" (Luke 15:16 NKJV).

In March 2020, the Coronavirus pandemic touched our lives in a way that we will never forget. I remember going into the grocery store and seeing the shelves that were once stocked full of hand sanitizer, disinfectant spray, antibacterial hand soap, cleaning agents, laundry soap, bleach, alcohol, paper towels, and toilet paper, emptied. Canned goods, frozen foods, water, soda, chips, peanut butter, eggs, milk, juice—everything was now in short supply in an instant.

At that moment I began to sense what the Prodigal Son must have felt. Wishing his father was dead by requesting his inheritance while his father was still living, he squandered his ill-gotten sustenance and ended up penniless, friendless, kinless, and caught in the clutches of a "severe famine" in a distant land. To his credit, touched by the pangs of starvation and stripped of arrogance and the Jewish code, he found employment as a swine herder with subsistence wages that could not reverse his destitution. He needed help!

It might be said that he reaped what he sowed. But I get the sense that in this parable, Jesus speaks to the deep-seated self-centeredness of broken humanity when He says, "and no one gave him anything." This starving stranger, abandoned acquaintance, lost son, needed help even after struggling to help himself. Clearly, some were weathering the storm—but "no one gave him anything." It suggests that his tragedy was known; he was not invisible, and had probably asked for help—"and no one gave him anything."

When I looked at those emptied shelves, I wondered did anyone think about others who would be in need as well? How comfortable we can become with the "every man for himself" mindset, and be at ease knowing there are those who need help, who are desperately doing all they can and know to do while working in jobs designed to marginalize and disenfranchise.

We all have a moral responsibility to respond to the needs of others as we are blessed. In short, those who have something ought to always share with those who have nothing! May the words of Amos 8:4 (NKJV) never be our reality: "Hear this, you who swallow up the needy, And make the poor of the land fail..." We must edit the narrative in our context to read, "and someone gave them something." Let that someone be me! ▮▮

— MARCELLUS T. ROBINSON

AUGUST 26

WHAT'S YOUR RESPONSE?

"Therefore I tell you that the kingdom of God will be taken away from you and given to a people who will produce its fruit" (Matthew 21:43 NIV).

This was Jesus' conclusion after telling the parable of the tenants. Parable teaching was popular in Jesus' day and conveyed one salient point. What was that point in this parable? Is it possible after spending one's whole life in church that one can lose out on the kingdom? What does it mean to produce fruit? Why were the hearers of this parable in danger of losing out on the kingdom? Could it be they were not producing fruit commensurate with kingdom life? The hearers of the parable were upset when they heard the message inherent in the parable.

"When the chief priests and the Pharisees heard Jesus' parables, they knew he was talking about them" (Matthew 21:45 NIV). So, what was Christ saying about them? What is Christ saying to us? At the heart of this parable is the question of one's response.

A wealthy land owner provided everything needed for a productive and bountiful harvest. The landowner then rented the vineyard to tenant farmers. This arrangement benefited both owner and tenants. Like this landowner, God has given us everything we need to have fruitful spiritual lives.

Unfortunately, at harvest time the tenant farmers decided they wanted it all. Their greed resulted in the abuse and murder of three waves of servants sent to secure the owner's portion. Finally the owner sent his son, thinking he would succeed where the others had failed. Instead, the son was summarily murdered. They thought, "Let's kill the heir and take his inheritance" (Matthew 21:38 NIV). What are your thoughts when God comes looking for fruit from you?

Since Jesus' audience (chief priests and Pharisees) concluded that He was talking about them, let's use their insight to facilitate our understanding. This parable exposed their greed, challenged their teachings and traditions, and exposed their hypocrisy.

God has given us everything we need to lead fruitful spiritual lives. (All true disciples will be fruit-bearing disciples). When, in spite of God's patient long suffering and grace we refuse to bear kingdom fruit, we will ultimately suffer kingdom loss. Fruitless disciples will not possess the kingdom of Christ. Those who receive Him and produce kingdom fruit will be the inheritors of His kingdom.

The question that people of Jesus' day had to answer was, what's your response when God comes looking for fruit in your life? This is the same question each of us must answer.

What has been your response to the God's love, mercy, grace, kindness, patience, and long suffering? Have you borne fruit? What has been your response to the sacrifice of Jesus? We can ignore Him, deny Him, abuse Him or reject Him. None of these responses will negate His Messianic claims.

If we want to inherit the kingdom of God, we must receive Jesus into our hearts and bear kingdom fruit in our lives. What will your response to Jesus be? ■

— MAX FERGUSON

AUGUST 27

MYSTERIOUS SEEDS

"And He said, "The kingdom of God is as if a man should scatter seed on the ground, and should sleep by night and rise by day, and the seed should sprout and grow, he himself does not know how. For the earth yields crops by itself: first the blade, then the head, after that the full grain in the head. But when the grain ripens, immediately he puts in the sickle, because the harvest has come" (Mark 4:26-29 NKJV).

The Lord's parable about the growing seed is so simple if you blink you just might miss it. How many times do precious lessons pass by countless thousands who miss another opportunity to understand essential truths that unlock the Kingdom of Heaven, principles that can lead to eternal life?

The man throws the seeds unto the ground (assuming it's the right time of year and the right kind of soil, or good ground as we learned about earlier in the chapter). He sleeps and rises day after passing day. And finally when the fruit ripens, he puts in his sickle because the harvest has come.

Did you miss it already? Quick recap: the man actively does his part, in Verse 26. In Verse 27, he waits. And in Verse 29, he reaps, but something special happens in between! Verse 28 says the farmer "does not know how," and I dare say we don't really know how either. The miracle of life and growth is that which only God can make happen! The Bible says, "first the blade, then the ear, after that the full corn in the ear" (Mark 4:28 KJV).

I'm a witness that He can take that which was little and make it much! We have to be careful because we will reap what we have sown. Galatians 6:7 says, "Do not be deceived, God is not mocked; for whatever a man sows, that he will also reap" (NKJV). I've also learned that the more you sow, the more you will reap later! 2 Corinthians 9:6 says, "But this I say, He which soweth sparingly shall reap also sparingly; and he which soweth bountifully shall reap also bountifully" (KJV).

This parable of the growing seed gives me hope that if I'm faithful to do what God has given me the strength to do and I wait on Him to do what only He can, then in time I will experience my harvest and receive my reward!

Let's sow kindness, good deeds, and positive words. Let's sow a good work ethic, morals, and stewardship principles! Let's sow by spreading the gospel, ministering to those in need, and praying for them! Let's sow the truth from God's word, with an example to match, exemplifying the love of God. And let God perform the necessary miracles that will reveal that no investment in the Lord will be in vain! ■

— MELVYN (TRÈS) HAYDEN, III

AUGUST 28

THE WHEAT AND THE TARES

"But he said, 'No, lest while you gather up the tares you also uproot the wheat with them'" (Matthew 13:29 NKJV).

In order to produce a successful harvest, the farmer must take into consideration how and when to sow seeds. Planting wheat requires the farmer to be diligent in the timing. It must be done while it is cool. I am led to believe early in the morning is the best time to sow. The soil must be watered well, with ample amounts of sunshine in order for the wheat, in time of harvest, to reach its full potential. There are two seasons wheat can be planted; fall and spring which can bring about a great harvest.

In between morning and the two seasons of planting, many calamities can occur during the growth process. There can be bad weather which can include heavy rains and enormous heat. These are the "who" that makes it incredibly difficult for a full harvest. There are expectations of loss, but the Bible points out that an enemy of the sower came and sowed tares amongst the wheat and went his way. The word "tares" is translated in the Bible as "zizania" which refers to the darnel. The darnel is a type of grass that resembles wheat in its early growth process. Many farmers would consider the tares to be what we consider weeds.

In making a garden look presentable we normally take time to pull weeds away from flowers and plants. The aesthetics of a weed-less garden is one that green thumbs desire.

The servants wanted to pull the weeds from around the wheat, but the danger in this extraction was that it would likely create confusion, causing them to pull up the wheat with the tares. The mistake would be easily made especially because the servants were not experienced in the field to make the distinction.

The command is that we must grow together until harvest. We all have a heaven to experience and a hell to shun. One will be bundled to burn while the wheat will be bundled to the barn.

Let us grow together till then. ■■

— PATRICK G. GRAHAM

AUGUST 29

PARABLE OF THE LEAVEN

"Another parable spake he unto them; The kingdom of heaven is like unto leaven, which a woman took, and hid in three measures of meal, till the whole was leavened'" (Matthew 13:33 KJV).

In today's text and in Luke 13:20-21, Jesus said: "The kingdom of heaven is like unto leaven, which a woman took, and hid in three measures of meal, till the whole was leavened." Because leaven was usually used as a representation of sin (Luke 12:1; 1 Corinthians 5:8), it is ironic that the Kingdom of Heaven is compared to leaven. Nevertheless, it is its speedy and absorbing quality that is represented here.

Just as leaven assimilates the whole bread, the grace of God takes over our whole being—our souls and spirits (our very essence), transforming us into His likeness. It is an inner working with an outward manifestation. This renewal is made effective by the Holy Spirit which permeates the heart of him who, being lost in sin, looks to Christ as his only hope and opens himself to His inner workings.

The kingdom of God then becomes hidden in the heart of every believer. Its process leads to conversion and sanctification. The leaven of truth functioning within purifies the thoughts, enables the ability to obey, and awakens the conscience, and love for God and mankind becomes natural. This love becomes the driving force that penetrates the whole character and personality. Our goals and outlook in life turn heavenward. We eventually become partakers in the divine life.

Having explained the process, it is obvious that this is not our reality today, not even in the church. Therefore, I exhort you to give Christ a chance to change your lives as sinful beings. We cannot do this for ourselves; we have fallen short of the glory of God. All the instructions, learning, and culture which the world offers cannot make a debased child of sin a child of heaven. All of our selfishness, unholy tempers, overbearing, and worldliness cannot be washed away unless transformed by the Holy Spirit that works within as leaven.

No matter how low you have fallen or how vile you have become, you are not beyond salvation. There is hope for you. Give Christ an opportunity to change your life and to rise in praise and worship to the One who is able, through His sacrifice and His will, to redeem. All heaven is waiting. ■

— RAMON ESCALANTE

AUGUST 30

VIPS AND THE UNWELCOMED

"Then the master said to the servant, 'Go out into the highways and hedges, and compel them to come in, that my house may be filled. For I say to you that none of those men who were invited shall taste my supper' "
(Luke 14:23-24 NKJV).

In His "Parable of the Great Banquet" (Luke 14), Jesus tells of a man who invited some VIPs to his dinner fair—a community developer, an entrepreneur and a newlywed. Each refused to come citing various excuses. The community developer had bought land that he had to go see. The entrepreneur bought oxen he had to examine. The newly wed just wasn't leaving his wife, no reason given, period.

The king then bids his servant to go out in the streets and bring in the poor, crippled, blind and lame. When the servant does that he tells his master, "Sir, what you commanded has been done, and still there is room" (Verse 22).

We learn first that the very important people were not interested. Often the people invited and intending to go to heaven can become distracted by the things of this world if they are not careful.

We also learn that there is plenty good room in the Father's house. We will run out of the less fortunate before we run out of room in heaven. Even after the first invitation went out, the servant told the king, "and still there is room" (Verse 22).

The servant is told to "go out to the highways and hedges and compel people to come in, that my house may be filled" (Verse 23). When the servant goes out this time, he's looking for "whosever" will answer his appeal to come and eat. He is to compel people and urge them to not miss the opportunity of a lifetime.

We learn God welcomes with abandon. He isn't looking to leave any space, if possible. Are we selective in whom we share the good news of God with? Are we particular in whom we want to be in fellowship with on this side of heaven?

The servant ventures out to the highways and hedges to fill the master's house. The Greek word for hedges refers to a fence or partition. There are people who are walled off, ostracized, marginalized, oppressed and depressed for various reasons in the market place of life. In the economy of the kingdom, Jesus tore down the wall of partition between the Jew and the Gentile (Ephesians 2:14). He welcomes with open arms "whosoever will." The kingdom of God is for everybody who is willing to accept God's gracious invitation. The unwelcome are welcomed by the open arms of Jesus that were spread open on a cross at Calvary.

Jesus warned the religious leaders then, and us today who find ourselves commissioned to share the everlasting gospel, "none of those men who were invited shall taste my banquet" (Verse 24). It's not that they weren't invited; they had various reasons for rejecting the invitation given them. The very important people were replaced by the unwelcomed so that God's house "may be filled." ■

— RONALD D. WILLIAMS, JR.

AUGUST 31

WELL DONE

"'Who then is a faithful and wise servant, whom his master made ruler over his household, to give them food in due season? Blessed is that servant whom his master, when he comes, will find so doing'" (Matthew 24:45-46 NKJV).

All Christians want to hear from Jesus, "Well done, good and faithful servant" (Matthew 25:23 NKJV). No one wants to hear, "Depart from Me, you cursed, into the everlasting fire prepared for the devil and his angels" (Matthew 25:41 NKJV). So how can we be sure to hear the commendation and not the condemnation? Jesus does not leave it up to us to figure it out. He tells us. Why? Because He delights in us and wants to be able to say to every child of His, "Well done."

Today's focus is Matthew 24:45-51. It is a story given in the context of the coming of the Son of Man (Matthew 24:42). If we are to be ready for His appearing, Jesus says that we must be as the faithful and wise servant who is found in the act of fulfilling the task which he was given.

Now, before we deal with what that task is, please notice that one servant is given two designations; faithful and wise (Verse 45) or evil (Verse 48). The potential exists for being called one or the other depending on what that servant is found doing at the time of the master's return. In other words, it is up to us which label we receive.

This story is found among a cluster of parables and instructions which concludes with the admonitions found in the parable of the sheep and the goats. In the story about the faithful and wise servant, he is called so precisely because of his proper treatment of those in the master's household. Who are those in the master's household? Since Jesus is the master, those the servant gives to are His family, who are given food when it is most needed. Notice in the parable of the sheep and the goats, Jesus' brethren are also in dire need of the bare necessities, and the faithful are found ministering to those in need. See the connection?

When Jesus walked the earth, His mission was to minister to those in need. Those who love Him and are filled with the oil of His Spirit will find themselves giving to those in need—the incarcerated, the hungry, the helpless, the naked. Those who are servants of Jesus are found doing justice, loving mercy and walking humbly with God. It is a faith that works by love.

When we live with an interested benevolence toward our fellow man, we will hear the words, "Well done, good and faithful servant." ▮▮

— VERNON WATERS

SEPTEMBER

DISCIPLESHIP

"Be like Christ" equals discipleship. Simple formula compromised by excuses, extenuating circumstances, and ethical considerations. In being like Christ, it requires a complete denial of self and transformation to Christ. Discipleship requires practice. Practice necessitates prayer, fasting, and a daily and fresh baptism of the Holy Spirit. And with discipleship, practice never ends.

In a world confused about the definition and character of Christians, discipleship represents an intentional effort to be like Christ in spirit and in truth. Through spirit, we worship God from totality of our heart with no ulterior motives, partisan persuasion, or self-interests from the totality of our hearts. And in truth, calls for a correct knowledge about the good news, not the fake news, about Jesus Christ.

As you ponder discipleship this month, please note that your character matters to Christ and it should matter to you. Buzz words like open, transparent, and authenticity require real meaning in a world that expects hypocrisy. Now more than ever, we need disciples to ensure discipleship. ■■

— EDWARD WOODS, III
Director of Public Affairs and Religious Liberty,
Allegheny East Conference of Seventh-day Adventists

SEPTEMBER 1

IMITATE GOD

"Follow God's example, therefore, as dearly loved children and walk in the way of love, just as Christ loved us and gave himself up for us as a fragrant offering and sacrifice to God" (Ephesians 5:1-2 NIV).

I love to read to my four children. One book I like to read is Caps for Sale, by Esphyr Slobodkina. In this book a peddler who sells caps goes into the country to take a nap under a tree. Upon awakening he finds that all of his caps, except for his own, have been stolen by a group of monkeys who are playing with the caps in a tree. The peddler points his finger and gets angry at the monkeys. The monkeys point their fingers and get angry. The peddler stomps his feet. The monkeys stomp their feet. Finally, in desperation the peddler throws down his cap and starts to leave. The monkeys throw down their caps and start to leave. So the peddler gets all of his caps back.

In Ephesians 5:1-2, Jesus asks that we imitate God. Children naturally imitate their parents. This has been a constant source of both joy and frustration for me as a father. I want my children to follow the best of who I am. Ephesians 5 tells us that we should imitate God just as Christ imitated God, by loving people.

This imitation is a childlike thing to do resulting in adult-sized self-sacrifice. Christ gave Himself for us. He asks us to give ourselves for others. I am very moved by the idea that Christ's primary attitude toward us is love. My primary attitude toward others is rarely "love from a pure heart" (1 Timothy 1:5). I find that I am at my best when my attitude is love. I am less selfish, I live in the moment, and I do not covet when my attitude is love. Differences in class, race, gender, and politics do not seem to matter as much when my attitude is love.

In the public affairs and religious liberty (PARL) work, we must constantly balance a firm belief in biblical Christianity with the idea that love is God's primary mode of operation. Too often in politics the primary driving focus of an interaction is to imitate others' unsavory characteristics instead of loving them. Our success in PARL likely depends on our ability to find ways to love others dramatically because we uphold the teachings of Jesus.

What if today I decided that my attitude toward others would be love first? Consider Jesus challenging us to "Love your enemy" (Matthew 5:44). I want to choose to imitate God today. I want to decide to be a disciple. Don't you? ■■

— JONATHAN FETRICK

SEPTEMBER 2

OLD MAN VS. NEW MAN

"Do not lie to each other, since you have taken off your old self with its practices and have put on the new self, which is being renewed in knowledge in the image of its Creator" (Colossians 3:9-10 NIV).

Jesus calls us to help one another—not lie to one another. He used the metaphor of an old man and a new man to describe the conflict which characterizes the life of a Christian (Colossians 3:9-10).

But what is it about the "old man" that makes it a good analogy for our spiritual condition? I believe the essential aspect captured by the image of the "old man" is the lack of awareness and the loss of contact with reality. The "old man" is full of sin and worldliness. The "new man" is the one that is full of righteousness and holiness of God. When the old self has been put away, the new Christian is renewed in knowledge according to the image of God who created him (Colossians 3:9-10). The new Christian will have compassion on others (Colossians 3:12) and be long-suffering toward others (Colossians 3:13).

The government of God is based on freedom of choice. The "new man" stands out because he has learned to put on love, to worship God according to conscience, and to share Christ's love, as cherished freedoms not universally enjoyed. God chose to create humanity with the power of choice. "See, I have set before thee this day life and good, and death and evil . . . blessing and cursing: therefore choose life, that both thou and thy seed may live" (Deuteronomy 30:15, 19 NKJV).

As followers of Jesus Christ, everything we do must be bathed in prayer, consumed with preaching a crucified, risen and soon coming Savior, and winning the lost to Christ, as our passion. As disciples, all of us must become imitators of Christ's life because we have felt the call to do something special for the Lord. We have been given a vision and guided to fulfill that specific plan tailored exactly for us.

In the later years of my childhood and early years of adolescence, I became a disciple of Jesus Christ. Today, in this very moment, I feel so good about Jesus that I want to tell others about the wonderful happiness I have found in Him. I want to tell my family members and neighbors.

Be self-determined disciples to speak the truth about Jesus, to seek justice, and to pray for justice! Let us speak out against injustice so that it never happens again. Believe that God will avenge His children who trust Him. Never give up asking God to avenge us! Model the life of Jesus ... Be a disciple ... Become involved ... Watch and pray! ▮▮

— DORIS GOTHARD

SEPTEMBER 3

WHAT'S YOUR PROBLEM?

"I am crucified with Christ: nevertheless I live; yet not I, but Christ liveth in me: and the life which I now live in the flesh I live by the faith of the Son of God, who loved me, and gave himself for me" (Galatians 2:20 KJV).

We all have problems in our lives. Some are vocal about them and share with anyone and everyone who will listen. Some air them out on social media for the entire world to see. Some confide in a select few. Some just bottle them up and pretend like everything is perfect.

We've all got problems, every one of us. Those problems can come from home life, work life, school life, church life, or a mix of all. It might be your boyfriend, or girlfriend, or wife, or husband, or kids. No matter who you are, no matter your age, no matter what, we all have problems.

The good news is that God can handle our problems. God is concerned about every area of our lives. God even cares about what others might deem "insignificant." Jesus stated that God takes care of sparrows and even counts the hairs on our heads. (Luke 12:6-7) There is no problem too big for God.

Perhaps the biggest problem we have is the battle with self. The warfare against self is the greatest battle ever fought. Let's admit it; surrendering all to the will of God requires a struggle. Our natural tendency is bent on selfishness. We want what we what when we want it.

I have two wonderful sons. They both are intelligent, outgoing, and followers of Christ. Yet, they both have tendencies of selfishness. As I try to disciple them into young men and eventually manhood, I am constantly at war with their selfish spirits. Where did their selfishness come from? Me! Yes, me. I passed down the selfish gene to my boys. I received the selfish gene from parents. Humanity's problem is self. Selfishness is nothing more than sin. Since Adam's sin in the Garden of Eden (Genesis 3), we have had a major problem. Yet we are not without hope.

There is no way to experience victory without death; in fact, your victory is in death. When we learn to die to self, we begin the process of living for Christ. Every disciple of Christ must die! How? There are two prayers I pray every day, James 1:5 and Luke 11:13. The Word of God and the Spirit brings victory; and as Christ lives in us, we have the victory! When despondency, gloom, and doubt arise, claim the blood of Jesus, for you are crucified with Christ. ▮▮

— WILLIAM J. LEE

SEPTEMBER 4

JUST LIKE JESUS

"You were taught to be made new in your hearts, to become a new person. That new person is made to be like God – made to be truly good and holy" (Ephesians 4:23-24, NCV).

One of the unpleasant outcomes of the social media revolution is that an individual can become obsessed with self, because they are looking for positive online responses from people who really do not care about them. Youth are depressed at not being liked by all their classmates, and even adults go online hoping for emotional strokes from their friends. This social phenomenon has produced a lack of socialization and, potentially, the loneliest people on the planet. We have become ever so more isolated by as many as 80 glances per day at our cell phone. We keep looking for validation of our self-image or, as some call it, personal brand. Rather than being impressed with oneself, I suggest, be impressed with someone else.

So, with whom am I impressed? You have already guessed it. It is Jesus. All the political personalities, stars represented on Hollywood's walk of fame, award winners of every type—from the Grammys to the ESPYs—or all of them together, cannot match the matchless charm of the One who gave Himself so that we can be restored to God's original design.

Talk about star power! How many celebs were visited by wise men because their coming was announced in Scripture long before their birth? How many were preceded by a prophet announcing a real star was on the horizon? Which of them neglected their selves by living the life of a homeless person when they could have been born in the lap of luxury?

What life is more compelling to follow than that of a selfless God-man who lovingly obeyed His Father's desire to save mankind? Did you know Jesus could have changed His mind with regard to giving His life on Calvary? He stated, "I have power to lay it down, and I have power to take it again. This command I have received from My Father" (John 10:18 NKJV). Jesus didn't have to give His life, as God never forces anyone to obey. Yet His surrendered life gave Him value beyond any home or online address in the world, and it does the same for you!

In all of my travels, board meetings, and other engagements, the most fulfilling thing I do is being there for people when they are in need, to share the love of Christ. May I again suggest an antidote for virtual loneliness is being a disciple of Jesus?

Today, may all your "likes" be heaven sent, because His love for you compels you to walk, talk, and relate to your fellow man, just like Him. ∎

— MAURICE VALENTINE

SEPTEMBER 5

ALL EYES ON ME

"For the grace of God has appeared that offers salvation to all people. It teaches us to say "No" to ungodliness and worldly passions, and to live self-controlled, upright and godly lives in this present age, while we wait for the blessed hope—the appearing of the glory of our great God and Savior, Jesus Christ" (Titus 2:11-13 NIV).

Flight experiences can be quite memorable. Once, aboard a flight headed back to Chicago, a gentleman boasted about our positioning near the front of the plane as opposed to those in the back enduring an infant's incessant shrieking. To my surprise and his chagrin, the infant and his mother exchanged seats with another passenger placing them directly behind us. The gentleman blurted out expletives and frantically looked for alternative seating to avoid enduring the boy's cries. Unfortunately, he was stuck. He began texting others concerning his plight while we remained on the plane, at the gate, delayed, frazzled, and impatient. We all wanted to get home, but we were still stuck there.

After a while, I pulled out a book and read. He observed that my behavior reflected one who seemed calm during this debacle. I did not appear shaken, rattled, or ready for a skirmish. Instead, I seemed to treat the unfortunate nature of my environment as a learning opportunity. You see, I realized that if I reacted in a way that did not reflect Jesus, I would potentially ruin my witness for Him in that moment. This is the essence of discipleship.

Discipleship is the combination of proclamation and demonstration. It is practicing what we preach. Today, there is a desperate need for greater consciousness concerning our discipleship. Our reactions to those things that seek to beset us and upset our equilibrium are often our greatest witnessing tools and platform.

Paul admonishes Titus to be conscious of his surroundings. Paul knows the societally expected lifestyle is the antithesis of discipleship. However, Paul says, live a life that is neither reflective of societal standards nor indulgent of rash behaviors. Live a life that reflects the auspicious anticipation of our Savior's arrival.

Finally, after an hour of sitting on the plane at the gate, we were cleared to leave the gate and prepare for takeoff. The gentleman unshackled his earbud from his ears and asked me a question I will never forget.

"How are you so relaxed right now?" The baby continued shrieking, the plane had not graced the sky, and the one-hour delay pushed our arrival late into the evening.

I responded, "I know it will all be over soon."

When you live with auspicious anticipation of Christ's imminent arrival, your September will be one to remember. ▮▮

— E.J. BELL

SEPTEMBER 6

GOD KNOWS BEST

"He cuts off every branch in me that bears no fruit while every branch that does bear fruit he prunes so that it will be more fruitful" (John 15:2 NIV).

Jesus in His characteristic fashion draws illustrations from the contemporary agrarian society to drive His point home to His disciples. He lays before them His discipleship strategy. He uses a metaphor that they would have readily understood. Jesus, in today's text, presents two ways by which this takes place.

He is the vine. The word translated "cut off" in Verse 2 is the Greek verb "airo." Its primary meaning is "to raise up"; to raise from the ground; to raise upward, elevate and lift up. It can also be translated "to take way" (cut off) as the NIV puts it.

In the spring in Jesus' time, two things were done to care for the vine. The fruitless vines that ran on the ground were lifted up. The fruit-bearing vines were pruned. The vines on the ground were not well aerated and did not have full access to the sun. Lifting them up gave the leaves opportunity to photosynthesize and create food that spurned growth and fruitfulness.

God repositions us for fruitfulness. I have personally experienced God's grace that has lifted me from fruitless ways of thinking and behaving, by exposing me to the light of His Son of Righteousness.

When vines are left to themselves, they create excess foliage but no fruit. Pruning redirects resources by removing what is superfluous. I need the Master Gardener to regulate my growth so that energies and resources are directed to what is important—fruit. "But the fruit of the Spirit is love, joy, peace, patience, kindness, goodness, faithfulness, gentleness and self-control…" (Galatians 5:22-23 ESV).

The deeper pruning is done in the fall after the harvest. The vine looks desolate with all its branches pared back. It looks like there is very little life in it. When the vine enters into a dormant state and nothing seems to be growing above the ground, the vine puts all its energy in extending and deepening its root system.

Our brokenness provides an opportunity for depth. As we sink our roots into the promises of God's Word and are strengthened in the inner man, we shall be launched into greater fruitfulness as the winter subsides and spring emerges.

May God help us to submit to His ways of discipling us. He knows best. May we allow God's grace to lift us up from the fruitless works of darkness. When He brings us to fruitage, may we submit ourselves to His pruning that ensures quality and abundant fruit. ▮▮

— FARAI NHIWATIWA

SEPTEMBER 7

WHY RENOUNCE?

"So therefore, any one of you who does not renounce all that he has cannot be my disciple" (Luke 14:33 ESV).

It was spring semester 1999. As a student at New York Technical College, I was heading to class when I heard protest chants. Being a city boy, it was too familiar. However, this time my interest was sparked because of the latest events on the news. I saw the crowd organizing together to shut down and cross the Manhattan Bridge.

They were protesting the February 4, 1999 police shooting of Amadou Diallo, a 23-year-old immigrant from Guinea, killed by four New York City police officers after they mistook him for a rape suspect. The officers fired a combined total of 41 shots. The crowd was chanting, "How many times, 41 times," repeatedly. It was another tragic result of racial profiling. No class for me today. I joined the cause, but for me this was going to be a short-term protest because I had class the next day.

However, for the person marching two rows in front of me, this was not short-term. He was completely sold out to this cause. This was neither his first nor his last protest. As a matter of fact, he was the organizer of several protests in many states. This was none other than Rev. Alfred Charles Sharpton, Jr. When I think about someone who has counted the cost and renounced it all, no matter the criticism, the name that pops up is his. Today, I believe many people do not understand discipleship or its cost, especially for Jesus Christ. I used to watch martial arts movies where grandmasters would cause their pupils to go through extremely rigorous training that would eliminate those who were not committed. Those who went on to be faithful disciples later become grandmasters themselves.

Although Jesus' disciples are not committed to an earthly match of human glory, they are required to surrender everything for the glory of Christ. Many apostles went as far as being executed for the Lord. John was exiled for his commitment. Old Testament disciples such as Abraham, Jeremiah and Daniel forsook all for God.

Now, I see too many of us Christians give up, church hop, abandon the calling, and some just don't have time for Christ. What if Martin Luther King, Jr. quit when he was first arrested? There would be no Al Sharpton.

Above all, what if Jesus abandoned His purpose at the first sign of criticism? There would be no us. Jesus renounced all for us to save us; could we not renounce for Him and receive a crown of glory? ▮▮

— DENRY WHITE

SEPTEMBER 8

GROWING INTO DISCIPLESHIP

"Like newborn babies, crave pure spiritual milk, so that by it you may grow up in your salvation, now that you have tasted that the Lord is good" (1 Peter 2:2 NIV).

When one looks up the meaning of "disciple," one will find words like follower, believer, acolyte, devotee, student, protégée, admirer, supporter...you get the point. The apostle Peter, in today's text, gives an imperative to the ardent follower of Christ to take the posture of a newborn and be nourished by the pure word of God.

It is obligatory that this invitation by Peter be considered in the context of what he said in the preceding chapter when he explicitly stated, "For you have been born again, not of perishable seed, but of imperishable, through the living and enduring word of God" (1 Peterl:23 NIV). Here, he is articulating that in order to be a disciple of Christ, one needs to receive nourishment from the pure, unadulterated word of God.

Peter is imploring the new believer to put away the old practices of being deceitful, hypocritical, and envious, and to desist from creating pain for others, brought on by gossiping. In other words, the disciple of Christ must behave like Christ. In declaring His mission on earth, Jesus said, "For the Son of man is come to seek and to save that which was lost" (Luke 19:10 KJV).

This means that the follower of Christ must engage in practices that seek to fulfill the mission of Christ. This mission cannot be accomplished by the weak and emaciated. The irony is disciples are sometimes malnourished while surrounded by an overabundance of food; the Word of God! It is really sad that we live in a country where Bibles of all sizes and versions are available; we even have electronic Bibles, yet malnutrition abounds.

Inherent in discipleship is the need to be disciplined—one must have a well-ordered and self-controlled life. A mother may have an abundance of milk for her newborn, but in order to be nourished this infant must rely on what is known as the rooting reflex. That is, somewhere between 28 – 30 weeks of gestation, a baby starts to develop rooting (sucking) motions, by turning the head when the cheeks or lips are touched. This rooting reflex precedes the development of the sucking reflex.

In order for me to grow, I need to develop the rooting reflex of turning my head towards the nourishment that comes from the Word of God. I was inspired in my discipleship by sharing a cabin one weekend with Pastor Gordon Martinborough, who would rise up early in the morning to read his Bible. He motivated me to greater discipleship. ▮▮

— ERROL LIVERPOOL

SEPTEMBER 9

POWER OF LOVE

"We love because he first loved us" (1 John 4:19 NIV).

I once heard a preacher relate the true story of twin boys who were in the foster care system. Appallingly, they had already been transferred to nine homes by the time they were only 18 months; and sadly, in some of these homes they had been abused. Finally, they were placed in the home of a Christian couple who had a deep love for children. However, by this time so much damage had been done to these little ones that developmental tests led social workers to conclude that they would never be cognitively and affectively normal. Yet after two years of nurture in their new home, tests demonstrated that the children were not only normal but thriving. What made the difference? It was the power of love.

This is the same transformative power that love has in the lives of Christian disciples. We too have been hurt, damaged and traumatized—not only by life experiences, but ultimately because of the ravages of sin. The record of our first parents, Adam and Eve, reveal how quickly sin and guilt distorts our nature to produce fear, control, blaming, and defensiveness. Sin makes us abnormal. It affects not only us, but also our relationships—poisoning them and making it difficult for us to demonstrate self-sacrificing, self-renouncing love.

Through Jesus Christ, His Son, and the power of His indwelling Spirit, God has provided a way for sinful people to live lives of authentic love. The apostle John describes this process in 1 John 4:18 when he says, "There is no fear in love, but perfect love casts out fear..." (NIV). By His perfect love, Jesus is continually and progressively teaching us that we can trust Him; teaching us that in Him we can be secure; teaching us that there is no need to be afraid.

Once we encounter the perfect love of Jesus and continue to experience it by the Holy Spirit every day, we begin to be normal again. We begin to experience freedom from the guilt, insecurity, control, and defensiveness that sin causes. This process starts to change how we relate to others. It causes us to become more self-giving rather than self-preserving. It makes us generous and kind. It even takes away the need to be vindicated, validated, or avenged! This transforming love makes us free to love. It even makes it possible for us to love our enemies! We love because He first loved us. ▮▮

— DWAYNE DUNCOMBE

SEPTEMBER 10

DISCIPLESHIP THROUGH SINGING AND MUSIC

"Let the word of Christ dwell in you richly in all wisdom; teaching and admonishing one another in psalms and hymns and spiritual songs, singing with grace in your hearts to the Lord" (Colossians 3:16 NKJV).

Truth be told, I am not a very good singer. My father was even worse and is considered by many to be tone deaf. Fortunately, my mother was a bit better. I can play the trumpet reasonably well and even the guitar a bit. My wife, on the other hand, is a tremendous musician, with a degree in violin and voice performance. Thankfully, my children have largely inherited their mother's musical gifts.

But I have discovered that great musical ability is not needed to be blessed by listening to praise and worship music. My father enjoys loud hymn singing and gospel music festivals (perhaps this is in part because he can sing loudly without being heard!). And I enjoy both those and more modern Christian praise music, tastefully but enthusiastically performed.

Our text today suggests that the emotions of music can be a powerful tool to teach and disciple others. Often, we think of Christian teaching as the transmission of ideas which involves mostly talking or reading, and the sharing of doctrine. But the text says that we are to teach and admonish one another through "psalms, hymns, and spiritual songs." God knows that we are not just mind and reason, but also heart, emotion, and soul. Music speaks to these other elements of our being more directly than words alone.

When I turned 40, I decided to learn to play the guitar. I never got very good, but learned well enough to strum some hymns and worship songs as part of my daily personal worship time. I found that it added an emotionality and spiritual lift to my spiritual experience that I previously lacked. Others have had a similar experience.

I had a Bible teacher in academy that actually left the church and God for many years. Later in life he returned to the Lord and the church. In his testimony he said that one of the things that re-awakened his spiritual life was listening to praise and gospel music.

In sharing with, and discipling others, especially young people, we should not overlook the power and importance of praise and worship music. It should be relevant to their generation, and such as will appeal to both their hearts and minds. This will help them develop holistically and fully as followers of Christ. It will give them not just right ideas, but also uplifted and worthy emotions and feelings as they sing with "grace in their hearts to the Lord." ∎

— NICHOLAS MILLER

SEPTEMBER 11

LIVING IN THE SPIRIT

"But the fruit of the Spirit is love, joy, peace, longsuffering, gentleness, goodness, faith, meekness, temperance: against such there is no law" (Galatians 55:22-23 KJV).

Naturally, I am not loving, joyful, peaceful, longsuffering, gentle, good, faithful, meek, and temperate. Why? Because my carnal mind is opposed to God and cannot be subject to His law (Romans 8:7).

So, every day I must ask for the gift of the Holy Spirit (Luke 11:13). Not only must I ask every day for the gift of the Holy Spirit because of the great controversy going on in my heart (Romans 7), but because the Greek verb translated "ask" in Luke 11:13 is in the present tense.

One of my greatest challenges is to ask for the gift of the Holy Spirit every day. I am not alone in this. The enemy of us all does not want us to ask for the Holy Spirit daily because he knows the dynamic power the Holy Spirit brings into our lives. Our common enemy wants us to remain powerless, but Jesus wants to give us dynamic ("dunamis" in the Greek, from which we get the word "dynamite") power through the Holy Spirit (Acts 1:8).

When the Spirit comes into our lives, He changes us. The fruit of the Spirit is manifest in our lives to the glory of God, regardless of our circumstances. This fruit is a composite gift. By the grace of God, all the composite parts are to be manifest in our lives.

Instead of having selfish love (Greek eros), by the Spirit we can have God's giving love (Greek agape). Instead of temporary happiness, we can have God's joy. Instead of being anxious, we can have God's peace (John 14:27). Instead of being impatient, we can have God's gift of longsuffering. Instead of being harsh, we can have God's gentleness. Instead of being normal human beings, we can have God's goodness. Instead of being unreliable, we can have God's faithfulness. Instead of being arrogant and proud, we can have God's meekness. And lastly, instead of being intemperate, we can have God's temperance.

When God's Spirit comes into our lives, it makes a difference. It obviously changes us. People start seeing Jesus in us and are drawn to Him (John 12:32). Because people start seeing Jesus in us, they want what we have. When this happens, evangelism will happen naturally. Then the Lord will not be adding to the church weekly—which would be wonderful—but daily (Acts 2:47).

By the grace of God, I am determined to ask every day for the Holy Spirit so that I can live in the Spirit and Jesus can be seen in me. How about you? ■■

— VIALO WEISS

SEPTEMBER 12

ROOTED AND WRAPPED IN CHRIST

"As you therefore have received Christ Jesus the Lord, so walk in Him, rooted and built up in Him and established in the faith, as you have been taught, abounding in it with thanksgiving" (Colossians. 2:6-7 NKJV).

Jesus, before he left His disciples, gave them a command in Matthew 28:19 to go therefore and make disciples of all nations. Paul's primary concern in Colossians was that they continue to grow in Christ as they disciple others. Though saved in Christ, they are tempted to look outside of Christ for a blessing. Paul encourages the Colossians not to forget the One in whom they live and move and have their being.

First Paul encourages the believers; as they receive Christ, they are to walk in Him. Discipleship begins with receiving Christ; then it moves on to living in Him. Walking with Christ is characterized by steady progress in discipleship. The metaphor of walking reflects the act of putting one foot in front of the other over and over again. It means to continuously live and behave in a Christ-like manner, not occasionally. When we stop going forward, we stall; when we stall, we can fall. Paul wants us to be doers of the Word and not just hearers of the Word, because information without application will not result in transformation.

The believers are to walk, take root, and be built up in Christ. Roots do not exist for themselves: they exist to convey nourishment to the branches and to keep the tree steadfast during a storm. Christians are not to be tumbleweeds with no roots, blown about by the wind. Nor are they to be "transplants" that are repeatedly moved from soil to soil. Once we are rooted by faith in Christ, there is no need to change the soil! As disciples, we should live lives that exemplify the Lordship of Christ only, by remaining like branches firmly attached to the vine.

As we walk, take root, and are built up in Christ, the intensity and the frequency of our sinful tendencies begin to decrease as we abide in Him. The word "in" is a preposition used as a function word to indicate inclusion, within something abstract or concrete. When a person is in Christ, it means they are enveloped with Christ.

A letter came to my house and it was addressed to my wife. I was not curious until I saw in the little window on the envelope, "Pay in the order to." I tried to see what the amount on the check was, but it was enveloped. The person that wrote the check placed it in the envelope and when they sealed it you could not see the check anymore. All you saw was the envelope. I put it next to the fire; I put it next to the light; but I could not see anything because it was enveloped. I shook it and rocked it; I rocked it and shook it, but I could not see it because it was enveloped.

When a person is in Christ they are enveloped, wrapped up, covered with Christ so you do not see the person anymore; all you see is Christ. ■

— STEVE BRAMWELL

SEPTEMBER 13

A NEW CREATURE

"Therefore, if any man be in Christ, he is a new creature: old things are passed away; behold, all things are become new" (2 Corinthians 5:17 KJV).

A man being a new creature begins with the death of the old man and the born-again experience of the new birth. This process does not end with being born of water, but commences with it. Christ told Nicodemus we must "be born of water and of the Spirit" (John 3:5 KJV). It is the result of the indwelling of the Spirit, the reproving of sin, righteousness, and the judgement that we become disciples of Christ.

This discipleship is when, through the Holy Spirit, we determine to let Christ live out His life in us. We develop the fellowship with God the Father, His Son Jesus Christ, and our fellow men. We are continually deployed to make disciples who follow that same process in their "new creature" being. Daily we are told that Christ sought for a fresh supply of the indwelling of the Holy Spirit to minister and go before the people. If the Son of God sought for this infilling on a daily basis, how much more do we need to seek the daily freshness of the Holy Spirit in our "new creature?"

While this process has not been perfected in my "new creature," it is a joy to know that He who has begun a good work in me has promised to complete it, as I die to self on a daily basis. He is working in me both to will and to do according to His good pleasure. As I wait each day to be filled with the Holy Spirit, I then move and walk in the Spirit. The fruit of the Spirit is manifested in my life. The Holy Spirit makes me a gift to the body of Christ, empowering me to be discipled and to disciple someone else.

The "new creature" no longer is walking or controlled by the flesh, nor living in a carnal, Laodicean state. Instead, old things have died and all things have become new. The "new creature" experiences the joy of being filled with the Spirit and then pouring themselves into someone else. The "new creature" enjoys watching that other person grow in their relationship with Christ, and that process being repeated in so many others.

Freely we have been received, and freely we give. ▮▮

— LEON BRYANT

SEPTEMBER 14

DISCIPLESHIP AND HATE

"If the world hates you, keep in mind that it hated me first" (John 15:18 NIV).

Discipleship is teaching biblical precepts while modeling for and guiding others. Discipleship empowers or equips the Christian with God's Word, prayer, doctrine, and discipline in worship. Discipleship training is also about relationships with others. Discipleship is an ongoing process. We should never quit learning from our daily walk with Christ.

Furthermore, we must keep ourselves spiritually fit. The path to spiritual fitness is as practical as the path to physical fitness. Anyone can become physically fit if he or she will regularly do certain exercises and practice good habits. Likewise, spiritual fitness is simply a matter of learning certain spiritual exercises and being disciplined to do them until they become habits. Character is shaped by the habits we develop as disciples of the Lord. Discipleship, again, is discipline!

As a disciple of Christ, you will become a target to be hated. In John 15:18, Jesus forewarned His believers that accepting Christianity was not at all a smooth road to travel. Enemies await us in the paths we are taking. He (Jesus) was aiming at something when He said in John 16:1, "I have told you these things so that you won't abandon your faith" (NLT). The hatred which besets Christians was first directed against Christ himself.

Christians are not of the world. The world loves its own but hates that which is out of harmony with it. If Christians do not adopt the world's spirit, language, and habits, this singularity and nonconformity naturally excites dislike and provokes ill treatment. The world knows not God, and hence hates the Church which is in possession of this knowledge. Had the world known God, it would have recognized among Christians the tokens of the Divine presence and operation. Because the world hated Jesus, we who follow Him can expect that many people will hate us as well.

If circumstances are going too well, ask yourself if you are following Christ as you should. We can be grateful when life goes well, but we must make sure it is not at the cost of following Jesus half-heartedly or not at all.

Jesus came with the greatest gift ever offered, so why did He often act secretly? The religious leaders hated Him, and many would refuse His gift of salvation no matter what He said or did. The more Jesus taught and worked publicly, the more those leaders would cause harm for Him and His followers. So it was necessary for Jesus to teach and work as quietly as possible.

There are so many stories of people I've known for years, myself included, of how the Lord delivered His believers from the hands of their enemies who hated righteousness. In order to make it, we must remain focused on the four Ds: devotion, dedication, determination, and detainment. ■

— KEYNEL CADET

MY EXPERIENCE WITH DISCRIMINATION

"When he saw the crowds, he had compassion on them, because they were harassed and helpless, like sheep without a shepherd" (Matthew 9:36 NIV).

I believe God puts certain people on our hearts for a reason. It might be a whole group of people or it might be specific people who come into our lives. God calls us to be His hands and feet here on earth. So in us exploring our feelings for others, we are in turn exploring the heart God has for His people. This is not a new concept. God's people have been caring for those less fortunate for thousands of years.

White privilege, as found in the United States, can be defined as the social, political, and cultural norms that give power or advantage to an individual or group of people because of their white skin color. According to Karen Brodkin, author of How Jews Became White Folk and What That Says About Race in America, through the institution of slavery, whiteness was continually defined in opposition against blacks and American Indians.

After coming to America June 6, 1976, I had my first experience with racism and social justice. My eyes were opened when I got hired as a receptionist while attending school. I was hired without a social security number because they were pressured to hire an African American person; but they considered me a foreigner. I stayed there for years, and received several promotions, but was still a victim of discrimination. Consequently, I filed a lawsuit and won my case for discrimination. They never hired another African American until I left five years later.

Micah 6:8 says, "He hath shewed thee, O man, what is good; and what doth the LORD require of thee, but to do justly, and to love mercy, and to walk humbly with thy God?" (KJV). ▮▮

— YVONNE COLLINS

SEPTEMBER 16

DISCIPLESHIP

"If anyone desires to come after Me, let him deny himself, and take up his cross, and follow Me" (Matthew 16:24 NKJV).

I have been blessed to have people professionally pour themselves into my life. Samuel Sampson was one such person. We met in college as theology students and remained dear friends until he passed late in 2018. My senior in ministry, Sampson took me under his wings and even opened up his home to me. Fresh out of seminary and totally new to ministry, I paid attention to everything he did. My relationship with him was truly transformational. We prayed together, studied Scripture together, shared ideas for sermons, and encouraged each other. He was a true mentor to me. I could say I was a disciple of his.

Do you know what it means to be a disciple? Knowing that Jesus Christ had 12 disciples who were close to Him during his three-year public ministry, people believe that discipleship is a life of commitment, sacrifice, and self-denial.

Christianity is not just about getting baptized and joining a congregation. Jesus wants His followers to be intimately connected to Him. He wants us to be like Him in profession and practice. The call to discipleship is a call to abandon all for Jesus. The disciples of Jesus were with Him 24/7, eating, sleeping, and ministering with the Savior around the clock. In fact, Jesus stated that those who are unwilling to leave all behind are not fit to be His disciples (Luke 14:26, 33).

Disciples learn more by observing and absorbing than by classroom instruction, making spending time with Jesus vitally important. The disciples of Jesus learned to pray by hearing Jesus pray, and they developed an appreciation for the Scripture by noticing how much Jesus relied on it. They observed how Jesus treated people, including those who were looked down upon.

It is alleged that the German theologian Dietrich Bonhoffer said that when God calls a person, He bids him come and die. Jesus said, "If anyone desires to come after me, let him deny himself, and take up his cross, and follow me" (Matthew. 16:24 NKJV). The cross signifies death, making discipleship not for the faint of heart and too costly for many.

What provides evidence that we are true disciples of Jesus? "By this all will know that you are My disciples, if you have love one for another" (John 13:35 NKJV). Love is the indisputable hallmark of true discipleship.

How does one grow in discipleship? By staying connected to the source of life and love (John 15:1-10). A life apart from Jesus Christ is destined to suffer and fail. A life of discipleship is fostered by prayer and the study of God's word. ■

— R. CLIFFORD JONES

SEPTEMBER 17

CHOSEN TO CHOOSE

"For whom he did foreknow, He also did predestinate to be conformed to the image of his Son that he might be the firstborn among many brethren. Moreover, whom he did predestinate, them he also called; and whom he called, them he also justified: and whom he justified, them he also glorified" (Romans 8:29-30 NAKJV).

The spiritual meaning of "disciple" denotes one who is a follower of Christ. For the Christian, it connotes an unswerving faith in His Redeemer, Jesus Christ. "He knows in whom he believes. He is fully persuaded that Jesus is the Son of God and the Savior of sinners" (Our High Calling, p. 331).

My father was a faithful Seventh-day Adventist pastor who understood what it meant to be a disciple. He was a committed follower of Christ, and through his teaching, nurturing, and encouragement, my siblings and I began to model the attributes of discipleship during our formative years. He used the Scriptures to teach us how to be totally dedicated and committed to the cause of Christ.

To foreknow, in the context of today's text, means that God chose to love us before the foundation of this world. Not only did He choose to love us, but He also chose to predestinate us through an adoption process that would empower us to make disciples (Matthew 28:19). God also predestinates His elect to be justified, and then glorified.

In other words, once we are made righteous in the sight of God, we are then honored by God as we begin and complete the process of disciple-making. In actuality, that is the function of the body of Christ. One does not have to be a leader in the body of Christ to encourage members to be followers of Christ. Each member has a responsibility to provide this kind of spiritual nurturing.

There is a story of a little boy who went through Bible studies and was charged by his pastor to return to his town and share the Lord with at least five non-believers. One month later, the pastor received a call from the little boy who asked him to come to his town to have a baptismal service.

"Do you have five souls to be baptized?" asked the pastor.

The young boy replied, "No sir!"

The pastor being a busy man, said, "Young man, do you realize how far a drive it will be to your town? I asked you to find five people for baptism."

The young boy interjected "I do not have five people. I have five villages."

The overwhelmed pastor found himself faced with the task of baptizing 753 people (Greg O'Connor, *Open Doors*, 1/97).

God is inviting each of us to be disciples. Ephesians 1: 4-5 says "According as he hath chosen us in him before the foundation of the world, that we should be holy and without blame before him in love: Having predestined us unto the adoption of children by Jesus Christ to himself, according to the good pleasure of his will (NAKJV). ▮▮

— GARTH GABRIEL

SEPTEMBER 18

THE CROSS OF CHRIST: THE LESSON OF GROWTH WE NEED

"But grow in grace, and in the knowledge of our Lord and Savior Jesus Christ. To him be glory both now and forever. Amen" (2 Peter 3:18 KJV).

There is a great temptation to believe that what is needed is more effort, more work, more accomplishment, better planning, more technology, and more effective execution of plans on the part of the members of the church of God. True enough. But Peter ends his second epistle with both an admonition and a prayer for us. He desires that we grow in grace and the knowledge of Christ Jesus, as both Savior and Lord. This is the work of the Holy Spirit and the Word of God in us, and there is no substitute for it.

We may know many things about Jesus Christ, we may be familiar with the biblical record, but our knowing Him must be personal, intimate, and experiential. Peter was drawn to Jesus. He was the first disciple recorded as confessing Him as the Messiah, saying "Thou art the Christ" (Matthew 16:16). But even then, Peter still had much growing to do. The greatest challenge for the disciples was embracing the idea that Christ was to be crucified.

To know Christ, we must know also the cross of Christ. It is there that we truly meet Him as the One who, while we were yet sinners, died for us. The fruit of such a walk with Christ will be manifest in character development and this is what Christ, as refiner, is looking for: "Christ is waiting with longing desire for the manifestation of Himself in His church. When the character of Christ shall be perfectly reproduced in His people, He will come to claim them as His own" (*Christ Object Lessons*, p. 69).

Knowing Him is the foundation of salvation, faith, and spirituality. His word is true, powerful, and settled in heaven and earth. But this knowledge comes only through a process of learning and growth.

Daniel describes God's people at the close of human history: "The people that do know their God shall be strong and do exploits" (Daniel 11:32b KJV). Knowing Christ is transforming: The Samaritan woman who met Him at the well, liberated and empowered by His love, evangelized a whole town in a few days.

Peter's training began with Christ's call, "Follow me, and I will make you fishers of men" (Matthew 4: 9). Peter's experiences with Christ on the sea, on the Mount of Transfiguration, in the Garden of Gethsemane, at the judgment hall where he denied Jesus, and at Calvary where He saw the ultimate love of God—that entire journey with Christ was an education, a growth in grace through trials that exposed self-sufficiency and produced self-denial. ■

— MICHAEL HORTON

SEPTEMBER 19

CHARACTER TRANSFORMATION

"That you put off, concerning your former conduct, the old man which grows corrupt according to the deceitful lusts, and be renewed in the spirit of your mind, and that you put on the new man which was created according to God, in true righteousness and holiness" (Ephesians 4:22–24 NKJV).

One of my greatest joys working as a pastor has been to watch the Gospel in real time transform the lives of individuals I've had the pleasure of serving. I remember it clearly. Late one evening my phone chimed, alerting me to an incoming text message. On the other end, a distressed teenager. The concern was so great that I jumped in my car and headed over to the house. This beautiful young lady not only persistently rebelled against authority, but had somehow come to believe that her life was no longer worth living. What does a pastor say?

Well, my first reaction in situations that are bigger than me is to pray, and that I did. As the emergency services were called, we still prayed. When we went to the hospital, we still prayed. Over time it was clear that the Lord was answering our prayer. This young lady went from being a rebellious troubled teen to the baptismal pool, knowing and loving Jesus for herself. She excelled in school and later graduated successfully from college.

Just like we choose which pair of pants to put on or which dress to wear, we must make the daily choice to put on a Christ-like character. The good news is we do not have to try to accomplish this on our own. In fact, we cannot. As Philippians 2:13 says, "For it is God who works in you both to will and to do for His good pleasure" (NKJV). The Holy Spirit is at work in those who invite Him in to help. It is no wonder that Ephesians 4:23 says, "and be renewed in the spirit of your mind" (NKJV). It is written in the passive tense. That is, we must allow God to do the renewing work in us. Then and only then will we be able to be true Christians.

The work of salvation, including character transformation, is God's work. We simply have to be willing to let Him do His work by choosing Him each day. Similar to looking in the mirror after getting dressed to make sure everything is looking just right before heading out the door, so we are to let God examine us and reveal what is not right and needs removing. Then we surrender it to Him, asking Him to help us let it go and walking in that victory step by step. If we are willing to allow Him to work in us, He will.

Choose Him to work in you today. ▮▮

— TRICIA WYNN PAYNE

SEPTEMBER 20

FREEDOM—PART 1

"Know that the Lord is God. It is he who made us, and we are his; we are his people, the sheep of his pasture" (Psalms 100:3 NIV).

We are living in a time when most people believe there is a disconnect between Christians and the issues of social justice. Some might even believe that Christians, at best, are silent bystanders and at worst, actively oppose those who live at the margins of the social strata. Their concern seems to begin and end with the unborn.

But this detachment from social involvement does not agree with God's position with the disenfranchised and dispossessed. God's concern for the social justice and liberty of all humanity is unquestioned in Scripture. Psalms.

Many, who question those that claim Christianity is silent on issues of social responsibility, have challenged this disengagement. In His masterful work, Jesus and the Disinherited, Howard Thurman writes,

It cannot be denied that too often the weight of the Christian movement has been on the side of the strong and the powerful and against the weak and oppressed—this, despite the gospel. A part of the responsibility seems to me to rest upon a peculiar twist in the psychology of Paul, whose wide and universal concern certainly included all men, bond and free."

As a Jew, Jesus was well aware of what it meant to live without the benefit of social equality as a vassal of the Roman Empire. He was a part of a people who were subjected to an unjust tax system and impoverished living conditions. The town He grew up in, Nazareth, was notorious as a place of residence. When He began His earthly ministry, He announced that it would be directed to those who lived on the margins of society; the poor, prisoners, the oppressed and the blind. Thurman writes, "The basic fact is that Christianity as it was born in the mind of this Jewish teacher and thinker appears as a technique of survival for the oppressed...Wherever his spirit appears, the oppressed gather fresh courage; for he announced the good news that fear, hypocrisy, and hatred, the three hounds of hell that track the trail of the disinherited, need have no dominion over them" (Thurman, 1949).

In Matthew 25 Jesus makes it clear that in the final judgment, the final destiny of His disciples will be determined by their involvement with humanity on issues of social justice. With Jesus as our model, what implications does this have for those who claim to be His discipleship? How does the word disciple relate to issues of justice, public policy and religious liberty? ■

— TIMOTHY P. NIXON

SEPTEMBER 21

FREEDOM—PART 2

"Know that the Lord is God. It is he who made us, and we are his; we are his people, the sheep of his pasture" (Psalms 100:3 NIV).

For any organization, movement, institution, or association to have any meaningful impact it needs to answer some important questions. Those basic questions center on identity, purpose, goals, and patterns. The answer to these core questions originates with God. God answers the important questions that we face in every aspect of our lives and sets for us the best pattern to follow in achieving our goals through Jesus Christ.

Psalms 100:3, centers us in God, and serves as a powerful biblical guide in helping us to develop a framework for personal, as well as organizational direction. Notice the structure of the text and the questions it answers.

It begins by calling us to "Know the Lord is God." This knowledge calls us to a personal relationship with Jesus Christ, as well as an understanding of His immensity.

Then the Psalmist goes a step further. He answers the question of origins, identity, and purpose. He says, "He made us," and "we are His people." Because all humanity has a common origin and brotherhood as God's creation and people, this gives us a responsibility to see that all people are treated justly, with dignity, decency, and equity. We are our brother's and sister's keeper.

The phrases "not we ourselves," and "sheep" are clear references to discipleship. The double emphasis used by saying, "God created us," and "not we ourselves," strengthens the assertion that He leads and we follow, because sheep always follow the shepherd.

Jesus has given us a powerful example to emulate and follow in seeking the justice and good will of all humanity. Micah 6:8 CEV says it best; "The Lord God has told us what is right and what he demands: "See that justice is done, let mercy be your first concern, and humbly obey your God."

Howard Thurman tells the story of an experience he had when he was a seminary student. A Korean student who was visiting America to observe the American educational system was asked to give her impressions of American education. The Korean student, who was very personable and somewhat diminutive said, with obvious emotion, "You have asked me to give my impressions of American education. But there is only one thing that a Korean has any right to talk about, and that is freedom from Japan."

Her words and sentiment bespoke the core desire of all oppressed and disenfranchised peoples no matter who they are or where they are from. Uppermost in all of their minds is justice, equality, and freedom. ∎

— TIMOTHY P. NIXON

SEPTEMBER 22

KNOWN BY THEIR FRUITS

"By this time, you ought to be teachers yourselves, yet here I find you need someone to sit down with you and go over the basics on God again, starting from square one—baby's milk, when you should have been on solid food long ago! Milk is for beginners, inexperienced in God's ways; solid food is for the mature, who have some practice in telling right from wrong" (Hebrews 5:12-14 MSG).

The writer of the above admonition in the book of Hebrews was not only challenged by the lack of spiritual maturity, but was appalled that those who were supposed to be teachers needed to be taught the ABCs of God. In other words, the "disciple" makers needed to be taught the rudiment of discipleship, i.e. a basic understanding of the priestly role of Christ.

According to Harris W. Lee, in his book *Effective Church Leadership: A Practical Sourcebook*, *"Leadership*, (discipleship) is more than awareness and understanding, more than perspectives and attitude. Leadership, (discipleship) is to be expressed in concrete ways in the life of the church" (Lee, 2003, p. 99). Disciple makers help those who are being discipled to understand the church, the ecclesia in terms of mission and ministry.

The Seventh-day Adventist church I joined had four spiritual strong male elders. They began to teach me the doctrines of the church. One of them in particular, Elder Nelson (now deceased) took a keener interest in me. He would give me religious books to read and invite me to his home, after church, to have dinner with his family. After dinner, we would retreat to his office where he told me the history of my new faith. The oral tradition of teaching was meaningful to me. Elder Nelson was the first person to say to me that "God was calling me into ministry."

As his way of preparing me for "the call," he asked the church board to appoint me to be the outreach leader of the church. A stipulation was that he would be my assistant and guide me because I'd only been a church member for one year. The church board agreed, and the summer of that year we invited an evangelist to run a four-week campaign. More than 30 people were baptized or re-baptized.

By the end of the summer, two ladies (sisters) in the local congregation told me that, "God was calling me to be a pastor." I dismissed it but, to my wonderment, the president of the conference called me and asked me to come see him. I did, and he told me that he heard what was happening at my local church and asked me if I considered that God was calling me to be a pastor. I dismissed it again, but he insisted and offered to assign me a church upon graduation if I would go to college and the seminary to become a pastor. I told him that I would talk to my mother about it and let him know.

I am a pastor today because one spiritually mature disciple understood the importance of disciple-making. ■

— RICHARD SYLVESTER

SEPTEMBER 23

SEEING THROUGH GOD'S EYES

"You, my brothers and sisters, were called to be free. But do not use your freedom to indulge the flesh; rather, serve one another humbly in love" (Galatians 5:13 NIV).

I am standing in line at my local library. The line extends out the room and the checkout counter is unbearably slow. I am feeling tense. In my 20-something year old mind, there are better things I could be doing right now. I hear someone speaking behind me. Turning, I see a blonde, middle-aged lady loaded with books.

"Can you believe this line?" she asks, apparently to me. "I can't believe they don't have another person helping out!"

I nod politely and slowly face forward, hoping that would end the conversation. It does not.

"Oh man, I think I'm going to miss my bus. And that bus may not come again for the rest of the day."

She pauses and I stare at her. We both know what the next question is going to be.

"You wouldn't mind if I go ahead of you, would you?" she asks quietly.

A flash of irritation rises inside me. My thoughts are churning out questions I dare not ask. How could this complete stranger ask this of me? Couldn't she have timed herself better? And how do I know if she is telling me the truth? Does she really think I am that gullible?

I reply that I am also in a rush. She understands. We spend the rest of the time in silence.

After I finally check out my books and head toward the exit, I pause and turn. The lady has walked out the other exit and is heading toward the bus stop. A wave of shame envelops me. I feel the Lord prompting me. "Go make it right." I fight the urge. I argue back. "Why, Lord? She is a stranger. Why should I feel anything at all?" The Lord gently speaks to me again. "She's my child, too."

Unable to repress the urge any longer, I run out the other exit and call out to her.

"I remember you saying you probably missed your bus. I have a car. Would you like me to drive you home?" Surprised, she accepts. As I drive her home, she tells me her story. She's a single mom, but studying to be a nurse. She has not always made the right choices in life, but wants to make them right. I tell her I will keep her in my prayers. She thanks me profusely as I reach her apartment.

"You really didn't have to do any of this," she says.

I am ecstatic, not at all because I see myself as some hero. I am thankful the Lord gave me love in my heart and used me to show love to one of His in need. ■■

— LAURA IM

SEPTEMBER 24

AVOIDING SHORTCUTS

"Don't look for shortcuts to God. The market is flooded with surefire, easy-going formulas for a successful life that can be practiced in your spare time. Don't fall for that stuff, even though crowds of people do. The way to life—to God!—is vigorous and requires total attention" (Matthew 7:13-14 MSG).

Reading this text and assessing my life, I took an introspective look at the progress in my Christian journey. Surely if it had not been for countless thousands of individuals who cared for me and took the time to reach out and give instructions, I would not be where I am today.

In considering this text and my mistakes, I raised the following questions and three points. Was I trusting God who saved me or was I trying to emulate man to feel that I really belonged? There are three things that are needed for a successful life with Christ: (1) Denial of self; (2) Death to self; (3) Determination to serve Christ!

We can't let our prejudices—whether it be race, differences of opinion, cultural backgrounds, religious affiliation, etc.—affect us to the point that our love will be so diminished that we will not want to reach out and share the love of Jesus with others.

To be honest with ourselves, wrong motives have been the dominating force behind what we say and do. Personal gain, position, or just thinking we look right and are accepted by our fellowman is really what motivates us instead of following the Master! That's a shortcut! It has taken nearly 68 years of ministry to bring me to the realization that I must die to self!

Living for Christ without letting Him have full control is not dying to self or living for Him. Whenever you are in a dilemma about what to do, go to the Word!

When the time came, Jesus set aside the privileges of deity and took on the status of a slave; He became human! Having become human, He stayed human. It was an incredibly humbling process. He didn't claim special privileges. Instead, He lived a selfless, obedient life and then died a selfless, obedient death—and the worst kind of death at that—a crucifixion.

On my 85th birthday, I came to understand that deliverance is found by allowing Jesus to completely absorb my every living moment. To be Christ-centered is to know peace! To be Christ-centered is to have joy unspeakable. Having known the joy of music, I find solace in this hymn of the church: "My hope is built, on nothing less than Jesus blood, and righteousness. I dare not trust the sweetest frame, but wholly lean on Jesus name! On Christ the solid rock, I stand. All other ground is sinking sand!" ■

— LAWRENCE LOGAN

SEPTEMBER 25

INSTRUMENTS OF RIGHTEOUSNESS

"Neither yield ye your members as instruments of unrighteousness unto sin: but yield yourselves unto God, as those that are alive from the dead, and your members as instruments of righteousness unto God" (Romans 6:13 KJV)).

Neither yield ye your members..." The apostle more fully explains what he means by obeying sin in the lusts thereof; a presenting, or making use of the "members, as instruments of unrighteousness unto sin."

By their "members," he means the several powers and faculties of the soul. The Ethiopic version renders it, "your souls"; or the several parts of the body, or both. By "yielding," or presenting of them, is designed the employment of them in the service of sin, as instruments of unrighteousness unto sin. That is, as a means of performing unrighteous actions, in obedience to sin, or the corruption of nature with its lusts.

The word translated "instruments" signifies "arms" or "weapons." The ancients formerly reckoned weapons the members of soldiers. Here, the apostle calls the members weapons, which he would not have the saints use in favor of sin, an enemy and a tyrant. That would be unrighteous in itself, and injurious to the cause of God and themselves.

Paul admonishes the saints to yield to God, as those that are alive from the dead. That means for them to present themselves, soul and body, to God and give up and devote themselves to Him, and to His service. Saints are to yield a cheerful obedience to Him, considering themselves as under great obligation to do so. Inasmuch as saints are free from condemnation and death by the righteousness of Christ; and quickened when dead in trespasses and sins, by His Spirit and grace; and therefore should yield.

The strongest motives against sin, and to enforce holiness, are here stated. Being made free from the reign of sin, alive unto God, and having the prospect of eternal life, it becomes believers to be greatly concerned to advance thereto. But, as unholy lusts are not quite rooted out in this life, it must be the care of the Christian to resist their notions, earnestly striving, that, through Divine grace, they may not prevail in this mortal state.

Let the thought that this state will soon be at an end, encourage the true Christian, as to the temptations of lusts which so often perplex and distress him. Let us present all our powers to God, as weapons or tools ready for the warfare, and work of righteousness, in his service. There is strength in the covenant of grace for us. Sin shall not have dominion. God's promises to us are more powerful and effectual for mortifying sin, than our promises to God. ■■

— BRITTON MCKENZIE

SEPTEMBER 26

LOVING GOD WITH EVERY STEP

Whoever fears the Lord walks uprightly" (Proverbs 14:2a NIV).

My best friend had just gotten his mother to lend us her car keys. It was a hot summer afternoon in Queens, New York, and we were on our way to a local fast-food chain. While at a stoplight, we noticed two young men who were walking the city block. One of them appeared to be walking in a very peculiar fashion. He almost seemed to be walking as if he had sustained an injury. The light turned green, and I proceeded to my destination.

On my way to the car after leaving the restaurant, I ran into the two young men again. I inquired about his injury and offered to give him a ride to his destination. He informed me that he had not sustained any injuries but had a justified reason for walking in such a manner. He told me that he was wearing a brand-new pair of "uptown" sneakers, also known as "Nike Air Force 1." He was walking in a cautious manner because tomorrow was the first day of school and he did not want any creases in his "ups." While he understood that he could not keep his sneakers in perfect condition, he still saw the value of walking differently than others.

As a young man, I have often spent immense amounts of time trying to measure up to other people's perception of success. People's opinions had determined the school I attended, the car I drove, and even the clothes I wore. Above all, my family's opinions mattered most. I yearned to hear the affirmation of those who were closest to me. Words of affirmation I often equated with love. Honoring one's parents is an essential behavior according to Scripture; after all, it is the fifth commandment.

Matthew describes the depth of love we should strive to have for Christ, as one that surpasses the love we have for family. Matthew states: "Anyone who loves their father or mother more than me is not worthy of me; anyone who loves their son or daughter more than me is not worthy of me" (Matthew 10:37 NIV).

Matthew is not encouraging us to love our families less. Instead, he is challenging us to love God more. We ought to love God more than anyone or anything else. It is a love that makes God a top priority in our lives. This supreme love for our Creator is one that sustains us when facing the hills and valleys of life.

Today, let us strive to walk in a way that pleases the God we love more than ever. ▮▮

— ABRAHAM HENRY

SEPTEMBER 27

THE COST OF DISCIPLESHIP

"Then Jesus said to his disciples, 'Whoever wants to be my disciple must deny themselves and take up their cross and follow me. For whoever wants to save their life will lose it, but whoever loses their life for me will find it'" (Matthew 16:24-25 NIV).

Let's be honest. Self is made up of our personal desires and ambitions. The Old Testament equates self with being "stiff-necked," which is really rejecting God. The denial of self comes when we sacrifice our earthly and fleshly ambitions. Self-denial is about what Jesus wants in me; "not my will, but thine, be done" (Luke 22:42b KJV).

Jesus is never afraid of challenging who we are. By making each decision in life, we are not only deciding our destiny but we are making ourselves into a certain kind of person. Are we willing to deny ourselves and take up our cross and follow Jesus?

If you live long enough, you will discover that life usually presents us with a variety of crosses. Some of them are more difficult than others. However, it is never easy to accept a cross, whether it is financial difficulties, illness, family issues, joblessness, depression, and the list goes on. How we view our cross is going to determine the impact it has on us. Do we view it as a punishment from God or do we believe that crosses are simply a part of our lives, just as joy and love are part of our human condition?

When we are carrying a cross, Jesus gives us an amazing gift—the gift of His presence; that He is with us and He will help us to carry our cross. Jesus will give us everything we need to deal with our cross. In dealing with our cross Jesus invites us to share our stories and experiences with others.

It is funny how as Christians we are always trying to make converts. God does not ask us to seek converts, He simply asks us to do discipleship. Discipleship is modeling and teaching Christians the principles in God's Word. It is my joy to witness lives being changed as a result of a total surrender to the Lord. There is a joy I got when I experienced that change in my life. Now I understand why Jesus calls it the new birth. Just like the miraculous conception of a newborn baby, something miraculous went on inside of me.

This new birth must take us into the highways and byways with the cross. We need to get outside the walls of churches to feed the hungry, quench the thirsty, invite the stranger, clothe the destitute, care for the sick, and visit the prisoners. We wait patiently for the day when we will hear, "Well, Done!" It is on that day we will fully comprehend, "For whoever wants to save their life will lose it, but whoever loses their life for me will find it." ∎

— MARLON GREGORY

SEPTEMBER 28

WHAT'S YOUR JOY QUOTIENT (JQ)?

"As the Father loved Me, I also have loved you; abide in My love. If you keep My commandments, you will abide in My love, just as I have kept My Father's commandments and abide in His love. These things I have spoken to you, that My joy may remain in you, and that your joy may be full" (John 15:9-11 NKJV).

General Massena of Napoleon's army suddenly arrived with 18,000 soldiers to conquer a defenseless Austrian town during Easter. Deciding to surrender, the town chose first to celebrate church services as usual while trusting God with their inevitable defeat. As usual, they rang the church bells joyfully.

The invading army construed that an Austrian army had come to defend the town, hence the enemies dispersed promptly! These Austrians won through the weapon of joy! Similarly, believers must ring the joy bells in the face of life's vicissitudes and trials. Satan cannot withstand joy-filled Christians who stretch their faith in God.

God, the Creator of joy, wants His full joy in His blood-bought child, while Satan determines to steal it. Christians should be the most attractive people because God's deep-seated joy fills them as bearers of His amazing grace. While the Intelligence Quotient (IQ) measures intelligence level and the Emotional Quotient (EQ) measures emotional intelligence, the Joy Quotient (JQ) measures the level of joy in our lives at any given time. It reveals our knowledge, understanding, and appreciation of ourselves and indicates the balance in our lives, or lack thereof. Jesus' joy is certain, satisfying, "unspeakable and full of glory" (1 Peter 1:8 KJV).

Joy comes into your heart when you appreciate and contemplate your salvation. You know that God loves you unconditionally and eternally. That God loves you as much as He loves Jesus, invokes joy!

Radical decisions to obey and honor God and His words ensure joy. It continues when you are God-centered, God-honoring, other-centered, and mission-centered, knowing your future is secured in God who has our best interest at heart always (Jeremiah 29:11). God rejoices over me to do me good (Jeremiah 32:41). Why won't I have joy?

Your level of joy is like your barometer measuring your right standing in Christ. Don't lose your joy in the busyness of life and ministry. Don't let worries, temptations, hustling, survival, distractions, and professional pursuits steal your joy! Unforgiveness or craze for revenge will destroy your joy. Salvation is not by works but by grace! If you downplay grace in your life or deny grace to others, your joy will diminish and deplete. If you over analyze your situation, you cannot have true joy.

If you are low on joy, you need a genuine revival. Joy evidences revival just like light evidences day dawn. ▮▮

— TUNDE OJEWOLE

SEPTEMBER 29

THE NAZARETH DECLARATION

"But you shall receive power when the Holy Spirit has come upon you; and you shall be witnesses to Me in Jerusalem, and in all Judea and Samaria, and to the end of the earth" (Acts 1:8 NKJV).

Since Jesus came to dwell with us, we know that God is acquainted with our trials and sympathizes with our griefs. Every son and daughter of Adam may understand that our Creator is the friend of sinners. For in every doctrine of grace, every promise of joy, every deed of love, every divine attraction presented in the Savior's life on earth, we see "God with us."

Jesus did not limit compassion to personal relationships. He left nothing to chance. His "Nazareth Declaration," announcing His strategic plan at the very outset of His public ministry, quoted the comprehensive charter of the prophet Isaiah:

"The Spirit of the Lord God is upon me
because the Lord has anointed me
to preach good news to the poor;
He has sent me to heal the broken-hearted,
to proclaim liberty to the captives,
and the opening of the prison to those who are bound;
to proclaim the acceptable year of the Lord
and the day of vengeance of our God;
to comfort all who mourn," (Isaiah 61:1-2 MEV).

When I was five years old, my mother took me to the Shed Aquarium near downtown Chicago. As we were traveling on Lake Shore Drive, we came to East McFetridge Drive and made a right to go towards Megs Field. As we were driving down, my mother and I saw a large white man dragging a small black boy by his arm down the street. My mother stopped the car in the middle of traffic and got out and confronted this man. My mom was only 5'2" and the man had to be over 6 feet tall. I was amazed to see her stop that man.

"Why are you dragging this little boy?" she asked.

He replied, "He tried to steal something out of my car. I am taking him to the police."

My mother said, "You can go get the police, but the little boy will stay with me." The man never came back, and my mom took that little boy home.

It is when I reflect back on this experience, that I truly understood what Jesus meant when He reveals to us His mission as well as ours; to "bring good news to the oppressed, to bind up the broken hearted, to proclaim liberty to the captives, and release to the prisoners; to proclaim the year of the Lord's favor." ■

— JULIUS R. EVERETT, SR.

SEPTEMBER 30

DISCIPLESHIP: ACTIONS AND IN TRUTH

"Dear children, let us not love with words or speech but with actions and in truth" (1 John 3:18 NIV).

John admonishes his readers not to limit their love to words, but include deeds motivated by genuine compassion. In 2020 we witnessed the affirmation of the principle Black Lives Matter too, not just here in America, but around the world. Through actions and in truth, we witnessed the outpouring of love through peaceful protests that affirmed the dignity of all humanity, and not to the exclusion of Blacks.

Women's Health magazine published, on June 9, 2020, that one week of protests (actions and in truth) regarding the principle that Black Lives Matter too did more than 18 months of conversation (words or speech). In that article, the editors cited how Dallas and Denver banned the use of chokeholds by the police. What would have happened if the church had stepped up?

In his book, *The Woke Church*, Eric Mason lamented that the Black Lives Matter movement started in the secular world versus the church. In referencing Isaiah 10:1-3, he states, "Christians of all ethnicities should have entered their pulpits and gone to war in the fight for black lives, both in these instances and holistically." In failing to produce actions and in truth to the principle of Black Lives Matter too, Mason assails that Christians' witness became compromised due to silence and inaction.

As Adventists may know, our founders affirmed the principle of Black Lives Matter too. According to the *Encyclopedia of Seventh-day Adventists*, John Byington, the first General Conference president, was an abolitionist in that movement. In Present Truth, James White labeled as "laggards" those who did not endorse freedom of the slaves. According to the *Adventist Review and Sabbath Herald* on June 17, 1862, Uriah Smith condemned the whitewashed villainy emanating from the pulpits. Ellen G. White states in *Manuscript Release, Vol. 11*, "While we will endeavor to keep the unity of the Spirit in the bonds of peace, we will not with pen or voice cease to protest against bigotry" (p. 229).

Where would Adventists be today if we followed the admonition of our pioneers in applying the principle that Black Lives Matter too?

Through recognition of the biblical principle of the *Imago Dei* found in Genesis 1:26-27, here is the integral question: Does our discipleship trump our politics or self-interests in exemplifying the principle that Black Lives Matter too?

In the *Discipleship Handbook*, a resource for Seventh-day Adventist church members, it states, "According to Jesus, discipleship involves self-denial and sacrifice. It is not for those seeking popularity or selfish desires." ■■

— EDWARD WOODS, III

OCTOBER

ENGAGEMENT

Every day we make decisions for Christ or for this world. Every day we pass by people who are hurting, who are suffering. Some have been treated unjustly and cannot defend themselves.

If we are honest, we too have experienced injustice at some point in our lives—either on our jobs, in our communities, schools, or even in our families. Social injustice wears many faces of discrimination—race, gender, age, disability, etc. Jesus, Himself, experienced social injustice. However, in spite of all that Christ endured for us and continues to do for us, He always points us back to the essence of who He is, love. This is the only way that we will be recognized as His disciples; if we love one another (John 13:35).

Love is the motivator that compels one to engage in the fight against injustice and mistreatment of others. Love seeks out the needs and best interests of others. "Not everyone who says to Me, 'Lord, Lord,' shall enter the kingdom of heaven, but he who does the will of My Father in heaven" (Matthew 7:2, NKJV). Christ is looking for a relationship with us and He wants us to express that same love relationship with others.

During the month of October, our hope is that you will experience the true nature of what it means to care about the wellbeing of others. We must be intentional when it comes to the way we treat people, knowing that we will one day have to give an account for all that we have done. ▮▮

— MOSES EDWARDS, SR.
Director of Public Affairs and Religious Liberty,
South Atlantic Conference of Seventh-day Adventists

OCTOBER 1

#STAY WOKE

"Open thy mouth for the dumb in the cause of all such as are appointed to destruction. Open thy mouth, judge righteously, and plead the cause of the poor and needy" (Proverbs 31:8-9 KJV).

In October 1964, at the age of 35, Dr. Martin Luther King, Jr. became the youngest person to win the Nobel Peace Prize. One month later, on November 13, he delivered a speech in the McDougal Gymnasium on the campus of North Carolina College. Though still a high school student, I, along with 5,000 other people of all races, packed that arena to hear the champion for civil rights in America inspire us from the subject, "Remaining Awake Through a Great Revolution."

I will admit to you that much of what Dr. King said that night escapes my memory. Here are some anecdotes, however, that I do recall: (1) the gymnasium was electric with excitement; (2) because I did not allow time for the traffic and the crush of people that turned out on a chilly November evening, the only place to sit was in the nosebleed section, on the steps or in the rear of the gym; and (3) I vividly recall that during his speech, the PA system failed for a few moments. Dr. King was unfazed. He continued to speak in that booming voice of his and could be clearly heard throughout the arena.

My research into this memorable night from my youth has turned up the following excerpt from this civil rights icon:

"We must realize that violence and hatred are dangerous and tragic forces to be alive in any society. Violence... is both impractical and immoral in the struggle for racial justice."

He concluded:

"If we will remain awake, standing up against evil in our societies, struggling in every creative movement to get rid of the evils that cloud our days, then we will see that brighter day; then we will see that new America... I have faith in that new day" (nccuarchives.wordpress.com).

We are nearly 56 years removed from that evening back in my hometown of Durham, North Carolina. And, "that new America," though much improved, still has a way to go to reach Dr. King's dream. Violence and hatred still persist. There is much left to do to advance the cause of social justice. As Dr. King admonished, we must remain awake and stand up against evil. We must!

History records that Dr. King was again invited to Durham in early April 1968, to help campaign for Black candidates seeking city-wide office. At the last minute he changed his plans, opting instead to go to Memphis to help in the sanitation workers' strike. ■

— WILLIAM L. WINSTON

OCTOBER 2

BLESSED TO BE A BLESSING TO OTHERS

"He that hath pity upon the poor lendeth unto the Lord; and that which he hath given will he pay him again" (Proverbs 19:17 KJV).

There is a song that says. "If I can help somebody, as I pass along. . . . Then my living shall not be in vain." God blesses us so that we can bless others. What greater blessing can there be than to help a young, faithful Christian realize a goal that God has placed upon her heart.

Upon learning of the Academy Days program at a school owned and operated by the Seventh-day Adventist Church, located in Pine Forge, Pennsylvania, a local pastor serving in Durham, North Carolina, decided to organize a trip for potential high school students to attend the program. He hoped that the trip would create some interest in the hearts of the students in attending the school for all or part of their high school years.

After the trip, one young lady expressed an interest in attending. Her family, with very minimal finances, enrolled her for her first year. She completed the school year and testified at her home church what a blessing it had been to have been able to attend the academy. She then stated that she wanted to continue her education there, but would not be able to do so because her family could not afford to pay the cost of a second year.

After the prayer service that evening, the pastor and several members of the church got together and decided that they would all contribute funds to help pay for the cost of the next school year. They wanted that young lady to return and continue her education at the academy. She and her family were excited and very grateful that the church family was willing to help the young lady continue to receive a Christian education. The church membership continued with the assistance, and the young lady was able to complete her high school education and graduate.

Inspired writings tell us that children are a gift from God and that His church family should treat them as a top priority. The church should invest in their futures to help them to prepare for life in this world and the world to come.

I was blessed to serve as the young lady's pastor and to be used by the Lord, along with members of the Immanuel Temple Seventh-day Adventist Church family in Durham, North Carolina, to help this youth get a Christian education. ■■

— DAVID A. SMITH

BLACK LINES IN MY HANDS

"A friend loves at all times, and a brother is born for a time of adversity" (Proverbs 17:17 NIV).

It was the late 1960s. I was the only black student in my first-grade class at a lovely Seventh-day Adventist (SDA) school in the Midwest. Despite my teacher's kind and attentive ways, on most days I felt sad and lonely, especially at recess time. Many of the children had never interacted with any person outside of their race. For that matter, neither had I. They were cautious and curious. I was timid and wary.

Occasionally, members of the class would approach me as a group, only to ask me to show them the black lines in my hands, or to demonstrate how my hair could stand up all by itself. I would always oblige, only to watch them walk away snickering, leaving me to stand alone.

One day at recess one of the popular girls in the class, Tammy, left the group and walked over to ask if I wanted to play with her on the swings. I did not answer at first, but finally I looked up to see eyes that looked like two blue marbles awaiting my answer. I joyfully agreed! From that day forward, Tammy, the girl with the blue marble eyes, became my playmate and best friend. Many times our classmates would tell her not to play with me because I was black. She would boldly let them know that I was her friend and she did not care about my color.

Soon our parents became friends and our families began to share time together. But, a year later my family decided to move to another region of the country. Tammy and I never saw each other again. I never forgot her bold stand.

During a break between classes while attending summer training for teachers, at an SDA university, a lady greeted me and asked my name and where I grew up as a child. As I responded, I saw the blue marble eyes. It was Tammy, my BFF. It was 30 years later, but it felt like yesterday. We immediately embraced and jumped around just like back in first grade.

When we returned to class, we were given an opportunity to tell our story. I was eager to thank Tammy for standing up and being my first civil rights hero.

Soon, God's faithful will be eager to thank Jesus, our Forever Friend, Advocate and Savior, for His infinite sacrifice and unfailing love! What a reunion that will be! ■■

— KIM GAITER

LOVE AND COMPASSION FOR ALL

Greater love hath no man than this, that a man lay down his life for his friends" (John 15:13 KJV).

Our country continues to see a rise in the number of homeless veterans. Many of our veterans are homeless due to mental health problems or economic hardships.

Just over nine percent of all adults experiencing homelessness in the United States are veterans of the U.S. military. That means that on any given day, an estimated 40,056 veterans experience homelessness in America, according to Point-in-Time counts conducted in January 2017 by communities across the country.

This weighs on my heart because I am a United States Army veteran. I served my country and stood for the right. I was trained in warfare strategies, and taught how to be a team player—to leave not one of my fellow soldiers behind. If any of my fellow soldiers were lacking in some way, whether in unit or company inspections and/or personal issues, I gave them my support. We were taught to work together to help strengthen the weak (nothing like what I sometimes find in the civilian world).

I trained by drilling, exercising, walking, marching, and running up to 15 miles throughout the day. I was no stranger to living in the woods for a week or more. It was mandatory in all weather conditions. I mean ALL weather conditions—high temperatures (80+ degrees), low temperatures (below freezing), in the rain, mud, icy snow, storms, and tornados. Sometimes it was very harsh living in field conditions. There were raccoons, armadillos, rats, rabbits, ants, spiders (even tarantulas), scorpions, and snakes. I shot an M-16 weapon and other military weapons from foxholes, fields, and target ranges.

Without a doubt, these things presented levels of adversity for me, but I also know these things made me a better person, shaping the person I am today. I find it disheartening that many of my fellow veterans are coming back from wars feeling like this country has turned its back on them. But I do find hope in the initiatives to address the homeless problem.

Awareness can help bring about change. I pray that as we continue to seek to address our homeless population, we will also strive to understand how many veterans are dealing with mental health issues that precipitated their homelessness.

I thank the living God of heaven for keeping me, and for the prayers of my family (especially my mother) and faithful prayer warriors of the Seventh-day Adventist Church.

My prayer is that we have compassion and love for one another, because we never know the struggle, and the struggle is real! ▮▮

— M. TERESA POSEY

DIVINE HEALING

"I beseech thee, O Lord, remember now how I have walked before thee in truth and with a perfect heart, and have done that which is good in thy sight. And Hezekiah wept sore" (2 Kings 20:3 KJV).

Looking at the life of King Hezekiah, at the age of 25 years old he took over the kingdom from his wicked father, King Ahaz. King Ahaz was known for his injustices, cruelty, and unfair practices. He even went as far as removing the priests from the temple. He built idols all over the nation for the people to worship. But King Hezekiah restored the priests to the temple and treated the people of Judah fairly. He replaced injustices with justice, and turned the hearts of the people back to the Lord.

God honored King Hezekiah's character, and even stopped time for this king. The Lord added an additional 15 years to King Hezekiah's life. His prayer is our text for today: "I beseech thee, O Lord, remember now how I have walked before thee in truth and with a perfect heart, and have done that which is good in thy sight. And Hezekiah wept sore."

"And it came to pass, afore Isaiah was gone out into the middle court, that the word of the Lord came to him, saying, 'Turn again, and tell Hezekiah the captain of my people, thus saith the Lord, the God of David thy father, I have heard thy prayer, I have seen thy tears: behold, I will heal thee: on the third day thou shalt go up unto the house of the Lord. And I will add unto thy days fifteen years" (2 Kings 20:3-6 KJV).

If our leaders today would have the fear and respect for God as this king did at the beginning of his reign, and lead by example, not only would we see an end to name calling, bigotry, racism, sexism, division among cultures, division among the rich and the poor; we would also see a religious awakening in our country.

If we adhere to this lesson as we deal with one another, let us remember what the Lord expects of us: "He hath shewed thee, O man, what is good; and what doth the Lord require of thee, but to do justly, and to love mercy, and to walk humbly with thy God?" (Micah 6:8 KJV).

No nation can be great without God! ▮▮

— DAVID M. JONES

OCTOBER 6

SHARING IS PLEASING TO GOD

"Do not neglect to do good and to share what you have, for such sacrifices are pleasing to God" (Hebrews 13:16 ESV).

Growing up in a home where love was not shown was a traumatic experience for me as a child. I made up in my mind at a young age that I would be different.

I can't say I made a decision at that early age to help people. However, as I got older I was touched when I saw someone in need and I always had the desire to help them.

I had only been in the United States about three years. My husband and I were not only newlyweds, but also newly baptized members of the Seventh-day Adventist (SDA) Church. One day I received a call from a friend who also had just arrived in the United States. She was thrown out of the home where she was living and had no place to go. I immediately told her she could stay with us. I am thankful for my husband, because I did not talk it over with him first, but he accepted her and treated her like his own sister.

After she moved in, we discovered she had a disease called Lupus. She spent five years with us. During that time there were many emergencies due to her medical condition. She attended church with us and we shared our beliefs with her. She eventually joined the church and became the first SDA in her family. Her time with us ended when my husband received the call to enter the ministry, and we relocated to Huntsville, Alabama for him to attend Oakwood College.

Years later she visited us. My husband was working for the church at that time. She remained a faithful member, witnessing to her family and others about her faith. She died a few years ago, while still working for the Lord.

God has moved many times in our lives, using us to share with others what He has blessed us with. Our doors have always been open to those whom God has sent.

I pray that our hearts remain open to continue sharing with those in need. When we share what God has blessed us with, He considers it a sacrifice, and it pleases Him. ■

— MARLENE EDWARDS

OCTOBER 7

THE HOARY HEAD IS A CROWN

"Therefore, it is lawful to do good on the Sabbath"
(Matthew 12:12 NKJV).

As I was leaving church one Sabbath afternoon in January 2017, I noticed a phone message from my friend and mentor Dr. Richard E. Tottress. He's usually still in church at this time, so I hastily returned the call.. He assured me everything was fine. Since it was raining so profusely, he'd decided to stay in and watch the Hope Channel.

I had a long drive through heavy rain and was eager to get home. But as I approached the exit to Dr. Tottress' house, I got the impression to go see him. Why? I thought to myself. I'd spoken with him and all is well; besides, it's a steady downpour. Yielding to my impression, I turned off the exit toward Dr. Tottress' house.

While ringing the doorbell, I could see him through the glass, rising slowly from his easy chair and laboriously making his way to the door. He usually had a sturdier stride for his age of 99. He opened the door and smiled brightly.

"Hello Partner," he said. "What a surprise, come on in!"

After a big hug, I said, "Well, I was impressed to come on by."

As soon as I stepped further inside I realized why—a whiff of natural gas hit my nostrils. Suddenly, the smell diminished but I felt a painful headache, which dispelled all doubt.

"I smell gas!" I told my friend.

"You do know there are no gas appliances in here," he replied, "everything is electric."

I inquired about his central furnace and asked if I could call the gas company and have them check it. He said he would leave it up to me. The technician came and confirmed there was a gas leak. He shut the gas off, pending repairs. I called the paramedics to check Dr. Tottress' vitals. They were amazed at how coherent he was and said his vital signs were better than theirs. The next day a plumbing company gladly performed the pipeline repairs and the gas service was safely restored.

It's a blessing to see how God moved to protect the hoary head, his servant of many faithful years who reached thousands of souls as the pastor of the Oakwood College Church, "Your Bible Speaks" radio ministry speaker/director for over 50 years, author of several books/tracks, and a dependable food pantry volunteer. Although he was nose blind to the gas and lurking dangers in his home, his guardian angel stood by, a firm sentinel at the gate.

Dr. Tottress lived to be almost 102. ■

— JAMES L. REID

OCTOBER 8

ME THE INNKEEPER

"'Which of these three do you think proved to be a neighbor to the man who fell into the robbers' hands?' And he said, 'The one who showed mercy toward him.' Then Jesus said to him, 'Go and do the same'"
(Luke 10:36-37 NASB).

While this famous parable is certainly focused on the kindness of the Samaritan to his would be Jewish enemy, we must not forget the innkeeper. Remember the theme for this parable is mercy and how those seeking eternal rewards achieve this, not by keeping the letter of the law, but instead by living it.

Jesus is teaching that one must be naturally able to show unbiased mercy to strangers. Jesus is the one who shows us how to see people in their distress. He puts in us a love that makes it impossible to ignore suffering. He gives us the desire and wisdom to take action for the health and benefit of the needy. As we care for those cast to the roadside by poverty, sickness, incarceration, racism, and violence, we are joining with Jesus. We are pouring the oil of His Spirit to soothe the pain, and offering the wine of His blood to heal the soul.

But like the Samaritan, Christ has gone to prepare a place for us. He has left the needy at the inn and we are the innkeeper there. Think about it. I have seen too many evangelistic events where the focus is on how many people are baptized and saved, but not so much on healing and long-term transformation. The church has a responsibility to care for the people who are brought to the inn. The saving and baptizing is reserved for the Holy Spirit.

When I married my wife, Kimberly, she definitely made sure the wedding was a focal highlight. But while we spent probably way too much money on just a few hours of celebration, we both knew that the wedding was a gateway to the more important lifetime of marriage. Many marriages do fail because of a lack of endurance. There are rough patches when you feel like giving up. But we remember we made a choice, a decision for God, a responsibility to be true to each other.

As people in a relationship with Jesus, we have the great responsibility of caring for others who have been brought to the inn. The work of discipling, restoring, rehabilitating doesn't happen in one day; healing takes place over time at the inn.

In your life today who is in your inn? Who has God placed in your life for you to care for and heal? It may be tempting to give up or pass by, but I challenge you to endure. God will be back soon and we must be found working for His children. ■

— JOSHUA NELSON

OCTOBER 9

STONES OF MERCY

"The Lord... is longsuffering toward us, not willing that any should perish but that all should come to repentance" (2 Peter 3:9 NKJV).

Social injustice is not a new phenomenon. It is as old as sin itself— beginning with the first crime committed on earth when Cain killed Abel. "The voice of thy brother's blood crieth unto me from the ground" (Genesis 4:10 KJV). It was a cry for justice.

The Bible is replete with stories of injustice. But the injustice is overshadowed by God's amazing grace and unexplainable mercy toward those who deserve it the least.

John 8:1-11, recounts a story of pious men who "caught" a woman in the act of adultery. In an effort to publicly discredit Jesus, they orchestrated the event (entrapment). They chose a willing participant to go undercover and at the right moment burst into the room. Barely clothed, perhaps with just a blanket to cover her, they dragged her through the streets to the temple where Jesus was teaching. Right away an injustice was perpetrated because the woman could not commit adultery by herself. Where was the other guilty party?

She is cast at the feet of Judge Jesus to pronounce sentencing without a trial. What would the verdict be? Actually, Jesus was the one on trial. If He pronounced her innocence, Jesus would be accused of violating the Law of Moses which called for both guilty parties to be stoned to death. If He pronounced her guilty, Jesus would be accused of assuming Roman authority.

Many recount this story and clearly see the mercy of God extended to the woman who was the center of their hypocritical plot. But upon closer inspection, we see even greater mercy extended to her accusers.

Instead of a verbal response, Jesus stoops and writes in the dust the guilty secrets of their own lives. Ellen G. White, in the *Desire of Ages* states, "Their eyes fell upon the pavement at His feet" (p. 461). Jesus wrote in the dust that sat on top of the stone pavement of the temple. The same finger that wrote the Ten Commandments on the stone tablets was the same finger that could have written their sins in the stone pavement of the temple! But in divine mercy, Jesus chose to write in the dirt that was so easily swept away.

Even those guilty of injustice are also benefactors of God's love and mercy. ■

— JAMES K. LAMB

ONE NURSE'S RELIGIOUS LIBERTY JOURNEY

"So Jesus said to them, 'Because of your unbelief; for assuredly, I say to you, if you have faith as a mustard seed, you will say to this mountain, 'Move from here to there,' and it will move; and nothing will be impossible for you'" (Matthew 17:20 NKJV).

When I was baptized into the Seventh-day Adventist (SDA) Church in 1976, I was working full-time as a registered nurse. Though I had studied and accepted the church's doctrines, my faith at that time was not strong enough to ask for a change in my work hours. So, I continued to work my day shift, Monday through Wednesday, and my evening shift on Thursday and Friday. This meant coming home at 11:30 p.m. on Fridays, and walking into church Sabbath morning by 9:20 a.m., with a four-year-old and a seven-year-old in tow.

In April 1977, we relocated to North Carolina. Prior to the move, my husband and I decided that I would go back to being a stay-at-home mom. One quiet Friday evening after worship, my husband announced that he was feeling a call from God to the pastoral ministry. After much prayer and many miracles, in August 1981, the North Carolina house was sold, our two girls and my husband were enrolled in Anna Knight Junior Academy and Oakwood College, respectively, in Huntsville, Alabama, and I was seeking employment.

Now, my faith had grown, and my job application stated that I was not available to work from sunset Friday to sunset Saturday. The Lord worked my schedule out in a wonderful way. Yes, it was the night shift with Sabbath hours off and I was thankful! I was at home when the kids came home from school, and Friday evenings were a delight.

It was a great three years in Huntsville, then on to Berrien Springs. I prayed for no more night shifts and God answered my prayer. I worked a full-time day shift, with my girls enrolled in the SDA junior and senior academies. During that time I was never scheduled to work during Sabbath hours, and my husband earned the Master of Divinity degree he sought.

Throughout my career, only once did I have to ask the Seventh-day Adventist Religious Liberty Department for help. A new Director of Nursing sought to change my schedule, but the corporate office quickly told her that she was to resume my hiring agreement and not schedule me to work on Sabbaths. I was grateful for the support of the Religious Liberty Department.

Our family moved often during more than 40 years of pastoral ministry. I pursued certifications, and the letters behind my name became RN, CRRN, and CCM. I became a case manager and my work hours were Monday through Friday from 8:00 a.m. to 5:00 p.m. God blessed; I had many nursing positions, but never again did I have to work on Sabbath. ■

— EULA P. WINSTON

OCTOBER 11

GET MAD

"But if ye will not hear these words, I swear by myself, saith the Lord, that this house shall become a desolation" (Jeremiah 22:5 KJV).

Get mad!

When we are angry at the action of injustice we are connecting with the heart of God. We learn to "be angry and sin not" as we are filled with righteous indignation. Being complacent in the face of injustice is being complicit with the wrongs in our communities.

Too many of us dismiss inequities because they do not seem to directly affect us. We are lost in our own world, aloof to the suffering of those on the other side of the tracks. We think that what we don't know won't hurt us. We are lost in "lala land" fighting over rubbish, while people are dying, unjust laws are passed, and our own liberties are being removed.

I have sat in too many church meetings that entertain pointless conversations, that do not address real life issues and whose conversation is about self. When we fail to observe our world through the lens of Christ, we miss opportunities. We love to hide behind the walls of the church, our homes, careers, relationships, instead of opening our eyes to the world around us.

Jesus needs our talents, our gifts, to do our part in weaving the fabric of love this world desperately craves. But too often the world's problems seem too big and we opt to focus on our own comfort and self-interests. These pursuits are often entangled with the devil's plan to keep us from engaging in the war against sin and from fulfilling our purpose. We must learn to get angry.

Anger is not always bad. God has given us this emotion for good. We often use it for our own desires. But if we lean into the emotion of anger, we will begin to hate what God hates and love what God loves. We will burn with passion to move into action and transform His world. Righteous anger fuels the engine of God's justice reformation.

So, reflect for a moment and allow God's Spirit to consume your desires. What disturbs you? What is He asking you to help change? Allow His anger to fuel your life's purpose.

My Father, You do not like what is happening to Your people, especially those who cannot help themselves. Help me to develop a distaste for wrong doing and mistreatment, and to be moved to do something to help someone who is being taken advantage of this week. Help me to keep an out for those who are unable to help themselves. Provide me with the resources needed to help in whatever capacity. Amen. ■■

— JOSHUA NELSON

OCTOBER 12

YES HE CAN!

"And Jesus looking upon them saith, 'With man it is impossible, but not with God: for with God all things are possible'" (Mark 10:27 KJV).

Have you ever been in a situation where the circumstances seem to be hopeless? When you see no way out, and no one to turn to? In those moments, it seems hard to bear. Sometimes you just want to throw your hands up in defeat. Life can be that way sometimes; too impossible to handle by yourself. It is when we are at that point, God always has someone to come through with a word or deed to encourage us to hang in there just a little while longer, so we don't give up.

I remember a certain church that had to deal with a situation that proved that very point. This particular church had a problem with a leaking roof. They tried to fix it many times. They patched the roof over and over again, but could not fix it. Every time they thought they had it fixed, it would rain and the leaky roof would show itself again. So, they gave up. The cry went out, "We tried, but we could not fix it!"

For five to six years the roof stayed that way. Until one day a new pastor came and saw the roof with its patchwork and realized that the members were totally embarrassed with the way their church looked. So, he prayed, "Lord, help me to be a blessing to this congregation by getting this roof repaired." Within a few weeks of praying about the situation, the answer came. Call the insurance company and report the leaky roof.

Within a few days, an adjuster came to look at the roof. He saw the images of large hail prints in the shingles, and ordered a new roof to be installed. Hallelujah! What a blessing! Five to six years had gone by and God opened the door by moving on the heart of the insurance company. God also moved on the heart of the roofer who did the work. He saw more rotten wood on the side of the building and was moved to replace that also, as a gift to the church. He confessed to them that he wanted his work to look good to the public. Hallelujah! What an act of love shown by a stranger who was moved by God's love to help those who had given up.

It is true, God is a way-maker. He puts people in the right place at the right time. When things are impossible with man, they are always possible with God. ■■

— MOSES L. EDWARDS, SR.

OCTOBER 13

STANDING IN THE GAP

"The King will reply, 'Truly I tell you, whatever you did for one of the least of these brothers and sisters of mine, you did for me'" (Matthew 25:40 NIV).

It was a hot blistering Tuesday in the summer of 1996. Although I was inside with cool air blowing in the building, beads of sweat were trickling down my face and my hands were sweaty. I was in Washington, D.C., inside the Senate Building in front of the office of the Speaker of the House.

At that time the Speaker of the House was Newt Gingrich (from Georgia). I was with a group of volunteers and staff from the Lupus Foundation of Georgia. We were there to talk with Speaker Gingrich about signing a bill to fund research for lupus, and appeal for equal access to specialists, treatments and services for people diagnosed with lupus. For a moment I hesitated before knocking on the door. I questioned, "God, what am I doing here?"

I was there because 12 years previously I was a patient needing access to those services (access to specialists, medications, housing, and employment/finances). I was diagnosed with systemic lupus erythematosus on the eve of Thanksgiving in 1984, and the following year with polymyositis—a rare muscular inflammatory disorder.

Three months after that diagnosis I lost my job, permanently "laid off" with a check of three months' pay and COBRA insurance. When that ran out, I was desperate and found myself standing in long lines, sitting in lobbies, and filling out mounds of paperwork in order to get minimum assistance to see doctors and get medicine. Because of my pre-existing condition, it was hard finding a job because few employers would hire someone with a pre-existing condition.

During those years and following, God kept me and sustained me. I was actually living Psalms 34:10: ". . . those who seek the Lord shall not lack any good thing" (NKJV).

It was during that time that disability rights were at a peak. The Americans with Disabilities Act was signed into law by President George Bush on July 26, 1990. It was created from the civil rights bill to ensure equal treatment, access, rights and opportunities for people with disabilities.

So, as I stood there knocking, I realized that what I went through prepared me to stand in the gap for my peers who would come after me. This social movement for human rights continues today. ■

— ROSEMARY GRAHAM

OCTOBER 14

WHEN YOU SEE A NEED, HELP

"If anyone has material possessions and sees a brother or sister in need but has no pity on them, how can the love of God be in that person? Dear children, let us not love with words or speech but with actions and in truth" (1 John 3:17-18 NIV).

As Christians we believe that God wants us to love. "Let all that you do be done in love" (1 Corinthians 16:14 NKJV).

Often in life we will come into situations where there is a need. With so many scams going on today we must ask God for direction. When we see others in need our hearts should go out to them.

One night as I was coming out of the local Walmart, I was met by a middle-aged Hispanic woman and her daughter. She told me that she lost her job and asked for financial help. All I had was five dollars in cash. After giving her the five dollars, her reaction really touched me. She and her daughter were overjoyed; it was as though I had given them one hundred dollars. I told her to wait for me—I needed to go to the ATM across the parking lot where I wouldn't be charged a withdrawal fee. (I wanted to give them more.)

As I went to my car, a Walmart employee came out of the store and started yelling at the lady. I could hear her telling the lady that she needed to leave or she would call the police. Unfortunately, the Hispanic woman and her daughter ran off to a car waiting on the other side of the parking lot.

I felt bad for the lady because I could feel her pain from the look on her face. She really seemed to need the help. I was not able to tell her to follow me to the ATM. I was hurt because I wasn't able to help her a little more.

There is a need for food, shelter and clothing among us. How do we call ourselves Christians and not try to meet these needs? God wants us to help any way that we possibly can. Don't look the other way. We must have trust in God and look to Him, so we may boldly say, "The Lord is my helper; I will not fear. What can man do to me?" (Hebrews 13:6 NKJV). ■

— CHARLES BROOM, SR.

OCTOBER 15

WE ARE HERE FOR ONE ANOTHER

"Honor thy father and thy mother: that thy days may be long upon the land which the Lord thy God giveth thee" (Exodus 20:12 KJV).

Approximately 10 years ago, I received "that call." You know, that call when your parent tells you they can no longer live alone. I had been telling my mother for years that she needed to move in with me because it wasn't safe for her to live alone anymore due to her health challenges. I couldn't believe she was finally giving in.

I knew I had to move quickly—especially with her temperament. It was either now or never! I obtained permission from my employer to leave, and within a matter of days I was on a plane bound for San Francisco.

It was an extremely emotional experience as we went through her things, giving away items she would have normally kept—good ole' cast iron skillets, quality furniture, and some of her clothing, which was neatly hung in a very organized closet (nothing was ever out of place in her home).

While we were packing her things, I ran across a housing verification form. This was the arduous form she filled out annually in hopes of qualifying to remain in her home. Oh, how she dreaded filling out that form. She never knew when the rules for qualifying would change. We all know too well how our senior citizens are oftentimes taken advantage of; unfortunately proprietors do not always follow the rules.

Believe it or not, according to the UIC John Marshall Law School Fair Housing Legal Support Center and Clinic, "some state and local laws prohibit source of income discrimination. A landlord may not institute a policy that all renters must earn a monthly wage that is 60 percent above the monthly rent. If a retired senior can easily afford a unit with his or her Social Security check and with additional funds . . . a landlord may not refuse to rent to the senior." How many seniors know this?

Regrettably, when it comes to those who fall prey to social injustice, our senior citizens (those who should be honored) are high on the list. But I am so grateful that there is an unseen Law Maker "whose eyes are over the righteous, whose ears are open unto their prayers, and whose face is against them that do evil" (1 Peter 3:12 paraphrased). "God requires more. He demands of you to love as Christ has loved souls. He demands of you compassion for the suffering, the erring, those who are subject to Satan's temptations. He demands of you kindness, courtesy to even the unfortunate, a generous consideration of the feelings of others" (Ellen G. White, *Sons and Daughters of God*, 271).

I am so grateful for the opportunity to share this extraordinary love, as I honor my mother. ▮▮

— OLIVIA MORRISON

OCTOBER 16

THE SOCIAL JUSTICE HOLIDAY

"Is this not the fast that I choose, to release the bonds of wickedness, To undo the ropes of the yoke, And to let the oppressed go free, And break every yoke? Is it not to divide your bread with the hungry and bring the homeless poor into the house; When you see the naked, to cover him; And not to hide yourself from your own flesh? Then your light will break out like the dawn, and your recovery will spring up quickly; And your righteousness will go before you; The glory of the Lord will be your rear guard" (Isaiah 58:6-8 NASB).

Growing up as a Seventh-day Adventist (SDA) Christian we often quoted Isaiah 58:13-14 outside the context of the entire chapter. We were taught to highlight the "no pleasure" stipulation for the Sabbath day. This was a great proof passage for the legalist to ensure that Saturday and fun never comingled. Some went as far to say sex was forbidden on the Sabbath since it involves pleasure. C'mon man!

I never knew how ridiculous such an interpretation was until actually reading the entire chapter. One will easily learn that the "pleasure" from which God's Sabbath was supposed to deter, was far worse than going to the beach or playing sports on the Sabbath. Isaiah 58:3 describes people finding pleasure in mistreating people. The insane posture of these people is that they are mistreating people and wondering why God is far from them. How naive to be so aloof to what truly concerns the heart of God.

Our personal piety is meaningless without public pity for those God loves. It is when we learn to love like God that our light begins to burst forth. When we truly respect the Sabbath, we begin to do and say what God wants. The Sabbath should be the social justice day of the week; a weekly reminder of our responsibility to rest from doing our own pleasure, which often leads to injustice. Instead, we rest on the day God created nothing but time, time for the created to reflect on the will of the Creator.

The will of the Creator is that we show love to His creatures. Imagine if everyone reserved the seventh day as the holiday that reminds us of our duty to God and man. God told us to remember—we have forgotten what we are to remember! Deuteronomy 5 says we are remembering God's power to deliver us from bondage. The Sabbath is also a day to praise God for His creative and re-creative power. The Sabbath is full of social justice implications and reminders. Have you considered the spiritual and biblical implications of worshiping God on His day for justice?

As I continue to embrace the true nature of a social justice Sabbath, Lord I pray that You will keep me busy doing your will on the Sabbath day and each day of my life. Help me to reflect on what the Sabbath really is about and give me opportunities to fulfill it. Allow me to serve the least, the lost, and the last. Amen. ▮▮

—JOSHUA NELSON

OCTOBER 17

MY RUDE AWAKENING

". . . Of a truth I perceive that God is no respecter of persons" (Acts 10:34 KJV).

Growing up in the southern United States, I had no personal social discrimination issues. My family kept to our side of the "track" and had literally no dealings with Caucasians (except those for whom my mother worked). Our work, play, worship, and schooling were all among African Americans in our neighborhoods.

At 13, I was culturally awakened when my family relocated to northeastern Ohio where I was enrolled in Warren G. Harding High School. The total enrollment was about 1,500, (huge, compared to my former school of maybe 200), and of those 1,500, maybe 250 were Black Americans. This was very new for me. As well, there were five, or less, Black American teachers on staff. My graduating class was 500 strong.

Our school was big in sports and had trophies for numerous championship wins. Despite the shock, Harding seemed OK, but simmering beneath the surface was a volcano that was about to erupt.

The details of the incident 50 years ago elude me, but a fight broke out in the school cafeteria that afternoon between a Black student and a White student, and someone was thrown into the glass trophy case. People ran in all directions. As students fled the building, me included, it occurred to "us" that 95 percent of the kids now locked outside were Black, and the others remained inside, gazing out at us. To this day, I'm unsure just how that was orchestrated.

Before we knew it, police "paddy wagons" swarmed the area and numerous Black students were carted off to police headquarters. The White kids and faculty were safely locked inside, away from "trouble-making" Black students, some of whom ended up in juvenile facilities and negatively labeled before finishing high school.

Yes, 50 years have passed but not very much has changed. People have only become more sophisticated, and even blatant at times, in carrying out their acts of social injustice. A sad reality is that the same I'm-better-than-you mentality often shows itself in our church today.

Numerous White members (not all) have left their churches, schools, and neighborhoods, running, it seems, from "other" members who have joined their company. Even sadder, we are going to heaven anyhow.

Only God can permanently solve the issue of social insolence and an attitude that seems to believe that one race is better than, or more important than another. Only God can, and in time, He, indeed, will. ■■

— GLORIA FELDER

OCTOBER 18

THE LEAST OF THESE MY BRETHREN

"For I was an hungred, and ye gave me meat: I was thirsty, and ye gave me drink: I was a stranger, and ye took me in" (Matthew 25:35 KJV).

Many people come to the city of Atlanta, Georgia seeking employment opportunities. Like most major cities, it has a sizable homeless population.

After just buying a car, I was driving it home through downtown when I decided to take the freeway. The entrance ramp has two lanes with a traffic light that causes a backup and creates an opportunity for the homeless to solicit the slow-moving traffic. They line up on both sides of the ramp, each one a soul for whom Christ gave His life.

I feel compassion toward the poor, realizing "there but for the grace of God, go I." There are churches and other organizations that provide for the homeless and I support some of these local charities. But God just blessed me with a new car and I wanted to be a blessing to someone else that day.

I lowered my driver side window and gave some money to a young man who happily thanked me.

"God bless you," I responded.

Another man was sitting on a retaining wall to my left and a woman was working the right lane. I handed her gift out of my passenger window and she joyfully screamed and waved it in the air, getting the attention of the man sitting on the retaining wall.

"Give me one!" he shouted out.

My generosity also caught the attention of someone else—Satan— who was enraged that I dared to bring a little joy to those he holds in an imprisonment of despair.

Suddenly my vision blurred as a can of partially opened soda whizzed by, landing inside my car, spewing soda everywhere. Looking around, I saw the angry man sitting on the retaining wall, now standing, preparing to throw something else. Dripping with soda and squinting through misty glasses, I had to speed off to evade a direct hit. I prayed for the man's salvation and relief from the mental anguish of Satan's daily torment.

Then I began to reflect upon how my God intervened on my behalf. The powerful throw of a one pound can, missed a midsize car and came fizzing through my open window, narrowly missing my head, bouncing off the inside passenger door and fell crumpled to the floor. What a mighty God we serve!

The very next day I saw a homeless man at the end of an off ramp and I blessed him with money.

"Thank you sir!" he said.

"You're welcome friend and God bless you," I replied.

Take that Satan! ■

— JAMES L. REID

OCTOBER 19

GIVE WHAT WE HAVE

"But Peter said, 'I don't have any silver or gold! But I will give you what I do have. In the name of Jesus Christ from Nazareth, get up and start walking'" (Acts 3:6 CEV).

Contemporary society is full of misery and pain. The wealthy oppress the poor, management abuses labor, and immigrants and strangers are turned away as Christians grapple with our responsibility. In Testimonies for the Church, Vol. 6, Ellen G. White writes, "In the world today, where selfishness, greed, and oppression rule ... For these the Lord has a special care, and He calls upon His people to be His helping hand in relieving their wants" (White, 1901, p. 255).

In the 1950s, African Americans were relegated to a second-class status as every social interaction was accompanied by a humiliating set of social customs. Many Blacks had given up hope that conditions could be changed until Rosa Parks' defiant act. However, though Rosa Parks and Martin Luther King, Jr. deserve honor, they are only part of the story. There are a number of unknown people who deserve credit for uprooting segregation. Jo Ann Robinson is one of them.

Born in Culloden, Georgia, Robinson graduated valedictorian of her high school class before completing her master's degree at Atlanta University. In 1949 she began teaching at Alabama State College in Montgomery, Alabama. Soon after arriving in Montgomery, she was verbally attacked by a public bus driver for sitting in the "whites only" section of the bus. She joined the Women's Political Council (WPC), a civil rights organization.

In 1950, when Robinson became president of the WPC, she refocused the organization on desegregating the public buses. She met with Montgomery's Mayor, William A. Gayle, to discuss her complaints. The city's leadership was not interested in integrating buses, so Robinson threatened a boycott. After Rosa Parks refused to give up her seat, Robinson convinced the Black community to boycott the buses to support Parks' protest. A 381-day boycott followed that eventually broke the will of the community and shook the foundations of segregation.

Though we celebrate Rosa Parks and Dr. Martin Luther King, Jr., it was the thousands of ordinary citizens who supported the boycott and brought it to success. As with much of life, the little things that we do to help others often get overlooked. However, God notices them.

There are millions of injustices going on in our society. We may not have gold or silver, but God expects us to give what we have to help those in need. That may mean walking, standing, or just speaking out when the time comes. ▮▮

— ABEL A. BARTLEY

TRUST IN GOD

"Commit thy way unto the LORD; trust also in Him; and he shall bring it to pass" (Psalm 37:5 KJV).

It was Friday evening. I was on my way home to prepare for the Sabbath. There was only one concern at the end of that work day—we were told by the superintendent (who was a very arrogant person) that we needed to report to work the following day (which was Sabbath). As you can imagine, my faith was being tested at a very high level. We were warned, if we didn't report to work, we better not show up on Monday.

When I arrived home my wife was waiting for me. I explained the situation to her and what would be the result if I didn't report to work on Saturday. We prayed about the matter and decided to place all our trust in God. We both decided that God would act on our behalf, and we had a happy Sabbath.

When Sunday night came, we had the dilemma of whether I should go to work or stay home. We finally decided that I should go to work, even though I fully understood that it would be in vain based on what the superintendent told me the previous Friday.

I arrived at work very early in the morning, I must admit, with some uncertainty, but with the confidence that God was leading me. When I arrived, it seemed strange because no one was working; they were waiting for all the workers to arrive. As I approached the area where my colleagues were, I asked them why they were all standing around and what they were waiting on. One of them asked me what I did to the superintendent. They said this in a joking manner.

"Why?" I responded. "What happened?'

"Don't you know?" they answered.

"No," I replied.

They said the superintendent suffered a heart attack and died over the weekend. When I heard those words, I felt so sorry for him. I then reflected on what he'd said that previous Friday, and thanked God for His mercy.

I'm telling you this story because perhaps you have felt fear, or are now dealing with this kind of situation regarding your religious freedom. It may seem that God is silent and is not responding to you. But I have learned that in situations like these, when your faith and the support of your family is at stake, it is better to fall into the arms of the One who knows the end from the beginning, and live your life trusting our loving Lord and Savior, Jesus Christ. ■■

— MAX BELTRÁN

OCTOBER 21

GOD THE PROTECTOR

"The eyes of the Lord are on the righteous, and His ears are open to their prayers… And who is he that will harm you, if you will become followers of that which is good?" (1 Peter 3:12-13, NKJV).

How safe are we in this world? Every time we turn on the news there are crimes of every sort—rape, sexual assault, robbery, car theft, and murder, just to name a few. Those who follow Christ know little of the plots that the adversary and his hosts are forming against them. Ellen G. White states in The Great Controversy, "No man is safe for a day or an hour without prayer. Especially should we entreat the Lord for wisdom to understand His word. Here are revealed the wiles of the tempter and the means by which he may be successfully resisted" (White, 1858, p. 530).

One sunny, breezy afternoon in the summer of 2003, in Washington, D.C., I was visiting a friend by the name of Lois, along with her three daughters. We decided to cook on the grill that day. Lois did the grilling while the girls and I prepared the side dishes. The dinner was great and that evening we played Family Feud, Jenga, and dominoes. It was getting late and I had three long D.C. blocks to walk. Lois invited me to spend the night, but I decided to make my way home.

As I was walking home I noticed two men walking toward me. My first instinct was to turn around and run, but I was too afraid, so I didn't. As I walked toward them I noticed that they were saying something to each other in a low tone while looking at me. I felt as though I was in real danger. I immediately started praying in my heart. Suddenly, a sense of bravery came over me.

As the two men got closer I looked straight at them. I felt a presence behind me, but I didn't turn around. And to confirm my feeling, the two men stopped looking at me and focused on who was behind me. Their countenance changed as they continued to look upon whoever it was.

I passed the men with a nod. I never looked back, but I believe an angel in disguise walked behind me to protect me. I continued my walk home, walking a little faster because I did not want to encounter another experience like that.

In my heart, I truly believe that God allowed a holy angel to protect me that evening. I thank Him and praise Him for His grace, mercy, and endless love for me. God looked beyond my faults and saw my need. Our only safety in this world is in our Lord and Savior, Jesus Christ! ▮▮

— PATRICIA BECTON

OCTOBER 22

PUTTING OTHERS BEFORE OURSELVES

"Do nothing out of selfish ambition or vain conceit. Rather, in humility value others above yourselves, not looking to your own interests but each of you to the interests of the others" (Philippians 2:3-4 NIV).

It warms my heart and gives me joy when I put others before myself. The Bible says in Acts 20:35 that it's more blessed to give than to receive. So whenever I can, I put others before myself.

One cold morning as I was driving home from the hospital, exhausted after spending several days and nights sitting with my mother as she fought to breathe on an oxygen machine, the hood of my car appeared to be lifting up with the force of the wind. The more I drove, the higher the hood lifted. I knew that if I didn't pull off to the side of the road, my life would be in danger.

As I pulled off the road I noticed a lady with five children walking past me. I got out of my car, then opened and securely shut the hood. When turning to get back into my car I was startled by the lady and her children, as they were standing up close to me.

The lady asked if I could give her some money. I gazed down beside me and there stood the youngest child looking up at me with deep, sad eyes. I told her I probably didn't have much to give because I was taking care of my mother, but I would check my wallet. When I looked in my wallet, I was impressed to give her all that I had. I paused, realizing that if I gave everything, I wouldn't have anything left for myself.

I often have a battle with doubt when it comes to situations like this, but that's when I go to one of my favorite Bible promises; "My God will supply every need of yours according to his riches in glory in Christ Jesus" (Philippians 4:19 ESV). Remembering the importance of making decisions based on what God wants instead of what I want, I made the decision to be obedient and give all.

Valuing others above ourselves is clearly defined in Hebrews 13:2, "Do not forget to show hospitality to strangers, for by so doing some people have shown hospitality to angels without knowing it" (NIV).

As we continue this walk as Christians, if we want people to put us first, then we should do the same. ■

— TERESA HAIRSTON

OCTOBER 23

GOD OF JUSTICE

"Seek good and not evil, that you may live; And thus may the Lord God of hosts be with you, Just as you have said! Hate evil, love good, and establish justice in the gate! Perhaps the Lord God of hosts may be gracious to the remnant of Joseph" (Amos 5:14-15 NASB).

We may think that God doesn't see the injustice happening in the nation today. We may think He sees but does not care. Or, maybe He sees and cares, but is unable to change it.

Through the prophet Amos, we discover that God sees all the dirt the nation does in the dark. He also calls out their hypocrisy as they claim to the world that they are God's servants, yet they continue to practice injustice. The way in which God solves the injustice problem right now is through the miraculous power, wisdom, and courage He puts inside of us, His followers. His message is simple to those who are doing, or allowing injustice; "hate evil, love good." Good versus evil, the great controversy, is the war that tips the tide of justice in our nation.

If we love good we will build up justice at the gate. The gate is the entrance of the city, the place where court was held and the fate of criminals was decided. This means that we must uphold justice at the beginning of everything in the city. All that enters into society must be filtered through the gate of justice. Leaders and politicians have a responsibility to do justice. Christians know justice because they know God.

When we fail to speak truth to power, we are depriving our communities of God's justice imperative. Who else can truly have a pulse for justice in our cities but the faith-based community? Justice should be best explained by the people in our communities claiming to be closest to the One who is just.

Father, develop in me a hate for evil and a love for good. Point out the good in all people so I can treat them like you treat me. Even in my filth, You look upon me and pour out Yourself to me. Lord, help me do the same for those who are deserving and undeserving. Though hard, help show me this week how to pour out myself to my brothers and sisters. Amen. ■

— JOSHUA NELSON

OCTOBER 24

HE KNOWS JUST WHAT YOU NEED

"So do not fear, for I am with you; do not be dismayed, for I am your God. I will strengthen you and help you; I will uphold you with my righteous right hand" (Isaiah 41:10 NIV).

Being a stay at home mom for more than seven years was truly a blessing from God. Despite funds being tight and having to be creative when shopping for our clothes, God always provided what we needed.

As my family's needs changed, my husband Charles and I knew it was time for me to go to work. Within a few months, I landed a temporary receptionist position at a home health care office. When that position ended, I was offered a payroll billing clerk position. The hardest part was to inform my supervisor that I had a history of acute myeloid leukemia (AML). Every three months required a doctor's visit. My supervisor said that she didn't see a problem with that, and would inform personnel.

Almost a year into my employment, my youngest son Christopher started having asthma attacks. I did not foresee this challenge. Here I was, thinking my doctor appointments would be an issue.

One day the owner of the company requested a meeting with our department. A new policy for attendance was introduced which only permitted three unexcused absences. To make sure that I understood the owner, I asked if that would include having a sick child with asthma.

"As good as you are Ortrene," she said, "I wish we had more of you, but yes it does. If anyone calls in for the third time, they might as well not come back to work."

At the end of her meeting she asked each employee to shake on the new policy. I could not. I explained that I understood her position as a business owner, but I couldn't shake and agree with her. She asked personnel to take note that I did not shake her hand.

Afterwards I was deeply disturbed—I needed a new job! I prayed to God, and within two weeks I became an employee of the South Atlantic Conference of Seventh-day Adventists, where I have been employed for the past 23 years. Today's text is the text that I stand by: "So do not fear, for I am with you; do not be dismayed, for I am your God. I will strengthen you and help you; I will uphold you with my righteous right hand." ▮▮

— ORTRENE GORDON

OCTOBER 25

FROM CARNALLY MINDED TO SPIRITUALLY MINDED

"For to be carnally minded is death; but to be spiritually minded is life and peace" (Romans 8:6 KJV).

Immediately, a class member shouted, "What! Are you telling me that one day I may be persecuted just like Paul, just because I am a Christian? I then reminded her that 2 Timothy said "all."

She quickly retorted, "I am sorry, no one is going to ever touch me, Paul just liked to be beat! Are y'all telling me that you are ready to go through this?"

There was a unanimous "Yes!"

She was reminded that in Matthew 28:20 the Lord says He is with us always. Jesus, the Christ, was beaten and scourged beyond the point of human endurance to provide salvation for all who love and trust Him.

Then someone thoughtfully commented, "What if Jesus would have felt like you feel, we would all be lost! Jesus Christ was a perfect example of Philippians 2:3 and 4."

This incident made me realize that we must change from a carnal mindset to a spiritual mindset where we are pleasing to the Lord. When someone observes a person performing a compassionate act, they become more likely to become motivated to help others, just like the following story.

It was on a day when the vast crowd was watching the gladiatorial show in the great arena. A Syrian monk by the name of Telemachus stood up. He was deeply grieved and outraged by the utter disregard for human life. He leaped into the arena in the midst of the butchery and boldly cried out, "This thing is not right! This thing must stop!" Because he was interfering with their entertainment, the emperor of Rome commanded that Telemachus be run through with a sword. Thus, the monk died.

But through his death, he kindled a flame in the hearts of thinking people. History records that because of his courageous sacrifice, within a few months the gladiatorial combats began to decline and soon ceased altogether. Why? Because one man dared to boldly speak out against the evil carnage.

The Bible says there is a battle in every person's heart between the carnal mind and the Spirit. What will win your heart's battle? ▮▮

— ROSIA A. PARKER

EMPOWERED TO ENGAGE

"Is not this the fast that I have chosen? To loose the bands of wickedness, to undo the heavy burdens, and to let the oppressed go free, and that ye break every yoke?" (Isaiah 58:6 KJV).

God has called each of us to a life of service. We are called to break yokes and lift burdens in the lives of those who have been oppressed, forgotten and marginalized. As Christians, we are called to share the love of Jesus Christ as His witnesses, and stand up against social injustice!

Homelessness, joblessness, food insecurity, mass incarceration, voter suppression, healthcare reform, criminal justice reform, human trafficking, addiction, mental illness, and discrimination in its many forms are serious issues that currently plague our society. We can't afford to stand on the sidelines as spectators. Jesus asked us not only to identify our neighbor, but to be willing to get involved and help our neighbor! God has given each of us gifts and talents to "engage" in effective ministry.

Many years ago I asked God to show me what He wanted me to do. He revealed that ministry is not just limited to the inside of a church, but ministry happens when we sacrifice our time, talents and resources, to do the will of God. God called me to do Workforce Development Ministry (WDM).

WDM provides training and development, jobs, housing, apprenticeship programs, food programs, job fairs, technical and higher educational opportunities, housing, and vital health services, which go hand in hand with the gospel that Jesus preached and practiced.

I recently shared an apprenticeship program with those who were looking for work. A woman in the group gave the information to her nephew, a high school senior. Her nephew took the information to his guidance counselor to find out if it was a legitimate apprenticeship program. The guidance counselor researched the program. As a result, not only will the woman's nephew begin a career as an apprentice working with a major power company in Georgia at $15 per hour, but 35 additional African American young men graduating in his senior class will also be employed at $15 per hour! These jobs will provide much needed income and stability for these young men and their families.

God is calling each of us to "engage" in ministry, and to use our gifts and talents to bless others. He is calling us to "undo the heavy burdens and help the poor and oppressed in our society go free!" ▮▮

— SANDRA REDDISH

OCTOBER 27

ENGAGEMENT

"And we know that all things work together for good to them that love God, to them who are called according to His purpose" (Romans 8:28 KJV).

Permit me to put this Scripture in a social justice context. It is especially vital. It tends to justify my personal engagement in the struggle.

Social justice is based on the concept of human rights and equality. Online it is defined as "The way in which human rights are manifested in the everyday lives of people at every level of society."

Wikipedia tends to agree that social justice is a concept of fair and just relations between the individual and society, as measured by the distribution of wealth, opportunities for personal activity, and social privilege.

In 1891, years before Wikipedia, social justice was defined in the Black Law Dictionary as, "That justice that conforms to a moral principle, such as that all people are equal" (p. 869).

It is an established fact that biblically, historically, and constitutionally, all people have basic human rights. According to the United Nations Declaration, "Human rights are rights inherent to all human beings, regardless of race, sex, nationality, ethnicity, language, religion, or any other status. Human rights include the right to life and liberty, freedom from slavery and torture, freedom of opinion and expression, the right to work, education, and many more."

While pastoring in Chattanooga, Tennessee, all basic human rights were not fully extended to my people. It was then that I chose to get involved or engage in social justice activities. I believed today's text; that, "All things work together for good, to them that love God." Social justice is important to God!

It is important because it is theologically sound, historically documented, philosophically moral, and constitutionally supported. It is the "Golden Rule" as recorded in Matthew 7:12: "Therefore, all things whatsoever ye would that men should do you, do ye even so to them" (KJV).

In Chattanooga, Tennessee, I became very active in the social justice movement. After joining the Inter-Denominational Ministerial Alliance, I was elected as the president. At this time in Chattanooga, schools, lunch counters, and waiting rooms in the bus and train terminals were segregated. As president, it was my responsibility to chair all strategy sessions for the desegregation of those facilities. All interested denominational thought leaders were organized, and mobilized. The outcomes were positive.

Engagement with others resulted in the desegregation of nine public schools. All the lunch counters were opened to all races. The Greyhound and Trailways bus terminals were opened to everyone, regardless of color or race.

I still believe that all things work together for good. Social justice is important to God. It is fair. It is moral. It is divine. ■

— RALPH PEAY

OCTOBER 28

DESTROYING THE KENNEL

"The righteous considers the cause of the poor, but the wicked does not understand such knowledge" (Proverbs 29:7 NKJV).

It was the summer of 1972. NBC news announced a disturbing special report coming up. The report was done by Geraldo Rivera and Jane Kurtin. It was a horrific story about Willowbrook, an institution for people with developmental disabilities.

Going on an inside tip, Geraldo and Jane snuck inside one of the buildings with a stolen key. What they saw were gruesome sickening conditions of neglected and abused children and adults—some were naked, clustered together in rooms that smelled of death. There were sounds of wailing and moaning.

This school was originally designed in 1942 as a place to educate children with mental disabilities, but by 1972 it had become "a kennel for humanity disguised as a school." Geraldo's report sparked an angry outcry from the nation and the world.

The institution's conditions were not new, and decades followed with continued frustration from parents dealing with poverty and stigma, having to relinquish (sometimes forcibly) their disabled children to the state for care. Reports of horrific conditions and abuse continued as the years rolled by—mostly hidden from public knowledge.

The angry outcry of the injustices at Willowbrook was the catalyst that provoked parents, and human and disability rights activists to come together and start a movement of reform to break down barriers of physical, institutional, and social barriers, and push for equal rights, opportunities, dignity, and respect. The hard work of these alliances resulted in President George Bush signing the Americans with Disabilities Act (a civil rights law) on July 26, 1990. It was amended in July, 2008 to broaden the coverage for people with disabilities. The work still continues today.

God admonishes us to care for the sick, poor, widows and homeless. Isaiah tells us in Isaiah 61:1-2, "to bind up the brokenhearted, to proclaim liberty to the captives, and the opening of the prison to those who are bound...to comfort all who mourn" (KJV).

Today, with the massive budget cuts that deeply slash services and care for the least, the last and the lost, it must be our mission to be the voices for those who are voiceless. We must become the arms, feet and hearts of those in need. ■

— ROSEMARY GRAHAM

OCTOBER 29

THE REMNANT

"And the dragon was wroth with the woman, and went to make war with the remnant of her seed, which keep the commandments of God, and have the testimony of Jesus Christ." "And I fell at his feet to worship him. And he said unto me, See thou do it not: I am thy fellow- servant, and of thy brethren that have the testimony of Jesus: worship God: for the testimony of Jesus is the spirit of prophecy" (Revelation 12:17; 19:10 KJV).

God's faithful, last day people will be identified by keeping the commandments of God and having the spirit of prophecy. Undoubtedly, Christians know that the commandments of God are the Ten Commandments (Exodus 20:1-17), and we should understand that these commandments are supported by the two great commandments (Matthew 22:34-40). These commandments point the faithful, last day Christians toward the moral responsibility of loving Yahweh, and through our love for Yahweh we should also love all people. Thus, by living with love toward God and our fellow man, and faithfully observing the Ten Commandments, we are fulfilling half of God's description of His faithful, last day people.

From my perspective, many Christians do not fully comprehend the depth of meaning regarding the spirit of prophecy. I hate to disappoint anyone who reads this, but the Spirit of Prophecy is not the writings of Ellen G. White—she is simply a part of God's prophetic voice that He has used throughout the ages. The Spirit of prophecy does not mean that we have the clearest understanding of God's prophetic messages. It has greater implications than that conclusion.

The Spirit of prophecy can best be understood when one considers how the Holy Spirit moved through the prophetic figures of the past; consider the messages of the prophets such as Amos, and Isaiah. They called people back to righteousness, to the abandonment of idolatry, and to fair treatment of their fellowman, with justice (Amos 2:6-7; 5:10-12, Isaiah 58). If one chose to study the messages of the Old Testament prophets, the reader would find God's messages through the prophets lamented idolatry because it dethroned God of His rightful honor. By dethroning God, it transformed Israel's moral ethos and made room for dehumanizing, unjust practices toward those vulnerable in society—like overcharging someone in need.

God's prophets called Israel to do good toward foreign widows and orphans, and other vulnerable populations. God's last day people must continue to do the same. It is no wonder God's prophets were despised; it's because prophets called the sins of greed and exploitation by their right names. It resulted in people wanting them dead because God's message was a call to assist the disadvantaged.

A holistic understanding of the Spirit of Prophecy calls people to the love of God and people in tangible ways. It calls them to cry out against injustice toward those marginalized in society. Although it may result in being despised by their fellow men, it promises a crown of gold in the New Jerusalem. ▮▮

— EVAN WILLIS

OCTOBER 30

GOD CARES, DO YOU?

"This is what the LORD Almighty said: 'Administer true justice; show mercy and compassion to one another'" (Zechariah 7:9 NIV).

I always wanted a job that would allow me to help others, especially those in need in my home country, Haiti. Haiti is the first independent nation in the Caribbean, and the first black republic in the world. We always had to fight for our freedom—we fought with the French as well as the Spanish.

Even today, the people of Haiti are still fighting for the basic necessities of life. It seems as though Haiti has been forgotten and no one cares. There is so much upheaval. Crime is at its highest, and we still haven't even recovered from the earthquake that killed over 300,000 people. My sister died in that earthquake. I felt so helpless; I still do. There still remains so much destruction, so many are still displaced. I kept asking God how I could help, and God had a plan for me.

I was working for a fairly large corporation when I received a call from a nonprofit Catholic organization, Food for the Poor. They needed an executive secretary to help them with various projects that served those in need. This was an answer to prayer. I immediately left the job I had and began working for Food for the Poor. I was able to help people obtain housing. We had orphanages, homes for the elderly, schools, several feeding programs, and even a hospital. I spoke with approximately 200 people per week. I cannot count the number of times that God worked through me to bless His people.

When you have a desire in your heart to serve others, God will always make a way. He has many doors to open, and your work will never be in vain. He made it very plain when He said: "... Then the righteous will answer him, 'Lord, when did we see you hungry and feed you, or thirsty and give you something to drink? When did we see you a stranger and invite you in, or needing clothes and clothe you? When did we see you sick or in prison and go to visit you?' The King will reply, 'Truly I tell you, whatever you did for one of the least of these brothers and sisters of mine, you did for me'" (Matthew 25:37-40 NIV).

God is still looking for people that have a heart to help others. It doesn't have to be in Haiti, it doesn't have to be in a nonprofit organization. God can use you right where you are. Why don't you let Him? ▮▮

— FARAH VANESSA GRACIA

OCTOBER 31

TO KNOW HIM

"Who says, 'I will build myself a roomy house with spacious upper rooms, and cut out its windows, paneling it with cedar and painting it bright red.' Do you become a king because you are competing in cedar? Did not your father eat and drink and do justice and righteousness? Then it was well with him. He pled the cause of the afflicted and needy; Then it was well. Is not that what it means to know Me? Declares the LORD"
(Jeremiah 22:14-16 NASB).

To know God is to know justice. What do people know about us? Are we known for how we plead for the cause of the afflicted and needy? A true king is not measured by how much power and money he has, but by how he gives. The King of Kings teaches us to look outward before seeking selfish pleasures. Our task is to seek first the kingdom of God and His righteousness (Matthew 6:33).

In other words, the very first of our desires should be the rulership of God and doing His justice. We have no right to have selfish desires when following after God. It is God who teaches us to seek the lost. It is Jesus who shows us the model of healing and touching the poor. It is Jesus who shows us a custom of liberation and prayer. It is Jesus who shows us the character of God. For God so loved the world that He gave. Yes, God loved, so it led Him to give. This is the direct action of love.

Love explains El as Elohim, the living God, our Yahweh; El Shaddai, the Almighty God; El Elyon, the Most High God; El Roi, the God who sees me; El Olam, the everlasting God. Love gave His only begotten son. Love gives all, from a place of value and endearment. Love creates so that it can fulfill. Love desires to save whoever simply has belief in love.

Our prayer is that you have discovered the God of love. May His love fill your heart and lead you to give like He gives. May we seek to offer people Jesus. May we be so consumed with His Spirit, that when people encounter us, they encounter God. May the actions we show the world reflect the God we worship. May our actions speak louder than our words.

Lord, may I be consumed with your love. Amen. ■

— JOSHUA NELSON

NOVEMBER

THANKSGIVING

November is the month of thanksgiving and praise. It's is a time when people get together with family and celebrate the liberties that this country professes to bestow upon every individual within the confines of its territory.

However, even in this American system that promotes freedom and justice, there are surges of the draconian voice that penetrates its streets, its people, and it laws. Therefore we have put together a few short devotionals from the Book of Psalms celebrating God's goodness in the midst of injustice. We have also included some prophetic comparisons using the books of Daniel, Revelation and The Psalms.

In these pages you will find various writing styles, as these devotionals have been penned by people of different backgrounds and different experiences. You will notices themes of justice, themes of liberty, and themes of praise interwoven into a perfect compact of spiritual edification.

Our prayer is that you come from each devotional refreshed, recharged, and empowered to make changes in the world through the power of Jesus Christ. "May the grace of our Lord Jesus Christ be with you all is our earnest prayer." Amen. ■

— KERWIN JONES
Former Director of Public Affairs and Religious Liberty
Southwest Region Conference of Seventh-day Adventists

THE EXCELLENT GOD

"O Lord, our Lord, How excellent is thy name in all the earth!" (Psalm 8:9 KJV).

Often times we are burdened with all the bad news we see and hear in our world. The shocking news we hear, many times throws us off of our spiritual guard as we concentrate on the tragedies. This spiritual shock sometimes causes us to forget who and who's we are. We forget that we belong to the Creator of the universe. We forget we are called by His name. We forget that the author of life, Himself, has complete providence of this universe and our lives. We forget that the Creator of this universe trusts sinful beings like you and me.

Within spiritual shock, we forget just how much trust and confidence God has in us, and that He is excellent! In Psalm 8:4-9, David expounded on that trust and the excellency of God. He said, "What is man, that thou art mindful of him? and the son of man, that thou visitest him? For thou hast made him a little lower than the angels, and hast crowned him with glory and honor" (Psalm 8:4-5 KJV).

David is in awe that the Ancient of Days will have anything to do with sinful man. He is in awe that we do not even have angel status, but yet we are the apple of God's eye. David continued, saying, "Thou madest him to have dominion over the works of thy hands; thou hast put all things under his feet" (Psalm 8:6 KJV). Here, David is showing us the trust that God has in us.

God trusts us and gave us dominion over the works of His own hands. In verses seven and eight, David lists some of the things that God gave us dominion over, and summed the whole matter up in verse nine—our text for today—by calling Him "excellent."

So, what was David calling excellent? It was the fact that the Creator of this vast world trusts you and me. Does David sound like someone who is in spiritual shock? No! God is using this Psalm to remind us today, that He loves and trusts us; that we are fearfully and wonderfully made; that we serve a God who is excellent.

So, the excellent God has much confidence and trust in us. We should not let the evil of this world cause us to forget His excellency. Today, let the world see the excellence of God through you. ▮▮

— PAUL LAWRENCE

NOVEMBER 2

THE DIVINE INTENT FOR SOCIAL JUSTICE

"You made them rulers over the works of your hands; you put everything under their feet" (Psalm 8:6 NIV).

In Psalm 8:4, David asks the question, "What is mankind that you are mindful of them, human beings that you care for them?" (NIV). He continues on, "You have made them a little lower than the angels and crowned them with glory and honor. You made them rulers over the works of your hands; you put everything under their feet" (Psalm 8:5-6 NIV). How amazing and wonderful is our God, who sees that we are capable of managing the world He created for us. If God designed a world where we can live in peace and equality within our community, why do we no longer feel at home or have control over our land?

Unfortunately, the result of sin has turned our world into a chaotic place where social injustice was born, but God has a plan to restore social justice in the new world to come. According to the Oxford reference, social justice is defined as the objective of creating a fair and equal society in which each individual matters, all rights are recognized and protected, and decisions are made in ways that are fair and honest.

God created us equal, but somewhere through the ages we were divided by gender, race and social status. We were made to rule over the works of His hands, but instead we became slaves in our lands. This was never God's design. Many people have chosen to turn a blind eye against the injustice that surrounds them, but God hears His children who suffer from the cause of inequality.

In Psalm 9:9, David reminds us that "The Lord is a refuge for the oppressed, a stronghold in times of trouble," (NIV). And Psalm 34:17-18 says, "The righteous cry out, and the Lord hears them; he delivers them from all their troubles. The Lord is close to the brokenhearted and saves those who are crushed in spirit" (NIV).

God is watching how we, as His children, represent Him to those who are in crisis. Jesus came to serve, and we are to continue His ministry in our communities. The American theologian and author, Jim Wallis, once said, "If you benefit from a system, you are responsible of changing it."

Let us change our community for the better. The consequences of sin may have caused the evil we see today, but as children of God, we must do our part by cultivating a world of hope until Christ returns.

Social justice begins with us. ■

— PEGGY FILOSSAINT

JUSTICE AND THANKSGIVING

"I will give thanks to you, Lord, with all my heart; I will tell of your wonderful deeds. I will be glad and rejoice in you; I will sing the praises of your name, O Most High" (Psalm 9:1-2 NIV).

As I write this, it is February 5, 2020, the day after the SOTU (State of the Union) address. One might ask, "What does this have to do Justice and Thanksgiving?" I believe that the SOTU address that I heard had more to do with Justice and Thanksgiving than we might have realized.

I heard the president artistically manipulate words and people to advance his agenda. As I watched the spectacle and interaction between the president, senate, congress and the Speaker of the House, Nancy Pelosi, I was painfully reminded of the many individuals who came before the president, who used the same tactics of verbal manipulation to move masses to do their bidding. Individuals like, the Pharaoh of Egypt, Nebuchadnezzar, Napoleon, Hitler, Stalin, Jim Jones, the prosecutor from New York who stole years from the lives of five young men by falsely prosecuting them—I am sure you can think of a few yourself.

The point I am getting at is that these individuals all seemed to operate outside of justice. They seemed to be able to do whatever they wanted, for a time, without facing any real consequences. So, I have to ask a couple of questions, as I am sure many other people have asked or maybe even thought, but not asked. "Where's the justice in their actions? And how can one be thankful with the knowledge of these actions?" The answer is found in Psalms, Chapters 9 and 13.

In Psalm 9:7, it states, "The Lord reigns forever; he has established his throne for judgment" (NIV). As painful as it is, in the moment, to see loved ones and people who we may never meet go through unjust situations, we have to remember that the Lord has the last word. We have to remember that God will, and some of us will, also judge those individuals when Jesus returns.

The good news of life and justice can be found in Psalm 13:3-6, which captures how I feel at this moment, and the reason we must be "thankful." Verses three and four remind me that in this world there will be trouble. But, there is hope in verses five and six which state: "But I trust in your unfailing love; my heart rejoices in your salvation. I will sing the Lord's praise for he has been good to me" (NIV).

These verses remind us that we can be thankful, because no matter what happens, God is still on the throne. ■

— R. NORWOOD

NOVEMBER 4

SOLUTION IN AN AGE OF CORRUPTION

"When the foundations are being destroyed, what can the righteous do?" (Psalm 11:3 NIV).

When threatened by his enemies and forced to flee for safety, David encouraged himself with songs of praise. He had committed no crime, nor was he guilty of any treasonous act against the ruler of the nation. Nonetheless, King Saul, in his heated jealousy of David, pursued him to take his life. Not only was David's life in danger, but also all who were loyal to him.

Hans LaRondelle, in his book, Deliverance in the Psalms, states, "The moral foundations—law and justice—of the covenant people as a society are at stake." In despair David cries out, "When the foundations are being destroyed, what can the righteous do?" (Psalm 11:3 NIV).

Present times demonstrate that corruption has entered the legislative councils of government, affecting the officers of law and order; and then "all the foundations of the earth are shaken" (Psalm 82:5 NIV).

Following the example of the psalmist, God's people must take their refuge in their God (Psalm 11:1). Although God is in heaven, His eyes are ever on the righteous. "The Lord tests the righteous, But the wicked and the one who loves violence His soul hates" (Psalm 11: 5, NJKV). The Lord fully guarantees the survival of His people, and He will execute righteous judgment on earth.

God is not unmindful of the injustice and travesties occurring. His timing is not always immediate or His intervention speedy. However, His mercy is demonstrated in the time allowed for mankind's repentance and time to return to Him. Those disconnected from God do not interpret this time of temporary prosperity in the same manner as those who profess and practice a relationship with God. Spiritual things are spiritually discerned. The righteous understand that good will be rewarded and evil will one day be avenged.

The comfort given is that we can never escape our responsibility to God. He cares for His creation and will bring about justice on the earth. As we look toward the future, we can take new courage and turn from the chaos on the earth to the Lord, for the Lord is "in His holy temple" (Psalm 11:4).

Psalm 11 concludes with the words, "For the Lord is righteous, he loves justice; upright men will see His face" (Psalm 11:7 NIV). To one day see the Lord face to face was the hope that supported the psalmist's trust and confidence in God's daily care.

May that same hope be our support and anchor. ▮▮

— PASTOR BUFORD GRIFFITH, JR.

NOVEMBER 5

THE LIBERATED MIND

"By you I can crush a troop, and by my God I can leap over a wall" (Psalms 18:29 NSRV).

I have seen it repeatedly and I know you have too. There is a task that needs to be done and you know the person assigned to the task can do it. But for some strange reason, they sabotage themselves. They talk themselves into failure. I have done it myself. Some folks call it, "Stinkin, Thinkin." I remember, in one instance, how my little sister had all this self-doubt while we were doing literature evangelism door to door in Canada.

One morning after breakfast I went to her to challenge her mindset and encourage her to raise her goals and expectations.

"Alicia, what is your book goal for today?" I asked.

"Eight books and 10 smaller books," she responded.

"Sis, you are aiming to low. God can provide you much more than that," I said.

"OK. How about 12 books and 15 smaller ones?"

"That sounds good, but how about a little more. What do you think about 20 large books and 20 smaller books?"

"Uh, I don't know, sure?" she faltered, not sounding confident.

In the van on the way to our territory, we reiterated that goal and the goals of the team. When I tell you God moved, it would be an understatement. That day there was a massive rainstorm which forced us to do literature work in several apartment complexes. The books were flying into homes. That rain was really a shower of blessings, prompting us to adjust our plans and be where God wanted us to be.

At the end of the day, my little sister had sold 20 big books and 20 little books. If we translate that into funds, it was over $450 generated by my 12-year-old sister. Our five-person team sold every book in the van. At the end of the day we all gathered together praising God. You should have seen us; I was crying, my sister was crying, and the team was crying and praising the Lord because He has used us so mightily.

It reminds me of these statements made by Ellen G. White in *Christ Object Lessons*: "[m]any whom God has qualified to do excellent work accomplish very little, because they attempt little..." (p. 331).

"Remember that you will never reach a higher standard than you yourself set" (p. 331). Release yourself from mediocrity and embrace the greatness of our God. With Him, we can crush a troop and with Him we can leap over walls. ∎

— ANDRE WALLER

NOVEMBER 6

THE KING OF GLORY AND HIS KINGDOM

"The earth is the Lord's, and everything in it. The world and all its people belong to Him...Who is the King of glory? The Lord of Heaven's Armies, He is the King of glory" (Psalm 24:1 &10 NLT).

In a world of so much chaos, confusion, and calamities; in a time where all manner of sickness and diseases, including COVID-19, has brought emotional, financial, and even spiritual trauma, it is sometimes difficult for human beings to find anything for which to be thankful. But then this Psalm of David shows up and reminds us that the Lord is still worthy of our praise for the following two reasons: He is our Lord, and He is our King.

In the first two verses of this Psalm, David highlights the creative power of God. He is Lord of everything on this planet. The physical planet, which He Himself created in six literal days, is still under His care. From the depths of the oceans and the deepest caves within the earth, where lie precious stones and minerals, to the top of the highest mountains and the widest plains—it all belongs to Him.

This wonderful reality pulls us into the majesty of Adonai, the Lord Who has ownership and rulership of everything. This truth helps us to not be discouraged when we see many assuming that they have power or authority on this planet. Adonai suggests "Lordship" on His part, and stewardship and submission on our part. We gain perspective that there is still literally a God Who sits high but looks low and cares deeply for us.

David then offers all the opportunity to be blessed by this great God if we have clean hands and pure hearts. Those who reject worshipping other gods or prioritizing anyone or anything above God, and those who remain honest and humble, are promised to receive blessings from the Lord and righteousness from the God of his salvation.

In the closing stanzas of this Psalm, described in Verses 7-10, it reveals that God is not only celebrated as our Lord, but He is worshipped as our King. The Matthew Henry Bible Commentary says, "It is supposed that the psalm was penned upon occasion of David's bringing up the ark to the place prepared for it..." However, because the ark is a symbol of the presence of God, biblical prophets and preachers describe the call of the gates to lift up their heads by the angelic host of heaven so the King of glory can enter, as Jesus' triumphal return to heaven after His resurrection. Oh, what a glorious sight.

Therefore, open up your hearts and mouths and give God thanks for being our Savior and Lord, and our conquering King of Glory. ■■

— CRYSTON E. JOSIAH

ETERNAL SANCTUARY

"One thing I have desired of the LORD, That will I seek: That I may dwell in the house of the LORD All the days of my life, To behold the beauty of the LORD, And to inquire in His temple. For in the time of trouble He shall hide me in His pavilion; In the secret place of His tabernacle He shall hide me; He shall set me high upon a rock" (Psalm 27:4-5 NKJV).

I am an unabashed animal lover; one of those types who has already determined the menagerie of furry species they plan to surround themselves with in heaven. Here on earth, any cuddly creature I spy immediately dominates my attention. While out on neighborhood walks, I have been known to greet dogs well before acknowledging their owners.

I'm also a huge proponent of both travel and justice. Whenever I have the opportunity to visit a new region, one of my itinerary mainstays is an excursion to the local wildlife sanctuary. These designated refuges provide an opportunity to experience vulnerable native species in an environment committed to their safety and security.

In Psalm 27, David yearns for such a place of refuge. Besieged by his adversaries, the psalmist is in desperate need of a stronghold. Yet he understands man-made shelters aren't adequate. Battling both worldly and spiritual warfare, David recognizes his deliverance rests in the shielding presence of his mighty God: "The LORD is my light and my salvation; Whom shall I fear?" (Psalm 27:1 NKJV). Though his enemies encircle him, he is confident in the sanctuary found in his Redeemer.

Yet David comprehends that the benefits of a life lived in Christ go far beyond comfort and protection. In these verses, he seeks the Savior for refuge, yes, but also for instruction and companionship. His greatest desire is "to behold the beauty of the Lord, And to inquire in His temple" (Psalm 27:4 NKJV). Simply put, a relationship with God is David's happy place.

Whether bombarded by difficulties or relaxing in a place of peace, David aspires to experience life through Christ. "Teach me Your way, O Lord" (Psalm 27:11 NKJV), he petitions, that he may "sing praises to the Lord" (Psalm 27:6 NKJV)

The psalmist ends his poem with an appeal and a promise: "Wait on the Lord; Be of good courage, And He shall strengthen your heart." (Psalm 27:14 NKJV).

I am so grateful for those around the world who dedicate their lives to the welfare of endangered animal populations. But how much more does our Father love His sons and daughters? What inexhaustible protection and provision are found when we tabernacle in Him. He is our refuge and our strength! ■

— MELISSA REID

NOVEMBER 8

WHEN THE STORMS COME

"The Lord sat as King at the flood; Yes, the Lord sits as King forever" (Psalm 29:10 NASB).

Perhaps you are facing a turbulent storm in your life. The rains are pouring down; the skies of your once bright and promising life have grown dark and menacing, leaving you filled with sadness and despair. The only light seems to come from the filaments of lighting connecting heaven to earth, while the claps of thunder shake your whole world to its core. Whether you're experiencing a family trial, financial hardship, news of a terrible disease, or countless other fears that turn your world upside down and take away your equilibrium, storms are part of life.

The psalmist, in this verse, watches as the storms bring to his remembrance the creation story of Genesis and the perils of the flood. He declares, "The Lord sat as King at the flood." Have you ever paused to consider how awesome God is as you see the power of torrential rain or the stunning flashes of lightning in the night sky?

In the passage the writer refers to God as Lord, or master. God's majesty and power are displayed in full array in the midst of the most powerful storm. What's more, God sits above the storm, enthroned in divine power and might. He is the master whose power transcends the threats of the storm.

Our storms seem overwhelming to us, but the psalmist reminds us that God remains omnipotent in His power. Your storm is an opportunity for the power of God to be displayed fully in your life. In the stormy seasons of this life God sits unchanging and unchallenged. He is the Lord of your life and the Lord of the storm. His throne gives us the picture of a seated, calm, omnipotent King who tells us to "be still and know that He is God" (Psalm 46-10a KJV). He gives strength to His people through each and every one of life's storms. He controls nature and He can control the chaos of your life. The rainbow of His covenant stands as a reminder that His promises are still available to you.

Are you facing a storm today? Rest in the knowledge that you will see Him in the storm, but more importantly, He will see you through the storm. And after the lightning and rain, and thunder and darkness, comes the calm. There you will experience the promised blessings of God where the Lord sits as King forever. ■■

— MELVIN WARFIELD

NOVEMBER 9

A SHELTER FROM STRIFE

"You shall hide them in the secret place of Your presence From the plots of man; You *shall keep them secretly in a pavilion From the strife of tongues" (Psalm 31:20 NKJV)*

Although this Psalm can seem to apply to many events in the life of David, it is believed that the events which transpired in the wilderness of Maon, found in 1 Samuel 23:19-26, serve as the backdrop. David is on the run from Saul. The Ziphites of Horesh have recently informed Saul that David is hiding among them. Saul gets them to find out David's exact location so that he can finally put an end to the man who threatens his dynasty.

Nevertheless, as Saul closes in on David so that only the crest of a mountain, and a few hundred yards, separate the two feuding warriors, David lifts up his cry to the heavens and God miraculously delivers him from his pursuer. In his heart-felt gratitude, David pens today's text in response to his Savior's faithfulness: "You shall hide them in the secret place of Your presence from the plots of man." David knew, that even in the most dire situation, he was never outside of God's presence.

It is in prayer where we experience God's presence as if we were in the very courts of heaven itself. It is through prayer that He preserves us and sustains us. Though the tumult of strife may assail us, the plans of the enemy have no true power against us as we keep our hearts lifted up to the Most Holy pavilion in which Christ intercedes on our behalf. He "hides" us, by faith, in His presence. By faith, we are seated there with Him, in the heavenly places, where no plot or enemy can reach us.

He also keeps us, "secretly in a pavilion from the strife of tongues." The word here used for "strife" carries with it the connotation of a public legal dispute over one's personal rights. Not even Satan's charges or verbal accusations can challenge our standing before God. Through faith, we have access to special legal protection. We have the "right" to be children of God.

In those times when you feel as if your challenging circumstances have closed in around you, you can trust that God will deliver you. Though the accuser disputes your legal standing before God, trust that you have been positioned before the Father, Himself, as if you have never committed a crime. Though Satan pursues you, the prayer of faith will keep you ever evading his attempts to overcome you.

Today, praise God that your life is hidden with Christ, and that He will keep you. ■

— MELVIN KINGS

THE WORD OF THE LORD HOLDS TRUE

"Rejoice in the lord, O you righteous! For praise from the upright is b eautiful. Praise the Lord with the harp; Make melody to Him with an instrument of ten strings. Sing to Him a new song; Play skillfully with a shout of joy. For the word of the Lord is right, and all His work is done in truth" (Psalm 33:1-4 NKJV).

The African American composer, Dr. Adolphus Hailstork, wrote a song based on Psalm 33 called, "Shout for Joy," featured on the album by the Aeolians of Oakwood University released in 2020. This majestic anthem begins with the invitation to "Shout for Joy all ye righteous... Sing to the Lord a new song... Give thanks to the Lord... Sing Him psalms; shout in triumph... and Praise the Lord." These phrases are sung with gusto and enthusiasm befitting the awe and magnificence that belong to God.

But then Dr. Hailstork explains why we should shout and sing, give thanks and praise the Lord. Based on Psalm 33:4 he says, "The Word of the Lord holds true. And all His work endures. His love never failing fills the earth, and the Word of the Lord holds true." In other words, our praise is in response to God's promise.

The next declaration Dr. Hailstork elucidates is that, "The Word of the Lord made the sky, and my Lord made the sea. He spoke and the world came to be; and the Word of the Lord made me." These phrases are sung with pathos and quiet reverence, with the understanding that the God who made the vast glorious world with His voice, also took the time to make human beings (namely me) with His hands.

Finally, Dr. Hailstork triumphantly proclaims, "The Lord is our help and our shield; we put our trust in Him; at the sound of His voice our hearts shall rejoice; for the Word of the Lord holds true." We are reminded that when we are in trouble or when we are in need, we can hold on to the promises of God because the Word of the Lord holds true.

Whether it's the promise of Hebrews 13:5 where God says He will never leave us nor forsake us; or the promise of Psalm 23:4 where we are told even though we walk through the valley of the shadow of death, the Lord is with us; or even the promise of John 11:25 where Jesus said that even though a person dies, yet shall that person live; we can rely on the promise and rejoice because, "the Word of the Lord holds true."

Wherever we are or whatever we are going through, we can shout, sing, rejoice, give thanks, and praise the Lord, because the word of the Lord indeed holds true.

So, the next time we wonder if God cares or if God means what He says, just read Psalm 33 and be reminded that "the Word of the Lord holds true." ■

— PAUL GOODRIDGE

REAL JUSTICE AND SOMETHING TO BE THANKFUL FOR! PART 1

"God is our refuge and strength, A very present help in trouble. Therefore we will not fear...The Lord of hosts is with us; The God of Jacob is our refuge. Selah" (Psalm 46:1-2a, 7 NKJV)

Psalm 46, in some circles, is called "Martin Luther's Psalm" because he would often quote and sing this passage in his times of trial. Therefore it has been dubbed, "Luther's Psalm." I submit to you today, that it's not just Luther's Psalm but it's a song of hope for all who trust in God and His son Jesus Christ.

We do not know the direct author of Psalm 46. We don't even know the occasion that prompted the writing of these words. Scholars link this psalm to the various instances in the history of Israel where enemies attacked and God intervened. And even though we don't have the specific historical occasion for the psalm, or the proper hermeneutical setting and contextual form, this doesn't limit us in finding a proper occasion to use it for our lives, when we need the God who intervenes to step in when the enemy shows up.

Psalm 46 is quite seasonal for any believer who is in today's rancid and wrecked society. From your side of the world to my side of the world, there is trouble on every side. I like Psalm 46, because for some of us, the devil and desperate situations have already arrived. But thanks be to our God, that when the enemy shows up in flood-like forces of tumultuous trials or the treacherous trauma of emotions, the Bible says in Isaiah 59 that God lifts up a standard against the enemy!

Is it not true, that the personal trials, political upheavals, racial tension, economic downturns, moral decline, world conflict, constant terrorist threats, nuclear proliferation, and spiritual struggles that we face all beg the question in life, "Is there any place that is safe in this world?"

The text submits to us that there is no safe place in this world. When you can be shot down in a the midst of worship and prayer, slain walking through your neighborhood, choked in front of a market in the middle of the day, shot down for simply looking suspicious or while on the run and unarmed—this lets us know there is no social coverage. Psalms 46 beckons us to recognize that the governments and world powers can't help, heal, or console; but that there is One who is on the scene who can, and will, console and comfort you in the midst of trouble.

The good news that I want to leave with you today is that even though there is no safe place in society, there is a safe place in God. In fact, that is the message of Psalms 46—that the only place you can find safety and security is in God, through His son Christ Jesus.

That news ought to bring you comfort; that news ought to make you realize that God is at His best when times and season are at their worst. That's real justice—that "God is" when I need Him most! The hymn says it best; "Jesus is near, just when I falter, just when I fear; Ready to help me...just when I need Him most" (Poole, 1907).

— JOHN POOLER, III

NOVEMBER 12

REAL JUSTICE AND SOMETHING TO BE THANKFUL FOR! PART 2

"God is in the midst of her, she shall not be moved; God shall help her, just at the break of dawn. The nations raged, the kingdoms were moved; He uttered His voice, the earth melted...Come, behold the works of the Lord..." (Psalm 46:5-6 & 8a NKJV).

The writer of Psalm 46 tells us that there is:

- safety in the power of God (Verse 1);
- safety in the presence of God (Verse 1);
- safety in the purpose of God (Verses 2 & 5).

Here is the good news and mandate for every believer! God's presence must become an actual shelter-like complex that gives provisions of peace in the midst of trauma (Psalm 46:7 & 11) .

The beginning of this Psalm challenges us to recognize who's in control. It is not by happenstance or chance, or merely by the lack of clear communication, that the writer of this Psalm starts with the announcement of who's in control. The very first name and proclamation of hope given in the first verse is God.

We would do well to pay close attention to this announcement of authority, for even in the midst of trouble—or even before trouble begins—God is. John tells us, "In the beginning was the Word and the Word was with God and the Word was God...all things were created by him" (John 1:1 & 3a KJV). If everything was created by Him, then everything must be checked by Him before it manifests.

You, as the believer, need to hear this today, for I believe that on all sides the enemy is attacking our understanding of the power of God, the presence of God, and our purpose in God. If we understand this triad of faith, there's no way that we can exist without the trust and the confidence that's in Christ! Here are our credentials of confidence in Christ: I'm safe to practice and produce in the midst of it all.

Yes, God expects you to produce and practice even while events and environments may not be favorable. As a matter of fact, that's why He died our death; so that we could live and thrive for His glory. For He took the most grueling and gruesome of deaths, and in spite of complete abject darkness, He produced eternal salvation!

Notice again with me, in Verse 1: God, or God is, not only is the announcement of divine and cosmic authority, but also a direct call to the believer to acknowledge that before anything happens, God is. I call this the "is-ness" of God. This is where God's presence and power transcends the existence of life and the problematic. Therefore, the answer to what we need is found in Him.

Furthermore the, "is-ness," or the authority and predated presence of God, is followed by the prescription. God is what you need for any circumstance of life and in any crisis of faith... God is!

Now, that's something to be thankful for. ■

— JOHN POOLER, III

NOVEMBER 13

THE FOLLY OF THE GODLESS AND THE RESTORATION OF ISRAEL

"The fool says in his heart, "There is no God." They are corrupt, and their ways are vile; there is no one who does good. God looks down from heaven on all mankind to see if there are any who understand, any who seek God. Everyone has turned away, all have become corrupt; there is no one who does good, not even one. Do all these evildoers know nothing? They devour my people as though eating bread; they never call on God. But there they are, overwhelmed with dread, where there was nothing to dread. God scattered the bones of those who attacked you; you put them to shame, for God despised them. Oh, that salvation for Israel would come out of Zion! When God restores his people, let Jacob rejoice and Israel be glad!"
(Psalms 53 NIV).

How often do we finish watching the news of the day and think these same thoughts as David, here in Psalms 53? We wonder, as David contemplates the same thing, "Do all these evildoers know nothing?" The temptation to deny there is a God is all the more poignant, because when those who refuse to believe look upon the world and its wickedness, they come to conclude that no God would allow such things to occur, therefore there must be no God.

And yet, we know that God exists. If by faith, alone, we believe, then we know that God can and does protect His people. Are we so caught up in life's woes that we cannot acknowledge God's saving grace toward us? David knows nothing of Jesus as he writes these words, but his knowledge of God and what God can do for Israel, if they would only allow it, shows he understands the nature of God and the restoration that comes from trusting and acknowledging Him.

As humans we tend to rank sin. We create numbered lists of sin, going from bad to worse. There is evidence that the greatest sin of all is to say in your heart, "There is no God." Maybe it is just as much a sin to know there is a God, but to fail to acknowledge all He does for you, and furthermore, to fail to show that to others. David laments this very thing in these today's passage.

Has God restored you in the last day or week? Have you shared and shown others what God can, and has done in your life? When others (the godless) look at you, do you reflect the love of a God that can restore? David directed the chief musician to set these contemplations to music.

How much more is it important that we sing the same song; a song that is sweet music to the ears of how God can restore; a song that brings the godless to the feet of God for the restoration possible, only through Him. ■

— AMIREH AL-HADDAD

NOVEMBER 14

REFLECTIONS ON PSALM 54

"Save me, O God, by Your name, And vindicate me by Your power. Hear my prayer, O God; Give ear to the words of my mouth. For strangers have risen against me And violent men have sought my life; They have not set God before them. Selah. Behold, God is my helper; The Lord is the sustainer of my soul. He will recompense the evil to my foes; Destroy them in Your faithfulness.Willingly I will sacrifice to You; I will give thanks to Your name, O Lord, for it is good. For He has delivered me from all trouble, And my eye has looked with satisfaction upon my enemies" (Psalm 54 NASB).

The ability for a person to oppress another requires a turning away from God's will. This opens two fronts wherein we can clearly see God's will: as oppression erupts on a voiceless people, so, too, does God's judgment against those who oppress, in favor of the voiceless. The appearance of God's judgment in turn promotes a hope that transcends the hopelessness of injustice, and that is why we pray.

Prayer is an active acknowledgment of God's judgment for oppression. Prayer serves as a moment of awakening that propels the hopeful into activism against oppressive forces. Prayer acknowledges that I, too, if given the chance, will gladly reciprocate violence with violence. It is recognition that I, too, can turn away from God and become an oppressor of God's people.

Prayer is the realization that submitting to God's justice and to God's actions cannot be equated with passivism or inaction. It is one of the most direct and forceful forms of protest one can secure. Prayer is so radical in its aims and power, that it topples the strongest of foes; even Satan himself.

The prayerful life results in an active life wherein we abide in the will of God. As the Psalmist declares in today's passage, "The Lord is the sustainer of my soul." Therefore, a life bent toward God is bent toward sustaining life. In turn, the act of sustaining life directly counters the act of oppressing life. In our text, the actions of the righteous are seen as violence by the oppressor. To secure life is to deny oppression, and therefore the systems that oppress. To the enemies of God, the spiritually active life manifests as the greatest subversion to their rule. God's faithful are revolutionaries, rebel rousers, untrustworthy.

In reality, the actions of the prayerful is, first, the recognition that violent action is oppression and that promoting life is the will of God. We can therefore look with "satisfaction upon our enemies" because we see their power as powerless. We live in an experience wherein cycles of oppression and revolution are broken by prayerful life giving. We stand on the side of Emmanuel!

Look around you today. Consider both the oppressed and the oppressor. Let your anger and helplessness push you to prayers for God's justice to rain down throughout the land. And then go. Bring life to the voiceless through your words. Subdue pain by bringing healing. Resist the abuse of the oppressor by creating strongholds for the oppressed. And as you do these things, recognize that God's judgment against the oppressor is life. And because oppression is against life, it will cease. ▮▮

— JON-PHILIPPE RUHUMULIZA

NOVEMBER 15

KNOCK THE TEETH OUT OF THEIR MOUTHS!

"God, knock the teeth out of their mouths; Lord, tear out the young lions' fangs" (Psalms 58:6, CSB).

OK, OK, I admit it! I have often quoted the sentiment of today's text, with the wrong motives. Mostly in traffic, when I feel I have been wronged and there is nothing I can do about it, I am tempted to call for lightning to strike from the heavens and make things right. Or those times I'm stuck in an airport without headphones and venture into a store within the terminal and a dead-eyed employee relays to me—with a straight face—that my same cheap headphones are now premium priced on this side of the security check in! I feel my temperature rise and my blood boil. What an injustice! But the foibles of my life are not even tapping at the door of the frustration expressed by the Psalmist, here.

This is not the anger of being cut off in traffic, the disdain that rises when the drive-thru two exits back forgot the French fries, or the indignation that manifests when somebody bumps into you without saying sorry. No, this is the rage of those facing a system of oppression that is protected and upheld by the powerful. (See Psalm 58:1.) This is the frustration that flows when power is used to hurt the people it is meant to help.

This was the rage in our Messiah that drove Him to craft a makeshift whip and sent the panhandling preachers who exploited the sincerity of the faithful for financial gain, scrambling out of the Temple. When witnessing the imbalance of power weaponized against others, there is an internal desire written upon our hearts to see fairness and equality restored.

The first defense my children uttered began with the words, "that's not fair!" From the cradle, we have a righteous indignation that is sparked when we encounter life being out of balance. This rage is not misplaced, it is not sinful; it flows from our Father. It is given as a call for us to participate in restoration. We do not wash away the bad taste of injustice with distractions, but take our charge to the highest authority in the universe. We stand in the fight for others and raise our voices for true justice to be poured out. We give the energy of our anger toward bringing about change.

So, in light of the oppressors in our time, our prayer and reflection today is simple, "God; knock the teeth out of their mouths." ■■

— JASON FRANCIS

NOVEMBER 16

BUT I WILL REMEMBER

"But I will remember the years of the right hand of the Most High. I will remember the works of the Lord; Surely I will remember Your wonders of old. I will also meditate on all Your work, and talk of Your deeds" (Psalm 77:10-12 NKJV).

When I was 13 years old, my life changed forever. Until then, I had been very close to my grandfather. One night, after being sick for a while, he passed away. My grandmother said she felt all alone.

After his death things were very hard for my family, causing us to feel as if we were in a dark pit and could not get out. But as time went on, we learned not to be afraid of the future. One night I just asked God to take care of my grandmother, and let her feel whole again.

David's life changed forever when he was a teenager and was anointed and appointed to be the next King of Israel. But although God said he would be king, David experienced days where he complained and felt that God was no longer there. In Psalm 77, the Psalmist said, "In the day of my trouble I sought the Lord; My hand was stretched out in the night without ceasing; My soul refused to be comforted. I remembered God, and was troubled; I complained, and my spirit was overwhelmed" (Psalm 77:1-2 NKJV).

David wondered aloud whether God had forgotten to be gracious. However, in Verse 10 it came back to him how good God had been throughout all of his trials. He finally stated, "But I will remember the years of the right hand of the Most High. I will remember the works of the Lord; Surely I will remember Your wonders of old" (NKJV).

It is not difficult to go through hard times and wonder if you are all alone. The Bible is clear when it says that God will never leave us or forsake us. I can now live every day of my life knowing that it is not about who I am, but it is always about who is with me.

Today my grandmother is doing fine. I even drive the car that she and my grandfather drove while I was growing up. My grandmother gave it to me as a gift. When I see my car outside of my house in Huntsville, Alabama, it always reminds me of my grandfather and how he loved God and how much God loves me.

If you accept the gift of peace from God, you can get through anything. The Bible is clear that God will never leave us nor forsake us. All we have to do is trust Him, and wait for Him to come through with yet another miracle. ▮▮

— ORLAN JOHNSON AND JAIR JOHNSON

NOVEMBER 17

HOLY DISSATISFACTION

"God calls the judges into his courtroom, he puts all the judges in the dock. 'Enough! You've corrupted justice long enough, you've let the wicked get away with murder. You're here to defend the defenseless, to make sure that underdogs get a fair break; Your job is to stand up for the powerless, and prosecute all those who exploit them.' Ignorant judges! Head-in-the-sand judges! They haven't a clue to what's going on. And now everything's falling apart, the world's coming unglued. 'I commissioned you judges, each one of you, deputies of the High God, But you've betrayed your commission and now you're stripped of your rank, busted.' O God, give them their just deserts! You've got the whole world in your hands!" (Psalm 82:1-8 MSG).

Justice must never be an afterthought for the believers in God. We are called to uphold the Bible's truths which declare liberty for the downtrodden and the oppressed. Not only are we called to support and live by it, but we must also speak truth to power to the people and systems that continue to create a permanent underclass.

In the book, Where Do We Go from Here, Martin Luther King Jr. said, "Let us be dissatisfied until America will no longer have high blood pressure of creeds and an anemia of deeds. Let us be dissatisfied until the tragic walls that separate the outer city of wealth and comfort battering rams of the fires of justice. Let us be dissatisfied until they who live on the outskirts of Hope are brought into the metropolis of daily security. Let us be dissatisfied until slums are cast into the junk heap of history, and every family will live in a decent, sanitary home. Let us be dissatisfied until the dark yesterdays of segregated schools will be transformed into the bright tomorrows of quality integrated education."

In our passage, Asaph is dissatisfied with the leadership, particularly the courts that have ignored the plight of the least of these. Because they have corrupted justice for so long, they have allowed the wicked to get away with murder. In our United States of Anxiety, black and brown people have expressed the same feelings of dissatisfaction. We witnessed George Zimmerman get acquitted of all charges for murdering Trayvon Martin. We witnessed the courts rule in favor of the police officers who choked Eric Garner to death. These are just a few examples of miscarriages of justice that we have had to contend with as children of God.

As Asaph expressed his displeasure, he also raised his voice by holding them accountable, saying, "You're here to defend the defenseless. Your job is to stand up for the powerless and prosecute all those who exploit them." When we do our job, we please God, and we protect His creation from unjust leadership that only seeks to abuse them.

For this devotion, let us pray that God will give us the courage to be an Asaph. Let us pray for the audacity to call out leadership that does the opposite of what God requires them to do. Let us pray that in our lives we "learn to do right; seek justice. Defend the oppressed. Take up the cause of the fatherless; plead the case of the widow.

Let us be dissatisfied with injustice until there is liberty and justice for all. ■

— JAIME KOWLESSAR

NOVEMBER 18

THE CALL TO CARE FOR OTHERS

"Give justice to the poor and the orphan; uphold the rights of the oppressed and the destitute. Rescue the poor and helpless; deliver them from the grasp of evil people" (Psalms 82:3-4 NLT).

We live in a world that teaches that we should look out for ourselves in order to find our happiness or success. This message of self-empowerment can be found from politics to education, and even from people who are closest to us. It is not that this idea is entirely wrong or evil, but rather the assumption that we should put ourselves ahead of others that can position us into dangerous territory.

As followers of God, the message of finding happiness and success is actually the opposite. Those who care for others and put others first tend to find themselves more satisfied and fulfilled in life. In Psalm 82, today's text focuses the followers of God on the message of caring for others. The writer of this chapter gives us behind-the-scenes footage of God's desire for how those who are societal leaders, as well as everyday people, should treat the less fortunate. And I believe that essentially, when we have this mindset that God encourages, we will find fulfillment.

The text suggests to us that there are two things we should be intentional in doing for our fellow mankind. First, we should "uphold the rights of the oppressed and the destitute." For societal leaders, God expects us to act as judges, or governors of law, and speak up for those who are voiceless and overlooked. Even further, God expects us to put into laws and policies, instruments that will serve as a vehicle to providing equality for the marginalized.

As regular citizens, God also expect us to defend those who do not have a voice and are being taking advantage of. Such action may include, using our right to vote, protesting injustice and running for local, state or national offices.

Second, we should "Rescue the poor and the needy." The word "rescue" in the Hebrew is in the similar context as the word "deliver" in the same verse. Essentially God says, help people who are shackled by the injustices of society, and wicked leaders, to escape from the bondage. We can do these things by showing up to school board meetings, and holding our educational system accountable. We can also accomplish this by educating ourselves on what our people are going through in underserved communities, fostering relationships with individuals in underserved communities and collaborating with our underserved communities by developing plans of liberation.

God ultimately shows us that His character is foundational in putting others first, over ourselves. ■

— S. ELIOT BROOKS, III

NOVEMBER 19

LIVING IN THE SIGHT OF A HOLY GOD WITHOUT AN INTERCESSOR

"All that the Father gives Me will come to Me, and the one who comes to Me I will by no means cast out" (John 6:37 NKJV).

I remember when I was a teenager, hearing sermons about last day events. I would hear the statement that, "we must live in the sight of a Holy God without an intercessor." Such statements made me tremble about last day events. How could I make it through? Could we be saved?

Such feelings caused me to doubt that I could even be saved. And here is just the problem; such emphasizing of this made me feel that "I" must live in the sight of a Holy God without an intercessor. Instead, how about we focus more on the Intercessor, Himself?

Jesus came into this world to save sinners. The whole foundation of the gospel is that God "so loved the world, that he gave his only begotten Son, that whosoever believes in him should not perish but have everlasting life" (John 3:16 KJV). We must place our eyes upon the plan of redemption and just how much salvation cost the Godhead. It cost the blood and life of the Son of God. He became sin, who knew no sin, that we might be made the righteousness of God in Him (1 Corinthians 5:21). Jesus submitted to suffer the penalty of sin, or second death on the cross. Let's take a moment to flesh this out.

Revelation tells us that the second death is the lake of fire and that the lake of fire is the second death (Revelation 20:14). These two terms essentially mean the same thing. This means to suffer the second death is no different than suffering the lake that burns with fire and brimstone (Revelation 21:8). These texts give us an insight into the mental anguish that Christ felt on the cross. He felt Himself being completely separated from the Father in place of every human being.

Christ is the mercy of God. Having suffered and paid such an expensive price for our sins helps us to understand that He will never leave us nor forsake us, even in times of trouble or in "the time of trouble" that Daniel speaks of (Daniel 12:1). We must realize that this same loving Jesus will carry us through in His arms and under His wings. He is our Savior.

Let's make this even clearer. In heaven, we will forever live in the sight of a Holy, Loving God without an intercessor—and that is OK, because the plan of redemption will be completed and no intercession is needed. Christ, Himself, has redeemed. ■

— KERWIN JONES

NOVEMBER 20

ALMOST PERSUADED

"It is a good thing to give thanks unto the Lord, and to sing praises unto thy name, O most High: To shew forth thy lovingkindness in the morning, and thy faithfulness every night" (Psalm 92:1-2 KJV).

A Shakespearean tragedy is a literary classification of written dramas in which there is a purported noble protagonist, who is flawed in some way, placed in a stressful heightened situation, and ends with a fatal conclusion.

In June of 2015, Dylann Roof, the man who was charged with nine counts of murder in a mass killing in a historic black church in Charleston, South Carolina, reportedly almost didn't go through with that Wednesday night massacre. The Charleston police said Roof almost didn't go through with it because, "everyone was so nice to him."

Roof reportedly spent about an hour inside Emanuel African Methodist Episcopal Church with the victims before the shooting.

Psalm 92:5-7 says, "Lord, how great are thy works! and thy thoughts are very deep. A brutish man knoweth not; neither doth a fool understand this. When the wicked spring as the grass, and when all the workers of iniquity do flourish; it is that they shall be destroyed forever" (KJV).

Dr. King once stated that, "The arc of the moral universe is long, but it bends towards justice." Many of us may miss out on our blessings because of the "tragedy of the almost." I almost went to college; I almost forgave my enemy; or tragically, I almost gave my life to Christ.

You remember that God's purpose for the children of Israel was for them to go directly into the Promised Land. One day they came to a little village known as Kadesh-Barnea and were on the very border of the Promised Land. Just a few more yards and they would be in the land which God had promised them. Yet, they were almost persuaded, but turned from Kadesh-Barnea and went back into the wilderness for another 40 years.

On another occasion, Jesus made a statement to a to a man who wanted to be saved. Jesus looked at him and said; "Thou are not far from the kingdom of God" (Mark 12:34 KJV). In other words, the man was almost there. Psalm 92:14-15 reminds us that if we don't "break camp" and hang on until the end, God has the power and authority to protect us for life. "They shall still bring forth fruit in old age; they shall be fat and flourishing; To shew that the Lord is upright: he is my rock, and there is no unrighteousness in him" (KJV).

I still believe that the greatest tragedy in life is for a person to almost see Jesus, and despite all their experiences with Him, still be lost. ▮▮

— ORLAN JOHNSON

NOVEMBER 21

A PRIMER IN PRAISE

"Make a joyful shout to the Lord, all you lands! Serve the Lord with gladness; Come before His presence with singing. Know that the Lord, He is God; it is He who has made us, and not we ourselves; We are His people and the sheep of His pasture. Enter into His gates with thanksgiving, and into His courts with praise. Be thankful to Him, and bless His name. For the Lord is good; His mercy is everlasting, and His truth endures to all generations" (Psalm 100 NKJV).

In five short verses, we are given a primer on how and why we should praise the Lord.

At the time of writing this devotional, the nation is gripped by contention as we seek to decide whether or not one of the most polarizing men in our nation's history will be given four more years to serve as president or not. With a cacophony of voices trading barbs, indictments, innuendo and allegations, Psalm 100 challenges the believer to rise above the fray and not just make noise, but make a joyful noise! It reminds us that the subject of our adoration is not a partisan political system, but is God Himself!

With the COVID-19 pandemic raging out of control because that same leader, along with others, failed to lead, with death and destruction all around and with fear and uncertainty abounding, this sweetest of Psalms urges us to come before God with singing. Why? Because He is the reason we exist, and our lives are in His hands! And in His hands we can sing in the face of fear! In His hands we can sing in the face of uncertainty! In His hands we can sing, even when the outlook is dire and our human nature shrinks from the task at hand.

And then, in a nod to its counterpart, Psalm 23, Psalm 100 reminds us that we are not a cosmic accident. We are here because the loving heart of God designed for us to be here. Evolution fails bitterly in its anemic attempts to account for our existence. Of a truth, we did not "create ourselves" as Darwin would have us to believe. And not only are we here, but we are here as the sheep of the Good Shepherd, meaning that we shall not want!

So with all of that in hand, we are invited to keep our regular appointment with the Lord by entering into His gates, not kicking and screaming, not going as against our will, not showing up as though we are doing God a favor by being there. Instead, with praise and thanksgiving we are to approach the Most High God.

We should be thankful for His grace! Thankful for His mercy! Thankful that He loves us! Thankful that we can trust Him! Thankful that anywhere with Him we can safely go! Thankful that even in the most dismal of circumstances, He is still God and we are still His people! And above all, thankful that trouble won't last always and that one day faith will become sight.

And we will have a blessed eternity to celebrate the God of our salvation! ▮▮

— LAWRENCE BROWN

NOVEMBER 22

GIVE THANKS TO THE LORD

"Oh, give thanks to the Lord, for He is good! For His mercy endures forever. Let the redeemed of the Lord say so, Whom He has redeemed from the hand of the enemy, and gathered out of the lands, from the east and from the west, from the north and from the south" (Psalms 107:1-3 NKJV).

Today's text reminds us to "give thanks to the Lord, for He is good, for His lovingkindness is everlasting. Let the redeemed of the Lord say so, whom He has redeemed from the hand of the adversary and gathered from the lands: from the east and from the west, from the north and from the south" (NASB).

Beginning with the end of this passage, we get a picture of the care and admonition of God, even as God's oppressed people travel through the troubles of life. The translated word "south" in this passage is better transliterated as "sea."

In general, in the Old Testament, the word "sea" is used for the west, because the western boundary of the land of Palestine was the Mediterranean Sea. However, in this text we see that the word "sea" is used to denote the southern boundary. This change is due to the location that the writer was referring his deliverance from.

While the western boundary of Palestine was the great Mediterranean Sea, from Babylon the great waterway was on the southern boundary. This text gives us a clue into a different perspective of the people of God, even while they were going through Babylonian exile. In short, the writer of this text is exclaiming to his readers to give thanks to a God who can bring us through every difficult, exilic place in our life.

God is telling us today, that even though life is not always easy, to give thanks to God anyway. God understands our plight and is keenly aware of the bad places that we go through in this life. But God also knows how He will be with us in those bad situations and carry us through to the other side.

I want to remind us to trust God even in situations that are less than desirable to us. Remember that God can bring us out in His time, and redeem us from the hand of those who oppress us. Oppression is not in charge of us; God is in charge of us, and therefore oppression cannot overcome us. If we hold on to God, trusting in His redeeming power on behalf of His children, we will be able to say like the psalmist: "He is good" and "His lovingkindness is everlasting" towards His children.

So today, because we are redeemed from the hand of the enemy, let us give thanks to God for His goodness and ever-loving kindness in our lives. ∎

— RODNEY GRISSOM

NOVEMBER 23

MY REFLECTIONS ON THE CONNECTION BETWEEN LAW AND LIBERTY

"Open my eyes, that I may see wondrous things from Your law" (Psalm 119:18 NKJV).

Many of us think of "law" as being confining and even oppressive, whereas love and freedom are liberating and joyful. But Psalm 119 reminds us of the important connection between law and liberty, and even between law and love.

Psalm 119 is the chapter of the Bible that mentions law more than any other, indeed more than almost all other entire biblical books. Indeed, if you consider words that are synonyms for law, like "statutes," "commandments," "testimonies," or "word," law is referenced in all but three or four of the 176 verses of the Psalm.

But despite having this strong focus on law, Psalm 119 also has a great focus on words like "love," "delight," "hope," and "rejoicing." Indeed, along with being the chapter that mentions law the most times in the Bible, this same chapter mentions "love" more times than any other, except for 1 John 4.

What connection did the Psalmist see between law and liberty, and even love and delight? A key verse in the chapter that directly brings out this connection is Verse 45, which says, "And I will walk at liberty, for I seek your precepts" (NKJV). The psalmist understood that far from being an instrument of oppression, that properly understood, God's law was a pathway to freedom. Why was this? Well, the rest of the Psalm tells us why.

It helps "a young man cleanse his way" (Verse 9), which helps him avoid the civil and spiritual consequences of moral failure. It causes us to "look away my eyes from worthless things," (Verse. 37) which only serves to distract us from our real life purposes and goals.

The law has "caused me to hope," (Verse 49) because it sets out the standards of success in this life and the life to come.

Its health principles cause us not to have a "heart as fat as grease," (Verse 70) giving us happier, healthier, more enjoyable lives.

It gives us "more understanding than all my teachers," (Verse 99), thus giving us success in academic and scholarly pursuits. Its principles provide a "lamp to my feet and a light to my path," (Verse 105), showing us where both earthly and heavenly success lie.

And these are just some of the benefits of the law and its wisdom. If we understand the true role of the law is not to save us, but to provide guidance, wisdom and direction to those that are saved by faith in Christ, we can say with the Psalmist that, "Therefore I love your commandments, more than gold, yes, than fine gold!" (Verse 127). ■

— NICHOLAS MILLER

NOVEMBER 24

LIBERTY FROM LYING LIPS

"Deliver my soul, O LORD, from lying lips, and from a deceitful tongue" (Psalm 120:2 NKJV).

That brother is a fanatic." "He thinks he knows everything."

These were a few of the words I heard one Sabbath morning. I had come to church early and sat in the back of sanctuary to quietly meditate and talk with God. After about ten minutes, you could hear church members beginning to come into the foyer and familiar voices talking. I paid them no mind until I heard my name. My ears perked up, now listening to every word. They had no idea that I was there.

"I don't even know why he comes to church here," one said.

Frustrated and saddened, I sat there considering what to do with myself. And then the unthinkable happened. They walked through the sanctuary doors. They saw me and, of course, looked shocked at my presence. Then the very ones gossiping, reached out their hands to shake mine.

"Happy Sabbath, Brother Waller," they said, smiling.

I could not believe it. Now, I don't know about you, but I don't like fake folks. Proverbs 26:24 says, "Enemies disguise themselves with their lips, but in their hearts they harbor deceit" (NIV). These types of people are a bane in the church. They reflect their father, the devil, who did the same thing in heaven, and for that reason was cast out. (See Revelation 12:4; Isaiah 9:15; and Psalm 101:5 & 7)

Lying, gossiping lips bring pain, suffering, and sadness into the world. Wars have begun based on lies. Lies are, without question, an abomination (Proverbs 12:2) The final crisis is to be provoked by the lies and deception of the devil, symbolized perfectly as a dragon working through the superpower of the earth (Revelation 13:11).

All the world will wonder after the Beast, receive his mark and number, making lies their refuge (Isaiah 28:15-17). The only safety one has is to make the Word of God their constant companion. As we are of the word, we will not be of the world. Jesus said, "Sanctify them through thy truth, thy word is truth" (John 17:17).

Liberation from those with lying lips will require us to be freed from lying and gossiping ourselves. Do you desire this liberty? If so, we must give God permission to take, keep and purify our hearts, refining us after His likeness (Malachi 3:1-3).

This is how we will be delivered. Then the prophetic word will be fulfilled that like Jesus "in their mouth was found no deceit" (Revelation 14:5 & 1 Peter 2:21-22). ■

— ANDRE WALLER

NOVEMBER 25

HE SHALL PRESERVE

I will lift up my eyes to the hills— From whence comes my help?" (Psalm 121:1 NKJV).

It was in my freshman year in college, where I found myself doing more than what my body was able to handle. It was only the beginning of the spring semester.

I woke up early that Sabbath morning after going to bed around midnight, and was unaware of what the rest of my day would be. Little did I know, taking a 50-minute drive, twice, for some free food, and getting to know new faces after church was probably not the wisest thing that I could have done. A new driver on the block, hanging out with friends late at night, and going for that second visit was the last time my Toyota Corolla saw the light of day.

Yes, you guessed it. While heading back to campus, listening to music, I fell asleep at the wheel. I was scared for my life when I woke up. When I opened my eyes, I was in the middle of some woods, in a ditch on the side of the road, and by train tracks. There was blood from my head injury, the car was totaled, and I had no idea where I was.

Through God's strength, my only option was to walk up a hill to find a Good Samaritan that would help me. I was cold, embarrassed, and only wondered how my parents would react. While I stood outside on the phone with them, waiting for the ambulance, they reminded me that I was still alive. My life was still spared. I was bruised, but not destroyed; disappointed that the car was lost, but grateful that I had breath still in my body.

At that moment, I remembered my grandmother's favorite Scripture: Psalm 121. It reminded me that no matter what comes, the Lord is forever a present help. We are helpless without Him and cannot make it on our own. We need the God who created the heavens and earth, to preserve us and keep us daily in His arms wherever we may go.

To paraphrase the Psalmist, "If it had not been for the Lord on my side, where would I be?" I could have been six feet underground, but the Lord preserved me. I could have been paralyzed, but the Lord preserved me. I may have fallen asleep at the wheel that night, but we serve a God that never sleeps or slumber. ▮▮

— ELIJAH RASHAD JOHNSON

THE LIBERATED HOME

"Except the LORD build the house, they labour in vain that build it" (Psalm 127:1 KJV).

Home should be a sanctuary; a place where peace and love abide; a place where people are given space to grow and develop. Where imperfections are not a death sentence, but rather learning moments. Where unkindness is not tolerated and where constant maturation takes place. Home should equal a little heaven on earth. Sadly, in most instances this is not the case.

One Sabbath after service, a dear sister came to me and asked a serious question.

"Brother Andre, I do not love my husband. Does God expect me to stay in a loveless relationship?"

This sister felt that she was in bondage; a slave to a relationship that was not bound by love, but by the dictates of the courts and expectations of church, friends, and family. Extensive cheating had taken place, and emotional distancing had been going on for years. What was she to do? Was she to stay in a loveless relationship?

"No." I said, "God does not expect you to stay in a loveless relationship." For a moment she looked relieved, but then I kept talking.

"You are looking for love from the wrong place. Your husband is not the source of love, and neither are you. The reason why your marriage is loveless is because neither of you have invited God to be the center of your relationship. If you go to God as your Source, you will have everything you need to love the one that you find unlovable. Will you allow God to help you?"

For a moment she looked disappointed, but then you could see a little hope flicker in her eyes. I am happy to say it has been many years later and that couple is still together and happy in Jesus.

So many homes are in bondage; slaves to sin, dysfunctionality being the norm. However, there is this most beautiful promise that states, "Behold, I will send you Elijah the prophet before the coming of the great and dreadful day of the LORD: And he shall turn the heart of the fathers to the children, and the heart of the children to their fathers, lest I come and smite the earth with a curse" (Malachi 4:5-6 KJV).

In order to save our world, God must first liberate our homes. Let us let Love liberate us all. ■■

— ANDRE WALLER

THE TEMPORAL JUDGEMENTS OF GOD

"Daughter Babylon, doomed to destruction, happy is the one who repays you according to what you have done to us" (Psalm 137:8 NIV).

It had been one of those weeks. A week when nothing seemed to go as planned. I realized that with each blessing there will always be at least one antagonist. I wanted God to "bring the pain" to my adversaries that week, swiftly and without reservation.

Ironically, when you juxtapose this harrowing week against the previous week that felt like life could not be any better, you can't help but agree with the adage that we all live in one of the three continuums of life: You are either in a storm; just got out of a storm, or heading back into a storm again.

I imagine that's how Jeremiah felt when he penned the powerful, but sad words that begin the 137th Psalm, "By the rivers of Babylon we sat and wept when we remembered Zion. There on the poplars we hung our harps, for there our captors asked us for songs, our tormentors demanded songs of joy; they said, 'Sing us one of the songs of Zion!'" (Psalm 137:1 NIV).

Bible scholars agree that "by the rivers of Babylon" generally refers to living in a repressive society and longing for freedom. So, Psalm 137 is expressing the anguish of God's people during their Babylonian exile. In its totality, this psalm demonstrates the longing to be back in Jerusalem—as well as extreme hatred for their enemies, with sometimes graphic imagery.

This particular psalm is one of several called imprecatory psalms, in which the writer calls upon God to bring down severe judgment and harsh punishment on one's enemies. And although we serve a God of love who is long-suffering, kind, redemptive and full of grace, there are times when He chooses to exact His temporal judgments on individuals and nations, according to His own will.

As a nation, Egypt experienced temporal judgements with10 plagues and its army drowning in the Red Sea. Ananias and Sapphira experienced temporal judgement when they chose to lie and rob God of His offerings. God, in His infinite wisdom, has the standing and the authority to hand down temporal judgments.

However, true servants of God should understand that imprecatory prayers should only be used against spiritual foes (Ephesians 6:12). Praying imprecations on human foes is never justifiable. It is only when you have the spirit of God coursing through your veins, will you be able to sing a song for your tormentors while living in a foreign land. Even when your body is in captivity, your spirit and heart can always be free. Because he who the Son sets free is free indeed. ■

— ORLAN JOHNSON

NOVEMBER 28

IN GOD'S SPACE

"My frame was not hidden from You, When I was made in secret, and skillfully wrought in the lowest parts of the earth. Your eyes saw my substance, being yet unformed. And in Your book they all were written, the days fashioned for me, when as yet there were none of them" (Psalms 139:15-16).

There are times when we may feel discouraged and alone. We may think that God is beyond our situation and unreachable amid our pain and affliction.

However, the God who created our vast universe also created our finite minds. He created space and time and set those as our earthly confines, which we call reality. While we are limited by those, God is not. He moves inside, through and beyond our boundaries, and therefore can see reality and what is yet to be.

In Psalm 139, David praises God as he portrays Him as an explorer who carefully searches the deepest part of our beings. He knows our hearts and our intimate thoughts, where we move and have our rest, and what motivates us to be and do.

While David praises the All-knowing God, David is awed by something even greater—the Eternal has known the part of us that is yet unknown to us and our position before we entered the human realm. It is not just an imagination about us, because we have existed in the Eternal's mind. Since then, He has written about us in His eternal book, and loved and cared for us before we were conceived. He precedes our experience and therefore has known our joys and pains. Our predicaments cannot hide us from Him because His Eternal presence has surrounded the space and time that He established for us.

Acknowledging that God already knows all about us, David cries out at the end of the Psalm, asking God to search him as an explorer in unknown territory. He gives God permission to search and reveal to him the part that he doesn't know about himself—his inclinations and aspirations. David's desire is to be brought in tune with God's thoughts and be led in His way.

The Bible affirms that God's thoughts are not our thoughts, yet He longs to reveal them to us. As we go through difficulties, we can be comforted in knowing that God already knows. As we surrender every part of ourselves to Him—including those yet unknown to us—God will walk with us and empower us with His thoughts, and lead us in His everlasting way. ■

— LESLIE SOUPET

SEARCH ME, OH GOD!

"Search me, O God, and know my heart" (Psalm 139:23a NKJV).

All you saw as a baby was a change of environment: from your mother's womb and into the real world. All you knew was that someway, somehow you are finally able to see the face of the woman who has been speaking to you for nine months. You do not know what you will become, because you are not aware of much.

The only one who knows what your future holds is God. He knew you before your mother met your father and before they laid eyes upon your face (Jeremiah 1:5). It was God that formed your inward parts, covered you in your mother's womb (Psalm 139:13), and installed a passion for you to complete whatever purpose He has for you.

As I grew up in the church, I personally was drawn to music ministry. No matter where you would find me, I made a vow to always be prepared to say "yes" to music. This mentality of always being ready for music has followed me all the way to today, but I have learned its dangers.

One day, I was so caught up in the music and the response of people, that I failed publicly and forgot the words to a song. Yes, God humbled me in front of the church (Matthew 23:12). I did not understand what happened because I practiced, I prayed, and I knew the song. However, my performance didn't reflect that. God told me about myself in my room and I could not believe it, but it was true. I was so caught up in the music and had forgotten about the ministry, so I had to pray like David.

In Psalm 139, David is praying after a revelation that he and mankind is messed up and that God is forever there, even when He knows the real you. There is wickedness hidden within our hearts because we have been shaped in iniquity, and in sin our mothers conceived us (Psalm 51:5).

In our eyes, we may not be as bad as our neighbors, but there is no one that is greater than the other. That is why David asked God to, "Search me, O God, and know my heart; Try me, and know my anxieties; and see if there is any wicked way in me, and lead me in the way everlasting (Psalm 139:23-24 NKJV)."

Do you want to be ready for everlasting life? I do. Let us pray that He will search us, try us, and renew us. ▮▮

— ELIJAH RASHAD JOHNSON

NOVEMBER 30

AND THEY OVERCAME HIM BY THE BLOOD OF THE LAMB

"O God the Lord, the strength of my salvation, You have covered my head in the day of battle" (Psalms 140:7 NKJV)
"And they overcame him by the blood of the Lamb and by the word of their testimony, and they did not love their lies to the death" (Revelation 12:11 NKJV).

Niccolò di Bernardo dei Machiavelli was an Italian Renaissance diplomat, philosopher and writer, best known for the famous treatise, The Prince. Machiavelli's name came to evoke unscrupulous politicians of the sort Machiavelli advised, most famously in his treatise.

Machiavelli proposed that immoral behavior, such as the use of deceit, was normal and effective in politics and necessary for political expediency while helping to maintain power. Many have a quest for power. Power reveals who you really are. Power reveals what you really value.

In the Revelation 12, we see the devil's quest for power and influence. John looks up and sees a woman in the original sundress; she's clothed with the sun, the moon under her feet, and she has a crown of 12 stars. This woman is pregnant with Child and the dragon, the devil, is there waiting to devour the child.

Since the beginning of time, the devil/snake/dragon has been seeking influence by seeking to destroy Jesus and His people. The devil has sought to prevent the crushing and final blow to his head from the One whose heel he could merely bruise. The devil used the little influence he had to draw a third of the angels. Yes, he has a little bit of influence, but the glorious gospel teaches us that his influence is shrinking day by day.

We are engaged in a great war, but our opponent, accuser and deceiver is ever losing ground. Believer, be encouraged that your greatest enemy lost ground when he was evicted out of the portals of glory. He thought he gained influence at the midday-midnight of Golgotha, however just a couple of days later, the enemy lost ground again. Your greatest enemy loses ground every time a soul comes to Christ in repentance, confession and faith. We can ascertain that our greatest enemy has shrinking influence, and very soon his influence will be naught. Yes, he is still roaming, roaring, seeking and devouring, but one day his roam shall cease; his roar shall be silenced; his search shall be halted; and his jaw shall be wired shut.

May your faith be increased, today, in knowing that we have overcome already the shrinking influence of the devil by the blood of the Paschal Lamb, Jesus the Christ. In the words of today's first text, 'O God the Lord, the strength of my salvation, thou hast covered my head in the day of battle." ▮▮

— LAURENT GROSVENOR

DECEMBER

PROPHECY

After millennia of injustice, oppression and disenfranchisement, the answer remains the same: Jesus! By showing up the first time, He spoke truth to power, rebuking all who would afflict the downtrodden and mistreat other sons and daughters of God. By showing up the second time, Christ will once and for all break the back of evil and all that comes in its foul train.

For the month of December, the devotionals are supplied by the ministry team of Northeastern Conference of Seventh-day Adventists. Our president at the time of this writing, Dr. Daniel Honore, was born on December 25, and you can find his devotional on that day.

Be blessed as we seek to remind you that Christ, the maker of Heaven and Earth, will return in power and great glory, delivering His faithful ones and ushering us into an unending eternity of peace and love. May this grand realization give us all the courage to continue the fight against oppression, wherever it may rear its ugly head! God bless you! ■■

— LAWRENCE BROWN
Director of Public Affairs and Religious Liberty,
Northeastern Conference of Seventh-day Adventists

IN NEED OF A CURE

"But when the fulness of the time was come, God sent forth his Son, made of a woman, made under the law" (Galatians 4:4 KJV).

As I write this, our world sits gripped in the iron-clad grasp of a pandemic that has singlehandedly changed the way life works for everyone. Like a perfect killing machine, the COVID-19 virus has disrupted parts of our lives that we perhaps once thought were bullet proof, snatching away time-honored traditions as easily as it has snatched away, in some cases, entire families. It has laid waste things as noble as school graduations and as mundane as the weekly visit to the barbershop or hair salon. Who saw this one coming?!

The ironic thing is that this moment has so much in common with another equally profound moment; another time when the world changed and the inhabitants of that time and space were slow to realize just how radical the change was.

Then, as now, the time for census had approached. (We are in the midst of the 2020 census at the time of this writing.) The need for everyone to be counted meant that folks had to make their way back home, whether they liked the idea of going or not. And in the midst of all that movement, a baby was born—and just by showing up—struck a blow for conscious and justice. Then, as now, may we exclaim: who saw it coming?

Before the arrival of Jesus in Bethlehem that night so long ago, things had gotten atrociously bad. Ellen White describes it this way in her seminal book, *Desire of Ages*: "The deception of sin had reached its height. All the agencies for depraving the souls of men had been put in operation" (White, 1898, p. 36). "Sin had become a science, and vice was consecrated as a part of religion. Rebellion had struck its roots deep into the heart, and the hostility of man was most violent against heaven" (White, p. 37).

But in one night, the cure was injected into the problem and the world would never be the same again! From that same book: "At the very crisis, when Satan seemed about to triumph, the Son of God came with the embassage of divine grace" (White, p. 37). "And when the fullness of the time had come, the Deity was glorified by pouring upon the world a flood of healing grace that was never to be obstructed or withdrawn till the plan of salvation should be fulfilled" (White, p. 37).

Jesus remains the answer for every problem in life that we face. Why not pause and have your own Bethlehem moment, right now, by inviting Him to be born anew in your heart? ▮▮

— LAWRENCE BROWN

DECEMBER 2

FIGHTING WORDS – SEED VS. SEED

"And I will put enmity between thee and the woman, and between thy seed and her seed; it shall bruise thy head, and thou shalt bruise his heel" (Genesis 3:15 KJV).

"Back in the day" when I was growing up, I remember having a few fights. Back then, fights began with fighting words. One would challenge the opponent with words describing how much hurting was going to be put on them; you talked yourself into being the winner of the fight. Sometimes I said more fighting words than I could back up, to the extent I wished I could back out. Fear gripped me as I thought about what might happen to me.

One of the most paralyzing feelings to overcome humankind is fear. Fear causes anxiety. Not knowing how things will turn out, you lose control. Your thoughts are no longer rational and your actions are stupefying. Fear will have you hide yourself because of its debilitating condition on the mind. That is what it did to Adam, causing him to hide from God (Genesis 3:9-10).

As God questioned Adam, being afraid and recognizing his nakedness, Adam remembered God's promise of dying. Fear gripped Adam and he blamed the woman, his "help meet," who was, in Adam's own words, "bone of my bones, and flesh of my flesh." She became the scapegoat for his actions. A man afraid seldom takes responsibility.

The final blame fell on the serpent, which God created. The war that began in heaven is now on earth (Revelation 12: 7-9). In the midst of the garden, at the tree of knowledge of good and evil, God declares a fight with the serpent on behalf of man, "your seed vs. my seed." God also declares the victor to be His seed—fighting words, if ever there was any.

Unlike me, God can back up His fighting words! On the day of the main event, they took the fight to Calvary. Jesus called the fight. He said, "I am going to Jerusalem, they are going to kill me, but it is not a knock out. Look for me in three days; I will be back with the keys to hell and to death (Revelation 1:18). He (the devil) will get me on the heel, but I will get him in the head."

This fight was called out for you and me, because of God's Love for us (John 3:16). ▮▮

— ROBERT CHANDLER

THE CONFLICT RESOLVED

"Now all this was done, that it might be fulfilled which was spoken of the Lord by the prophet, saying, Behold, a virgin shall be with child, and shall bring forth a son, and they shall call his name Emmanuel, which being interpreted is, God with us" (Matthew 1:22-23, KJV).

The birth of Christ is surrounded by a couple of conflict-filled events. These conflicts are utilized by Matthew as a means of moving his narrative about Jesus toward the climax of prophecies being fulfilled through Him. This is the blood coursing through the veins of this Gospel, because Matthew writes with the intent of proving that Jesus is the fulfillment of the prophecies recorded in the Old Testament.

In the first episode of Jesus' life, concerning his paternity, both Mary and Joseph are placed in a compromising position. In the eyes of their community, Mary would have been considered an adulterer, while the society that they lived in would have expected Joseph to respond to her "infidelity." The only way to begin to imagine the internal conflict that Joseph experienced is to place yourself in his shoes. He probably had a difficult time processing how to respond to the news of Mary's pregnancy. Therefore, the Lord shows up to provide a resolution to the conflict. This occurs through God's clarification and Matthew's explanation of the event's occurrence.

After Joseph makes up his mind to put Mary away privately to avoid disgracing her publicly (Matthew 1:19), the Lord clarifies to him in Matthew 1:20-21 why this event transpires. The presence of God here should cause us to see that He is intentionally invested in helping us resolve the internal conflicts that we experience. The reason for this is because anything that disturbs the peace that God wants to be present in our minds prevents us from conceptualizing His saving grace.

In other words, conflict often functions to inhibit our ability to see the hand of God moving in our problems. While Joseph is thinking about how to save Mary, God initiates the process of revealing to him how all people, including himself , will be saved. Without this clarification it would be impossible for him to comprehend the reason why he is placed in this position. Therefore, God shows up to make it clear to him how and why this happens. This then gives rise to Matthew's explanation of God's clarification.

Matthew 1:22-23 acts as a commentary that functions to diffuse an already escalating conflict. This should reveal to us that when conflicts in our lives start to escalate, the word of God provides insights that help to deescalate it. As a result, God's word can be trusted to restore the peace that once occupied our minds. ■■

— CORY MARSHAll

DECEMBER 4

GROW IN GRACE

"And Jesus increased in wisdom and stature, and in favor with God and man" (Luke 2:52 NKJV).

Many people who grew up in small towns or communities compare growing up there with living in a glass house. Everybody seems to know everybody, and everything about everybody. It can feel that way growing up in the church too.

Looking at the early life of Jesus, Luke says that Jesus grew physically, mentally and spiritually. The results of such a life brought Jesus into favor with both God and man. Jesus was a good citizen. He was an honest hard worker. He regularly attended the synagogue, and He paid taxes whether He "needed" to or not.

The social, political and economic times in which He lived did not escape His notice. Roman law required that any request for assistance to carry out an official duty must be complied with. Jesus' response to this law: "And whosoever shall compel thee to go a mile, go with him twain" (Matthew 5:41 KJV). Some might call this nonviolent resistance or nonviolent protest.

While Jesus responded to this social issue, He also had another agenda. Perhaps Jesus was looking to the very near future when, on a brutal journey up Golgotha's hill, this law would be evoked and a man named Simon would have to respond.

Growing up in the grace of God, and experiencing favor with God and man, is a good thing. But the most important thing to remember while growing up with this kind of favor is to always seek God's favor. There will always come a time when going the extra mile has to be set aside in order to continue in the favor of God.

When Jesus fed the multitude with two small fish and five loaves of bread, the Fishermen's Union and the Brotherhood of Bakers were not in harmony with Jesus. When Jesus left a town or village and healed every person of every disease, big pharma was not in harmony with Jesus. When Jesus turned over the tables of the money changers, all those crooked check cashers were not in harmony with Jesus. Nevertheless, Jesus kept on feeding, healing, and preaching.

Growing in grace requires that when it comes to a choice between God and man, each one of us must make the decision that Jesus made; "I seek not mine own will, but the will of the Father which hath sent me" (John 5:30 KJV) ■

— RICHARD H. CALHOUN SR.

THROUGH THICK AND THIN

"But now thus saith the LORD that created thee, O Jacob, and he that formed thee, O Israel, Fear not: for I have redeemed thee, I have called thee by thy name; thou art mine. When thou passest through the waters, I will be with thee; and through the rivers, they shall not overflow thee: when thou walkest through the fire, thou shalt not be burned; neither shall the flame kindle upon thee" (Isaiah 43:1-2 KJV).

Have you ever felt alone? Have you ever felt abandoned? Have you ever felt like giving up? Oft times the Christian race is a long, rough, rigorous, arduous, and exhausting journey. There are obstacles, blind-spots, treachery, adversity, and countless other dangers that lie in ambush. We are knocked down so often that the temptation to give up is always in tow; whispering, taunting, beckoning, even cajoling us to give up. But brothers and sisters, we need not give up because there is hope!

The prophet Isaiah assures us of this hope. He informs us that this is no false hope, because it comes from God: A message of revelation, creation, and redemption. He admonishes us that when problems strike, it is not time to give up because God has promised to be with us through thick and thin. He has promised to be with us now; while we are still locked on the horn of our dilemma; now, while we are facing difficulties; now, while we are going through great turmoil. There is hope because God is not just God of the past and of the future, He is also God of the present.

God has promised to reveal Himself to us even in our adversities and trials. This revelation reminds us that our God is the one who created us, who formed us from the dust of the ground; and when we strayed, He redeemed us. He bought us back and restored us as children of God.

The Bible does not guarantee, promise, or even stress that the life of the Christian will be free from trials. Instead it stresses—it assures us—that when problems strike, no matter how long the journey, dark the night, fierce the enemy or few the friends, God, our Creator and our Redeemer, will always be with us.

However, the Bible does not stress the awareness of His presence. Although He is with us, we may not always feel His presence. His presence, therefore, is not a feeling. It is a guarantee God promises and God delivers. The Christian lives under constant attack, constant danger, and constant adversity. Nevertheless, we keep on hoping because God has promised His constant presence, His constant deliverance, and His constant redemption.

You may be experiencing some great struggle, heartache, disappointment, betrayal, ruptured relationship, job loss, or even a serious medical diagnosis. Don't give up! There is hope! God has not abandoned you. The waters of adversity will not overwhelm you; the floodtides of anxiety will not sweep you away; and the fire of affliction will not consume you! God has promised and He will be with you.

God is with you, through thick and thin. ■

— STAFFORD BYERS

DECEMBER 6

TOKENS OF EXPECTANCY

"So Christ was offered once to bear the sins of many. To those who eagerly wait for Him He will appear a second time, apart from sin, for salvation" (Hebrews 9:28 NKJV).

Like us, the children of Israel expected the coming of their Messiah. The Messiah coming filled their Bible. It was the focus of their prophecy; but "He came unto His own, and His own received Him not" (John 1:11). How do you expect Jesus to come and miss Him when He comes?

Because Israel was full of talk on expectation but empty on preparation, they made no meaningful preparation to receive their Messiah. In her book The Great Controversy, Ellen White considers the birth of Jesus in this context.

"An angel visits the earth to see who are prepared to welcome Jesus. But he can discern no tokens of expectancy...The angel hovers for a time over the chosen city...but even here is the same indifference...There is no evidence that Christ is expected, and no preparation for the Prince of life. In amazement the celestial messenger is about to return to heaven with the shameful tidings, when he discovers a group of shepherds who are watching their flocks by night, and...contemplating the prophecy of a Messiah to come to earth, and longing for the advent of the world's Redeemer" (White, 1858, p. 313).

"Oh, what a lesson is this wonderful story of Bethlehem!...How it warns us to beware, lest by our criminal indifference we also fail to discern the signs of the times, and therefore know not the day of our visitation" (White, p. 314).

"All the people should have been watching and waiting that they might be among the first to welcome the world's Redeemer" (White, p. 313). But, no, there was no longing, no searching, no tokens of expectancy, no preparation for the Messiah's coming. So they failed to receive Him when He came and they were left out in darkness to perish.

Sincere expectation must accompany meaningful preparation. You expect to go to college—you prepare to pass the SAT. You expect to marry—you prepare a bank account. You expect Jesus to come—you prepare for His coming.

Expecting our children from school, my wife salvages their rooms to welcome them home. Others expecting their loved ones, cook favorite dishes (rundown snapper or veggie fry pat) and light some candles.

Waiting for Jesus, as for a date, means you shower (wash your sins away); put on your best apparel (His robe of righteousness); look out every so often (long for His coming); and tell your friends about Him (witness about Jesus).

What are your tokens of expectancy? "... unto them that look for him shall he appear the second time without sin unto salvation" (Hebrews 9:28 KJV). ■

— SEDNAK KOJO DUFFU YANKSON

DECEMBER 7

BE THE VOICE FOR THE VOICELESS

"Open your mouth for the speechless, in the cause of all who are appointed to die...And plead the cause of the poor and needy" (Proverbs 31:8-9 NKJV).

It was a bright and beautiful summer day in June. The sun kissed the plants and flowers and their hues exploded with brightness. I decided to mow my lawn. I would bend my head as I passed under an overarching tree branch which impeded my progress. Usually, the birds would fly away as I approached the tree. This day, however, was different. Suddenly their voices exploded in a cacophony of shrieks and screeches. I was startled and stopped. Unexpectedly, about five birds dove at my head with such loud twitter and chatter that I had to stop.

It was then that I noticed my neighbor. She had interrupted her morning jog to look at me.

"What's the matter with these birds?" I exclaimed.

"Well, quite possibly they may have young ones and think you are too close, and they are just trying to protect their babies" she responded with delight. She wanted to see my next move.

I peered through the leaves to see if there were any nests among the thick foliage. I saw no nests, but was astonished at what had caused the surprise attack. There, perched on a branch was a sick adult bird with its eyes closed. He looked faint, weak and tired. He looked as though he was near the point of death. I had seen birds fearlessly do all to protect their young, but never an old, sick bird.

This was the very first time that I had ever witnessed the strong adult birds coming together to protect an old adult bird that was vulnerable, weak and helpless. They were all vigilant and wary of anyone or anything which would cause any harm to the infirmed older member of their family.

That family of birds came together to protect that vulnerable and infirmed bird. What about us? Shouldn't we do the same and be the voice of the weak, the vulnerable, the infirmed, and the voiceless among us? ▮▮

— HERMAN CHARLES

DECEMBER 8

FOREIGN VISITORS AND EXPENSIVE GIFTS PART 1

"I have other sheep, which are not of this fold; I must bring them also, and they will hear My voice, and they will become one flock with one shepherd" (John 10:16 NASB).

The Bible calls Job the "greatest man in the east" (Job 1:3). The east refers to the place where the Black descendants of Abraham resided. These Black descendants included the Midianites, who taught Moses about Horeb, "the Mount of God." These people from the east, which included the wise men who came to acknowledge the birth of Jesus, were worshipers of the true God and keepers of His commandments.

The Bible never mentions the number of Magi. Whatever the number, there was undoubtedly an entourage. The number of men could have exceeded the three types of gifts they brought. Although the wise men (Magi) were foreigners in bearing their gifts, given other actions, they demonstrated love. This word love is the Greek word ἀγάπη. It means, "the quality of warm regard for and interest in another, esteem, affection...love [without limitation to very intimate relationships, and very seldom in general Greek, of sexual attraction]." This love "refers almost exclusively in the New Testament to the love of persons for persons."

Love can't help but give. The Magi visited Jesus after His birth, bearing gifts of gold, frankincense, and myrrh. Their contributions were meaningful, doable, and within their means. After the Magi saw the Child with Mary, His mother, they fell to the ground and worshiped Him. Then, opening their treasures they presented to Him gladly.

The foreign visitors, magi, wise men, truly lived up to their reputation by studying astronomy (not to be confused with astrology) and the prophecies. They believed what they studied and observed.

In the implementation of their understanding, they traveled, bore gifts, and manifested a godly discernment. Having been warned by God in a dream, they didn't return to Herod. The Magi left for their own country by another way, thereby not giving aid to Herod's fear, anger, and murderous plot.

God has people in many places outside the significant center of religious leaders, scholars, or those who profess to know the "the truth." ■

— CHARLES MCNEIL

FOREIGN VISITORS AND EXPENSIVE GIFTS PART 2

"Give, and it will be given to you. They will pour into your lap a good measure—pressed down, shaken together, and running over. For by your standard of measure, it will be measured to you in return" (Luke 6:38 NASB).

Yesterday, we shared that the Magi brought gifts (Matthew 2). Note one of the two Greek words, "doron" and "charisma," can be translated as "gift" in the New Testament. The one we're concerned with today is the word "doron," translated into English that means "a gift or present that one receives"—interpreted as Jesus, the Holy Spirit, a spiritual quality or characteristic (e.g., Matthew 2:11; Matthew 5:23-24; Matthew 7:11; John 4:10; Acts 2:38). Under this definition, comes the three gifts the wise men gave the baby Jesus.

The first was gold. It's a chemical element with the symbol Au (from Latin: aurum) and atomic number 79, making it one of the highest nuclear number elements naturally. Gold is bright, slightly reddish yellow, dense, soft, and malleable.

Gold is a transition metal. It is one of the least reactive chemical elements and is solid under standard conditions. Gold is resistant to most acids. Gold dissolves in mercury. A relatively rare element, gold is a precious metal used for coinage, jewelry, and other arts throughout recorded history. Infrared shielding, colored-glass production, gold leafing, and tooth restoration all use gold. Even today, some anti-inflammatories in medicine use certain gold salts.

A clue to the meaning of gold is found by looking at Smyrna, the poor-rich church ("I know your tribulation and your poverty [but you are rich]," Revelation. 2:9). Smyrna possessed the character riches that Christ most desired—fidelity to the point of death (Revelation 2:10). "Refined by fire" refers to the tribulation (as in Smyrna, Revelation 2:9-10) that purifies character. According to His messages to the churches, fidelity and love are the character traits Jesus values most.

Notwithstanding all the precious gems and minerals, gold is the most valuable of all. The wise men gave their best. They did what many Christians haven't learned after years in the church. That is: "The silver is Mine, and the gold is Mine,' says the LORD of hosts" (Haggai 2:8 NKJV). ■

— CHARLES MCNEIL

FOREIGN VISITORS AND EXPENSIVE GIFTS PART 3

"...For by your standard of measure it will be measured to you in return" (Luke 6:42 NASB).

In the previous two parts, we discussed the foreigners' obedience to God's leading to travel and to give generously. In part two, we spoke of the opening of the first of the three gifts the wise men brought the baby Jesus.

The second gift in the chest was frankincense. It is an aromatic used in incense and perfumes, that is produced by five main species of Boswellia. It is also found throughout the Bible (Leviticus 2:1; Matthew 2:11; Revelation 18:13). Sanctuary incense, which was "sweet," used frankincense as its main ingredient. Exodus 30:34-37 outlines one recipe for sanctuary incense combining "pure frankincense" with three other aromatic substances: stacte, onycha, and galbanum.

The third gift the Magi presented to the infant, Christ, was myrrh. This natural Arabian gum is extracted from several small, thorny tree species. When crushed, it gives a beautiful fragrance. Myrrh resin has been used throughout history as a perfume, incense, and medicine. Myrrh was also used to embalm the dead (John 19:39). Nicodemus donated about 100 pounds of myrrh and aloes to anoint Jesus' body after the crucifixion.

In Revelation 2, one of the seven churches, Smyrna, derives its meaning from myrrh. Smyrna means sweet-smelling, but the church passed through an experience of death. Smyrna appeared to be weakened and effectively destroyed. But in fact, the death experience preserved the church, much like the myrrh Nicodemus donated to Christ's burial. Smyrna's death experience purged out corruption and selfishness, enabling the church to give a sweet-smelling fragrance in its expression of real Christian virtues.

Each gift reflects the character of the givers, the Magi, and foreshadows the life of the receiver, the Christ-child. The Magi were obedient to the prophecy of Christ, and faithful to the study of the prophecy of the coming Messiah.

Similarly, Christ was faithful and obedient to His heavenly Father in giving His life for the salvation of humanity (John 3:16). His death was as a sweet savor to the Father.

What does your giving say about your character? Are you giving generously, willingly, and of the highest quality? ▮▮

— CHARLES MCNEIL

WATCH

"Watch therefore, for you know neither the day nor the hour in which the Son of Man is coming" (Matthew 25:13 NKJV).

At different times during my teenage years I have seen a very thought-provoking skit. A woman is busily preparing her house because "Jesus" is coming to visit. In the midst of her preparation three strangers knock on her door at three separate times of the day. One of them is hungry and needs food; another is lost and needs direction; and the final stranger urgently needs guidance from the Bible. However, this church lady is so busy preparing for her imminent guest that she turns each stranger away without providing help. She tells each stranger that she doesn't have time to help at the moment and that he should come back another day.

By late afternoon, the lady's house is immaculate; everything is in perfect order as she eagerly awaits the coming of "Jesus." Sadly, it's 10:00 p.m. and her Special Guest has not arrived. All of a sudden she hears a voice saying, "I came to your house today and you did not receive me."

She cries out in chagrin "Lord, I prepared my house and waited for your visit but I did not see you."

"But indeed, I came to your house today," says the voice. "I came as a hungry stranger and you gave me nothing to eat; I came as a traveler who lost his way but you provided no direction; I came as one seeking after truth but you claimed that you had no time to open the Bible and guide me. I came but you were not prepared for me!"

As we reflect on this skit, it is hard to ignore the reality that we must be vigilant to love and care for our fellow human beings while we wait for Jesus to return. This principle is highlighted in an important parable concerning preparation for Jesus' second coming in Matthew 25. The moral of the parable is encapsulated in the following words: "Assuredly, I say to you, inasmuch as you did it to one of the least of these My brethren, you did it to Me" (Matthew 25:40 NKJV).

As we await the imminent return of Christ, let us be diligent in caring for the poor, the oppressed, and the imprisoned. Such demonstration of love to those who are less fortunate than us is evidence of the transforming power of the Holy Spirit in our lives. ■

— MICHAEL G. COLEMAN

DECEMBER 12

STEWARDSHIP AND THE SECOND COMING

"So then each of us shall give account of himself to God" Romans 14:12 NKJV).

What does stewardship have to do with the second coming of Jesus?

"So Christ was once offered to bear the sins of many; and unto them that look for him shall he appear the second time without sin unto salvation" (Hebrews 9:28 KJV).

For Christians, the second coming means the final act performed by Jesus to save all believers from sin. It is the most precious promise that God has given to us. It is a gift for all those who have accepted Christ's offer of salvation. Let me be clear, here, as I speak about salvation. I am not talking about a religious concept or an event in the future, but rather I am speaking of Jesus, the embodiment of our salvation. We are looking at what it means to have an intimate relationship with Jesus and to be ready for His second coming.

The direct question that needs to be asked is: can someone be saved and not be a good steward at the second coming of Jesus? The answer is an emphatic "No!" To be saved means to be obedient to the Word of God as a result of allowing the Holy Spirit's power to control our lives. To be saved means to accept by faith the death and resurrection of Jesus Christ as the ultimate price for our sins.

To be a good steward of salvation means that I allow the Holy Spirit to guide me into making decisions that reflect my love and commitment to Jesus for saving me. It means, therefore, how much time I spend in prayer, Bible study, and sharing Jesus with others. It further means how my life reflects that I am ready to meet Jesus at His second coming.

As a good steward of the salvation that I have received from God, my responsibility is to demonstrate in all areas of my life that I am blessed with this gift. This should be easily seen in my stewardship of the other gifts I receive from God. How I manage the time that I am entrusted with each day should reflect the fact that the gift of salvation is the most important thing to me. The same should be true with how I use the talents God has entrusted unto me. These talents are given to me to be used to glorify God as an expression of my appreciation to God for the salvation He has given me.

Being a good steward is a natural response to God for all of His blessings. We are looking forward to the second coming of Jesus with joyful expectations, because by the aid of the Holy Spirit, we have learned to be good stewards of all of His blessings. ■■

— FERRON F. FRANCIS

DECEMBER 13

DONNING YOUR SPIRITUAL PPE

"Finally, my brethren, be strong in the Lord and in the power of His might. Put on the whole armor of God, that you may be able to stand against the wiles of the devil" (Ephesians 6:10-11 NKJV).

When the COVID-19 pandemic struck America, there was a shortage of Personal Protective Equipment (PPE: masks, gowns, gloves, face shields, etc.) for frontline workers (FLWs: doctors, nurses, therapists, EMS, etc.). Experts agreed that because the disease is communicable, if FLWs didn't get PPE, they would be exposed, the virus would spread, and many people would die.

The apostle Paul tells of a virus that is more lethal than COVID-19, namely the sin virus. All Christians must be protected against this virus for while COVID-19 destroys the body, sin destroys the soul.

The apostle exhorts, "Put on the whole armor of God" (Ephesians 6:11). In order for us to be fully protected spiritually, we must be fully dressed for battle in our spiritual PPE.

Moreover, our fight is not against flesh and blood, but against the powers of darkness (Ephesians 6:12). We are up against a destructive force that is invisible, and many people believe that because it is invisible, it doesn't exist. In order to combat sin, we must put on the whole armor of God and be watchful. But what are the elements of the armor?

First, we need the girdle of truth. Just as the girdle held the soldier's armor together, truth holds our spiritual armor together. We must pursue truth, embrace truth, and live truth. Second, we need the breastplate of righteousness. Only Christ's Righteousness can transform our stony hearts into hearts of flesh that are receptive to the Holy Spirit. Third, just as soldiers wore greaves to protect their legs and sandals to give them a firm footing, we need the protection and the surety of the Holy Spirit in order to stand firm.

Next, we need the shield of faith to withstand the fiery darts of the wicked. The enemy is constantly on the attack, hence, we need the shield of faith to withstand him. Next, we need the helmet of salvation. Traumatic brain injury and post-traumatic stress disorder are two of the consequences of war. In this spiritual war, as in the physical, our heads are very vulnerable. In order to live the truth, we must first know the truth. If the enemy is able to convince us to believe a lie, that could be eternally detrimental. We need the helmet of salvation as a protection against the deceptions of the enemy.

Thus far, the armor is purely defensive. Now, comes the sword of the Spirit, which is the Word of God. In addition to being vigilant and on the defense, we need the Word of God to wage offences against the enemy. Finally, we must pray; we must persevere in prayer, and we must watch unto prayer.

Brothers and sisters, we can all be strong in the Lord. Thanks be to God that there is no shortage of Spiritual PPE. There is enough for everyone, but we must desire it, accept it, and wear it, and God will guarantee the victory over the craft and deceits of the enemy. ▮▮

— STAFFORD H. BYERS

DECEMBER 14

A DEFENDER OF JUSTICE

"He has shown you, O man, what is good; and what does the LORD require of you but to do justly, to love mercy, and to walk humbly with your God?" (Micah 6:8 NKJV).

Though not explicitly stated, Micah, one of the most prominent Minor Prophets, addressed the problem of social justice of his days, decrying leaders and "rulers of the house of Israel" (Micah 3:1) of neglecting the ethical and moral aspects of the Law. Instead of advocating justice for the most vulnerable in society, namely the widow, orphan, immigrant and poor, the leaders enriched themselves at the expense of the underprivileged.

Being filled with the power of the Holy Spirit, this bastion of justice wasn't afraid to defend the weak and innocent against the injustices of leaders who had forgotten that they were called to rightly represent a just God, (Micah 3:8-12).

It is obvious that the prophet was deeply moved that Yahweh, the God of justice, wanted to see this attribute replicated in the lives of His people. However, even at the threats of divine judgment the leaders refused to repent. God intended that the Promised Land would be a model society for the other nations, not just a land flowing with milk and honey. It was to be:

- A place where God wanted His glory to be on full display;
- A place where justice and mercy would reign supreme;
- A place that would be a witness to the Gentiles; and
- A place where the nations would recognize the justice of God as demonstrated by the actions of His people.

According to the *SDA Bible Commentary* Vol. 4, "The promises and predictions given through the Old Testament prophets originally applied to literal Israel and were to have been fulfilled to them on the condition that they obey God and remain loyal to Him" (*Review and Herald*, 1954, p. 25).

Although Israel's rulers never gave justice to the oppressed, Micah prophesied that Jesus, the True Ruler of Israel, "whose goings forth are from of old, from everlasting," (Micah 5: 2) would eventually bring justice for His people. Jesus spoke with the same power of the Holy Spirit that empowered Micah, when He declared, "The Spirit of the Lord is upon Me, Because He has anointed Me to preach the gospel to the poor; He has sent Me to heal the brokenhearted, to proclaim liberty to the captives and recovery of sight to the blind, to set at liberty those who are oppressed; to proclaim the acceptable year of the Lord" (Luke 4:18-19 NKJV). ■

— HANSON DRYSDALE

DECEMBER 15

THE GOD WHO'S THERE; THE GOD WHO CARES PART 1

"Behold, a virgin shall be with child, and shall bring forth a son, and they shall call his name Emmanuel, which being interpreted is, God with us" (Matthew 1:23 KJV).

Have you ever been separated from someone you really love?

It is very painful; especially when they reject you for no real reason. So it is with God and man. God's heart painfully suffers separation from His creation. Every day He yearns to be with the people who have forsaken Him. He's been seeking a relationship with fallen humanity ever since man's guilt severed that closeness. The Eternal One yearns for everyone. None are unnoticed or unloved by Him.

God first searched for Adam and Eve, whose guilt at the tree drove them from His presence. He, who intimately formed man out of earth's clay and kissed him with the breath of life, is the one who seeks us every day.

It was Jesus who commanded, "let them make me a sanctuary; that I may dwell among them" (Exodus 25:8 KJV). He delivered God's people from slavery that, "they shall know that I am the LORD their God, that brought them forth out of the land of Egypt, that I may dwell among them: I am the LORD their God" (Exodus 29:46 KJV).

In the same way, Christ delivers us from sin to be entirely His. The Scriptures say, "I will give them an heart to know me, that I am the LORD: and they shall be my people, and I will be their God" (Jeremiah 24:7 KJV).

Finally, when the world was ripe for the need of a Savior, Christ came. Matthew records, "Behold, a virgin shall be with child...and they shall call his name Emmanuel, which being interpreted is, God with us" (Matthew 1:23 KJV).

When leading them by a pillar of fire and smoke, dwelling in a wilderness tent, speaking through prophets, and His Shekinah Glory radiating in the Sanctuary were no longer good enough, God does the unimaginable. God's Eternal Divine Son enters human flesh. God's age-long desire to be with us is fulfilled. He became one with us by becoming one of us. Divinity could never be closer to humanity than when He was in Christ. Through Christ we are reconnected to God. And He wants that personal closeness with you so you won't be or feel alone.

May God give you the strength and knowledge to know that He is there, and that He cares. ■

— MARTY VEGAS

DECEMBER 16

THE GOD WHO'S THERE; THE GOD WHO CARES PART 2

"And the Word was made flesh and dwelt among us" (John 1:14 KJV).

God wanted to be so close to us that He became one of us. The Divine Word entered human flesh to demonstrate God's living love towards us.

Through entering human flesh God was bringing us back to Himself. He reconciled us at so many different levels. Notice the reasons why the Son of God became a man:

• To redeem fallen humanity by being the Second Adam. He conquered temptation and sin where Adan failed so miserably. He was obedient, even to the torturous ignominious death on the cross. He satisfied Divine Justice with His life and death, and now we can be free from guilt, shame and impending punishment.

• To demonstrate the Father's love to a lost and blind humanity. "He that hath seen me hath seen the Father" (John 14:9 KJV). In healing the blind we see that God desires to open our eyes. In His invitation to the children to come, we see a God who loves little ones. Touching the infected leper demonstrated God's alleviation of pain, suffering, and life-eroding sin. Jesus's patience with the vindictive thunder bolt brothers—James and John—who wanted descending fire to devour the unreceptive Samaritans, reveals a God who transforms angry men into ones that selflessly love.

• To be our example of such love that we should follow in His footsteps. He showed us how to love, care, and forgive. Through Him we see the love of God and how to love others. Through Him we find faith and trust in the Father.

• To experience, through His humanity, the pain, rejection, and hurtful wounds we suffer from the people we love. "He was despised and rejected— a man of sorrows, acquainted with deepest grief. We turned our backs on him and looked the other way" (Isaiah 53:3 NLB).

The perfect loving Son of God experienced the pain of human rejection because man's sin is so harmful and selfish.

He felt all of our pain, trials, and sorrows and came to give us eternal hope by showing us the way to the Father and to Eternity. He is with you during this time no matter if you have no one else.

Reach out to the God that is there, and who cares, and you will have peace and courage to face every day. ▮▮

— MARTY VARGAS

DECEMBER 17

SELF-LIBERATION

" O LORD, you have searched me and known me...Search me, O God, and know my heart; Try me, and know my anxieties; And see if there is any wicked way in me, And lead me in the way everlasting" (Psalm 139:1 & 23-24 NKJV).

Some people have been hurt by others and others have carried burdens of their pasts into their present life. Those burdens often create a sense of self-imprisonment and cause our minds to be traumatized by hateful ways we have been treated by other people. God's plan, however, is to set us free from all heavy burdens of the past that are blocking our future. "Come to me, all you who are weary and burdened, and I will give you rest" (Matthew 11:28, NIV).

We are the guardians of our souls. As we open ourselves to Jesus, He will tend to all that concerns us when we make Him the Lord of our lives. It is then that He will set us free; "If the Son therefore shall make you free, ye shall be free indeed," (John 8:36). Religious freedom must start within. We need to liberate ourselves from all past stories and be set free by the blood of the Lamb. We need to confess our sins so that God can help us let go of the past and be set free.

Paul depicts the notion of self-liberation in Christ as he states, "It is for freedom that Christ has set us free. Stand firm, then, and do not let yourselves be burdened again by a yoke of slavery" (Galatians 5:1 NIV).

True self-liberation occurs when we seek God's forgiveness, mercy and sanctification. There could be no self-liberation without true self-confession. It is not easy to let of go negative past stories, afflictions, humiliations, thoughts, or wrong doings in our hearts from those who've offended us. Those unforgiving or neglecting thoughts or behaviors have blocked and hindered you from being set free from the slavery of decades of negative emotional thoughts. We need to unblock those barriers so that the blessings can flow easily.

Let's invite God to search our hearts and our past and present deeds so that we can be self-liberated from them as we pray like David: "Search me, O God, and know my heart; Try me, and know my anxieties; And see if there is any wicked way in me, And lead me in the way everlasting" (Psalm 139:23). ∎

— BRIAN LADINY

DECEMBER 18

CHRIST, THE PHOS AND PHOTOS

"In [Christ] was life; and the life was the light of men. (John 1:4 KJV).

The Bible states that John the Baptist was not that Light, but was sent to bear witness of that Light (John 1:6-7).

The science of photos (and photography) operates as light bounces from an object and hits a chemically sensitive paper and burns that image into the paper. Likewise, the human eye receives light bouncing from images that burn that image into the brain.

Light has burned images into the human mind since the beginning of time. Christ is God's image burned into our hearts. He is the "Photos." Christ's character, words, deeds, and actions burned an image into the minds of those who encountered Him, thus transforming them.

It was noted of the apostles, "Now when they saw the boldness of Peter and John, and perceived that they were unlearned and ignorant men, they marveled; and they took knowledge of them, that they had been with Jesus" (Acts 4:13 KJV). Each apostle—who suffered great cruelty, derision, persecution and, for some, even death because of who Jesus was—was forever burned into their minds.

Paul saw the light on the Damascus Road when he met the "Photos" of God—Jesus. He was blinded by the "glory of the light" (Acts 22:11). Only when blinded and groveling in the dust did he see; "I am Jesus, the one you are persecuting" (Acts 9:5 NLT). This encounter was forever printed into Paul's mind. Jesus' life, presence, and power deeply impressed his soul.

It is the gospel's powerful light shining into our minds that changes us. Hence, Satan, "who is the god of this world, has blinded the minds of those who don't believe. They are unable to see the glorious light of the Good News. They don't understand this message about the glory of Christ, who is the exact likeness of God" (2 Corinthians 4:4 NLT).

"For God, who said, 'Let there be light in the darkness,' has made this light shine in our hearts so we could know the glory of God that is seen in the face of Jesus Christ" (2 Corinthians 4:6 NLT).

So, "while ye have light (Phos), believe in the light (Phos), that ye may be the children of light (Photos)" (John 12:36 KJV).

I pray we will see the burning "Photos" of Christ so His image will ever be etched into the deepest recesses of our mind and transform us into what we are to be. ▮▮

— MARTY VARGAS

DECEMBER 19

INTERCESSION 5.0

"Then the men turned away from there and went toward Sodom, but Abraham still stood before the LORD. And Abraham came near and said, "Would You also destroy the righteous with the wicked? Suppose there were fifty righteous within the city; would You also destroy the place and not spare it for the fifty righteous that were in it?" (Genesis 18:22-24 NIV).

The story of Abraham's intercession for Sodom and Gomorrah introduces the concept of prayer, for every believer. Abraham had just been promised a nation of his own, with descendants beyond stars counted in the sky. He has his own family and future to worry about, yet he is met with an opportunity to save a city destined to be destroyed. Abraham hears the plans of destruction from God and remembers he has family residing in that city.

Have you prayed for your family lately—cousins, aunts, uncles, grandparents?

Lot was kin to Abraham and had a large household himself. His family and servants grew so much that there was constant trouble between his herdsmen and Abraham's herdsmen. They decided to divide the team and Lot went down to the beautiful plains by Sodom and Gomorrah. By the time we arrive in Genesis 18, Lot is found living in these cities slated for a tragic end.

Have you prayed for places condemned by God?

Abraham knew how many family and friends went with Lot to the city. Therefore, he begs God to save the five cities of the plain if God can find 50 righteous people. This is not just the cities of Sodom and Gomorrah. There are five cities prophetically scheduled for demolition. Surely Abraham reasons there must at least be 10 righteous in each city. However, he decreases the number until he gets to 10 righteous people. God can't find 10, and Sodom and Gomorrah go down in smoke.

We have a problem in our cities today!

The main reason for the destruction of Sodom and Gomorrah wasn't just sexual indecencies. Ezekiel 16:47 speaks of their injustice. God is upset at the violence and sins against His Word and His people. God speaks against any nation that is constantly participating in oppressing people, and He seeks to address the problem.

Today we have a nation like Sodom and Gomorrah to intercede for. It seems we are hearing of a killing of some young black man for jogging, standing on the corner, sitting in his car, or a young woman in her own house almost weekly. It's time for the church to intercede for our nation, black young men, police, and politicians.

I challenge you, today, to intercede for young men and women who can't pray for themselves. Write down 50 people that you can pray for today. See what God can do for 50 people, like Abraham. Lot was blessed because of Abraham's prayer of intercession. One thing we can believe in today, God answers prayer! ■

— PHILLIP WESLEY, II

DECEMBER 20

BOTTOM OF THE NINTH—PART 1

"And I saw one of his heads as it were wounded to death; and his deadly wound was healed: and all the world wondered after the beast. And they worshipped the dragon which gave power unto the beast: and they worshipped the beast, saying, Who is like unto the beast? who is able to make war with him? And there was given unto him a mouth speaking great things and blasphemies; and power was given unto him to continue forty and two months. And he opened his mouth in blasphemy against God, to blaspheme his name, and his tabernacle, and them that dwell in heaven. And it was given unto him to make war with the saints, and to overcome them: and power was given him over all kindreds, and tongues, and nations. And all that dwell upon the earth shall worship him, whose names are not written in the book of life of the Lamb slain from the foundation of the world. If any man have an ear, let him hear," (Revelations 13:3-9, KJV).

For the 46 years that I have been a part of the Adventist church, we have made use of the phrase, "last days." This phrase comes to mind when I think of Jorge Mario Bergoglio, aka Pope Francis, who, with increasing frequency, has been on a whirlwind tour connecting with religious leaders and political figures.

These global rendezvous are not meaningless excursions to vacation hot spots so the "holy father" can chill out. Instead, the Pope is on a purposeful mission. The red shoe wearing pontiff—the 266th in Roman Catholic history, first ever Jesuit pope, and first Pope from the Americas—is operating methodically. Since assuming his role, he has become an overnight sensation, exploiting his celebrity, and pontificating. Pope Francis is on a roll.

In 2019, the pope stepped up his efforts, with subtlety, hawking to all who would listen a need for a so called "day of rest." This proposition is nothing more than a lurking national Sunday law, to usurp God's Sabbath, and its observers, in contravention of the law of God. The pontiff's 2015 speech to a star-struck, mummified joint Congress wasn't a Sunday school lesson. Instead, that convocation was about the need for seismic changes in the U.S. Constitution, a re-defining of freedom of religion.

You, no doubt, have heard about a future "global educational alliance," which will be hosted by the Vatican. In my humble estimation, this so called "alliance" is nothing more than a back door tactic to implement mandated worship on Sunday. In the NFL, this is called an "end run."

Using terms like, "protecting our common good," fraternity, universal solidarity, new humanism, and global pact, the pope's prophetic thrust will ultimately result in the introduction of the mark of the beast. ▮▮

— HARRIS THOMPSON

DECEMBER 21

BOTTOM OF THE NINTH—PART 2

"For when they shall say, Peace and safety; then sudden destruction cometh upon them, as travail upon a woman with child; and they shall not escape. But ye, brethren, are not in darkness, that that day should overtake you as a thief" (1 Thessalonians 5:3-4).

To summarize yesterday and today's lessons, the entire planet— every living person—has for six millennia, because of our sinful natures, been quarantined from the other worlds lest we contaminate them and they end up like us. Now we are in the final phase of this great controversy.

It is late in the game. The Seventh- day Adventist church, as they say in baseball, is now in the bottom of the ninth inning. The angels and the community of sinless other worlds, that when Lucifer came knocking didn't even bother to answer the door, are on their feet, cheering us on to the finish line. For thousands of years the inhabitants on this blue and gray ball have been doing battle with the enemy; some battles won, other battles lost.

Any time now, Jesus and His angels will come to extricate us from this earth, which has been traumatized by incomprehensible acts of evil. The recently signed global pact between Pope Francis and the Grand Imam in Abu Dhabi—the birth place of Islam—with promises of human fraternity, world-peace, and mutual cooperation, will result in none of it. There can be no solution for the sin problem down here unless it comes from above. I'm talking about from Jesus!

Jesus and the angels are in a holding pattern. A holding pattern is defined as the flight path maintained by an aircraft awaiting permission to land. A holding pattern keeps an aircraft in air space, while awaiting clearance from air traffic control, to descend. Jesus, our captain pilot, is about to put down the landing gear. Anytime now, He's about to announce to the cabin those long-awaited words, "preparing for descent."

To you, I say, "lift up the trumpet and loud let it ring, Jesus is coming again! Coming again! Coming again! Jesus is coming again!" ▮▮

— HARRIS THOMPSON

DECEMBER 22

NOW HEAR THIS

"And I will put enmity between you and the woman, and between your seed and her Seed; He shall bruise your head, and you shall bruise His heel" (Genesis 3:15 NKJV).

Only Jesus could have done it. Jesus stood before a hateful serpent and the hopeless human couple. The first sight that Adam saw was the face of Jesus, and the first breath he ever breathed was borrowed from Jesus. The second face Adam saw was Eve. The reverse was true for Eve; first she saw the face of Jesus then the face of Adam. How could this couple allow the serpent to get in between them and Jesus? If we are honest, that is a question that each of has asked ourselves time and time again.

The four of them were face to face in the Garden. Adam gives his pitiful excuse, followed by Eve's excuse. The serpent is silent. Satan already knows that there is no excuse for sin. Jesus breaks the silence. He addresses the tempter and the tempted. Only Jesus could have looked down the long and troublesome passageways of time and predicted His own birth. Not only this, but He also gave His own job description, accurately prophesied the outcome of His actions and rated His job performance.

Standing in a perfect garden with a fallen angel and a sin-cursed man and woman, Jesus reveals Himself as the Savior of the world, the Lamb of God, the Friend of sinners, and the Hope for the hopeless. For the sake of the entire world, Jesus would be born in the "fullness of the time" (Galatians 4:4).

Jesus was born into a world not much different from our own; a world of crime, corruption and callousness. The world then was ripe for the Cross and the world today is ripe for the Second Coming! Jesus' job description: Heaven-sent enmity establisher and heel-bitten head-crusher. Jesus' job rating; "Those whom You gave Me, I have lost none" (John 18:9). Why? Only Jesus can read an encrypted heart. Only Jesus can give you a brand new start.

Now hear this. "Jesus said to him, "I am the way, the truth, and the life. No one comes to the Father except through Me" (John 14:6 NKJV). Now hear this. Only Jesus can save a sin-sick soul. Jesus went looking for us in the Garden. He hung on a cross for us, and He is coming back to get us. Only Jesus! ▮▮

— RICHARD H. CALHOUN SR.

DECEMBER 23

KEEPING WATCH BY NIGHT

"And there were in the same country shepherds abiding in the field, keeping watch over their flock by night. And, lo, the angel of the Lord came upon them, and the glory of the Lord shone round about them: and they were sore afraid" (Luke 2:8-9 KJV).

It was night, the time when most men are at home in their own beds, asleep, and oblivious to the world around them. But the Bible reports, "the shepherds were abiding in the field, keeping watch over their flock by night." While others slept, the shepherd stayed awake. He knew there were dangers that lurked in the night, enemies that would destroy the flock. Wolves, lions, and sheep stealers worked best under the cover of darkness, waiting to pick off the vulnerable. And so the shepherd could not sleep. He lit the fire and watched, with staff in hand, ready to foil the plans of the attacker.

It is night. Our world is steeped in the spiritual darkness of fear, oppression and sin. Isaiah predicted of our time: "For, behold, the darkness shall cover the earth, and gross darkness the people: but the Lord shall arise upon thee, and his glory shall be seen upon thee" (Isaiah 60:2 KJV).

There is evil afoot in the land. Our sons are being snatched into the prison system. Our daughters are being valued for their bodies and not their brains. Our lives and liberties are under assault. The flock is in danger and some can neither see, nor sense the danger. And so, the shepherd must watch by night, with the blaze of truth and the staff of justice. We cannot sleep now as others. We have a work to do.

But we do not labor alone or in vain, for it is into the night the angel of Lord came upon them and the glory of the Lord shone round about them.

Oh shepherds, in these dark days, grow weary of the night but do not sleep. Be not weary in well doing for in due time we shall reap if we faint not. Light is about to break into the darkness. The Shepherd of Our Souls is about to appear. He shall snatch us from the jaws of our Predator and deliver us from evil. And the glory of the presence of our Lord shall illumine the long night of sin. Watch therefore, for in the hour that you think not, the Son of Man comes. ▮▮

— DEDRICK BLUE

DECEMBER 24

THESE KINGS!

"And in the days of these kings shall the God of heaven set up a kingdom, which shall never be destroyed: and the kingdom shall not be left to other people, but it shall break in pieces and consume all these kingdoms, and it shall stand for ever" (Daniel 2:44 KJV).

Few things are as disconcerting as watching a police officer kneel on the neck of another human being as casually as if he were kneeling on a couch cushion. And yet that is exactly what the nation witnessed on that awful day in May 2020. In what would turn out to be his dying words, George Floyd, an African-American man being detained by police in Minneapolis, Minnesota allegedly for a nonviolent infraction, declared: "I can't breathe! I can't breathe!"

In that awful moment, we were dragged back to a similarly distressing event when Eric Garner, another African-American man, several years earlier was choked to death by police in New York; he, too, for the entire world to see. And he, too, made the same dying declaration: "I can't breathe! I can't breathe!"

There is something wrong with a system that allows the repeated murdering of its own citizens at the hands of those who are sworn to protect and serve. And there is something even more wrong when too many people are willing to treat these murders as merely unfortunate, random events that have no bearing against the greater good. Far from being random, unfortunate acts, there is, instead, a very clear pattern where encounters between white police officers and minority citizens end with the citizens mortally injured.

So while righteous indignation demands that we raise our voices in protest of the clear reality of systemic injustice, the greater, grander truth hovering over all is the fact that God has weighed this system in the balances and found it wanting. He has declared, in no uncertain terms, that even while the morally bankrupt leadership pontificates and holds itself out as all powerful, that the outcome has been determined. The Maker of Heaven and Earth is going to interrupt this party called life, as we know it. He is going to interrupt lying lips, interrupt blatant discrimination, and interrupt racist rhetoric. He is going to knock down, shut down, throw down, and put down this order of things and establish, in its place, His kingdom of love and light. In the days of "these kings," God will show who is truly in charge. And to that blessed reality I declare, "I can hardly wait!" ▮▮

— LAWRENCE BROWN

DECEMBER 25

IN THE SHADOW OF GOD'S WINGS

"Be merciful unto me, O God, be merciful unto me: for my soul trusteth in thee: yea, in the shadow of thy wings will I make my refuge, until these calamities be overpast" (Psalm 57:1 KJV).

During childhood my brother and I were each given a beautiful hen, and my sister a rooster. We watched as these hens began to have chicks. On one occasion, my hen laid a number of eggs but four of them did not hatch. She seemed content with the hatched chicks and lost interest in the remaining eggs. Seeing this, my parents removed the unhatched eggs and placed them with my brother's hen as she incubated her own eggs.

Sometime later, all of the eggs from my brother's hen hatched. I was not happy that his hen had more chicks than mine. I hatched a plan to grab four of her chicks and place them in my hen's coop. After all, they were my eggs.

While executing my plan I was taught a lifelong lesson about coming between mothers and their offspring. After securing the chicks under her wings, my brother's hen taught me what pecking meant.

In our Biblical passage David finds himself in danger. The king wants his destruction, and many trusted friends have betrayed him. His passion for God led him to great conquests in life while arousing the insecurity, envy and jealously of those seeking to destroy him. As such, David was an early victim of religious persecution. Nevertheless, he understands that the more passionate we are about God, the more protective God is of us. He recognizes that God is zealous in the protection of His children.

In his longing for refuge, David concludes that the safest hiding place is under the wings of the Almighty. He pledges to shelter in place for the duration of that crisis, and later emerges unscathed. The psalmist also declares, "He shall cover thee with his feathers, and under his wings shalt thou trust" (Psalm 91:4 KJV).

The Lord yearns to shelter you and give you peace. Jesus lamented the failure of His children to claim His protection; "how often would I have gathered thy children together, even as a hen gathereth her chickens under her wings, and ye would not!" (Matthew 23:37 KJV).

What crisis are you facing today? May you discern that God is ready to spread His protective wings over you. ■

— DANIEL L. HONORÉ

DECEMBER 26

THE NEW JERUSALEM

"In my Father's house are many mansions; if it were not so, I would have told you. I go to prepare a place for you. And if I go and prepare a place for you, I will come again and receive you to Myself; that where I am, there you may be also" (John 14:2-3 NKJV).

The text is a direct quote from Jesus Christ. "In my Father's house are many mansions." Jesus went back to heaven to prepare a place for us, His followers. He is coming again when things are ready to receive us to Himself. This text is pregnant with hope that there is room for many in the mansions of heaven. Are we able, using Scripture, to find out how many? The answer is yes!

Revelation 20:4 tells us that following the saints being caught up to meet the Lord in the air, we live and reign with Christ in heaven for 1,000 years. At the end of the thousand years, something dramatic occurs. Revelation 21:10 states that at the end of the thousand years, the great city—the New Jerusalem—descends out of heaven from God. It is glorious, beautiful, and big. Its walls are tall and majestic.

The City has 12 gates and 12 foundations. Its length, breadth, and height are equal. According to the *Living Bible* and the New Revised Standard Version, the walls are some 75 yards wide and the length, breadth and height is 1,500 miles each. This means that the first floor alone has 2,250,000 square miles. Nothing like this has been seen or experienced before. The entire United States is 3,800,000 square miles with a population of 350 to 400 million individuals. And we are just looking at the ground floor of the New Jerusalem being 2,250,000 square miles.

Given that these are mansions, allowing for 15-feet ceilings means the City can have 528,000 floors. This is a majestic City. This means that, when compared to the population density of the United States, the City can hold some 130 billion individuals. There is room in the New Jerusalem for some 17 times the present population of the entire world. Only God is capable of such a majestic accomplishment.

In Revelation 7:9, John beheld "a great multitude which no one could number, of all nations, tribes, people, and tongues, standing before the throne and before the Lamb, clothed with white robes with palm branches in their hands." John 3:16 says, "For God so loved the world that He gave His only begotten Son that whosoever believeth in Him will not perish but have everlasting life" (NKJV).

Jesus will be there with the saints. What a day of rejoicing that will be. Come Lord Jesus ■■!

— VERNON JORDAN

DECEMBER 27

WHAT SHALL I RENDER?

"And Jesus answering said unto them: Render to Caesar the things that are Caesar's, and to God the things that are God's. And they marveled at him" (Mark 12:17 KJV).

The United States of America is deeply divided. We are divided into two camps: us against them—Republican against Democrat, conservative against liberal, rich against poor, white against black.

Our religious communities reflect this divide, both claiming to speak for God on the political questions of the day. Each party demands that their followers embrace the party's position with absolute fidelity. There is simply no basis for the two parties to agree. If a Republican supports limited government, the Democrat must argue for expanded government power. If a Republican believes in adding pineapples to pizza, a Democrat will reject that practice as an abomination.

In the first century, Jesus found Himself ministering in a similarly divided community. The Pharisees opposed the Sadducees, and the Herodians wanted nothing to do with the Sadducees. All lived under Roman dominion and sought to either overthrow that domination or be reconciled to it. By the time Jesus completed His ministry, He managed to unify each party within the Jewish community of faith and the Roman government. They all sought to persecute Him. Why? Jesus came to set captives free.

The Roman government and the Jewish religious establishment saw Jesus as a threat. His pronouncements rebuked the Roman government that would tax without representation. He also rebuked the Jewish religious political system that would bind the people to the traditions of the scribes. He preached about a kingdom that would supersede Rome and undermine the economic exploitation imposed upon the people by the synagogue.

When God's church resumes preaching the gospel of the kingdom preached by Jesus, she will experience the same persecution Jesus experienced on His way to Calvary. The fact that the church in America is not experiencing persecution, suggests that she is rendering her all to the political and spiritual traditions of Caesar.

Let us begin to render to God what is due to Him. Let us preach a gospel that will set captives free. ■■

— JOHN ASHMEADE

DECEMBER 28

OPERATION E.L.

"But when the fulness of the time was come, God sent forth his Son, made of a woman, made under the law" (Galatians4:4 KJV).

When you look at the Plan of Salvation, there are parallels to modern-day military operations. The Plan of Salvation, or Operation Eternal Life, has three parts: Phase One—entry (Jesus' Birth); Phase Two—completion of mission objectives (Jesus' life, death and resurrection); Phase Three—extraction (Jesus' second coming). Let us focus on Phase One.

Phase One-Part A

All military operations have a point of entry. In the case of Operation E.L., the entry point was Bethlehem (Micah 5:2). There are soldiers, called paratroopers, whose job is to step out of a plane, up high in the air, and parachute into a drop zone in enemy territory. Jesus, like a heavenly paratrooper, was high up in glory; He stepped out and came low to the drop zone, Bethlehem. Any other location would have jeopardized the mission. Not only did Jesus come down in proximity, but He also came down in stature (Philippians 2: 6-7).

Phase One-Part B

Most of the time when paratroopers carry out their mission, they have air support. When our heavenly warrior, Jesus, came to fulfill His mission, He too had air support. Angels and a multitude of the heavenly host provided the Savior with air support, and they heralded the coming of the Messiah (Luke 2: 13-14).

Phase One-Part C

Often when paratroopers land, they are met by ground support. Jesus also was met by ground support upon His arrival. Angels alerted the shepherds that the King of kings and Shepherd of shepherds was born. The shepherds said one to another, let us now go even unto Bethlehem, and see what the Lord hath made known unto us (Luke 2:15). Phase One of Operation E.L. was a complete success.

After the completion of Phase One, the devil was shocked and disheartened that Jesus would humble Himself and become the ultimate sacrifice for humankind.

I am so glad that before the earth entered existence, our Heavenly Father had a plan (Ephesians 1:4). There are days when you feel like you are surrounded in enemy territory. Remember that you have air support; angels who excel in strength camp round about those who love the Lord.

Remember that you have ground support. You are rooted and grounded in God's love, a love that strengthens us as brothers and sisters in Christ (Ephesians 3:14-19).

Most importantly, remember that our Heavenly Father, Loving Lord, and Commander in Chief has not, and will never, lose a battle. ■

— RICHARD CALHOUN JR

DECEMBER 29

IN THE MAGI'S FOOTSTEPS

"Therefore, I urge you, brothers and sisters, in view of God's mercy, to offer your bodies as a living sacrifice, holy and pleasing to God—this is your true and proper worship. Do not conform to the pattern of this world, but be transformed by the renewing of your mind" (Romans 12:1-2 NIV).

Following the footsteps of the Magi on their way to Bethlehem, we will inevitably end up at the doorsteps of the hostel where Mary and Joseph found solace; where the expecting mother delivered the Messiah baby slated to deliver the world from the harsh and unforgiving dominion of the dragon.

Unlike them we carry no gold, no myrrh and no frankincense since the new dispensation demands mostly, if not always, the sacrifice of self on the altar of self-surrender. In a manger, we too will see the newborn King surrounded by domesticated, unthreatening beasts, yet born to be killed by an unseen but ever present ferocious beast called, the devil.

T.S.Eliot in the *Journey of the Magi*, a literary eavesdrop of the royal visitors' conversation as they returned to their kingdoms in the East, heard them say: "We should testify having seen a birth; Birth or Death? There was a Birth...This Birth was hard and bitter agony for us...We returned to our places, these Kingdoms, But no longer at ease here, in the old dispensation, With an alien people clutching their gods. I should be glad of another death."

The Magi, those pagan royalties having beheld the beauty of Christ and tasted the meaning of true adoration, were no longer at ease in their own cultural settings. They were no longer willing to receive the adoration of men, for only the Child deserved such honor. Their submission to the newborn King opened their eyes to the futility of idol worship, to the point of referring to their own people as aliens clutching their gods. They talk of dying, in their last sentence. Die to self, die to pride, die to materialism, die to arrogance, die to exploitation.

So, it's imperative to wonder how could God's church, waiting for the coming King, live so comfortably in a culture where self-adoration, self-exaltation, self-promotion, and self-satisfaction are the daily currency in human interactions? How?

Maybe it's high time to follow the footsteps of the Magi, these pagan kings, so that we too can vie for death at the feet of the King who deserves all our honor and praise and glory forever. ■■

— EDDY LAGUERRE

WITHOUT NOTORIETY

"But made himself of no reputation, and took upon Him the form of a servant, and was made in the likeness of men" (Philippians 2:7 KJV).

Mark Twain's well known novel, *The Prince and the Pauper*, was released in 1881. It tells the story of two young boys; one, a prince in line for the throne of England and the other, a pauper. In an amazing turn of events the two boys end up exchanging their stations in life. Their rags-to-riches swap fades away, in comparison to the exchange that Jesus made for us.

For our sake, Jesus was born a second-class citizen amongst a subjugated nation state that was demoted to second-class citizenship. Born in Bethlehem then relegated to refugee status in Egypt, Jesus finally grew up in Nazareth. Nazareth was a village so notorious that even as an adult, Jesus could not escape the stigma of having grown up there. Jesus, aka "Wonderful Counselor, Mighty God, Everlasting Father, Prince of Peace" (Isaiah 9:6), was born into a peasant's life. Jesus—who is, was and forever will be God, the Creator of the Universe—was born into the life of a peasant.

Jesus came without notoriety into our world and called no undo attention to Himself. The Nazareth that Jesus grew up in, according to historians, was a town of between 500 and 2,000 people. The literacy rate amongst the wealthy was approximately three percent. To be able to read and write would place you in the upper levels of society. But Jesus humbly and willingly lived a life without notoriety.

Jesus, just like Moses, was a first-hand witness to the cruelty and injustice heaped upon the poor and disenfranchised. Jesus heard their cries for deliverance and He felt their pain. But unlike Moses, Jesus gives life. Jesus was just like us, "in all points tempted as we are"; and on the other hand, Jesus was not like us, as He was "without sin" (Hebrews 4:15 KJV).

There was no accidental case of mistaken identity that engrafted Jesus into the human race, no not at all. The Bible clearly and unequivocally proclaims that He, "made Himself of no reputation, and took upon him the form of a servant...And being found in fashion as a man, he humbled himself, and became obedient unto death, even the death of the cross" (Philippians 2:7-8 KJV). And that has made all the difference in the world. ▮▮

— RICHARD CALHOUN SR

OVERCOMING DECEPTIONS IN THE LAST DAYS

"To the law and to the testimony! If they do not speak according to this word it is because there is no light in them" (Isaiah 8:20 NKJV).

The issue in the Great Controversy between Christ and Satan is that Satan wants to be God and is determined to deceive everyone to worship him. "For thou hast said in thine heart, I will ascend into heaven, I will exalt my throne above the stars of God...I will be like the most" High (Isaiah 14:13-14 KJV).

"And there was war in Heaven. Michael and his angels fought against the dragon... And the great dragon was cast out...which deceiveth the whole world: ...and his angels were cast out with him" (Revelation 12:7-9 KJV).

The war began in Heaven. Satan tried to deceive the angels to join him in rebellion against God. In the book, *Patriarchs and Prophets*, author Ellen G. White says, "Not content with his position, though honored above the heavenly host, he ventured to covet homage due alone to the Creator. Instead of seeking to make God supreme in the affections and allegiance of all created beings, it was his endeavor to secure their service and loyalty to himself" (White, 1890, p. 36). And he did it by deception! "He began to insinuate doubts concerning the laws that governed heavenly beings..., angels, being more exalted, needed no such restraint, for their own wisdom was a sufficient guide" (White, 1890, p.36). Thank God, Christ was victorious, the holy angels stayed loyal, and Satan was cast out.

The war continued in Eden. "And the serpent said unto the woman, Ye shall not surely die" (Genesis 3:4 KJV). Eve yielded to deception and disobeyed God. Sin came into the world and death came to all.

The war continued in the wilderness. After 40 days of fasting, Satan said: " . . . All these things I will give thee, if thou wilt fall down and worship me. Jesus said, 'Get thee hence, Satan, for it is written, Thou shalt worship the Lord thy God, and him only shalt thou serve'" (Matthew 4:9-10 KJV). Same purpose and same method of deception! But Jesus was victorious. It is written!

The war continues today. The test will come to everyone. If it is possible, Satan will deceive the very elect (Mathew 24:24). How do we overcome Satan's deceptions in the last days?

- Defend your faith by the Word. "It is written."
- Test truth by the Word: "To the law and to the testimony: if they speak not according to this word it is because there is no light in them" (Isaiah 8:20 KJV).
- Claim the victory in the blood (Revelation 12:11).
- Be in the Remnant: "Here is the patience of the saints: here are they that keep the commandments of God, and the faith of Jesus" (Revelation 14:12 KJV). ■

— SEDNAK KOJO DUFFY YANKSON